Shakespeare's Grammatical Style

A COMPUTER-ASSISTED ANALYSIS OF

Richard II AND Antony and Cleopatra

by DOLORES M. BURTON

University of Texas Press, Austin & London

*The publication of this book was assisted
by a grant from the Andrew W. Mellon Foundation.*

Library of Congress Cataloging in Publication Data

Burton, Dolores.
    Shakespeare's grammatical style.

    Originally presented as the author's thesis, Harvard,
1968.
    Bibliography: p.
    1. Shakespeare, William, 1564-1616–Language–
Grammar. 2. Shakespeare, William, 1564-1616–Style.
3. Shakespeare, William, 1564-1616–Antony and
Cleopatra. 4. Shakespeare, William, 1564-1616–King
Richard II. 5. Electronic data processing–English
language–Style. I. Title.
PR3078.B8 1973   822.3'3   73-6795
ISBN 0-292-77504-0

For my mother

CONTENTS

TABLES

FIGURES

PREFACE

In this book I have sought to achieve two ends: to determine the role played by syntax in Shakespeare's stylistic development and to formulate a theory of style and a method for applying that theory to works of literature. *Richard II* and *Antony and Cleopatra* became the basis for the study of stylistic development because they are generally considered to be good examples of distinct stages in Shakespeare's career. The expression "grammatical style" designates my concentration on formal linguistic features, to the exclusion of imagery, vocabulary, rhetorical figures, and other aspects of style. Failure to include these features is not a denial of their importance but an acknowledgment that they have often been studied, whereas syntax, particularly that of Shakespeare's blank verse, has been generally neglected.

The decision to restrict the investigation of Shakespeare's style to formal language features is one of many limitations that were imposed in order to simplify the complex task of formulating a theory and a method of stylistic analysis. Another is the decision to use the Kittredge edition of Shakespeare's plays, accepting the editor's decisions about emendations, spelling, punctuation, and format, rather than working directly from Quarto or Folio. Finally, since the formal theory and explicit methods of modern linguistics provide better guidelines for a theoretical discussion of style, the terminology, categories, and assumptions of linguistic science have been preferred to those of classical rhetoric and traditional grammar.

Systemic grammar, a theory of language developed by M. A. K. Halliday and his colleagues at the Universities of Edinburgh and London, is the basis for the description of Shakespeare's syntax. Because it preserves many distinctions of traditional grammar (subject/object, theme/rheme, sentence/clause/phrase), because it adopts the Saussurean axes of paradigm and syntagm, and because it uses Firthian ideas of meaning, systemic grammar offers, in addition to the thoroughness and formality characteristic of linguistic theory, the flexibility and subtlety needed for a discussion of literary style. The categories of systemic grammar used throughout are based on materials available in 1966, when the research for this study was initiated.

The term "syntax" comprehends several levels of language, including not only sentence type, mood, word order, subordination, and so on, but also the modification of nouns by determiners, the structure of adjectives, and the semantics of adjective-noun relations. That these levels of language are the province of syntax may surprise those accustomed to thinking of syntax in terms of larger units like the sentence or the clause, yet the fact that a word can be labeled a determiner or an adjective is a statement about syntax.

In accordance with the prevailing spirit of modern linguistic description, explicit value judgments have been avoided, although the choice of Shakespeare as the subject for stylistic analysis and the selection of plays that have been generally praised for their style constitute implied value judgments. The general intention, however, was to record differences in syntax between *Richard II* and *Antony and Cleopatra* without claiming that the features ascribed to either play or the differences between them will explain why one is considered a fine example of lyric style or why the other is often viewed as the pinnacle of Shakespeare's stylistic achievement. Above all, there is no attempt to explain why or how a reader makes judgments of stylistic excellence or to account for the "aesthetic effect" of style. Such explanation requires a knowledge of human psychology and of experimental method that lies outside my competence, although it belongs to a general theory of style, and its place in such a theory is discussed in Chapter One.

The formal requirements of tabulating data and of statistical testing were added to that of linguistic description. This decision meant that counts had to be recorded in table form and that the criteria for assigning an item in the text to one grammatical category rather than another had to be spelled out in appendices so that the basis for the statistical study would be as explicit as possible. Since little is known about the style of long texts, it was decided to analyze the plays in their entirety rather than to draw samples from them. To facilitate the analysis of many syntactic features in two full-length plays, an electronic computer was used to compile a selective concordance of the two plays. This research was undertaken in 1965 before the concordances of Trevor Howard-Hill and of Marvin Spevack were published. The selective concordance had as its headings conjunctions, prepositions, pronouns, determiners, and other formal markers of syntax. These words appeared in their blank-verse line context, with reference to act, scene, line, and speaker.

The natural ambiguity of English (e.g., the fact that a word like *that* might be a pronoun, a determiner, or a subordinating conjunction) meant that the data yielded by the computer had to be analyzed further. This analysis and the further counts that it entailed were carried out manually. The criteria used for parsing appear in Appendix A. Where greater explicitness seemed desirable, citations to syntactic features in the plays were listed in Appendix B. Should it become feasible to automate the techniques of stylistic analysis described in this study, the material in Appendix A might provide a preliminary survey of the difficulties to be solved in programming, while the output of the computer might profitably be compared with the data in Appendix B.

The goal of devising a formal theory and a method of stylistic analysis dictated the organization of chapters in this book. The first chapter outlines a general theory of style, which is applicable to any discipline that uses the notion as an instrument of inquiry—architecture, dance, music, psychology, anthropology, linguistics. The three methodological chapters that follow examine questions often raised by students of style in literature: In what part of the text is style located? What techniques of analysis are useful for the study of style? How can one use the results of formal analysis to interpret a text? The attempt to answer these questions is illustrated throughout by reference to *Richard II* and *Antony and Cleopatra*. To lend substance to the illustrations and to provide a consistent description of differences between the two plays, it was necessary in each of these chapters to anticipate material from subsequent chapters. Thus, the second chapter, on locating style, makes its point by using techniques of analysis that are not fully explained until Chapter Three and offers interpretations of data on the basis of premises that are not justified until Chapter Four.

Each methodological chapter has roughly four sections. The first poses the question to be treated; the others suggest various answers. These provide the substantive analysis of Shakespeare's style. They identify a syntactic feature (e.g., interrogatives and imperatives), tabulate its frequency, and suggest ways in which the presence of the feature can be used to interpret the text. The methodological requirement that each syntactic feature ascribed to the style of a literary text must contribute something to our knowledge and appreciation of the work as literature follows from the definition of style proposed in the first chapter. Style is there defined as a function of a given object; it cannot be described until the object is defined. Defining literature is the task of literary criticism. While this tradition is by no means monolithic, most critics would agree that fictionality is a distinguishing mark of literature. Hence, the analysis of style in a work of literature means, among other things, that one must show how stylistic features build the fictional world of the literary work. The content of a particular interpretation is certainly arguable, but the need for interpretation is an axiom of the stylistic theory on which this study is based.

The last two chapters may be of greatest interest to readers interested in a summary statement about the style of the plays or to those seeking a general interpretation of the plays apart from considerations of style. The fifth chapter summarizes what has preceded, suggests an application of the general theory of style, and discusses briefly aspects of style that were neglected because of limitations created by time or methodology. The final chapter moves beyond stylistics to poetics with a discussion of Shakespeare's view of the poet's role in the dramatization of history as this emerges from statements about imagination in *Richard II* and *Antony and Cleopatra*. Chapter Four, with its emphasis on interpretation, will also be of interest to the general reader.

As far as the study of Shakespeare's style is concerned, I hope that this book will serve to enhance the reader's awareness and enjoyment of Shakespeare's linguistic virtuosity by calling attention to a neglected aspect of his style. Certainly other plays of Shakespeare invite study. I am particularly interested in determining whether the prose of the romantic comedies and of the Falstaff plays was an important factor in the changes in syntax that became manifest in *Antony and Cleopatra* or whether plays like *Hamlet* and *Julius Caesar* exhibit transitional features of syntax that mark a clear stage in Shakespeare's movement from the lyrical style of *Richard II* to the brilliance of *Antony and Cleopatra*. The style-function theory itself can be applied to the entire corpus of Shakespeare's work, creating an array whose dimensions might be compared with similar arrays established for Marlowe, Jonson, and other dramatists and poets of the period.

Whatever the merits and shortcomings of the method proposed in this book, I hope that it will prompt other students of style to join in the search for a generally accepted method of stylistic analysis. Only concerted effort to analyze works by many writers of different genres and different periods will make it possible to compare data and to learn more about the operation of style in literature.

ACKNOWLEDGMENTS

Every book requires extensive acknowledgment of assistance, and when the book was first a doctoral thesis, thanks must be a twice-told tale. On the first account, therefore, I wish to thank my thesis directors, Morton W. Bloomfield and Reuben A. Brower of Harvard University, for the open-mindedness with which they accepted my proposal to undertake a linguistic and computational study of Shakespeare's style, for their guidance and advice on the problems presented by the research, and for their continued encouragement. I am personally indebted to Michael A. K. Halliday, Ruqaia Hasan, Rodney D. Huddleston, and Vivian Salmon for their generosity in sharing with me information and material on systemic grammar during my year at London University. An American Association of University Women Fellowship and a Radcliffe Grant-in-Aid helped to finance that year of study and to defray the expense of keypunching the plays. Through conversation and correspondence, Sally and Walter Sedelow helped me to understand how I might use the computer for the study of style and how to prepare the plays for processing. Ralph L. Kent of the Harvard School of Public Health wrote the concordance program; members of the computation centers at MIT and Boston College assisted in running the program; and the IBM Corporation furnished cards and tapes for the data. I owe special thanks to the students who keypunched the plays, to the library staff at Emmanuel College, and to many Sisters of Notre Dame who encouraged and assisted me in countless ways.

To my former colleague, Elizabeth Michaels, SND, Chairman of the Department of Mathematics at Emmanuel College, Boston, must go the credit for developing the mathematical theory of style on which my work is based and for helping me to understand its implications for stylistics.

The transition from thesis to manuscript was aided by my chairman,

Harry H. Crosby of the Division of Rhetoric at Boston University, who through example and advice encouraged me to publish my research. The Graduate School of Arts and Sciences at Boston University supported the cost of revising and preparing the manuscript by grants-in-aid. Celia Millward of the English Department at Boston University and Richard E. Barbieri of the English Department at Emmanuel College read the revised manuscript, offering extensive and most helpful commentary. Particular thanks are due to Margaret Shaw, who typed the manuscript, and to Cecilia M. DiBella, who proofread it with me.

SHAKESPEARE'S GRAMMATICAL STYLE

CHAPTER ONE

Style as a Function

The Problem of Style

Style has always been among the most tantalizing aspects of literary study. Among the intrinsic difficulties are those of deciding what style is, where in a literary text style resides, how one describes style, whether there are kinds of style, and why a given style is good.[1] In order to create a comprehensive frame of reference for discussing these questions, especially the first, this chapter presents a theoretical definition of style. To propose a scientific study of literary style is to assume that the study of literature is, among other things, an intellectual discipline. One cannot simply continue accumulating facts, describing and reinterpreting texts, or taking exception to some hypotheses while filling out and clarifying others without considering from time to time new methods of studying literature. The new criticism has exhausted its original impetus in that its methodology has

[1] These questions, together with those discussed on pp. 11-16, define some of the phenomena that a general theory of style must encompass. They are derived from an examination of some major documents of stylistics, a field provisionally defined as the study of the language of literature. "Literature" refers, generally, to concepts drawn from the tradition of new criticism, especially as these are embodied in René Wellek and Austin Warren's *Theory of Literature*. "Language" corresponds to the object of twentieth-century linguistic science. In brief, literature is marked by the property of fictionality and language by a system of formal rules of grammar.

been generally assimilated, and students of literature seeking fresh perspectives are faced now with the broad alternatives of abandoning analytic method for increasingly intuitive and existential responses to literature or of developing more rigorous analytic techniques to make the study of literature more explicit. The latter course seems a logical extension of new critical theory.

Theoretical discussions of literary style run the risk either of implying that a piece of literature *is* a style or of appearing to reify terms like *style* if they insist that literature *has* a style. Richard Ohmann has described this dilemma well and has formulated the central question of stylistics simply and accurately: "How can we tell style from not-style?"[2] If, as Ohmann contends, style is a way of saying *it*, the critic's task consists as much in defining *it* as in describing style. Ohmann defines *it* in this fashion:

If the critic is able to isolate and examine the most primitive choices which lie behind a work of prose, they can reveal to him the very roots of a writer's epistemology, the way in which he breaks up for manipulation the refractory surge of sensations which challenges all writers and all perceivers. In this Heraclitean flux, and not in the elusive forms of thought, is the common source of all perceptions, all sentences, all prose. The stream of experience is the background against which "choice" is a meaningful concept, in terms of which the phrase "way of saying it" makes sense, though "it" is no longer a variable. Form and content are truly separate if "content" is not bodiless ideas, but the formless world-stuff. And if such a hypothesis carries forward the analysis of style only a comfortless millimeter or so, at least it offers to that discipline a firm theoretical base, and a justification as well, inasmuch as it establishes an accessible and interesting connection between style and epistemology.[3]

While Ohmann's statement of the problem of style seems an accurate one and while charting a relation between style and epistemology is a valid way of solving the problem he has defined, it seems preferable to seek a solution that remains within literature. Instead of positing a relation between

---

[2] Richard Ohmann, "Prolegomena to the Analysis of Prose Style," in *Style in Prose Fiction*, ed. Harold C. Martin, p. 3. The discussion of style throughout presupposes a serious pondering of the first two pages of Ohmann's essay, which deserves as much attention for the problem he raises there as for the solution he suggests, although it has received less on that account. Abstract though it is, the solution proposed in this chapter is an attempt to espouse and to reaffirm in the context of stylistics the organicist view of literature and, at the same time, to answer affirmatively the question, if literature is organic, "is there anything at all worth naming style" (ibid., p. 2).

[3] Ibid., pp. 9-10.

style and epistemology, I wish to examine the connection between style and the language of literature. Language, as the medium of literature, seems more directly accessible than the writer's epistemology, since the latter is too often derived from a writer's language, while the relationship between language and literature or between literature and epistemology is poorly defined, if at all. Furthermore, if style is a way of saying *it*, where literature is concerned, it would seem preferable to designate *it* in some immediate sense as a literary work rather than as "the formless world-stuff." To say, however, that style is a way of writing a literary work appears to make the literary work something that preexists style and is subject to a set of stylistic modifications. This drift toward Platonism can be overcome by taking refuge in the well-defined abstractions of mathematics.

The Style Function

Mathematically, the relationship of style to all objects of which style is predicated can be expressed as a propositional function $S(A)$.[4] This function is a correspondence between two well-defined sets, one of which is the domain of the function and the other of which is the range. The domain of the style function is A, the set of all well-defined objects. A contains as proper subsets the works of Chaucer, Picasso, Brahms, and any other objects to which style is ascribed. An element of A is any object, for example, a literary object like Shakespeare's *Richard II*. An element of A is designated by the symbol a. Thus, style is defined as a continuous qualitative function on A, and the style of *Richard II* is expressed as $S(a)$. Since a function can exist only between two well-defined sets, to define A, the domain of style, is the first step in the analysis of style.[5] A can be defined by specifying the structural components of its individual members, that is, by defining each element a. The problem of defining a can be

[4] This definition and the subsequent explanation were formulated by Elizabeth L. Michaels, SND, Chairman, Department of Mathematics, Emmanuel College, Boston, Massachusetts. Throughout this chapter terms like *function, domain, range, specify*, etc. are used in a technical sense. Readers unfamiliar with the terminology will find a fuller explanation in Charles J. A. Halberg, Jr., and John F. Devlin, *Elementary Functions*, especially pp. 9-14, 105-112.

[5] Charles F. Hockett's arguments against the notion of language as a well-defined system (*The State of the Art*) would seem to apply *a fortiori* to a theory of style as a function of the set of well-defined literary objects. F. R. Palmer, in his review of Hockett (*Language* 45 [1969]: 616-621) points out that the book is really an attack on the distinction between competence and performance and ultimately on that between *langue* and *parole*. It is safe to say that these distinctions have been produc-

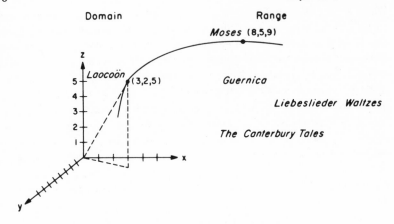

Fig. 1. Diagram of the style function

compared to that of plotting a point in space. Let us imagine an indeterminate point (x, y, z) in three-dimensional space. The values that will
constitute the coordinates of the point are real numbers. When x, y, and z
are assigned specific values (e.g., 3, 2, 5), we have a uniquely determined
point a. Figure 1 is a plot of the point $x = 3$, $y = 2$, and $z = 5$. Assuming
that this point represents the dimensions of the sculpture *Laocoön*, the
style function associates these structural components of the *Laocoön* with
the work itself and in this manner distinguishes it from all other works of
sculpture (e.g., the *Moses* of Michelangelo) and all other objects (paintings,
music, literature, etc.) in the style space. Any actual work of art is so
complex, of course, that many more dimensions than three would be
needed to define its structural components; but only three dimensions can
be represented on a flat surface, such as is shown in Figure 1. While style
can be regarded as a qualitative function, it can also be viewed as a quantitative function. When it is viewed quantitatively, the theory is applied in
mathematical rather than spatial terms.

   In a work of literature we hypothesize an indeterminate set of structural
components with n dimensions. The values that will constitute the coordinates of this structure are to be derived from language. When the structural
components of a work of literature have been defined in terms of specific

tive. Even Hockett admits the utility of entertaining the hypothesis of language as
well defined. Thus, whether literature is or can be well defined, we assume it is so in
order to formulate a theory of style.

linguistic values, the result is a well-defined and unique literary work *a*. When a given *a* is well defined, the style function will associate with it a specific style. Style thus differs logically from the chain of specific linguistic values that define the structural components of a given work, although it depends intrinsically upon them.

One could, of course, define style as the set of all mapping functions of *A* to *B*, where *B* is the range of style. Each function in the set would define a given aspect of the text, such as the proportion of end-stopped to run-on lines or the presence or absence of rhyme. This formulation would assign one function to each parameter of style. Hence, style would be defined by an aggregate of features rather than by a point where many features converge to form an entity. The broader formulation *S(A)* allows for the supposition that style is a unified phenomenon, a single function of the entire literary work.

A second reason for keeping the theoretical definition at this high level of generality is the fact that one can thus handle the related question of what meaning the term *style* has when it is predicated of personality, culture, other art forms, or language forms other than literature. In the section devoted to consequences of the style-function theory, the manner in which style can be predicated of these terms is discussed, as well as the kinds of comparative studies that are made possible among these areas of knowledge when the notion of style has the same meaning for each discipline.

It should now be clear that the theory of the style function relegates many venerable notions about style and style elements to the domain of style. Most studies that claim to be analyses of style are, in terms of the theory, studies neither of style nor of elements of style. They are specifications of segments of the structural components of literary works or an enumeration of elements that might ultimately be related to one another in a structural description. The point is a theoretical one that need not bother most devotees of stylistic analysis. When it has been made they are no worse off than Molière's prose-speaking gentleman who, after all, had the good sense to be delighted with his discovery.

Two Models of Literary Structure

Since structural description must logically precede the definition of the style space, one needs to clarify the notion "literary structure." The term *structure* has many definitions. Sometimes it can refer to the work as a whole; sometimes it refers to segments of that work. The distinction between the two uses could be maintained by reserving the word *structure* for the total work and by using *substructure* to designate the part. I wish now to examine two models of literary structure in order to indicate the possible relations between language and literature. The first model was developed by the Polish phenomenologist Roman Ingarden and given currency in this country through the critical writings of René Wellek. The second model belongs to the theory of the style function.

The aims of both models are similar: to maintain the autonomy of literary study (as opposed, e.g., to the purely linguistic study of literature), to acknowledge the central place of language as the medium of literature, and to develop a theory and a method of literary study that are at once value based and formal. The models differ chiefly in their statement of the relation of language to literary structure. Wellek and Warren's adaptation of Ingarden's model is summed up in this passage: ". . . there is, first, the sound-stratum, which is not, of course, to be confused with the actual sounding of the words . . . this pattern is indispensable, as only on the basis of sounds can the second stratum arise: the units of meaning. Every single word will have its syntagmas and sentence patterns. Out of this syntactic structure arises a third stratum, that of the objects represented, the 'world' of a novelist, the characters, the setting."[6] This statement suggests that literature has three components related hierarchically: sound, linguistic meaning, and the fictional world. The fictional world is the hallmark of literature in this theory. The first two strata belong to language, and the third stratum is an abstraction composed of the characters, events, and objects that comprise the fictional world.

Let us consider this model as a description of the relationship between language and the literary work. The fictional world arises from language, but it is not clear how this ascent occurs, what becomes of language once the third stratum is abstractly isolated from it, or, most important, to what degree the third stratum remains indebted, so to speak, to its linguistic underpinnings. The world appears to arise from language, detach itself from it, and constitute a distinct component of the total work. Similarly, language (syntagmas and sentences) remains abstractly isolated on its own level from the higher stratum *in a state of pure language*. The flaw in the model is that, conceptually, one begins with a unified entity, the work of literature, and then describes a set of strata that in effect separates language from the fictional world. Since the latter is the hallmark of

[6] Wellek and Warren, *Theory of Literature*, pp. 139-140.

literature, the work is thus divided into something that is and is not literature.

A more recent formulation of essentially the same model has been proposed by Charles F. Hockett:

Literary scholars have a battery of terms, *plot, counterplot, introduction, climax, anticlimax, denouements*, with which they describe the larger-grained structure of certain types of literary discourse. A whole novel, we must assume, has some sort of indeterminate IC-structure, its ICs in turn consisting of still smaller ones, and so on down until we reach individual morphemes. The terminological arsenal of the literary scholar applies, often very well, to the largest size-levels of this structure; that of the linguist applies equally well to the smallest size-levels; but there is at present a poorly explored terrain in between.[7]

What would be the units of this presumably middle size level? Would it lie somewhere between Ingarden's fictional world and his second stratum of sentences? A review of Samuel Levin's *Linguistic Structures in Poetry* has proposed that notions like Levin's "couplings" would occupy this middle terrain.[8] Like the idea of the paragraph or of cohesion, "couplings" applies to stretches of language that lie beyond sentence boundaries.[9] That such stretches of language might be the proper territory of stylistics was proposed over a decade ago by Archibald Hill.[10] Showing how or what linguistic relations obtain above the level of the sentence is not useful for defining the relation between language and literature, for, even if one could describe larger units like the paragraph, one would still face the central literary issue of showing how the larger and the smaller linguistic units combine to produce a literary world. There is no distinct terrain between the smaller language units and the larger fictional world, because the linguistic strata have no existence apart from the fictional world they create.[11]

---

[7] Charles F. Hockett, *A Course in Modern Linguistics*, p. 557.

[8] William O. Hendricks, review of *Linguistic Structures in Poetry* by Samuel R. Levin, *Language* 42 (1966): 641.

[9] Samuel R. Levin (*Linguistic Structures in Poetry*) defines "coupling" as "a structure in which semantically and/or phonically equivalent forms occur in equivalent positions, the forms so occurring thus constituting special types of paradigms" (p. 18).

[10] Archibald A. Hill, *Introduction to Linguistic Structures*, p. 408.

[11] For the structuralist aestheticians, to describe the process of perception and the structure of literature would presumably be similar activities, since the literary work

The description of literary structure as an indeterminate set of *n* components is one that begins with a set of ultimate linguistic variables and, by defining their relations to one another, generates the fictional world. As was mentioned earlier, the two models do not differ in aim. The difference between them lies in the way of thinking about the relationship between literature and language. And this distinction would have little significance unless it made a big difference elsewhere. It does make a difference in method for the analysis of style, which affects in turn the attainment of the goals of literary study. The practical result of using the first model is that one can talk about language in literature and ignore the fictional world that subsumes it; or one can discuss that fictional world without reference to language. Most linguistic studies of style shy away from the fictional world, while literary criticism tends to discuss it either with no reference to language or with reference only to the idiosyncratic, nonsystematic aspects of language.[12]

Fred Householder once wrote that, when linguistics and literary criticism are combined, "one discipline has to give in and usually it is linguistics."[13] Which one suffers probably depends on the sympathies of the researcher. Given the complex nature of literature and the poverty of semantic theory in linguistics, critics are faced with a choice of continuing their intuitive but illuminating exegesis or of confining their explications to the comparatively narrow scope offered by linguistics. Whether stylistics will survive attempts to describe literary works in formal terms is a question that must remain open until sufficient theoretical speculation and application have been undertaken. It seems more important now to address the prior question of whether the attempt is worthwhile.

---

is constituted by being perceived aesthetically. It is possible that, at the level of the fictional world, language no longer exists, because it is no longer perceived as such. But, if this interpretation is correct, how is it to be reconciled with the formalist-structuralist tenet that by definition literary (poetic) language calls attention to itself? If language calls attention to itself at the level of the fictional world, it is by virtue of some interaction between that world and language itself. And, if that is the case, there is no need for a lower, linguistic, stratum of literary structure.

[12] That literary criticism requires some defense of its approach to literature is evident from Yakov Malkiel's review of *Style in Language*, ed. Thomas A. Sebeok, *International Journal of American Linguistics* 28 (1962): 271. Malkiel's charge is somewhat unfair in view of the failure of the social scientists to contribute to the Style in Language conference a theory or method of literary study superior to the existing body of literary criticism and theory.

[13] Fred W. Householder, review of *Language and Style* by Stephen Ullmann, *Language* 42 (1966): 632.

Consequences of the Style-Function Theory

To demonstrate the value of a theory, one needs (*inter alia*) to derive from it nontrivial consequences. The chief advantage of the mathematical formulation is one already mentioned: In this manner one can discuss the relation of style to literature without falling into a form-content dichotomy, on the one hand, and without reifying terms, on the other. A second advantage is the formality of a mathematical theory. A formal theory may be adequate or inadequate to account for the data it was constructed to explain. In either case, it will prove illuminating. If the theory is adequate, it will explain the data to which it is applied. If it is inadequate, it will not fit certain aspects of the data, but one can state more precisely than otherwise what those aspects of the data are and why they defy definition. Finally, a good theory should enable any individual student of a given subject to define narrowly his particular task, to relate it to the work of his predecessors, and to view his field of inquiry as a coherent whole.

The last point bears elaboration, since, if it is possible to relate in a logical framework existing studies of style, it is also possible to define within that framework a means of solving many problems of style. These problems can be specified as questions: Can there be groupings of literary styles or does the uniqueness of each style make grouping impossible? How can one account for the fact that some literary styles are called excellent, while others are judged mediocre or poor? When a term like *baroque* is applied to the style of different objects (e.g., paintings, poems, cantatas), is there a real correspondence between the styles of these objects or is one dealing only with analogy and metaphor? What is the etiology of the problem of style? How "valid" are stylistic studies that seek the style of the man in the style of his writing? Should a theory of literary style postulate a model of style in terms of the author's "poetic competence" or a model based directly on the author's literary work? By reference to the theory of the style function one can formulate testable hypotheses that will assist one in answering these questions. The following paragraphs address themselves to each of these questions in turn.

The first is a question of typology: Can there be groupings of styles? Since style is a function of the set of all well-defined literary works, those works that have similar structural components will have similar styles, even though each work has a unique style as well. There is no theoretical reason, therefore, why one cannot group styles according to historical period (*Jacobean*), kind of influence (*Ciceronian*), or some impressionistic label (*learned*). These terms are external principles of classification. Such principles supply the only means in terms of which the style space can be segmented.[14] They must, of course, be well defined. The knowledge that a group of works written in English during the reign of James I appeared close together in the style space, while no works written outside that reign appeared in the same space, would be a rigorously defined reason for calling the style of these works *Jacobean*.

Principles of classification of a more interesting kind can be proposed, but they are harder to define. The problem of accounting for intuitions of stylistic excellence is essentially one of finding a good principle for establishing sets in the style space. One could use a set of intuitive judgments that some works of Shakespeare have a better style than other works of Shakespeare. One would then examine the style space to see whether the stylistically better works and the stylistically poorer works formed two distinct sets. The basis of stylistic excellence would in this case lie chiefly within literature. This method of accounting for intuitive judgments of stylistic excellence would fail to satisfy those who want to know why people respond favorably to good style or what enabled them to make intuitive judgments of excellence in the first place. Empirical evaluation of the aesthetic effect is just conceivable in terms of the theory of the style function, but the formulation of the method must wait until two prior problems have been discussed.[15]

[14] This point follows from the definition of a continuum as something absolutely continuous and homogeneous of which no distinction of content can be affirmed except by reference to something else. In his discussion of Aristotelian views of style, Edward H. Tenney lists seven external principles of style classification: author (*Homeric*) style; time (*medieval*); medium (*lyric, Germanic*); subject (*philosophical*); geography (*Billingsgate*); audience (*popular*); purpose (*humorous*). See his "Style," in *Dictionary of World Literature*, ed. Joseph T. Shipley, pp. 398-399. But even with a set of principles, the problem of determining what features of the style space correspond to these principles remains unsolved. Louis T. Milic adduces the methodological problem as sufficient reason for abandoning style typologies: ". . . descriptions of style usually proceed by generalization, by abstraction of qualities from masses of detail. Style is difficult to handle simply because it is a mass of detail. To classify a particular set of such details by means of an abstraction is to make a claim that these details are more important than others, that they fall into a configuration and that this abstraction outweighs others that might be constructed out of the same materials" ("Against the Typology of Styles," in *Essays on the Language of Literature*, ed. Seymour Chatman and Samuel R. Levin, p. 447).

[15] Monroe C. Beardsley, in *Aesthetics from Classical Greek to the Present*, notes that empirical research in psychology has had an important effect upon the aesthetician's way of thinking about art; he recounts the history of this influence and

The first is the problem of ascribing a common stylistic label to struc-turally disparate objects like painting, music, and literature. Because of its higher order of generality, the theory of the style function can be used as a theoretical model for any academic discipline that employs the term *style* as an instrument of inquiry and explanation. Style, broadly speaking, is a way of doing it. *It* may be a game, a suit of clothes, or a cathedral. If one wished to establish as the domain of the style function the set of all games, suits of clothing, or cathedrals, one could use the theory to describe the style of these objects. The problem is to find a set of values (like the real numbers used in plotting points or the linguistic units used to specify the structural components of literature) that will adequately define these ob-jects.[16] We can assume that a group of cantatas, a group of cathedrals, and a group of poems are well-defined sets in their respective domains. We can further assume that the label *baroque* is well defined and correctly at-tached to each of these sets. If we can define a rule of correspondence that translates the structural descriptions of each of these objects into more general terms, then there is a real basis for ascribing a baroque style to structurally disparate objects.[17] If not, the ascription is made by way of analogy, and one would not be able to speak of a baroque style but only of the baroque styles of music, architecture, and literature. Alternatively, one could define a domain that has as its elements all works of art and then proceed by the method for establishing groups in the style space that was described in the last paragraph. Undoubtedly, a cultural anthropolo-gist or a student of semiotics could establish such a domain.[18]

---

discusses the efforts of aestheticians to explain value in empirical terms (pp. 376-388).

[16] A. L. Kroeber produced a study of clothing styles that has a mathematical model. An account of it can be found in his *Anthropology: Culture Patterns and Processes*, pp. 139-144.

[17] M. W. Croll described baroque art as one that "displays itself best when it works in heavy masses and resistant materials; and out of the struggle between a fixed pattern and an energetic forward movement often arrives at those strong and expres-sive disproportions in which it delights." This description is a good example of the more general terms that might apply to structurally disparate objects. Croll's essay, "The Baroque Style in Prose," is reprinted in Chatman and Levin, *Essays on the Language of Literature*, pp. 341-361. This essay and other important articles on "Attic" prose and Euphuistic rhetoric have been collected and reprinted in *Style, Rhetoric, and Rhythm: Essays by Morris W. Croll*, ed. J. Max Patrick et al.

[18] On the other hand, in *Elements of Semiology*, Roland Barthes points out that the study of the system of signs must at some time "find language . . . in its path, not only as a model, but also as a component, relay or signified" (pp. 10-11). For this reason the student of style in literature can make an important contribution to the

We are now in a position to review the history of the problem of style by reference to the theory of the style function. In the classical rhetorical tradition, which remained intact in English literary history at least through the age of Milton, *style* was normally ascribed only to linguistic discourse. Its extension to the visual arts in the eighteenth century ascribed the term to objects whose structural components were defined by values other than linguistic. To do this was, in effect, to define a new domain for the style function. Another shift in the domain occurred when Buffon used the term in reference to the human personality: le style est l'homme même. This shift was still more radical, since it fused the styles of two theoretically different domains. With the development of the social sciences, *style* gradually became associated with a collectivity and was identified with notions like a *Zeitgeist*.[19] It applied, therefore, to increasingly abstract domains. Because its domains were confused or poorly defined, the notion of style lost content until it is today the most tenuous of terms. The ancients had made the mistake of equating style too narrowly and atomistically with elements of linguistic discourse, but at least their theory of style had a specifiable content. The moderns learned to see style holistically as a property of a total object but tended not to define the object well and so could not successfully discuss style. Either style tended to become the unique object, or the term was discarded as meaningless. This last point brings us full circle to the philosophical dilemma that the theory of the style function was designed to resolve.

Studies that seek the man in his literary work not only postulate a correspondence between two structurally different objects but also appear to assume further that the correspondence is a one-to-one relation. They imply that the style of the personality as a whole is mapped onto the literary style as a whole. Since style, as well as personality, may be viewed as a total configuration (in terms of this theory), there is a theoretical basis on which to propose that a real correspondence may exist between the

---

advancement of semiotics if he can define the nature and operation of style. His work might then serve as a model for the study of other areas of culture that are partly though not wholly comprised of language.

[19] Karl D. Uitti, in *Linguistics and Literary Theory*, shows how the work of Karl Vossler, which embodies an idealist philosophy and equates language with "spiritual expression," gives as much attention to language as cultural process as it gives to the individual work. Vossler's method of linguistic analysis was called *Stilforschung*, since he felt that style was the preeminent aspect of language (pp. 127-129). Uitti's book, a historical account of the way in which linguistics and literary studies became distinct disciplines, holds special interest for those who see stylistics as an attempt to effect a rapprochement between the two areas of knowledge.

style of the text and the style of its author's personality. Furthermore, some psychological studies lend support to this assumption.[20] If it could be demonstrated that the two styles (of the man and of his writing) exist in a mapping relation, one would not need every time to validate the analysis of literary style by independent study of the author's personality.

One can use the assumption that the style of a man's personality is a mapping onto the text to define a method of explaining the aesthetic effect in psychological terms. If a man as author can map a personal style onto what he writes (or, rather, if his act of writing constitutes such a mapping), it is conceivable that a reverse mapping relation could exist between the style of the text and its reader. The pleasurable effect of good style could then be viewed as a mapping of excellent style (in some sense to be defined) onto, for example, human emotional structure.[21]

This matter of the relation of the man to his work raises a final question: Why do we not take the author's "poetic/stylistic competence" as

[20] Gordon W. Allport, *Personality: A Psychological Interpretation*, p. 489. Allport describes an experiment in which themes of seventy college students written at various times were studied for stylistic indices of the individual personality. Here are his comments: "The point of interest here is the method by which successful matchings [of papers of individuals] were made. Occasionally, to be sure, some striking mechanical feature caught the eye and aided in identifications. Addiction to semicolons would mark the writing of one student, or some other oddity of punctuation or spelling. But most of the identifications were not made on this basis but through a diagnosis of the *personal traits* of the writers. The investigators found themselves searching for a 'form-quality' of the individual. [The productions showed] a feeling for atmosphere; a well-balanced sense of humour; a quiet, amused tolerance of social relations and situations; . . . a positive self-assurance; definite, but neither prejudiced, nor opinionated; sense of humour. . . . [A third] was constantly bored. One concludes that style is not a matter of mechanical arrangement of grammatical and rhetorical figures" (pp. 491-492). Finally, Allport notes that style is interestingly revealed in the individual's narration of events he has seen or books he has read (p. 492).

[21] Jacques Lacan in "The Insistence of the Letter in the Unconscious," *Yale French Studies* 36-37 (1966): 112-147, discusses from a psychiatrist's viewpoint the possible specific relationship between emotional structure and style elements: "Freud defined the ego by the resistances which are proper to it. . . . But this resistance . . . is only secondary in relation to the specific resistances of the journey in the signifying order of the truth. That is the reason why an exhaustion of the mechanisms of defense . . . manifests itself . . . as simply the underside or reverse aspect of the mechanisms of the unconscious. Periphrasis, hyberbaton, ellipsis, suspension, anticipation, retraction, denial, digression, irony, these are the figures of style (Quintilian's *figurae sententiarum*); as catachresis, litotes, autonomasia, hypotyposis are the tropes, whose terms impose themselves as the most proper for the labeling of those mechanisms. Can one really see these as mere figures of speech when it is the figures themselves which are the active principle of the rhetoric of the discourse which the patient in fact utters" (pp. 139-140).

the domain of the style function rather than make his literary works the elements of the domain? The question is really a quibble. In the first place, it would be difficult to imagine how one would discuss a writer's competence without reference to his literary output. One would have to invoke linguistic values of some kind, presumably, and the only others available exist in the language spoken by him and his contemporaries. In the second place, a major reason for formulating the theory of style as a function is to work toward writing a system of rules that will generate a writer's style. This would be an account of the author's stylistic competence.[22] But, unlike the linguist who can rely on intuition or on near mastery of a language, the analyst of style cannot claim an analogous productive mastery of an author's rules of style. He must depend on the text, as the linguist ignorant of a given language uses an informant, and, just as that linguist in writing his grammar is not necessarily limited to the surface data or the particular performances of his informant, so the analyst of style is not textbound.

[22] "We thus make a fundamental distinction between *competence* (the speaker-hearer's knowledge of his language) and *performance* (the actual use of language in concrete situations). . . . The problem for the linguist, as well as for the child learning the language, is to determine *from the data of performance* [emphasis added] the underlying system of rules that has been mastered by the speaker-hearer and that he puts to use in actual performance." This definition of competence appears in A. Noam Chomsky's *Aspects of the Theory of Syntax*, p. 4.

For other attempts to discuss style with reference to generative grammar, see Samuel R. Levin, "Poetry and Grammaticalness," in *Proceedings of the Ninth International Congress of Linguists*, ed. Horace G. Lunt, pp. 308-314. Levin developed his notion of "poetic competence" at the Bowdoin College Conference on Linguistics and English Stylistics, which was held in Brunswick, Maine, May 4-6, 1967. Two years earlier James Peter Thorne proposed what was, in effect, a competence model in his "Stylistics and Generative Grammars," *Journal of Linguistics* 1 (1965): 49-59. Richard Ohmann has called the same notion "mentalism" in his essay "Mentalism in the Study of Literary Language" (in *Proceedings of the Conference on Language and Language Behavior*, ed. Eric M. Zale, pp. 188-212). None of these is a fully developed theory and most are illustrated from brief poems or passages of prose.

It is instructive to reflect upon these discussions in the light of a subsequent critique by Harold A. Gleason, Jr., "Probings into No Man's Land—The Marches of Linguistics, Semantics, Stylistics," lecture delivered at the Bowdoin College Conference. Gleason does not cite specific works on style, but he generally censures atomistic style methodology: "There has recently been a small amount of discussion of stylistic problems allegedly based on transformational-generative grammar, and generally reckoning *Syntactic Structures* in its conceptual genealogy. . . . There is a limit to the progress that can be expected in this direction, and I doubt that it is very far ahead of us. We have been observing and describing isolated facts of style, not the style of a whole text, and not really building a stylistic theory. There has been little cohesion and no comprehending framework."

Naturally, we are far from being able to formulate such rules. This kind of rigor and generality will be possible only when linguists have perfected their description of the semantic component of language. For present and practical purposes, the theory of the style function has provided in this chapter a coherent framework in which some key problems of stylistic analysis can be discussed and to which the methodological issues raised in succeeding chapters can be referred.

CHAPTER TWO

Locating Style in Literature

Methodological Preliminaries

In the remaining chapters of this study Shakespeare's *Richard II* and *Antony and Cleopatra* will be used to apply the theory of style as a function, particularly to develop a method of specifying the structural components of a literary work.[1] To expect that an exhaustive account of the linguistic properties of a piece of literature will yield its structure is to espouse the Baconian notion that if we are precise and patient enough in

[1] The original purpose of this study was to describe two phases of Shakespeare's style as exemplified by three English history plays and the Roman plays. For this purpose a computer-generated function-word concordance of these plays was obtained. So vast was the output that, for pragmatic and other reasons to be discussed later, the study was restricted to these two plays. A prospectus of the original plan, together with remarks on preparing the texts for computer processing, appears in *Shakespeare Newsletter* 15 (December 1965): v.

Citations to *Richard II* and *Antony and Cleopatra* throughout this book will be to the Kittredge edition of the *Complete Works*, 1936. The format of the line references replaces the traditional mixture of roman and arabic numerals by all arabic numbers, since it was impossible to represent roman numerals on the equipment available when the concordances were generated. One hopes that the reader will not be seriously inconvenienced by this practice.

The Folio was not chosen as the basic text, because it seemed that decisions about the definition of a sentence or a particular mark of punctuation were better made by a good editor than by one who lacked specialized knowledge of compositorial prac-

our observations we will learn the secrets of nature. Since there is no such mechanical discovery procedure, one is free to develop virtually any method that will fulfill the theoretical requirement of defining the segments of structure by reference to language. The method, of course, must be explicit so that others can verify its results, extend it to other data, or suggest modifications of it if the method should prove to be inappropriate or should produce erroneous results.

The method adopted here has three constraints, namely, to begin with a formal feature of the language (e.g., syntax, phonology, some well-defined aspect of the lexicon); to determine by some formal criterion whether that feature of the language behaves in a way that is peculiar to the text (is, in traditional terms, a stylistic feature); and, if so, to suggest what it contributes to the dramatic character of the text. The method does not solve the practical difficulty that rigorous and thorough analysis of a long text must be conducted in stages, and that, therefore, one needs a principle of selection that allows one to examine some parts of the text and to ignore others.

Although it is seldom discussed, the problem has been solved in ways that vary according to the end for which stylistic analysis is undertaken. Those interested in cases of disputed authorship have tended to choose as their starting point linguistic items that appear stable, are easy to define, and are therefore quantifiable.[2] The purpose of these writers is to distinguish texts, and they are interested only in that aspect of a work which will distinguish it from other texts. Others are less concerned with variation between texts and seek to define the literary use of language in terms of grammatical rules. Their studies may take the form of defining figures of speech, and their interest in the text tends to be confined to utterances that deviate from some grammatical rule.[3] While differing in their methods of getting at style or the language of literature, both groups seem to define

---

tice, textual history, and Renaissance theories of punctuation. Reference to Kittredge was supplemented by consultation of the Variorum edition of *Antony and Cleopatra*, John Dover Wilson's Cambridge edition of *Richard II* and *Antony and Cleopatra*, and Irving Ribner's revision of Kittredge.

[2] Interest in statistical studies of function words as a clue to authorship was greatly stimulated by the work of Frederick Mosteller and David L. Wallace entitled *Inference and Disputed Authorship: The Federalist*, which argues on the basis of words like *an*, *of*, and *upon* that Madison, not Hamilton, wrote all twelve of the disputed papers.

[3] In "Poetry and Grammaticalness" (in *Proceedings of the Ninth International Congress of Linguists*, ed. Horace G. Lunt), Samuel R. Levin suggests, for example, that in the interpretation of sequences like *a grief ago* one's knowledge of grammar "limits

their object of study as a deviation from some norm, statistical or grammatical.

Michael Riffaterre has been more concerned with identifying stylistic excellence than has either of these groups, and he has argued against using any norm on the ground that it is both unobtainable and irrelevant.[4] It is not impossible to obtain a norm. The difficulty of establishing a statistical norm for the language as a whole can be, and often is, circumvented by comparing texts in order to obtain a relative norm. Grammatical norms are not so elusive as was formerly supposed, since intuition and the insights of traditional grammarians are now more widely recognized as valid sources of information about rules of grammar. Riffaterre holds that the norm is irrelevant because "a linguistic unit acquires, changes, or loses its stylistic effect according to position" in the text.[5] He seeks to identify the starting point of stylistic analysis in the reader's response to a given passage. The problem he defines is not so much one of locating style in a text as it is one of explaining the aesthetic effect of style. This matter, it was suggested earlier, is one of charting a relation between the style of the text and human emotional structure, after both of these have been adequately described.[6] Merely to define this task is to indicate that it has scarcely been attempted.

These approaches to locating style in a text share a common tendency to identify it by reference to something outside the work of literature—a grammatical rule, a statistical norm, or an ideal reader's response. With the exception of Riffaterre's theory, they leave unexplained the relationship between "stylistic" elements in the text and the rest of the text. They imply, too, that some sections of the text "have" style while others have not, thus violating the traditional critical assumption that every item in a work of literature contributes to its total aesthetic character. Finally, they take as their starting point a number of discrete variables—a portion of the vocabulary, a figure of speech, or passages containing special effects. Style thus becomes fragmented rather than a function of the entire work.

As statements about the location of style, therefore, these approaches

---

the framework within which the attempts to render the sequence grammatical" occur. The result is that one can assign a grammatical structure to this kind of expression, and the attempt to do so brings it into association with narrow, well-defined meanings. This latter confrontation, he points out, "probably lies behind all metaphor" (p. 314).

[4] Michael Riffaterre, "Criteria for Style Analysis," *Word* 15 (1959): 425.

[5] Michael Riffaterre, "Stylistic Context," *Word* 16 (1960): 207.

[6] See p. 15.

have serious inadequacies, but if they are viewed as positing systems of oppositions—between grammatical rule and deviation, statistical norm and significant fluctuation, stylistic context and stylistic function—they become useful tools for stylistic analysis. The description of style as a set of oppositions may well be as useful for stylistics as that method was in structural linguistics.[7] Since these methods for undertaking stylistic analysis can be indifferently adopted, or even used to supplement one another, the question of deciding where to begin the analysis of style would appear to be a pseudo problem. Style is a *continuous* function, however; any cut into the system must be made in virtue of some principle external to style itself. But choosing that principle, defining a starting point for stylistic analysis, is a theoretically indifferent matter. The problem is to keep going until the system of style has been thoroughly described and its elements coordinated. One might wish to begin systematically by pursuing a single feature of syntax (e.g., nonfinite verbs, adjectives) or by sampling sentences, words, or passages randomly. On the other hand, there is no reason why intuition should not provide a starting point. In Shakespeare there are many similar contexts of situation (death scenes, quarrel scenes, or ceremonial scenes), of content shared by two or more plays (the passages on sleep in *Henry V* and *Macbeth*, for example), or of passages that seem characteristic of one play or another. Intuitions about style in such passages can easily provide a starting point for analyzing style. Since style is a function of the entire work, ideally "we should be able to start at any given point and should arrive at the same results."[8] It seems desirable now to support these remarks by illustrating some principles of selection, by exemplifying the method of specifying the structural components of literature in terms of linguistic values, and in this manner initiating the stylistic analysis of *Richard II* and *Antony and Cleopatra*. Hence, in this chapter three methods of locating style in a text will be illustrated: a study of sentence mood, an analysis of passages thought to be representative of the style of each play, and an examination of selections from each play that have similar content and different styles.

Sentence Mood: Interrogatives and Imperatives

Syntax operates at several levels of linguistic structure and enters into

---

[7] The possibilities of this method are best illustrated by the work of Roman Jakobson, especially his essay with Claude Lévi-Strauss "*Les Chats* de Baudelaire," *L'Homme* 3 (1962): 5-21, and his book with Lawrence G. Jones, *Shakespeare's Verbal Art in Th'Expence of Spirit.*
[8] René Wellek and Austin Warren, *Theory of Literature*, p. 172.

various systemic choices.[9] One system is that of mood, the choice of making a sentence declarative, interrogative, or imperative. Conditional sentences are a special kind of sentence, and a preliminary study of their behavior in *1 Henry IV* indicated that Shakespeare's choices in the system of mood might serve a quite conscious artistic purpose.[10] A manual count of the conditional sentences spoken by Falstaff, Hal, and Hotspur assigns 66 percent of them to Falstaff, 22 percent to the Prince, and 12 percent to

[9] M. A. K. Halliday first outlined systemic grammar in his "Categories of the Theory of Grammar," *Word* 17 (1961): 241-292, and he developed it in articles like "Class in Relation to the Axes of Chain and Choice in Language," *Linguistics*, no. 2 (1963), pp. 5-15; "Some Notes on Deep Grammar," *Journal of Linguistics* 2 (1966): 57-67 and "Notes on Transitivity and Theme in English," *Journal of Linguistics* 3 (1967): 37-81, 199-244; 4 (1968): 179-215.

In collaboration with Halliday, members of the Communication Research Centre at University College, London, undertook a grammatical and statistical study of scientific English based on systemic grammar. They designed a handbook of analysis "to ensure that the description is applied as consistently as possible" and included in it definitions, examples, criteria of analysis, suggestions for diagramming, and categories for coding information. This handbook is the basis for most of the discussion of Shakespeare's syntax, unless otherwise noted.

Interested readers may consult a more recent, published, and fuller account of materials in the handbook and results of the study of scientific English in Rodney Huddleston, R. A. Hudson, E. O. Winter, and A. Henrici, *Sentence and Clause in Scientific English*.

[10] The analysis of conditional sentences in *I Henry IV* was a pilot study undertaken to determine what problems would arise in a linguistic and computational study of Shakespeare's style. Results seemed sufficiently interesting to warrant their inclusion here.

For a full grammatical discussion of how the system of mood operates in the prose of the Falstaff plays, see Vivian Salmon's "Sentence Structure in Colloquial Shakespearian English," in *Transactions of the Philological Society, 1965*, pp. 105-140. Salmon, using the prose of the Falstaff plays, points out the range of statement, question, and imperative forms open to an Elizabethan speaker and suggests what factors led him to select one of a set in free variation.

A few critics have found this aspect of Shakespeare's syntax a source of interpretative hypotheses in plays like *Macbeth* and *Lear*. Arnold Stein ("*Macbeth* and Word-Magic," *Sewanee Review* 59 [1951]: 271-284) sees questions as an expression of doubts in *Macbeth*, Winifred M. T. Nowottny ("Lear's Questions," *Shakespeare Survey* 10 [1957]: 90-97) finds Lear's insistence upon asking questions to be the source of his tragedy, and, in the same play, J. C. Maxwell ("The Technique of Invocation in 'King Lear,'" *Modern Language Review* 45 [1950]: 142-147) sees questions as related to inquiry about the meaning of the universe and the source of power in Lear's world. Maynard Mack, on the other hand, notes that *Lear*'s distinctive coloring onstage comes from "its commands, its invocations and appeals that have the quality of commands, its flat-footed defiances and refusals" (*King Lear in Our Time*, p. 90). Hazel Guyol analyzes the imperatives of Goneril in this play ("A Temperance of Language," *English Journal* 55 [1966]: 316-319), notably IV.ii, *Wear this. Spare speech. Decline your head.* Most recently, David Parker has pointed out

Hotspur.[11] There appear to be two kinds of conditionals in the play, one. in which the apodosis is an optative imperative and a second where the protasis is a verifiable statement, illustrated, respectively, by the following:

> An I have not ballads made on you all, and sung to filthy tunes, let a cup of sack be my poison.
>
> (2.2.47-49)

> *Fal.* Give me a cup of sack. I am a rogue if I have drunk to-day.
>
> *Prince.* O villain! thy lips are scarce wip'd since thou drunk'st last.
>
> (2.4.168-171)

The optative imperative relates the first type to oaths, promises, vows, boasts, and prayers.[12] The truth of these statements cannot be verified, or, at least, it is verifiable only contingently, depending on what happens in the future. The truth or falsity of the second type is immediately evident. The Prince has just watched *Titan kiss a dish of butter*, and the audience can easily adjudicate between the two statements. Because the Prince has given the lie to his premise, Falstaff is, by his own admission, a rogue. Conversely, when the Prince later says to Falstaff *if there were anything in thy pocket but tavern reckonings ... I am a villain*, the audience knows well that the Prince is not a villain, for they have heard

---

the role played by the imperative in the sonnets ("Verbal Moods in Shakespeare's Sonnets," *Modern Language Quarterly* 30 [1969]: 331-339). Few of these critics engage in extensive commentary, but their interpretative comments suggest that choices in the mood system might well prove a fruitful area for further study.

[11] Conditionals include sentences with an explicit *if* (variant: *an*) or an implied one (*were it not here apparent that thou art heir apparent*). Percents were obtained by dividing the total conditionals spoken by these three characters (94) into the number spoken by each. Falstaff spoke 57 in his 621 lines; Hal 27 in 575; and Hotspur 10 in 562.

[12] Walter Coppedge, who studied oaths in twelve of Shakespeare's plays (but did not include *1 Henry IV*), makes two points that are germane to this study of conditionals: "Superficially considered, an oath would appear to be a blasphemous exclamation; but a closer examination reveals the oath to be a conditional self-imprecation." According to the categories of analysis derived from this point by Coppedge, Hal's conversion speech would be more like a vow than an oath. Second, Coppedge notes the fact that the audience was actively involved as witnesses to oaths spoken on the stage: "The careful reader must keep in mind the double audience—the one addressed on stage and the other whose comprehension of the speaker's oaths will allow a richer and broader interpretation" ("Shakespeare's Oaths and Imprecations," *Dissertation Abstracts* 28 (1968): 2644A).

him itemize the bill. The conditional in these scenes contrasts the Prince's integrity and Falstaff's roguery. These exchanges foreshadow the field of Shrewsbury, where Falstaff will characteristically ask, *But how if honour prick me off when I come on? What then?* Verifiable conditions are not to his liking and he refuses to formulate them. Hal's conditions are almost always verifiable, either by the event or by their logical form. We cannot take seriously Hal's apostrophe to the presumably dead Falstaff, because it is a counterfactual conditional whose protasis is by definition false: *O, I should have a heavy miss of thee | If I were much in love with vanity!*

Hotspur's hybris expresses itself in conditional clauses that are curses:

> Speak of Mortimer?
> Zounds, I will speak of him, and let my soul
> Want mercy if I do not join with him!
>   (1.3.130-132)

> I'll keep them all.
> By God, he shall not have a Scot of them!
> No, if a Scot would save his soul, he shall not.
>   (1.3.213-215)

Hal must steer a middle course between Falstaff's vanity and Hotspur's false honor. His promise to reform is concluded in a conditionally expressed oath:

> This in the name of God I promise here:
> The which if he be pleas'd I shall perform,
> I do beseech your Majesty may salve
> The long-grown wounds of my intemperance.
> If not, the end of life cancels all bands,
> And I will die a hundred thousand deaths
> Ere break the smallest parcel of this vow.
>   (3.2.153-159)

This oath contrasts with the rash vows of Hotspur and the false boasts of Falstaff, despite the hyperbolical vow to die a hundred thousand deaths. Hal's humility is expressed in the second line, which means that, if God is pleased to have Hal perform his promise, Hal will keep it. Because Falstaff's false brags have been undercut throughout by his behavior, we are not surprised that he does not fulfill his promise to kill Percy: *Well, if Percy be alive, I'll pierce him.* But we are able fully to verify Hal's fulfillment of his promise. One might say, incidentally, that the action of this play is a fulfillment of a verifiable conditional expressed by the Bishop of Carlisle in *Richard II*:

> O, if you raise this house against this house,
> It will the wofullest division prove
> That ever fell upon this cursed earth.
>
> (4.1.145-147)

We might finally ask why Falstaff speaks so many conditionals. Falstaff's social status is ambiguous: as a knight he has dim notions about chivalry, honor, and oaths, but his real occupation is roguery. The apodoses of his conditionals, with their references to valor and villainy, admirably reflect his various roles. The salvation-damnation theme of Hotspur's oaths also appears in Falstaff's conditionals:

> Before I knew thee, Hal, I knew nothing; and now am I, if a man should speak truly, little better than one of the wicked. I must give over this life, and I will give it over! By the Lord, an I do not, I am a villain! I'll be damn'd for never a king's son in Christendom.
>
> (1.2.104-109)

Such remarks are, of course, entirely appropriate to Falstaff as the reverend vice of dramatic convention:

> If I do not beat thee out of thy kingdom with a dagger of lath and drive all thy subjects afore thee like a flock of wild geese, I'll never wear hair on my face more.
>
> (2.4.150-153)

Falstaff's brags, modeled on oaths, thus provide a simultaneous vision of two worlds, heroic and antiheroic. The verifiable condition removes the ambiguity from this double vision, for its verbal signs can always be checked against the external reality they claim to represent. They allow the audience to compare a statement with a situation and to draw its own conclusions about the truth value and the implications of that statement. Although these remarks about Falstaff and the themes of this play are common critical knowledge, the dramatic function of the conditional has not been discussed elsewhere.[13]

[13] In *Every Man in His Humour*, it seems clear that Ben Jonson also uses oaths in conditional form for comic purposes, and especially to characterize swaggerer types. In the England of that time conditionals undoubtedly saved many a braggart's honor

This pilot study of conditional sentences in *1 Henry IV* suggested that a full-scale investigation of sentence mood might yield interesting insights into the style of *Richard II* and *Antony and Cleopatra*. It would seem, for example, that stylistic development meant in part recognizing how to use grammatical options effectively. To appreciate this point, one need only compare the questions that constitute the opening lines of *Richard II* and *Hamlet*. *Who's there?* is a *wh*-question; it cannot be answered by a simple yes or no. The answer to it must yield new information. The epistemological problem of determining the ghost's honesty need not be one's favorite explanation for Hamlet's procrastination to recognize that the question (though it may not, as John Dover Wilson contends, adumbrate the entire dramatic action) has overtones beyond its immediate context. At the very least it furthers the dramatic action in a way that the opening question of *Richard II* fails to do:

> Old John of Gaunt, time-honoured Lancaster,
> Hast thou, according to thy oath and band,
> Brought hither Henry Hereford, thy bold son,
> Here to make good the boist'rous late appeal,
> Which then our leisure would not let us hear,
> Against the Duke of Norfolk, Thomas Mowbray?
> (1.1.1-6)

That this elaborate *yes/no* question elicits only the simple affirmative *I have, my liege* is not surprising, since it supplies all the information ordinarily requested by *wh*- questions. Before it is completed we have learned *who* is present on stage (Gaunt, Hereford, Norfolk), *why* they have assembled (to settle an earlier argument), *how* the speaker is related to those he addresses (by feudal oath), and, incredibly, *where* everyone is (*here, hither*). Moreover, Richard must ask a second question before the dramatic action can begin.[14]

---

and neck, as Touchstone's remarks in *As You Like It* indicate: *All these you may avoid but the Lie Direct, and you may avoid that too, with an If. . . . Your If is the only peacemaker. Much virtue in If* (5.4.101-102, 107-108). In *Merry Wives* Falstaff has few conditionals, although those few occur in some of his best speeches, where he uses them to boast. The humor of the play lies more in his being subject to conditions imposed on him by others, for example, when it is suggested that he hide in the basket: *If he be a man of any reasonable stature, he may creep in here* (3.3.137-138). The humor here does not proceed from Falstaff's wit undercutting itself; the joke in a sense is not on Falstaff but on the speaker, Mrs. Page.

[14] It is commonplace for critics to defend elaborate speeches of this kind as functioning dramatically to characterize Richard. Many speakers besides Richard speak in

Table 1
Sentences Classified by Mood

	Exclamatory	Interrogative	Imperative
R2	12	236	460
Ant.	8	261	780

To initiate the study of the system of mood in the two plays, exclamatory, interrogative, and imperative sentences in *Richard II* and *Antony and Cleopatra* were counted. Their frequencies appear in Table 1.[15] Exclamatory sentences decreased by 25 percent in *Antony*, a fact that is not so important as the different manner in which they are used in the plays. Clustering in the early acts of *Richard II*, they contribute to the mood of lamentation and sighing that not only belongs to King Richard but also permeates the speech of every other character:

How long a time lies in one little word!
(1.3.213)

---

the style ascribed to him. Many speeches, like this one, are simply awkward. Consider these lines spoken by the less self-dramatic Bolingbroke:

Be he the fire, I'll be the yielding water;
The rage be his, whilst on the earth I rain
My waters—on the earth, and not on him.
(3.3.58-60)

Here there is an attempt at parallel structure that results in a syntactic ambiguity that serves no dramatic function. *Be he the fire* can be a suppressed conditional, or, by analogy with *the rage be his*, an optative imperative. Compare also the conversation between Bushy and the Queen (2.2) and the scene where the gardeners comment on the condition of the kingdom (3.4) for examples where speakers other than Gaunt or Richard indulge in conceited language.

[15] Strictly speaking, mood is best viewed as a system of the clause rather than of the sentence. Hence, if a sentence contains three verbs in the imperative form, one can say that it contains three clauses in the imperative mood. In this study such a sentence would be counted as three imperatives to match the clause count rather than as a single imperative to match the sentence count. The same procedure was followed for interrogative frequencies. Further notes on procedural matters are provided in Appendix A, pp. 273-278.

Because the style of *Antony* presents a greater challenge to formal analysis, comparative statements about the two plays will normally be made with reference to the later play, even though this procedure introduces a certain bias in its favor. Throughout this study the prose lines of *Antony* have been eliminated so that the plays are of equal length when length is determined by word count: *Richard II*, 21,809 verse words; *Antony*, 21,777 verse words. These figures are taken from Marvin Spevack's Concordance to the *Complete Works*.

O, how that name befits my composition!
(2.1.73)

Used in indirect statement, the emotion of these statements becomes self-conscious:

Nay, rather every tedious stride I make
Will but remember me what a deal of world
I wander from the jewels that I love.
(1.3.268-270)

These feelings seem to culminate in York's helpless cry:

God for his mercy! what a tide of woes
Comes rushing on this woful land at once!
(2.2.98)

While Shakespeare uses the exclamatory sentence seriously in *Antony* to express the remorse of Enobarbus (4.6.32), most often the context is lighthearted, even mocking:

How much unlike art thou Mark Antony!
(1.5.35)

Eno.   O,how he loves Caesar!
Agr. Nay, but how dearly he adores Mark Antony!
(3.2.7-8)

The mood of lightness prevails at the deaths of both Antony and Cleopatra:

Here's sport indeed! How heavy weighs my lord!
(4.15.32)

What poor an instrument
May do a noble deed!
(5.2.236-237)

The strong emotion that these forms convey is here controlled and rendered more poignant by the blend of lightheartedness and solemnity that seems the special mark of Cleopatra's language in the closing scenes of the play.

Although the frequency of interrogatives was relatively stable from play to play, when different types of interrogatives were distinguished, important differences between the plays emerged. The major division of interrogatives is between *wh-* and *yes/no* questions, but there are certain vari-

Table 2
Types of Interrogative Sentences

	Wh-	Yes/No	Variant	Total
R2	122	101	13	236
Ant.	122	94	45	261

ants like echo questions, disjunctives, tags, questions with declarative form, and minor or verbless questions. Taken together, these variants increased in *Antony and Cleopatra*, especially declarative and verbless questions.[16] Table 2 provides the frequencies for *wh-*, *yes/no*, and variant questions. The more colloquial variants, declarative and verbless questions, are exemplified respectively by these quotations:

> Now, sirrah, you do wish yourself in Egypt?
>
> (2.3.10)
>
> Cold-hearted toward me?
>
> (3.13.158)

They are associated with Antony, Cleopatra, and their followers rather than with Caesar. Verbless questions do not occur at all in *Richard II*.

Among *wh-* questions the word *what* was the favorite interrogative term in both plays. Other *wh-* words occur far less often, tend to be adverbial types, and exhibit some difference of rank. In *Richard II* the words *how*, *who*, and *where* are favored in that order; in *Antony* the favored words are *where*, *how*, and *why*. A greater tendency to repeat words and phrases explains the high frequency of *who* in the earlier play:

> Than your good words. But who comes here?
>
> (2.3.20)
>
> Stands for my bounty. But who comes here?
>
> (2.3.67)
>
> Hath power enough to serve our turn. But
> who comes here?
>
> (3.2.90)
>
> Against their will. But who comes here?
>
> (3.3.19)

[16] Frequencies for each these variants appear in Table A-1, and examples of each are given in the explanatory notes that accompany this table.

                          May happily bring forth. But who comes
                                           here?
                                                      (5.3.22)

Whereas this line or a variant of it occurs five times in *Richard III* and
Romeo and Juliet, it appears only twice in *Julius Caesar* and *King Lear* and
not at all in *Antony*. In the later style it is rivaled by an imperative, such as
Look where they come (*Ant*. 1.1.10).

Questions do not always exist for the answers they elicit about the
dramatic action. The Czech critic Jiří Veltruský has shown how a dagger
can, variously, serve as a prop in the action, as a sign of a character's social
status, or as a symbol of some idea, such as violence.[17] A linguistic form
like the conditionals of *1 Henry IV* or the questions in *Richard II* and
Antony can also dramatize a character, evoke a mood, or symbolize some
aspect of the theme. The questions of Cleopatra and of the women in
Richard II occur at a much higher than average rate, and it may be that
questions are associated with women or with some quality ascribed to
them like powerlessness or a tendency to display emotion. Bolingbroke
and Caesar have far fewer than Richard or Antony; moreover, those of the
latter two characters occur with greatest frequency in the third and fourth
acts, which witness their disgrace and defeat.[18] Antony's questions, for
example, express his rage at finding Cleopatra with Thyreus and center
around the events leading to his death.

In *Richard II* questions present both the political theme of rights and
the psychological theme of man's internal source of power and control.
The Duke of York, whose ratio of questions is identical with King
Richard's, raises the issue of a subject's claim to his inheritance on behalf
of Bolingbroke (2.1) and of Richard's title to the crown (2.3). Richard,
just before his capitulation to Bolingbroke at Flint Castle, explores the
relationship between his name of king and his ability to stave off misfor-
tune: *Am I not King? Is not the King's name twenty thousand names? Are*

[17] Jiří Veltruský, "Man and Object in the Theater," in *A Prague School Reader on
Esthetics, Literary Structure, and Style*, ed. and trans. Paul L. Garvin, pp. 83-91.
[18] The chief method of determining the relative frequency of a construction in the
speech of a given character is to establish proportions, e.g., of interrogatives to
imperatives. This procedure eliminates problems created by varying line lengths.
These problems are not necessarily solved by determining the ratio of an item to the
lines spoken, since ratios give undue emphasis to speakers with a very small number
of lines. For comparative purposes, proportions are given in Table A-2 for most of
the major characters and their ratios in Table A-3.

we not high? Sometimes the questions take the form of a catechism or an examination of conscience designed to achieve resignation to the will of God:

> Say, is my kingdom lost? Why, 'twas my care;
> And what loss is it to be rid of care?
> Strives Bolingbroke to be as great as we?
> Greater he shall not be; if he serve God,
> We'll serve him too, and be his fellow so.
> Revolt our subjects? That we cannot mend;
> (3.2.94-99)

> What must the King do now? Must he submit?
> The King shall do it. Must he be depos'd?
> The King shall be contented. Must he lose
> The name of king? A God's name, let it go!
> (3.3.143-146)

At other times the questions have a distinctly literary and rhetorical flavor. One thinks of the stichomythia of the exchange with Gaunt (2.1.88-92) or of this direct echo of the *ubi sunt* formula:

> Where is the Earl of Wiltshire? Where is Bagot?
> What is become of Bushy? Where is Green?
> That they have let the dangerous enemy
> Measure our confines with such peaceful steps?
> (3.2.122-125)

The imitation of Marlowe's *Doctor Faustus* is, of course, well known:

> Was this face the face
> That every day under his household roof
> Did keep ten thousand men? Was this the face
> That like the sun did make beholders wink?
> Was this the face that fac'd so many follies
> And was at last outfac'd by Bolingbroke?
> A brittle glory shineth in this face.
> As brittle as the glory is the face,
> (4.1.281-288)

The notion of a rhetorical question—one asked for effect and for which no answer is expected—is clearly exemplified in these passages. Richard seeks no reply; even when he supplies an answer, the response carries no greater conviction than the original request for information. The recital of the catechism is glib and the note of resignation hollow. By contrast, in the soliloquy of Act Five, there are no rhetorical questions. Still, these should not be dismissed as pseudo syntax or as an element in the generally rhetorical style of this play. Like Richard's reliance on analogy and like the catechetical form that they often assume, these questions are a futile though sincere effort to arrive at truth and explanation through language and the exercise of reason. As such they display the poetic and imaginative powers that make Richard one of Shakespeare's most engaging kings.

Though it lacks poetic and dramatic impact, there is one occasion when Richard by asking questions achieves some truth and gains a measure of psychological power over Bolingbroke. After the latter's exile the two men meet only at Flint Castle (3.3.187-209), where Bolingbroke protests his innocence of ambition, asks his followers to show respect to the King, and repeats that he has come only for his rights. They meet again in the deposition scene, but the future King Henry is relieved of the onus of guilt, since the legal formalities are carried out by York and Northumberland. As the scene closes, however, Richard calls Bolingbroke's bluff:

> *Rich.*   I'll beg one boon,
> And then be gone and trouble you no more.
> Shall I obtain it?
>
> *Boling.*   Name it, fair cousin.
>
> *Rich.*   Fair cousin? I am greater than a king;
> For when I was a king, my flatterers
> Were then but subjects; being now a subject,
> I have a king here to my flatterer.
> Being so great, I have no need to beg.
>
> *Boling.*   Yet ask.
>
> *Rich.*   And shall I have?
>
> *Boling.*   You shall.
>
> *Rich.*   Then give me leave to go.
>
> *Boling.*   Whither?
>
> *Rich.*   Whither you will, so I were from your sights.
>
> *Boling.*   Go some of you, convey him to the Tower.
>
> *Rich.*   O, good! Convey? Conveyers are you all,
> That rise thus nimbly by a true king's fall.
>
>   (4.1.302-318)

The trivial questions create in Bolingbroke a hope that he will be allowed to show kingly magnanimity, but they succeed as nothing previously had done in arousing his anger. They betray him into a public and an unjust sentence of imprisonment, which counteracts the sense of fair-minded justice evoked by his earlier judgments of Richard's allies. Unfortunately, compared with the dramatic thrust of the entire play, the incident is trivial, the stylistic quality of the dialogue is poor, and the possibilities opened by it are left unexplored.

Compared to Richard, Bolingbroke speaks significantly fewer questions and a higher number of imperatives.[19] When he issues commands, he uses optative forms and terms of address sparingly, with the result that his imperative style is more brusque than Richard's. The optatives that he does use cluster in the ritual scenes of the first act; his commands increase as he challenges Richard's authority and gains power. Nearly all of these appear in scenes where he acts as minister of justice: his sentence on Bushy and Green in the third act, his arbitration of the quarrel between Bagot and Aumerle in the fourth act, and, in the last act, his pardon of Aumerle and Carlisle. The imperatives used by him in these scenes of judgment are nearly twice as numerous as those used by Richard when he presided at the trial of Bolingbroke and Mowbray in the first and third scenes of Act One. Richard's imperatives are generally ineffectual, whether they be the moral directives to Mowbray and Bolingbroke in the opening scene, *Forget, forgive; conclude and be agreed,* or the apostrophes to the earth

---

[19] The only test of statistical significance used in this study was the chi-square test, which is defined as "the sum of the squared discrepancies between observed and expected frequencies, each divided by the expected frequency" (Quinn McNemar, *Psychological Statistics,* p. 212). The test was used to determine whether two sets of proportions (e.g., of interrogatives to imperatives in *Richard II* and *Antony and Cleopatra*) are significantly different. Throughout this study a second set of observed frequencies has been substituted for the expected frequencies. This change could present problems for interpreting results if the texts were not of the same length or if the chi-square table consisted of more than two sets of proportions, but in the fourfold table used here (with the correction for continuity) there is little difficulty deciding which factor in a set of proportions accounts for a given difference. Thus, it is clear that imperatives are virtually equal in the speeches of King Richard (137, or .1814) and Bolingbroke (82, or .1985), so that interrogatives must account for the significant difference in the proportion of imperatives to interrogatives in the speeches of these two characters (where the interrogatives for King Richard are 84, or .1112, and those for Bolingbroke are 27, or .0653). Chi-square tests were carried out with the aid of an electronic desk calculator. Because numbers sometimes exceeded the capacity of the machine, the last five figures of numerator and denominator were eliminated before dividing to obtain the chi-square.

and to his name in the fatal events prior to Flint Castle. His most famous
imperatives, like his questions, appear to be futile exercises in rhetoric:

> Of comfort no man speak!
> Let's talk of graves, of worms, and epitaphs,
> Make dust our paper, and with rainy eyes
> Write sorrow on the bosom of the earth.
> Let's choose executors and talk of wills.
> . . . .
> For God's sake let us sit upon the ground
> And tell sad stories of the death of kings!
>   (3.2.144-148, 155-156)

It may be argued, however, that these lines and later uses of the imperative
by Richard have a special force and authority, but it is an argument more
conveniently developed in the final chapter of this study.

Because the ratio of interrogatives in the lines spoken by Cleopatra is
quite extraordinary, questions would appear to be a hallmark of her style.
While it is not unusual for characters in either play to raise a great many
rhetorical questions and to answer them in one fashion or another, this
trick of raising and answering questions assumes special significance in her
language:

> O Charmian!
> Where think'st thou he is now? Stands he, or sits he?
> Or does he walk? or is he on his horse?
> O happy horse, to bear the weight of Antony!
> Do bravely, horse! for wot'st thou whom thou mov'st?
> The demi-Atlas of this earth, the arm
> And burgonet of men. He's speaking now,
> Or murmuring 'Where's my serpent of old Nile?'
> For so he calls me. Now I feed myself
> With most delicious poison. Think on me,
> That am with Phoebus' amorous pinches black
> And wrinkled deep in time?
>   (1.5.18-29)

By enumerating the possible circumstances of Antony, these questions
answer themselves. They create and sustain a mood of speculation that
merges into a series of dialogues between Cleopatra and Charmian, between her and Antony's horse, between her and Antony. By these means
she retreats into an imaginary world where the lovers alone exist, yet it is

not wholly imaginary, for we soon learn from Alexas that Antony in Rome was thinking of Cleopatra and of his hope to make her mistress of the entire East. We even learn that he *soberly did mount an arm-gaunt steed.*

That Cleopatra's questions are an instrument for achieving truth and that the answers to them merit belief is further suggested by the scene in Act Three where she asks her messenger about Octavia. The messenger understands what is expected of him and answers accordingly. Cleopatra seems to fashion Octavia to her own desire, yet her picture may very well be the "real" one. Octavia is thirty and a widow. It would not be surprising if a woman of her *holy, cold, and still conversation* were *low-voic'd*, and, though Lear may think this an excellent thing in woman, Cleopatra does not value it and suspects rightly that Antony will not do so either. Hence, there is reason to believe that, despite the barbed selectivity of her inquiries, Cleopatra's questions conjure up no unrealistic picture.

At times the context of situation supplies the answer to the questions raised by Cleopatra. When Antony returns safe from battle she asks one of her most enigmatic questions:

> Lord of lords!
> O infinite virtue, com'st thou smiling from
> The world's great snare uncaught?
>
> (4.8.16-18)

We may be hard pressed at one level to state exactly why Cleopatra asks this question at this point, but we have no doubt of the answer: Antony stands, safe and alive, before the eyes of the questioner. Earlier in this scene, when Caesar had offered Cleopatra clemency if she would betray Antony, her reply took the shape of a question:

> *Ant.* To the boy Caesar send this grizzled head,
> And he will fill thy wishes to the brim
> With principalities.
>
> *Cleo.* That head, my lord?
>
> (3.13.17-19)

Antony's interpretation of this as a negative answer is never contradicted nor is his reply to Caesar countermanded.

This tendency to answer her own questions, to ask questions that will furnish her with an expected but realistic answer, or to raise questions whose answer is obvious needs to be considered when interpreting Cleopatra's other speeches. After the Thyreus episode, which is a second attempt by Caesar to win Cleopatra's allegiance, Antony is not so sure of her behavior:

> *Ant.*   To flatter Caesar, would you mingle eyes
>   With one that ties his points?
>
> *Cleo.*   Not know me yet?
>   (3.13.156-157)

Antony counters with another question but is at last satisfied by her protestation of fidelity, and well he might be, since it is an all-encompassing curse on herself, her children, and her country that will befall her if she does not speak the truth (3.13.158-167). In view of this oath and of earlier opportunities to judge the truth of the answers to Cleopatra's questions, there seems no good reason to doubt the sincerity implied by *Not know me yet?*

Given this evidence, we are in a better position to judge the truth of Cleopatra's answer to the most important of all her questions:

> *Cleo.*   Think you there was or might be such a man
>   As this I dreamt of?
>
> *Dol.*   Gentle madam, no.
>
> *Cleo.*   You lie, up to the hearing of the gods!
>   (5.2.93-95)

Up to this point Cleopatra's questions have been answered, and, for the most part, we have been able to judge the validity of their answers and have found them accurate. This method of allowing the audience to judge the truth of the response is not unlike the way the audience was invited to determine the truth value of Hal's and Falstaff's conditionals.[20]

Both plays have more imperatives than interrogatives, but imperatives increase significantly in *Antony and Cleopatra*.[21] Table 3 gives the frequencies for the jussive, or ordinary, imperative; the optative imperative introduced by *may*; the optative imperative introduced by *let*; and the verbless imperative. The column with the heading "Address" shows how often a term of address was used with jussive and optative *let* or *may* imperatives. One explanation for the increase of imperatives in the later play

---

[20] This discussion of Cleopatra's dream vision is developed in Chapter Six.

[21] The chi-square for the proportion of interrogatives to imperatives listed in Table 1 yields a significant difference between the plays.

Table 3
Types of Imperative Sentences

	Jussive	*May*	*Let*	Address	Verbless	Total
R2	326	49	59	(83)	26	460
Ant.	576	32	100	(131)	72	780

may be the fact that it has three major characters who throughout the action have absolute power to command others; certainly it is the case that the combined speeches of Antony, Cleopatra, and Caesar have a higher ratio of imperatives than those of Richard and Bolingbroke together. A second reason may be that *Antony* is a play with more physical activity, such as battles and the frequent dispatch of messengers and ambassadors between Rome and Egypt. This point is supported by the higher proportion of verbs of motion (*go, come*, etc.) found in the imperatives of *Antony* compared to the number of verbs of speaking and perception (*call, know, see*, etc.).[22] It would be difficult to make a simple statement about the imperative style of the two plays. The fact that verbless imperatives increase in *Antony* suggests a simpler, more informal style. On the other hand, *let* optatives and terms of address, which create an impression of formality, also increase. The notable rise in verbless imperatives like *Away, my Thetis!* or *From Sicyon, ho, the news!* corresponds to the increase in this play of minor interrogative forms and of verbless sentences generally, and these are associated again with the language of Antony and Cleopatra rather than with Caesar's.

Another aspect of the more informal character of the imperatives spoken by Antony and Cleopatra is their tendency to use the contracted form *let's*. Elsewhere in the play it occurs only in carefully defined situations: prior to and during the feast on Pompey's barge and in the speech of the soldiers who witness the death of Enobarbus. Apart from these incidents it is found almost exclusively in the speeches of Antony, who uses it in moments of recklessness: *Let's not confound the time with conference harsh* (1.1.45), *Let's have one other gaudy night* (3.13.183), *Let's to supper, come, / And drown consideration* (4.2.44-45); and of Cleopatra, where it appears with that lightness of tone which she brings to solemn moments: *Help, friends below! Let's draw him hither* (4.15.13).

For every question asked, Cleopatra has two imperatives, Antony four,

---

[22] This is a rough measure, as all counts of lexical items must be. In *Richard II* there were 129 common imperatives of speaking and perceiving, 45 common imperatives of motion. In *Antony*, speaking and perceiving, 186, motion, 124.

and Caesar eight.[23] Thus, Caesar, like Bolingbroke, has a higher proportion of imperatives to interrogatives than the protagonists, although the ratio of his imperatives to the total lines spoken by him is lower than the like ratios for either Antony or Cleopatra. Caesar and Cleopatra here, as on other occasions, show greater contrast in their language than appears when either of them is compared to Antony. With its higher rate of address, its more frequent use of optatives, and its fewer verbless imperatives, Caesar's imperative style is more formal than Cleopatra's, which is its mirror image. Antony's speech resembles Caesar's in the proportion of jussive to optative imperatives but is like Cleopatra's in the other two features.

Beyond these formal considerations it is difficult to discern a pattern that yields any special insight. When Caesar and Antony are together, their commands are cautious (neither will be seated before the other at the beginning of the quarrel scene, though each invites the other to do so) and courteous (optatives occur with roughly equal frequency, as if neither will be outdone by the other in ceremony). There may be a slight tendency for Caesar, when at a distance from Antony, to issue commands to him, as in the apostrophe *Leave thy lascivious wassails* or in several directives sent by messenger after Antony is defeated. In the early scenes of the play Cleopatra's commands, many of which are addressed to Antony, exceed his when they are together, which seems to verify the opinion *So our leader's led*. It is indeed the case that Cleopatra's commands are only one percentage point fewer than Antony's. One might note that many of Antony's commands are issued on occasions that little warrant the exercise of his authority—the feast on Pompey's barge, the attempt to dismiss his followers after his first defeat, his cruel treatment of Thyreus—but his commands are too numerous, too varied, too likely to follow the main pattern of events to make this argument very strong.

The most interesting imperatives in the play, however, are the *let* optatives, which increase significantly and which comprise some of its most notable passages.[24] Many of these contain other syntactic features that are shown later in this study to characterize the style of *Antony and Cleopa-*

[23] There is no significant difference for the proportions of Caesar and Antony. For *Antony and Cleopatra*, $\chi^2 = 9.2380$, for Caesar and Cleopatra, $\chi^2 = 13.6237$. See Table A-2 for the two sets of proportions.

[24] The proportion of jussive to optative imperatives shows a significant increase of the latter in *Antony*: $\chi^2 = 5.9428$. *Let* optatives are higher in *Antony*, volitives in *Richard II*: $\chi^2 = 10.8888$. See Table 3 for the proportions on which these tests are based.

tra. They include such linguistic items as proper names, superlatives, and unusual word order:

> If Caesar move him,
> Let Antony look over Caesar's head
> And speak as loud as Mars.
>
> (2.2.4-6)

> Let our best heads
> Know that to-morrow the last of many battles
> We mean to fight.
>
> (4.1.10-12)

> Let me lodge Lichas on the horns o' th' moon
> And with those hands that grasp'd the heaviest club
> Subdue my worthiest self.
>
> (4.12.45-47)

The second passage exhibits unusual word order, since the subordinate clause has a complement, *the last of many battles*, which precedes its subject, and the verb appears last, as it often does in a periodic sentence. Two passages have two superlatives each, and allied to the superlative, of course, is the rhetorical figure of hyperbole, which is an oft-noted characteristic of this play.

Other stylistic features that appear in the context of optative imperatives are intensive and reflexive pronouns, past participles used as adjectives, and a note of vagueness (defined by various syntactic properties) used to express a sense of horror or menace:

> Let that be left
> Which leaves itself.
>
> (3.11.19-20)

> Be you not troubled with the time, which drives
> O'er your content these strong necessities;
> But let determin'd things to destiny
> Hold unbewail'd their way.
>
> (3.6.82-85)

> Rather on Nilus' mud
> Lay me stark-nak'd and let the waterflies
> Blow me into abhorring!
>
> (5.2.58-60)

All the nonverbal constituents of the first passage are pronouns of the vaguest type: *that which* has no antecedent and *itself* is neuter gender. With these words, Antony, after his first defeat at sea, asks his followers to abandon him. *That which leaves itself* expresses his sense of dishonor and of disintegrating identity, a concept that is often expressed in these plays by indefiniteness and circumlocution. Other indefinite terms are the substitute word *things* in the second passage and the verbal expressions *determin'd* and *abhorring*, which imply human subjects but for which no overt subject can be found. The decision-making force of *determin'd* and the revulsion of *abhorring* cannot be located in a single person or a group and are for that reason the more frightening. In noting the conjunction of these features with optative imperatives, it has been necessary to anticipate material that cannot be further explained here, but the fact that one can hardly point to an optative that does not occur in the context of one or more demonstrable stylistic traits suggests the force and dominance of this construction in the play.

The volitive optatives with overt or implicit *may* reveal certain characteristics of each play. In the ceremonial and prayerlike volitives of *Richard II*, the subject is usually *God* or *Heaven*, but, even when they are governed by abstractions, words like *guilt, soul,* or *Book of Life* show that Christian mythology is the source of the power invoked:

> O, sit my husband's wrongs on Hereford's spear,
> That it may enter butcher Mowbray's breast!
> Or, if misfortune miss the first career,
> Be Mowbray's sins so heavy in his bosom
> That they may break his foaming courser's back
> And throw the rider headlong in the lists,
> (1.2.47-52)

> God in thy good cause make thee prosperous!
> (1.3.78)

> Terrible hell make war
> Upon their spotted souls for this offence!
> (3.2.133-134)

In *Antony* Shakespeare provides the volitive imperatives with subjects that are human or abstract or suggestive of pagan mythology:

> Henceforth
> The white hand of a lady fever thee!
>
> (3.13.138-139)

> Upon your sword
> Sit laurel victory, and smooth success
> Be strew'd before your feet!
>
> (1.3.99-101)

> The elements be kind to thee and make
> Thy spirits all of comfort!
>
> (3.2.40-41)

When a Christian term finds its way into one of these expressions, the context and the effect are naturalistic:

> Now the witch take me if I meant it thus!
> Grace grow where those drops fall!
>
> (4.2.37-38)

The witch suggests superstitious mythology; *grace* is presented as growing from the earth with a spontaneous generation reminiscent of the myth of Deucalion. Certainly, the gods are invoked on several occasions in *Antony*, but with a significantly lower frequency than God and Heaven are invoked in *Richard II*.[25] The source of the power to curse and bless appears often to be the speaker himself, and it argues a certain divinity or absoluteness in all the characters in this play:

> Yon ribald-rid nag of Egypt
> (Whom leprosy o'ertake!) ...
>
> (3.10.10-11)

> If he fill'd
> His vacancy with his voluptuousness,
> Full surfeits and the dryness of his bones
> Call on him for't!
>
> (1.4.25-28)

---

[25] When the subjects of all optative imperatives were divided into those that refer to deities or supernatural powers (*God, heaven, the devil; the gods, Neptune, Jove*) and those that refer to human beings and natural objects, there were twenty-nine of the former in *Richard II* as opposed to seventy-one of the latter; the proportion in *Antony* was twelve to ninety-seven.

Sink Rome, and their tongues rot
That speak against us!

(3.7.16-17)

The *let* optatives that permeate the language of this play are associated less with the speech of any individual than with the imperial world these imperatives call into being by their echo of the original creative fiat:

Let Rome in Tiber melt and the wide arch
Of the rang'd empire fall!

(1.1.33-34)

Melt Egypt into Nile! and kindly creatures
Turn all to serpents!

(2.5.78-79)

Even as they call for their dissolution, these parallel references to the ancient empires and the rivers on which they stood, to the martial grandeur and the architecture of the one and to the mystery and wisdom of the other, re-create the worlds of Rome and Egypt. Uttered as they are by the protagonists of the drama, these lines epitomize the evocative effect of *let* optative imperatives in *Antony and Cleopatra*.

This discussion of sentence mood was undertaken to illustrate the notion that one can commence the analysis of style at any point in a text. It has also exemplified the method of analyzing style by starting with a well-defined linguistic unit (interrogative and imperative sentences), of determining statistically that they are characteristic of the text, and of using the results of analysis to interpret the text. In the following section a second method of locating stylistic differences between texts will be illustrated, namely, that of choosing passages felt to be representative of each text under consideration.

Representative Passages: Hypotaxis

Often the critic of style selects for comparison sentences considered typical of the texts he wishes to examine, a method that is especially useful for exploring intuitive feelings about stylistic variation. For example, there are times when the syntax of the sentences in *Richard II* strikes one as rather "loose," even quite careless:

Part us, Northumberland—I towards the North,
Where shivering cold and sickness pines the clime;

> My wife to France, from whence, set forth in pomp,
> She came adorned hither like sweet May,
> Sent back like Hallowmas or short'st of day.
>
> (5.1.76-80)

Or one may feel that sentences like the following characterize not only the style of *Antony and Cleopatra* but also a certain "Roman" quality of that style:

> Our slippery people,
> Whose love is never link'd to the deserver
> Till his deserts are past, begin to throw
> Pompey the Great and all his dignities
> Upon his son; who, high in name and power,
> Higher than both in blood and life, stands up
> For the main soldier; whose quality, going on,
> The sides o' th' world may danger.
>
> (1.2.192-199)

Normally, in comparing such representative passages, one would explore their language from several points of view (diction, syntax, rhythm), would emphasize what is distinctive in each, and would stress differences between them. Thus, sentences may be chosen that will highlight felt differences so that, if parataxis is considered typical of one text and hypotaxis of another, seldom will an effort be made to see how both texts handle hypotaxis or how parataxis operates in each. But the study of representative passages can be made quite as illuminating and more rigorous if, instead of examining passages for all possible features, the same feature is compared in both texts. The sentences cited above share a number of hypotactic group complexes, and it seems reasonable to assume that an investigation of this construction common to both sentences may explain both the looseness of the first sentence and the Roman character of the second.

Hypotaxis is a construction consisting of at least two constituents, one of which is loosely subordinate to the other. In group hypotaxis a subordinate clause is governed by a clause constituent (a nominal group serving as subject, complement, or adjunct in another clause) rather than by an entire clause. The following sentences exemplify clause and group hypotaxis, respectively, and in each case the governing element is italicized:

> *You have broken*
> *The article of your oath*, which you shall never
> Have tongue to charge me with.
>
>   (*Ant.* 2.2.81-83)
>
>   . . . take Antony
> *Octavia* to his wife; whose beauty claims
> No worse a husband than the best of men;
>
>   (*Ant.* 2.2.129-131)

It seems clear enough that in the first example the entire clause *which you shall never . . . with* is related to the whole of the clause that governs it, whereas in the second sentence *whose beauty . . . men* has for its antecedent only the word *Octavia*, which serves as a constituent of the preceding clause. In this sentence *Octavia* is the governing element, or "alpha," and *whose beauty* is the subordinate element, or "beta." Beta clauses in these hypotactic group complexes usually take the form in Shakespeare of nondefining relative clauses, of past or present participial clauses, of nouns or phrases in apposition with another noun, and of adjective phrases. The italicized clauses of the following sentence exemplify three of these four types of beta clause:

>   The condemn'd Pompey,
> *Rich in his father's honour*, creeps apace
> Into the hearts of such as have not thriv'd
> Upon the present state, *whose numbers threaten*;
> And quietness, *grown sick of rest*, would purge
> By any desperate change.
>
>   (*Ant.* 1.3.49-54)

Since it is attached only to part of a clause, has an independent rhythm, and often furnishes relatively superfluous information, the hypotactic group complex is a naturally rather loose structure. It is important therefore that the clause that serves as its matrix (the clause that contains the alpha) should itself have a clear and coherent structure. The first of these sentences shows the difficulties that can arise when the matrix clause is problematic:

>   Or if of grief, being altogether had,
> It adds more sorrow to my want of joy;
>
>   (*R2* 3.4.15-16)

> And drink carouses to the next day's fate,
> Which promises royal peril.
>
> (Ant. 4.8.34-35)

Expanded, the first passage would read *Or if* [you tell tales] *of grief,* [grief] *being altogether had,* / *It* [your telling tales of grief] *adds more sorrow to my want of joy.* The preposition-complement construction *of grief* supplies the alpha for *being altogether had.* *Of grief* is qualifier to *tales,* a suppressed constituent that serves as complement in the sentence *Madam, we'll tell tales,* which appeared five lines and three speeches earlier. In creating the matrix, then, Shakespeare eliminated the head of a core clause constituent (*tales*), retained a marginal element in that constituent (the qualifier *of grief*), and attached to it a beta clause. Moreover, the matrix of the group complex is a beta clause in hypotactic relation with *it adds . . . joy,* an arrangement that would not be problematic if the antecedent of *it* were firmly established. As the expanded version of the sentence shows, the antecedent of *it* is *if of grief,* but the pronoun is attracted to the single word *grief* or even to *grief* as the covert subject of *being altogether had.* The reason for the potential ambiguity lies in the suppression of major constituents in the real antecedent, which, so to speak, is not strong enough to attract and hold the pronoun. This ambiguity makes little difference to the meaning, but, added to the structure of the matrix, which is stripped of essential constituents, on the one hand, and elaborated by this extraneous complex, on the other, the ambiguity pulls the sentence in different directions, creating the impression of looseness.

By comparison, the sentence from *Antony* provides a very simple matrix for the group complex. The alpha, *day,* has been preposed from the normal qualifier position *fate of the next day,* with the result that empty words have been suppressed but important constituents are fully explicit. All constituents in the matrix appear in normal order, and the complex itself appears in sentence-final position, where it cannot disrupt or distract core constituents. Ambiguity appears for a more obvious reason in this sentence from *Richard II*:

> For that our kingdom's earth should not be soil'd
> . . . .
> And for we think the eagle-winged pride
> Of sky-aspiring and ambitious thoughts

With rival-hating envy set on you
To wake our peace, which in our country's cradle
Draws the sweet infant breath of gentle sleep;
Which so rous'd up with boist'rous untun'd drums,
With harsh-resounding trumpets' dreadful bray
And grating shock of wrathful iron arms,
Might from our quiet confines fright fair peace
And make us wade even in our kinred's blood:
Therefore we banish you our territories.

(1.3.125, 129-139)

The first relative clause offers no problem; its antecedent is *peace*, and normally that would be the antecedent for the second relative clause, which appears to be recursively related to it. *Sleep* is also a possibility. But neither peace nor sleep, once roused up, is likely to frighten peace away. Conceivably, the antecedent of the second clause is *eagle-winged pride*, although too much material intervenes to make this clear.

A related problem appears in this sentence:

From forth thy reach he would have laid thy shame,
Deposing thee before thou wert possess'd,
Which art possess'd now to depose thyself.

(*R2* 2.1.106-108)

The alpha to the clause *which art possess'd now to depose thyself* is probably *thee*. At least immediate constituent analysis and rhythm suggest this interpretation. But the subject form *thou* in *before thou wert possess'd*, together with the fact that both clauses (*before thou . . . possess'd* and *which art . . . thyself*) share parallel structures and the repeated word *possess'd*, makes *thou* a strong rival candidate for the alpha. Here the ambiguity is not misleading, because logically the same person is involved whether *thee* or *thou* serves as alpha, but there is confusion generated by the interposition of an embedded clause between the real alpha and the beta clause. At a later date when Shakespeare wished to convey two subordinate pieces of information successively, he might have solved the problem by the kind of hypotactic recursion found rarely in *Richard II* and quite often in *Antony*:

. . . like seely beggars
Who, *sitting in the stocks*, refuge their shame,

>   That many have, and others must sit there.
>   *(R2* 5.5.25-27)

>   But you are come
>   A market-maid to Rome, and have prevented
>   The ostentation of our love, which, *left unshown,*
>   Is often left unlov'd.
>   *(Ant.* 3.6.50-53)

Everything before *sitting* and *left* has been suppressed and the referent for each beta clause is entirely clear. The consequent brevity makes it more difficult to confuse antecedents in the manner of *R2* 1.3.125-139.

Other attempts at this type of ellipsis in *Richard II* are less successful partly because the covert subject is not clearly specified in the context; indeed, in the following example it is hard to determine whether *buried once* is in clause or group hypotaxis with *And . . . why not upon my head*:

>   Or I'll be buried in the king's highway,
>   Some way of common trade, where subjects' feet
>   May hourly trample on their sovereign's head;
>   For on my heart they tread now whilst I live,
>   And buried once, why not upon my head?
>   (3.3.155-159)

Expanded, the last line might read *And* [once I am] *buried, why* [should they] *not* [tread] *upon my head?* The covert subject of *buried once* is clearly *I*. No such subject can be easily recovered from explicit constituents in the immediate context of *buried once.* The governing clause in the complex can only furnish *my head*; the clause paratactic to the complex, *for . . . live*, supplies either *my heart* or *they*. None of these are acceptable, of course. One obvious source is the *I* of *I'll be buried*, but there are several syntactic levels between that construction and *buried once.* Less obvious is the reading of *my head* as *head of me buried once* where *me* is the covert subject, but there is still ambiguity between *head* and *me.* There is also the subject of *whilst I live*, which is explicit, conveniently near, and of the appropriate case. The rhythm militates against its selection, as does the fact that both, *whilst I live* and *buried once* are subordinate in different ways to different clauses so that it is difficult to trace the syntactic path by which they can be related. Hence, whether one chooses for the subject of *buried once* the *I* of the first line, that of *whilst*

I live, or the *me* of *head of me* (from *my head*), there is a problem in the first instance of depth, in the second of the oblique relationship, and in the third of ambiguity.

In addition to ambiguities created by weak structure in the matrix clause, by the suppression of important constituents, and by the presence of embedded clauses that interrupt the constituents of the hypotactic complex, there is a problem created by constituent order in the matrix clause:[26]

> . . . else, if heaven would,
> And we will not, heaven's offer we refuse,
> The proffered means of succour and redress.
>   (*R2* 3.2.30-32)

In this passage, *the proffered means of succour and redress* is in hypotactic relation to *heaven's offer*, which is the complement of the matrix clause. That complement has been preposed, leaving the matrix verb *refuse* between the constituents of the hypotactic complex. It happens that, because the beta clause has nominal-group structure and a meaning that is congruent in every respect with the true complement of *refuse*, it becomes a potential complement for that verb. Reordering of constituents in the matrix clause has created ambiguity in the beta clause of the group complex. Rhythm, as often happens, prevents the ambiguity from being too noticeable.

This example and *R2* 2.1.106-108 suggest that at times Shakespeare wished to interrupt the constituents in a hypotactic group complex, perhaps to delay the change in rhythm that occurs when the beta clause appears. In *Antony* there are several instances of this interposition, but the device is more successful, partly because the intervening material does not take the form of an embedded clause and partly because core constituents appear in normal order:

[26] Observations on group complexes are based on a set of sentences drawn at random from each play. Line references to these sentences are given in Table B-1, and italicized items in this table indicate those sentences that contain group beta clauses. In the random sentences from *Richard II* there were thirty-eight hypotactic group complexes: eight nonfinites, fifteen appositives, and fifteen relatives (only one of which was not a *wh-* relative). The sample from *Antony* yielded thirty-nine complexes: eight nonfinites, seventeen appositives, and sixteen relatives (all of the *wh-* kind). These figures show how similar are the results of the sample in frequency and type of complex.

> Why should I think you can be mine, and true,
> Though *you* in swearing shake the throned gods,
> *Who have been false to Fulvia?*

(1.3.27-29)

> But how, when *Antony* is gone
> *Through whom I might command it?*

(3.3.5-6)

Even when formal ambiguity does arise due to unusual word order, the context of situation resolves the ambiguity, as in this instance:

> *A sister* I bequeath you, *whom no brother
> Did ever love so dearly.*

(2.2.152-153)

An interesting feature of this last example is the fact that the relative should be restrictive, since it specifies *a sister* in the manner of a qualifier but, by the inversion of constituents in the main clause, the relative takes on the rhythm pattern of a group beta.

Apart from the rhythmic variation created by this type of discontinuity, one might fancy in the discontinuous constituents a certain classical flavor, such as is obtained by translating the first lines of the *Aeneid* literally: *Of arms and the man I sing, who first from the shores of Troy, . . .* Shakespeare had used this type of discontinuity in *Richard II*, of course, but a complete study of discontinuity between antecedent and relative clauses introduced by *which, who, whom,* and *whose* shows that it increases by 21 percent in the later play. If *which* is omitted, the increase is significant.[27] Table 4 shows the frequency with which these relative beta clauses appear in their normal position, that is, immediately following their antecedent, and the frequency with which antecedent and relative are discontinuous.

This discussion has indicated that Shakespeare experienced occasional difficulty in *Richard II* when he tried to coordinate the demands of syn-

---

[27] Relative clauses are analyzed in Table A-10. The data in Table 4 analyze those hypotactic group complexes introduced by *which, who, whose,* and *whom.* The table provides separate figures for *which,* for the personal relatives, and for the four words combined. *Which,* with its higher frequency and greater stability, tends when the words are combined to neutralize the effects of the personal relatives, but the latter reveal significant differences between the two plays. The figures in Table 4 represent all group complexes introduced by these words; they are not based on a sample.

Table 4
Frequency and Position of Relative Group Beta Clauses

	Which		*Who, Whose, Whom*		Total	
	Discontinuous	Normal	Discontinuous	Normal	Discontinuous	Normal
R2	10	26	7	24	17	50
Ant.	12	26	15	23	27	49

tax, semantics, and rhythm. The difficulty seems to arise when he is striving for some rhetorical effect like the witty repetition or parallel structure of 3.4.15-16 or 3.3.155-159, which were discussed earlier. The next example illustrates potential ambiguity in imagery as well as in syntax:

> That blood already, like the pelican,
> Hast thou tapp'd out and drunkenly carous'd.
>   (*R2* 2.1.126-127)

Like the pelican is a preposed group beta whose alpha is *thou* in the second line. This constituent order is quite rare even in *Richard II*, where high-level constituents often occur in sequences that deviate from the normal.[28] By the addition of a genitive ending on *pelican*, the beta clause could as easily take for its alpha the noun group *that blood*; the line would then read *that blood, like the pelican's*. The reading would be an appropriate one, since in mythology the pelican was supposed to nourish its young by piercing its breast and offering its blood as food. According to one commentator on this passage, the young of the pelican symbolized ingratitude, and certainly the sentence as it appears in the text makes more sense if the young bird is meant, since it is incongruous to imagine the parent carousing with its own blood.[29] Even so, it is not unreasonable for the reader to expect *pelican's* in the first line because *that blood* appears in the normal alpha position for group hypotaxis so that *like the pelican* could be read as its beta and because without such a reading the analogical source of the blood is left unspecified. While the suggested change *pelican's* would clarify this, the mythological analogue of the carouser would then be

[28] Constituent order is discussed in the last section of Chapter Three.

[29] Irving Ribner in his version of the Kittredge edition of *Richard II* makes this observation about the young of the pelican. Separate and unambiguous facets of the pelican image appear in two other plays: *And, like the kind life-rend'ring pelican, / Repast them with my blood* (*Ham.* 4.5.146-147) and *'Twas this flesh begot / Those pelican daughters* (*Lear* 3.4.76-77).

unclear. By placing *like the pelican* in an ambiguous position Shakespeare manages to have it both ways, although the result is perhaps more distracting than illuminating.

The next passage, although it has no hypotactic group complex at the section in question, illustrates further the idea that syntactic ambiguity is sometimes related to an attempt to resolve the conflicting demands of rhythm and imagery:

> As a long-parted mother with her child
> Plays fondly with her tears and smiles in meeting,
> So weeping, smiling, greet I thee, my earth,
> And do thee favours with my royal hands.

> (*R2* 3.2.8-11)

In the first two lines the phrases *with her child* and *with her tears* can equally receive the action of the verb *plays*. Indeed, it makes more sense to play with a child than with tears, but the latter is the more likely interpretation of the second line. One reason for choosing *with her tears* as properly receiving the action is that the first line undoubtedly means *as a mother long-parted with her child*. It is difficult to see what metrical advantage is gained by the order of the first line, unless the ambiguity was deliberately invoked to create a run-on line.

The foregoing analysis suggests that precision of syntax and adequate expression of imagery are sometimes related. The ambiguities detected may not be the kind that delight linguist and critic, but their presence does shed light on some of the problems that confronted Shakespeare in 1595, when he was striving to write blank verse that would be metrically and rhythmically adequate, express ideas by analogy and image, and exploit the rhetorical devices of repetition and parallel structure. That he succeeded more often than he failed in *Richard II* is granted; that he failed on occasion is a happy fault, since it reveals, just a little, Shakespeare at work.

It is time, therefore, to inquire why and how the group hypotaxis that revealed the looseness of syntax in *Richard II* contributes to the Roman quality of certain sentences in *Antony*. One reason is that on occasion Shakespeare arranged these hypotactic clauses in the same way that *cola* or *membra* were arranged in the classical periodic sentence.[30] Today the periodic sentence is usually defined as one in which the thought is not

---

[30] In his *Logic and Rhetoric in England, 1500-1700*, Wilbur Samuel Howell defines the *colon* or *membrum* as a thought expressed in something less than a complete sentence and in something more than a phrase, that is, a clause. He notes, moreover,

complete until the end of the sentence, but in the older rhetorical tradition the term *period* was restricted to sentences with a structure rather like an onion, where minor syntactic elements surrounded the main clause that lies at the center of the sentence. Morris W. Croll expresses this idea more technically: "In the oratorical period the arrangement of the members is 'round' or 'circular,' in the sense that they are all so placed with reference to a central or climactic member that they point forward or back to it and give it its appropriate emphasis. This order is what is meant by the name *periodos*, *circuitus*, and 'round composition,' by which the oratorical period has been variously called. And it is the chief object of the many revisions to which its form is submitted."[31] These sentences seem to be the most successful imitations of the full period in *Antony*:

> When thou once
> Wast beaten from Modena, where thou slew'st
> Hirtius and Pansa, consuls, *at thy heel*
> *Did famine follow*; whom thou fought'st against
> (Though daintily brought up) with patience more
> Than savages could suffer.
>
> (1.4.56-61)

> To hold you in perpetual amity,
> To make you brothers, and to knit your hearts
> With an unslipping knot, *take Antony*
> *Octavia to his wife*; whose beauty claims
> No worse a husband than the best of men;
> Whose virtue and whose general graces speak
> That which none else can utter.
>
> (2.2.127-133)

The true period is achieved here by enclosing the simple clause at the center of each sentence within embedded and hypotactic clauses, half of which are hypotactic group complexes. But English is not Latin and such sentences as these are not easily produced in abundance nor, in drama, is it desirable that they should be.[32]

---

that terms like *colon* and *period* referred, not to punctuation, but "to the whole question of rhythm in style" (p. 121).

[31] *Style, Rhetoric, and Rhythm: Essays by Morris W. Croll*, ed. J. Max Patrick et al., p. 224.

[32] Thomas A. Dunn, in his *Philip Massinger*, observes that the blank-verse syntax of Massinger has more periodic sentences than Shakespeare's and that Shakespeare's more frequent use of colloquial loose sentences makes his language more suitable for drama.

It is possible, of course, to simulate the oratorical period by constructing sentences where one or two group beta clauses are attached to the initial constituents of the main clause in order to offset the weight of several beta clauses attached to the final constituents of the main clause. These left-branching sentences produce the effect of roundness, even when the number and the position of the constituents are not so perfectly balanced around a centrally located main clause. The resulting sense of fullness is typical of many of the Roman sentences in *Antony and Cleopatra*:

> *Our slippery people,*
> Whose love is never link'd to the deserver
> Till his deserts are past, *begin to throw*
> *Pompey the Great and all his dignities*
> *Upon his son*; who, high in name and power,
> Higher than both in blood and life, stands up
> For the main soldier; whose quality, going on,
> The sides o' th' world may danger.
>
> (*Ant.* 1.2.192-199)

The constituents of the main clause are relatively simple and appear in the most normal order possible. The lack of embedded clauses among them and the absence of any counterrhythm that might be established by re-ordering these constituents allow full play to the independent rhythm of the group complexes. The elaboration of the subject by the comparatively long group complex *our slippery people, whose love . . . past* and the consequent rhythmic weight prepares for and supports the four complexes that form the coda of the sentence.[33] This device of elaborating the subject is mirrored in the complexes themselves, where the clause-initial weight (*who, high in name*, etc.; *whose quality, going on,*) has the effect of rhythmic as well as structural recursion. The rhythmic suspense is increased and varied, however, even as it is repeated. Thus, we have the paratactic construction *high . . . higher.*

Evidence for the increase of left-branching sentences comes again from the relatives introduced by *who, whom*, and *whose*. The information in Table 5 indicates that there are virtually three times as many of these with clause-initial antecedents in *Antony* as are found in *Richard II*; there are half as many with clause-final antecedents in *Antony* as one finds in the

---

[33] At every stage in the analysis of Shakespeare's syntax one is confronted with the issue of rhythm, but through a lack of descriptive categories rhythm has been discussed only in the most subjective and cursory manner in this study.

Table 5
Position in Clause Structure of Relative Group Complexes

	Which			*Who, Whose, Whom*			Total		
	Initial	Medial	Final	Initial	Medial	Final	Initial	Medial	Final
R2	8	4	24	5	9	17	13	13	41
Ant.	9	8	21	14	16	8	23	24	29

earlier play. The figures in Table 5 show how often the antecedent of a given relative clause appears as the first, middle, or final constituent in the matrix clause.[34] It would appear from the data that there is an increase of left-branching in *Antony and Cleopatra*. This increase seems to be associated with Shakespeare's attempts to imitate the round structure of the oratorical period and thus to create a Roman style within the play.

More important than the arrangement of members around the central clause is the periodic *rhythm*, the balancing of clause against clause to create the effect of roundness. One factor that makes the rhythm of group beta clauses more prominent in the later play is that Shakespeare trimmed away excess constituents, especially those of embedded clauses:

> Harry of Hereford, Lancaster, and Derby
> Am I, who ready here do stand in arms
> To prove, by God's grace and my body's valour
> In lists on Thomas Mowbray, Duke of Norfolk,
> That he is a traitor, foul and dangerous,
> To God of heaven, King Richard, and to me;
> And as I truly fight, defend me heaven!
>
> (*R2* 1.3.35-41)

> Now I must
> To the young man send humble treaties, dodge
> And palter in the shifts of lowness, who
> With half the bulk o' th' world play'd as I pleas'd,
> Making and marring fortunes.
>
> (*Ant.* 3.11.61-65)

In the first sentence, the beta clause itself has six constituents, the last of which is an embedded clause, *to prove . . . me*, which contains a second embedded clause, *that he is . . . me*, which in turn contains the group

---

[34] Clause-initial position means that the antecedent of the relative serves as theme or secondary theme in the matrix clause; clause-final position means that the antecedent is the last constituent in the matrix; medial is any position between these two.

complex *foul and dangerous.* The first group complex thus comprises five lines and is so laden with further structure that it lacks the resilience such constructions have in *Antony* or, on occasion, in some of the passages from *Richard II* (5.5.25-27, e.g.) that were cited earlier. By contrast, the complex *I . . . who with half the bulk o' th' world* has only four constituents, and, although the final one is an embedded clause, it is quite short.

Group complexes in the speeches of Roman characters tend to be recursive; that is, one group beta clause may be hypotactically related to its predecessor or one may follow another by parataxis. Recursion prolongs and varies the independent rhythm established by the beta clause and contributes to the suspensory rhythm associated with the periodic sentence:

> . . . 'tis to be chid
> As we rate boys *who, being mature in knowledge,*
> *Pawn their experience to their present pleasure*
> *And so rebel to judgment.*
>
> (1.4.30-33)

In the passage above, *who . . . judgment* is a beta clause that serves as a matrix for the second beta clause, *being . . . knowledge,* which is hypotactically related to it. Recursive group betas contribute in no small measure to the rhythmic effects of Enobarbus's description of Cleopatra's appearance on the river of Cydnus:

> On each side her
> Stood pretty dimpled boys, *like smiling Cupids,*
> *With divers-colour'd fans,* whose wind did seem
>
> (2.2.206-208)
>
> Her gentlewomen, *like the Nereides,*
> *So many mermaids,* tended her i' th' eyes,
>
> (2.2.211-212)

Shakespeare's use of group betas in the barge speech constitutes an important departure from the syntax of his source.[35]

---

[35] In North there are, exclusive of relatives, four group betas. These average six words apiece, they are discontinuous with their antecedents, and three of the four occur singly. Shakespeare has ten group betas exclusive of relatives; they average four words apiece, and only three occur singly, all others appearing in recursive structures. Relative clauses, as well as further comparisons between the syntax of North and Shakespeare in the description of Cleopatra's barge, are discussed in Chapter Five.

Further evidence for the feeling that group beta clauses are associated with a Roman style is the fact that in a random sample there were twenty-three sentences containing group betas; eighteen of these sentences were spoken by Antony, Caesar, Pompey, Ventidius, Agrippa, and Enobarbus on occasions like the quarrel scene, battles, discussions of policy, and Caesar's apostrophe to Antony (see Table B-1). There is some overlap in a second piece of evidence, but the facts are even more convincing: Of the thirty-eight complexes created with relative *who*, *whose*, and *whom* only two are spoken by Cleopatra and none by her servants, yet Cleopatra speaks more lines in the play than any other character but Antony. Finally, the ratio of all group betas spoken by Antony, Cleopatra, and Caesar to their total lines reveals that Cleopatra has a ratio of .0134, compared to .0602 for Antony and .0622 for Caesar. The speeches of Antony and Cleopatra generally have similar ratios for stylistic features, while Caesar's language is normally quite different from theirs (see Table 41). The fact that Caesar and Antony have a similar ratio of group betas while Cleopatra's is much lower may suggest that this feature is intended to signify a Roman style.

In sum, a study of group hypotaxis in representative passages from each play indicates that different ways of treating the same syntactic structure account for what seems to be a characteristic looseness of syntax in *Richard II* and for the Roman quality of many passages in *Antony and Cleopatra*. In the earlier play, group beta clauses were loosely or ambiguously attached to their alphas because important constituents in the matrix clause had been suppressed, because embedded clauses in the immediate context offered a second possible alpha, because constituents in the matrix clause had been transposed, or because syntax was neglected in order to produce a particular rhetorical effect or to develop an image. In *Antony* Shakespeare places the complex in a simpler matrix, which is often a single clause and in any case has fewer constituents. The constituents themselves tend to occur in normal order and they are seldom realized as embedded clauses. Both these factors reduce the possibility of ambiguity and loose structure. All these factors—fewer constituents, normal order, and fewer embedded clauses—throw into sharper relief the independent rhythm of the beta clause, which has itself been pruned and simplified. Finally, the beta clause is placed in syntactic and rhythmic arrangements that create the round structure and sound of the classical period.

Considering these syntactic differences between the two plays, one wonders what besides the passage of time and the accumulation of experience in writing blank verse accounts for the changes in syntax that occurred between 1595 and 1608. *Richard II* is entirely in verse, as are many of the plays that preceded it. After the important transitional year in which *Richard II*, *A Midsummer Night's Dream*, and *Romeo and Juliet* appeared, Shakespeare turned to the composition of the romantic comedies and the rest of the English history plays. All of these contain prose in abundance, and that prose has always been praised for its excellence, although few critics have studied its style and fewer still have examined its syntax. Jonas Barish has pointed out some of its features, particularly the logical clarity achieved by repetition, balance, parallel structure, and disjunctive schemes like *the one . . . the other*; *if . . . if not*; *either . . . or*.[36] It is conceivable that the Shakespeare who experienced occasional difficulty with parallel structure, clear syntactic nexes, and rhythmic balance when composing the blank verse of *Richard II* learned, from writing the prose of this period, something that influenced the blank verse syntax of the later style.

Constant Topic and Varied Style: Adjectives

Because many passages in Shakespeare contain verbal echoes of other passages, it is often possible for purposes of differentiating between texts to find a constant semantic content, such as these descriptions of civil war in *Richard II* and *Antony and Cleopatra*:

> Like an unseasonable stormy day
> Which makes the silver rivers drown their shores
> As if the world were all dissolv'd to tears,
> So high above his limits swells the rage
> Of Bolingbroke, covering your fearful land
> With hard bright steel, and hearts harder than steel.
> White-beards have arm'd their thin and hairless scalps
> Against thy majesty. Boys with women's voices
> Strive to speak big, and clap their female joints
> In stiff unwieldy arms against thy crown.
> Thy very beadsmen learn to bend their bows
> Of double-fatal yew against thy state.
> Yea, distaff-women manage rusty bills
> Against thy seat. Both young and old rebel,

---

[36] Jonas A. Barish, *Ben Jonson and the Language of Prose Comedy*, pp. 23-40.

And all goes worse than I have power to tell.
(*R2* 3.2.106-120)

This long description by Scroop of Bolingbroke's return to England resembles Antony's account of Pompey's growing popularity in Rome:

> The strong necessity of time commands
> Our services awhile; but my full heart
> Remains in use with you. Our Italy
> Shines o'er with civil swords. Sextus Pompeius
> Makes his approaches to the port of Rome.
> Equality of two domestic powers
> Breed scrupulous faction. The hated, grown to strength,
> Are newly grown to love. The condemn'd Pompey,
> Rich in his father's honour, creeps apace
> Into the hearts of such as have not thriv'd
> Upon the present state, whose numbers threaten;
> And quietness, grown sick of rest, would purge
> By any desperate change. My more particular,
> And that which most with you should safe my going,
> Is Fulvia's death.
> (*Ant.* 1.3.42-56)

The rebels in the passage from *Richard II* are old men, young boys, women, and clerics. They represent the marginal segments of the society, and their participation in the rebellion indicates its depth and gravity. This method of dividing the social order into categories defined in terms of age and sex rather than by function is characteristic of primitive tribes and testifies to the essentially feudal world of this play. Disorder is symbolized in the second part of the passage by a set of semantic oppositions: boys as females, women as warriors, clerics as archers. But in every instance ordinary human beings perform human actions, a fact that is conveyed grammatically by subjects that are human, animate, and count plural.[37]

The groups who threaten civil war in *Antony* are also marginal, but they are composed of the politically disaffected members of society. In contrast to the neat domestic census of *Richard II*, one finds groups designated by vague substitute heads like *the hated, such as have not thrived, whose numbers*. Contributing to the sense of impersonality are the abstract nouns

---

[37] Including proper names and titles, twelve of the twenty-eight nouns in the passage from *Richard II* designate human beings; in *Antony* the proportion is seven to thirty.

necessity, equality, quietness, and *faction.* While the passage from *Richard II* states that Bolingbroke's rage is like a flood that leaves in its path a trail of steel, it is not clear in the passage from *Antony* who holds the swords that make Italy shine. The words *Our Italy shines* introduce the note of passive terror before the nameless threat of strife, and this note dominates the sentences that follow. Combined, these grammatical categories of abstract nouns and substitute heads evoke the faceless mob presented more dramatically but not less terribly in the other Roman plays. Critics have explored in *Macbeth* a similar use of vague expressions to create a sense of horror. There the pronoun *it,* the verb *do* used intransitively, and various euphemisms and circumlocutions are used by the witches and by the protagonists to avoid clear reference to the murder of Duncan.[38]

The substitute heads in *Antony* contrast markedly with Pompey's name. G. W. Knight, discussing Shakespeare's use of names, shows how names like *Crispin* or *Harry* in *Henry V* serve as verbal talismans to create a sense of personal dignity or royalty.[39] *Bolingbroke* and *Pompey* function in like manner as verbal standards and rallying cries in these two descriptions of a civil uprising. A study of their syntax in these passages reveals Shakespeare's method of using names as talismans in his early and late styles. The intended dominance of Bolingbroke's name is obscured on the semantic level by the elaborate Homeric simile comparing his rage to a flood; moreover, on the level of syntax, *rage* governs the entire sentence, since it is the subject. *Bolingbroke* appears only in an oblique form as qualifier to *rage.* Pompey's name appears twice, each time as subject, each time in sentence-initial position, and each time with a special internal structure. The first structure is the full name, *Sextus Pompeius,* with its conspicuous Latin endings. Second is the phrase *the condemn'd Pompey,* which is triply specified by the fact that it is a proper noun, by the adjective, and by the definite article. The extraordinary degree of care taken with this name further emphasizes the abstract and substitute nouns surrounding it.

The passages differ, not only in their choice of words, but also in the more general semantic category to which those words belong. In *Rich-*

---

[38] Paul A. Jorgensen, "A Deed without a Name," in *Pacific Coast Studies in Shakespeare,* ed. Waldo F. McNeir and Thelma N. Greenfield, pp. 190-198. M. M. Badawi makes a similar point in "Euphemism and Circumlocution in *Macbeth*," in *Cairo Studies in English,* ed. Magdi Wahba, pp. 25-46, but stresses the primitive world of taboo as the source of the protagonists' linguistic behavior.

[39] G. W. Knight, "What's in a Name?" in his *The Sovereign Flower,* pp. 170-174.

ard II the category "human" contains the oppositions male/female and old/young, which are quite conventional compared to the name/nameless contrast created in the same category in *Antony* by opposing the highly specific mention of Pompey to the vague terms that refer to his followers. Further differences at this syntactic-semantic level of the language can be discerned in sentences where the verbal echoes between the plays are unmistakable:

> Boys with women's voices
> Strive to speak big, and clap their female joints
> In stiff unwieldy arms . . .

> . . . I shall see
> Some squeaking Cleopatra boy my greatness
> I' th' posture of a whore.
>
> (*Ant.* 5.2.219-221)

> . . . covering your fearful land
> With hard bright steel, and hearts harder than steel.

> Our Italy
> Shines o'er with civil swords.

In the first set of sentences, where boys and women are compared, some differences can be revealed by converting the lines to "kernel" sentences:[40]

> boys have voices
> women have voices
> boys strive to speak big
> boys clap the boys' joints in arms [armor]
> the boys' joints are female
> the arms are stiff
> the arms are unwieldy

> Cleopatra shall see Cleopatra
> some Cleopatra squeaks

[40] The notion of the kernel sentence was first defined by A. Noam Chomsky in *Syntactic Structures* as "the set of sentences that are produced when we apply obligatory transformations to the terminal strings of the . . . grammar" (p. 45). He specified it further in *Aspects of the Theory of Syntax* as "sentences of a particularly simple sort that involve a minimum of transformational apparatus in their generation" (pp. 17-18). Richard Ohmann has used the notion to distinguish the syntax of Hemingway and Faulkner in "Generative Grammars and the Concept of Literary Style," *Word* 20 (1964): 423-439. George M. Landon employed it to define metaphor in "The Quantification of Metaphoric Language in the Verse of Wilfred Owen," in *Statistics and Style*, ed. Lubomír Doležel and Richard W. Bailey, pp. 170-177.

Cleopatra V_t a boy
A boy V_t Cleopatra's greatness
Cleopatra has greatness
A whore has a posture

The set of underlying sentences from the *Richard II* excerpt contains only one violation of selectional rules, *the boys' joints are female*.[41] The intended incongruity is conveyed largely at the surface of the sentence, and this fact might explain the relative weakness of the figurative language. Essentially the same comparison exists in Cleopatra's speech, but at the level of kernel sentences it is stated with greater frequency, variety, and further resonances. Thanks to the conversion of the noun *boy* to a verb, the male/female comparison occurs twice. Moreover, where in *Richard II* that contrast moved in one direction only, that is, from male to female, in *Antony* it moves in both directions simultaneously (*Cleopatra* V_t *a boy*; *a boy* V_t *Cleopatra*), underscoring the histrionic character of this passage where the real boy actor in the voice of Cleopatra imagines another boy actor playing that role. The meta-theatrical quality of the language is further conveyed by *Cleopatra shall see Cleopatra* and, perhaps, by *a whore has a posture*. The use of functional shift, or conversion, can be said in its own right to reinforce this quality by its transitoriness. Added to these central figures in the language of this sentence is the contradiction in the coupling of the nonspecific determiner *some* with the intrinsically specific proper name. And, while there seem to be no formal categories to explain it concisely, one senses a certain discrepancy between the young/ immature denotation of *boy* and the connotation of power/control/a kind of maturity implied by *greatness*.

If one represents the adjective-noun and noun-verb relations in the two descriptions of a civil uprising as a set of kernel sentences, the greater density of this type of deviance becomes quite obvious:

rivers drown shores; *world dissolves to tears*; *rage swells high*; *whitebeards arm scalps*; day is stormy; day is unseasonable; rivers are silver;

---

[41] Chomsky discusses the notion of selection restrictions throughout *Aspects*; perhaps the most convenient reference for the general reader is pp. 148-153. Briefly, these restrictions define a relation between two positions in a sentence, that of the verb and of the noun that immediately precedes or follows it; but the choice of verb is constrained by certain features of the noun (p. 113). Thus, the verb *frighten* may have a subject that is human or abstract but must take a human object, so that *Sincerity frightens John* observes this rule but *John frightens sincerity* violates it.

land is fearful; steel is hard; steel is bright; scalps are thin; scalps are
hairless; joints are female; arms are stiff; arms are unwieldy; *yew is
double-fatal*; bills are rusty; *rage covers land with steel*; *rage covers
land with hearts*; *hearts are hard*

Italy shines; *swords are civil*; *necessity is strong*; *heart is full*; *powers
are domestic*; *faction is scrupulous*; Pompey is condemn'd; *change is
desperate*; *quietness grew sick*; *quietness would purge*; *equality breeds
faction*; *numbers threaten*; *necessity commands services*

The italicized kernels are suggested violations of selectional restrictions.
One can note in *Richard II* the marginal effectiveness of *rage covers land
with hearts* or *white-beards arm scalps*, which border on the grotesque, and,
further, the dead metaphor of *hearts are hard*, compared with the highly
original and striking quality of the pairings in *Antony*, where a sentence like
equality breeds faction or *quietness would purge* has double violations in
that *equality breeds* is one violation and *breeds faction* a second; similarly,
quietness would and *quietness purges* can be apprehended separately because
of the strong modality of *would* in this context. Finally, in *Our Italy shines
o'er with civil swords* there is a suggestion that the adjectives have been
transposed from a further underlying reading, *Italy is civil* and *swords shine*.
The last point would not add to the violation of selectional rules, but it might
suggest a higher degree of organization at some point in the structure.

   This greater degree of organization allows more information to be conveyed in the same number of words, for the passages are of nearly equal
length and on the surface exhibit patterns of nearly equal frequency. For
example, the number of nouns modified by preposed adjectives in the
description of Bolingbroke's uprising is nine, in the other description, eight;
but about half the nouns in the first are modified by two adjectives in various
types of doubling (compounds, parataxis, simple repetition). Here, Shakespeare, again, is working on the surface of the language, attempting to gain
by repetition and by variety of form the effectiveness he achieves on the
deeper level of language in the later play.

   A careful search would turn up in Shakespeare's work many passages
with the same kinds of content and verbal echoes noted in these.[42] One

   [42] Many books define stretches of Shakespeare's text by some consistent principle
that would allow for such comparisons. One thinks, for example, of Morris Palmer
Tilley's *Dictionary of the Proverbs in England in the Sixteenth and Seventeenth
Centuries*; Wolfgang Clemen's work *Shakespeare's Soliloquies*; John Draper's various
studies, especially his "Shakespeare's Use of the Grand Entry," *Neophilologus* 44
(1960): 128-135; and other works like Anne-Marie Tauber's study of death scenes in

thinks, for example, of the dilemma of women whose beloved men engage in war on opposite sides (*King John* 3.1.331-332; *Antony and Cleopatra* 3.4.10-11). Then there are the numerous exhortations to battle in *Henry V* and *Coriolanus*, the reactions of Brutus and Macbeth to the death of their wives, and the manner in which Coriolanus and Hamlet mock other people, especially when they are imitating their style of speaking.

The possibilities opened up by this kind of analysis for a formal study of imagery are attractive, but to pursue them with the thoroughness they deserve would require a separate volume. Nevertheless, since some treatment of diction seems warranted in a study of style, to extend the data yielded by the passages on the civil uprising, all adjective-noun relations in the two plays were examined.[43] First the morphological structure of the adjectives was analyzed; then the types of imagery created by the violation of selection restrictions between adjective and noun were tabulated. A count of syllables per adjective revealed that two-syllabled adjectives (*happy, tawny*) decreased remarkably in *Antony* compared to those of four and five syllables, which increased slightly, or to monosyllabic adjectives, which increased noticeably.[44] Table 6 supplies the data on syllables per adjective. There are some interesting qualitative differences in the polysyllabic adjectives. In *Richard II* one finds words like *disordered, expedient, sacrificing, tumultuous*, and *immaculate*; in *Antony* the list includes *unparallel'd, penetrative, prophesying, victorious*, and *considerate*. Several words are common to both: *honourable, discontented, injurious, lascivious*. In each set the adjectival suffixes are rather evenly distributed in kind and number, and no single suffix seems to account for

---

the drama (*Die Sterbeszenen in Shakespeares Dramen*) or Clara Howe's briefer compilation of passages on the subject of death, "The Streaks of the Tulip–Shakespeare's Commentary on Death," *University of South Florida Quarterly* 3 (1964): 33-36. Similarly, there is John M. Lothian's interesting *Shakespeare's Charactery*, an anthology of over four hundred character portraits selected from the plays and grouped by type (nobles, women, lovers, etc.). Georg von Greyerz has compiled some fifty passages that re-create a dramatic scene by description (*The Reported Scenes in Shakespeare's Plays*) and Ludwig Borinski, for the express purpose of stylistic analysis, has studied recurrent types of expression in the prose ("Konstante Stilformen in Shakespeares Prosa," *Deutsche Shakespeare-Gesellschaft West, Jahrbuch* 1969: 81-102). These and similar collections furnish the interested student of Shakespeare's style with passages that have a similar message but that may manifest variation of language.

[43] Procedures for the study of adjective-noun relations are described in Appendix A on pp. 278-282.

[44] For the proportion of two-syllabled to four- and five-syllabled adjectives given in Table 6, $\chi^2 = 3.1053$, which lies between the .10 level of significance and the .05 level normally accepted where $\chi^2 = 3.841$.

Table 6
Adjectives Classified by Syllables per Adjective

	1	2	3	4-5	Compound	Total
R2	313	485	124	30	45	997
	.3139	.4864	.1243	.0300	.0451	
Ant.	248	248	101	26	24	647
	.3833	.3833	.1561	.0401	.0370	

the quantitative increase of polysyllabic adjectives in *Antony*. But when the words that derive their polysyllabic character from a combination of prefix and suffix are counted, it develops that 25 percent of the polysyllabic adjectives in *Richard II* are created in this manner: *dishonourable, discomfortable, unseasonable, discontented, disordered, unreverent, misbegotten, overweening*. In *Antony* only the single instance of *discontented*, representing less than 1 percent of the total set, depends on two affixes for its "extra" syllables. The fact that in *Richard II* many polysyllabic adjectives are created by adding relatively "empty" morphemes to common lexical bases like *honour, order, season*, and *comfort* makes this aspect of its diction less interesting than that of *Antony*, where the base of the adjective is polysyllabic. When Shakespeare does use two affixes to create extra syllables, there is often some novelty in the device, as happens, for example, in the verbal noun *discandying*, where the base *candy* is a noun converted to a verb and then nominalized by the suffix -*ing*. Similarly, though *unpolicied* does not derive its fourth syllable from the suffix, even if that were the case, the functional shift of *policy* from noun to verb and of the whole to an adjective would lend it special interest.[45]

Bernard Groom describes three aspects of Shakespeare's diction, the first being conventional terms like *silver* and *golden*, which are undistinguished enough in the early style but whose effect in the later plays (e.g., *Macbeth* 2.3.118) is quite striking. Shakespeare's earlier, Spenserian, vocabulary is

---

[45] There is much more to be said about these adjectives, which can be mentioned only briefly here. One can hardly ignore the context of words like *unparallel'd* and *unpolicied*: the transposition of noun and adjective, the phonological echoes of the two phrases, their proximity in the text, their use at the moment of Cleopatra's death, and the contrast of classical polysyllabic adjectives with monosyllabic nouns—one of which at least is Germanic. That such trains of thought are frequently suggested only demonstrates how starting at any point in the text will lead to others, but it is impossible to pursue every point and one hopes that occasional failure to note certain obvious directions will be attributed to lack of time and space rather than to severe limitations of method or insensitivity to finer nuances of style.

seen to contain a "high proportion of epithets," verbs with the prefix *en-* (*enring, endart*), and the adjectival suffixes *-y*, *-less*, and *-ful*. Functional shift, especially the conversion of nouns to verbs, is described as the new and characteristic method of the later style, which also exhibits a notable use of the negative prefixes *un-* and *dis-* with verbs and "a profusion of new words, mostly of Latin origin, some peculiarly harsh in form."[46]

Statistical analysis of the morphology of the adjectives in the two plays supports these observations in whole or in part as far as they pertain to the diction of adjectives. It also reveals some properties of adjectives not noted by Groom. Although the proportion of suffixes per adjective is identical in the two plays, prefixes decrease markedly in *Antony*.[47] The favorite prefix in both plays is *un-*, with *dis-* and *in-/im-* ranking next in *Richard II* and *in-/im-* in *Antony*. Nonnegative prefixes are rare, with *over-*, *up-*, *out-*, and *en-* occurring once each in *Richard II*. There is little more to be said on the subject of prefixes, since an adequate study must also include verbs. It is quite possible that in the later style *dis-* began to rival *un-* as a verbal prefix (*dislimn, discandying, disquiet, disprais'd*). To the list of Spenserian suffixes can be added *-ly*. These four suffixes are twice as numerous in *Richard II* as in *Antony*. To list a few words containing them is to capture the style of adjectives in the earlier play: *flinty, greedy, bloody; tongueless, spotless, stringless; restful, fearful, wasteful; knightly, stately, deadly*. Only two suffixes really increase in *Antony*—those of the group *inevitable, corrigible, miserable, honourable* and those created when the classical proper names are converted to adjectives. One easily recognizes these as special features of this play: *Roman, Egyptian, Herculean, Thracian, Ionian, Alexandrian, Philippan*.

Perhaps the most interesting suffixes are the less frequently studied inflectional morphemes used in the comparison of adjectives and in the creation of participial adjectives. In *Antony* there is a significant increase of superlatives, and no one will dispute that they contribute in an important way to its style.[48] In several passages they are doubled in frequency:

> They are so still,
> Or thou, the greatest soldier of the world,
> Art turn'd the greatest liar.

(1.3.37-39)

---

[46] Bernard Groom, *The Diction of Poetry from Spenser to Bridges*, pp. 26-47.

[47] The notes that accompany Table A-4 supply the data for suffixes and prefixes.

[48] For the data used in this discussion of superlatives and quantification, see Table A-5 and the notes that accompany it.

Thy palate then did deign
The roughest berry on the rudest hedge.

(1.4.63-64)

Then, noble partners,
The rather for I earnestly beseech,
Touch you the sourest points with sweetest terms,
Nor curstness grow to th' matter.

(2.2.22-25)

When the word *most* is added to the inflected superlatives, the hyperbolical meaning conveyed by this form is four times greater in *Antony* than in *Richard II*: The distribution of *most* in *Antony* suggests that its increase is largely due to its use with vocatives in titles, where it is also frequently collocated with *noble*: *most noble Caesar, most noble sir, most noble empress, most noble Antony* (2), and *a most unnoble swerving*. Its effectiveness seems due in part to the rhythm achieved by placing it before a group of words that end in unstressed syllables:

Now I feed myself
With most delicious poison.

(1.5.26-27)

The most infectious pestilence upon thee!

(2.5.61)

. . . cold and sickly
He vented them, most narrow measure lent me;

(3.4.7-8)

Since *most* is semantically emphatic and phonologically a strong monosyllable, its initial position in these passages strengthens words that might otherwise be weakened by their feminine endings.[49]

Comparative and superlative adjectives are types of quantification, and, in view of the increase of superlatives and the over-all decrease of qualifying adjectives in *Antony*, a general measure of the degree of quantification and of qualification is desirable. Numbers of a highly specific sort appear in both plays:

---

[49] The word *most* used as a quantifying adjunct increases also in *Antony*. This use is exemplified in a line like *Fortune knows | We scorn her most when most she offers blows* (3.11.73-74).

> Thy sad aspect
> Hath from the number of his banish'd years
> Pluck'd four away. Six frozen winters spent,
> Return with welcome home from banishment.
>
> (*R2* 1.3.209-212)
>
> He thinks, being twenty times of better fortune,
> He is twenty men to one.
>
> (*Ant.* 4.2.3-4)

When numbers used as numeral adjectives are added to the frequencies of *more, most*, and the adjectives inflected for comparison, quantifying adjectives increase significantly in proportion to qualifying adjectives in *Antony*.[50] The language of this play relies less than that of *Richard II* on the description of object, event, and person and more on their mode of specification and measure.

Participial adjectives, being created from verbs, may enter into different relations with the nouns they modify. While in some instances the relationship is oblique (*teeming date, numb'ring clock*) or the verbal element seems tenuous (*gnarling sorrow*), nearly all the participial adjectives in both plays are strongly verbal, and in most of the present participles the noun modified serves as subject of the verb. The main difference between the present participial adjectives in the two plays is in the type of noun they modify. In *Richard II* there is a higher ratio of human nouns, especially of parts of the human body; in *Antony* the human nouns decrease.[51] This difference is really independent of the participial adjectives, since it appears under other conditions as well, but the following citations afford some notion of the effect of concatenating present participles with certain types of nouns: *usurping steps, searching eye, daring tongue, helping hands, dancing soul; approaching Caesar, darting Parthia, squeaking Cleopatra, censuring Rome, blossoming Caesar*. The effect in both sets is strangely restrictive though in opposite directions. In the first set, activity that is usually associated with the total person is limited synecdochically to a part of that person. The second set suggests that entities like Rome and Caesar, which normally have many activities, are here restricted to those named by the participles. The first type of restriction suggests a fierce concentration of energy in the noun; the second suggests that the

---

[50] See Table A-5 and accompanying notes.
[51] See Table A-6.

Table 7
Frequency and Types of Participial Adjectives

	Present	Past	Total
R2	98	123	221
	.4434	.5565	
Ant.	35	89	124
	.2822	.7177	

total force of a powerful nation and a vehement personality have been thrown into the verbal action.

As Table 7 shows, adjectives formed from the past participle increase significantly in *Antony*.[52] They also create some of the most striking phrases in that play. Even when their function is attributive, the verbal element lends them an energy that creates the impression of action caught and rendered static: *anger'd ocean, rear'd arm, dimpled boys*. Sometimes the movement seems hardly to have ceased, especially when there is a hint of light on a reflecting surface: *plated Mars, tawny-finn'd fishes, scal'd snakes, gilded puddle, burnish'd throne, beaten gold*. At other times, however, the passive relation between noun and verb is exploited to create the impression of the hidden agent, whose activity is the more terrifying: *the condemn'd Pompey, a hired knife*. Several groups in which the noun is the object of the verbal action are associated with the instruments and the effects of warfare: *arm'd rest, mangled shadow, riveted trim, bruised pieces, well-paid ranks, conquer'd kingdoms, war-mark'd footmen, wounded chance, conquer'd Egypt*. The unnamed source of this activity is Rome, whose force and presence are perhaps felt as often as stated in the play. Nowhere is the state of helpless passivity before the Roman juggernaut expressed better than in these lines:

> Eros,
> Wouldst thou be window'd in great Rome and see
> Thy master thus with pleach'd arms, bending down
> His corrigible neck, his face subdu'd
> To penetrative shame, whilst the wheel'd seat
> Of fortunate Caesar, drawn before him, branded
> His baseness that ensu'd?

(4.14.71-77)

[52] For the data in Table 7, $x^2 = 7.8701$. The ratio of all participles to all adjectives is .2216 for *Richard II* and .1916 for *Antony*; hence, participles decreased slightly in the later play, making the increase of past participles all the more significant.

Table 8
Frequency of Compound and Multiple Adjectives

	Compound	Multiple	Total
R2	45	46	997
	.0451	.0461	
Ant.	24	12	647
	.0370	.0185	

Past participles, all in passive relation to their nouns, outnumber active verbs and dominate the passage.

While it is commonplace to say that compound epithets characterize the middle, or lyrical, style to which *Richard II* is usually assigned and while it is true that in simple frequency the epithets of *Richard II* nearly double those of *Antony*, it is also the case that in proportion to the number of adjectives in each play compound epithets do not decrease significantly in *Antony*, as the data in Table 8 shows. What does distinguish the adjective-noun pattern in *Richard II* sharply from that of *Antony* is the high proportion in the earlier play of nouns modified by two or more separate adjectives:[53]

> These high wild hills and rough uneven ways
> Draws out our miles and makes them wearisome;
>> (2.3.3-4)
>
> See, see, King Richard doth himself appear,
> As doth the blushing discontented sun
> From out the fiery portal of the East
>> (3.3.62-64)

But the felt prominence of compound epithets in *Richard II* does not lack justification. One does not find in *Antony* (or indeed elsewhere in *Richard II*) the high density of compounds revealed by this well-known passage:

> And for we think the eagle-winged pride
> Of sky-aspiring and ambitious thoughts
> With rival-hating envy set on you
> To wake our peace, which in our country's cradle

[53] $\chi^2 = .4048$ for the proportion of all compound adjectives to all adjectives in both plays; for all multiple adjectives to all adjectives, $\chi^2 = 7.4593$.

Draws the sweet infant breath of gentle sleep;
Which so rous'd up with boist'rous untun'd drums,
With harsh-resounding trumpets' dreadful bray
And grating shock of wrathful iron arms,
Might from our quiet confines fright fair peace
And make us wade even in our kinred's blood:
Therefore we banish you our territories.

(1.3.129-139)

Sometimes a passage where one or two features cluster in a striking manner suffices to create a stylistic tone that pervades the entire play and that is reinforced whenever the features are met singly in later lines. This comment seems especially true when the passage appears early in the play.[54]

The chief effectiveness of these and other adjective-noun phrases, of course, lies in the imagery they create. Following a method described by George Landon in his study of metaphor in the lyrics of Wilfred Owen, the adjective-noun collocations were analyzed to determine what constraints on lexical cooccurrence were violated.[55] The major finding was that in *Antony* personification decreases while reification increases; the tendency to personify objects and abstractions remains the favorite type of figure, but the language tends more often to reify abstract nouns by assigning them concrete attributes. The latter point is not new. Wolfgang Clemen calls the mingling of abstract and concrete images a characteristic of the imagery of Shakespeare's middle period, to which he assigns plays like *1* and *2 Henry IV*, *King John*, *As You Like It*, and *Twelfth Night*, all written within the five or six years following the composition of *Richard II*, but the phenomenon is even more characteristic of the mature than the middle style.[56]

There are many instances of reification in *Richard II* that typically ascribe to an abstraction some physical property like temperature or color: *dark dishonour, scarlet indignation, hot vengeance, pale cold cowardice.* Occasionally, the concrete element assumes a more dynamic form: *frozen admonition, weav'd up folly, brittle glory, blushing discontented sun.* Personification often results from assigning adjectives descriptive of human emotions to abstract and concrete nouns: *wrathful arms, sullen passage,*

---

[54] For further discussion of this point, see p. 88.
[55] The data for reification, animation, and personification in the two plays are given in Table A-7 together with corresponding information about Wilfred Owen as provided by Landon in "The Quantification of Metaphoric Language," p. 174.
[56] Wolfgang Clemen, *The Development of Shakespeare's Imagery*, p. 79.

rash blaze, eager feeding, envious siege, shrewd steel. The volatile, often malevolent, nature of these emotions suggests a kinetic energy that increased as Shakespeare's style developed.

Personification in *Antony* takes a more specific form. Adjectives like *envious, wrathful,* and *sullen* are relatively generic terms; to ascribe them to abstract or concrete nouns is simply to suggest that these nouns have the general property of humanness. But one would almost need another term to differentiate them from the personifications in this list: *vagabond flag, conquering banner, auguring hope, prophesying fear, visiting moon.* It is not simply that these adjectives express human activity, since there are many such participial adjectives in *Richard II,* but that they describe human beings in special roles and occupations—*wanderer, conqueror, seer.* The activity of the emotions is generally internalized; the activity here is social and extroverted.

In *Antony* there is a new type of reification as well. Normally one finds a concrete adjective modifying an abstract noun: *smooth success, beauteous freedom, swift thought;* however, in half a dozen of the adjective-noun images the movement is from concrete adjective to human noun, although the result is quite the opposite of the personification one normally gets when these semantic categories are concatenated: *wrinkled Cassius, slippery people, salt Cleopatra, full Caesar, wan'd lip, ebb'd man.* In the underlying comparison of lips to a waning moon, of a man to an ebb tide, or of people to a wet, greasy, or slimy object, the noun has been suppressed and its attribute retained so that one gets that oblique, compressed, associative image commonly found in the later style. Most of these form a cluster of images associated with change—the fickle mob, woman, the moon, the sea. Curiously enough, many of these expressions are associated with Pompey: he is the *ebb'd man;* he speaks of Cleopatra's *wan'd lip;* and Menas when deserting him says, *I'll never follow thy pall'd fortunes more. Pall'd* does not manifest the same tendency to reduce human beings to concrete attributes, but like *ebb* and *wane* it has a peculiar syntax. One cannot say *she waned the moon* or *he ebbed the tide.* Like *sun set* and *sun rise* these verbs evoke an older-world picture where sun, moon, and tide were quasi-animate objects capable of initiating motion. There is, then, an interesting dynamism in the figures from human to concrete to animate and perhaps a tendency in Shakespeare's creative imagination not only to create image clusters but also to pursue such associations at other linguistic levels even to the type of syntax (adjective-noun), the same violation of selection restrictions (human to concrete), the same image content (images of change), and even the same character, Pompey.

Finally, one might note the tendency of figures to be built from other figures. In *wrinkled Cassius*, Cassius is first equated with his skin (by synecdoche) and the wrinkled appearance of that skin is then attributed to the whole man by a reversal of the synecdoche from whole to part and part to whole. Or, in *the noble ruin of her magic, Antony*, Antony is first compared with the concrete noun *ruin*, which is then personified by the adjective *noble*. In *downy windows, close*, the conventional and explicit metaphors *eyes/windows* or *eyelashes/down* are conflated and the metaphoric elements in both statements are equated with each other. There is a dynamism not only in the pursuit of image by image but even in the fact that one type of image (personification, reification, synecdoche) will replace another, build on another, or become another.[57]

The first chapter of this study was devoted to answering the question "what is style?" This second chapter has considered the problem of where style is to be found in the text. Since style was defined as a continuous function of the literary work, it seemed logical that it might be found in any segment of the text however it might be divided. These excursions into different aspects of *Richard II* and *Antony and Cleopatra* are offered as evidence that any way of segmenting the texts can yield insight into their style. To introduce the method of specifying the structural components of the plays in terms of linguistic values, the analyses have depended on the formalism provided by linguistic analysis to a great extent and on quantitative data to a slighter degree. Further discussion of methodology, especially of linguistic and quantitative analysis, will be the subject of the next two chapters.

[57]What has been described here is not unlike the point made by Winifred M. T. Nowottny in *The Language Poets Use*, where in describing metaphor with reference to *R2* 5.5.1ff. she speaks of a metaphor inside a metaphor that "breaks the hold of the convention and enables us to become aware of the subjectivity of objects and the objectivity of subjective processes" (p. 86) or where she states that the real peculiarity of poetic structure "is that in it one constituent is used to develop the potential of another" (p. 98).

CHAPTER THREE

Reflections on Stylistic Analysis

Style as Proportions

Whether the starting point of stylistic analysis is chosen formally or intuitively, one can find significant differences between texts provided that the implications of the starting point are pursued with careful attention to the method of analysis. Syntax is a good basis for the analysis of literary style, since it mediates between the semantic and phonological components of grammar and often leads one to many other aspects of the language. Thus, the study of kernel sentences in representative passages led to an examination of semantic features of the nouns in these sentences and to the stylistic difference that in *Antony* selection rules were broken more frequently than in *Richard II*. Similarly, concentration on the hypotactic group complex suggested that Shakespeare handled this structure differently in the two plays because he sought another kind of rhythm in *Antony* than he had used in *Richard II*. Both these pieces of information—one semantic, the other phonological—were derived from a study of syntax. Another reason for emphasizing syntax is the fact that, while there are many studies of Shakespeare's style based on imagery and vocabulary, there are few assessments of the contribution made by syntax to his verbal art.[1] Finally, because syntax

[1] Among the earliest and best is E. K. Chambers's study of the relationship between syntax and meter in *William Shakespeare: A Study of Facts and Problems*. For more

operates at a more abstract and general level of language than does vocabulary, the description of it in these two plays might be valid for other plays
belonging to the same period in which they were written. *Richard II*, a
good example of the middle style, should yield some hypotheses about the
syntactic features of *Romeo and Juliet* and *A Midsummer Night's Dream*,
while a study of *Antony and Cleopatra* should tell us something about the
style of *Macbeth*, *Coriolanus*, and other later plays. When such information has been gathered for several plays, it should reveal something about
the number and nature of the stages in Shakespeare's stylistic development.

Comparison of texts, then, becomes a subsidiary aspect of method. Even
though they may well be stable for the language as a whole, linguistic
elements whose frequency is relatively stable in both plays can be provisionally regarded as an index of Shakespeare's personal style—that which,
on the one hand, differentiates him from other authors and, on the other,
identifies him as the author of each of his plays no matter how else these
may differ from one another. The peculiarities of the two plays, by virtue
of which they are distinguished from each other, will be said, again tentatively, to constitute their individual styles. This assumption will be maintained until similar studies of other plays show what features of *Richard II*
and *Antony and Cleopatra* are shared with others and which ones are
peculiar to these two plays. In comparing texts it seems advisable to keep
as many factors as possible stable so that when variation appears it can be
the more reasonably called a stylistic variation. Factors to be kept stable
would include subject matter (both are histories), genre (these are both
dramas), and sound structure (both are in blank verse, the prose of *Antony*
being omitted). There is some variation that cannot be completely controlled. The two plays have different sources, and *Antony*'s is a source that
is itself stylistically superior to the chronicles and histories that furnished

---

recent studies, one thinks of Thomas A. Dunn's comparison in his *Philip Massinger* of
Shakespeare's syntax (loose and colloquial) with that of Massinger (periodic and
formal); the admirable study by Jonas A. Barish of the logical character of the prose
as it is revealed by disjunctive terms (*Ben Jonson and the Language of Prose
Comedy*); Vivian Salmon's thorough description of statements, questions, and commands in the Falstaff plays ("Sentence Structure in Colloquial Shakespearian English," *Transactions of the Philological Society, 1965*, pp. 105-140). To these might
be added Francis Berry's remarks on pronouns, verb tense, and mood in *The Poet's
Grammar*; Sr. Miriam Joseph Rauh's discussion of the rhetorical figures of grammar
in *Shakespeare's Use of the Arts of Language*; and comments on rhetoric and sentence structure in Brian Vickers's *The Artistry of Shakespeare's Prose*. As can be
seen, half of these deal with the syntax of the prose rather than of the blank verse.

the material of *Richard II*. Most problematic is the fact that the English language was changing rapidly during the thirteen years that elapsed between the composition of these plays, and it will be difficult to determine at times whether a change is to be attributed to the language or to Shakespeare's stylistic development. Considering the many factors that can modify the tentative results of a limited study like this one, it becomes increasingly obvious that stylistic analysis is not unlike a game of croquet played in Looking-glass Land, where the hoops and mallets may at any time remove themselves to another position.

Quantitative analysis, whether it consists of a quick intuitive assessment of images or a rigorous tabulation, has traditionally been used to answer the question of how one can tell whether a given feature is characteristic of a text. The numerous quotations, references, and allusions cited to buttress arguments about the existence of image patterns in Shakespeare have been a favorite critical technique since Caroline Spurgeon's work on Shakespeare's imagery was first published, and these constitute an intuitive count of stylistic features. To formalize this technique by giving exact figures or by subjecting these to statistical tests of significance is not to break radically with that tradition so long as formal analysis is sensitive to the needs and interests of literary criticism and is productive of information that could not be obtained more easily by intuitive methods. The various sections of this chapter define some of the tasks for which the student of style needs statistical assistance.[2]

---

[2] There are few statistical studies of Shakespeare's work, fewer still of his syntax. Alfred Hart's vocabulary counts in "The Growth of Shakespeare's Vocabulary," *Review of English Studies* 19 (1943): 242-254, are counts of lines and words arranged in tables. A. C. Partridge has used percents of features like colloquial contractions to differentiate between Shakespearean and Fletcherian parts of *Henry VIII* in *The Problem of Henry VIII Re-opened*. B. F. Skinner calculated the probability that alliteration in the sonnets was due to random distribution and concluded that, as far as any conscious attention to this sound pattern was concerned, Shakespeare "might well have drawn his words out of a hat" ("The Alliteration in Shakespeare's Sonnets: A Study in Literary Behavior," *The Psychological Record* 3 [1939]: 191). Paul E. Bennett used Yule's characteristic K to compare the richness of vocabulary in two plays in his "The Statistical Measurement of a Stylistic Trait in *Julius Caesar* and *As You Like It*," *Shakespeare Quarterly* 8 (1957): 33-50. A little-known study by M. R. Yardi, based on figures drawn from the work of E. K. Chambers, determined the percentage of lines with extra final syllables and of split lines and suggests possible dates for plays whose chronology is uncertain ("Statistical Approach to the Problem of Chronology," *Sānkhyā: The Indian Journal of Statistics* 7 [1946]: 263-268). Two pioneer studies are those of Carson Hildreth, who repunctuated the sentences of the prose in fifteen plays on principles established by Skeat and calculated the average

The first problem encountered with large bodies of linguistic data is not often remarked by those who hold that style involves favoring certain linguistic patterns: When a text is long enough to admit the full variety of linguistic choices to operate, one will probably discover upon counting that the most favored choice in the text will be one favored by the language as a whole. Of what value is it to know that short *i* sounds predominate in Shakespeare's text if these also predominate in the English language? But if one were to learn that the proportion of short *i* to short *e* and long *i* sounds presented a rather different configuration in Shakespeare's phonology than it did in the English language, one might begin to have some knowledge of Shakespeare's special orchestration of sounds. Stylistic features will be revealed, not by the fact, for example, that one play has 10 percent more declaratives than another, but by the proportion in each text of imperative, interrogative, exclamatory, and declarative sentences to one another. Systemic grammar provides the student of style with an excellent rationale for establishing such proportions. The linguistic units of sentence, clause, and group arranged along the scale of structure ensure that comparable aspects of the language can be derived from the texts, and within each grammatical structure one can move along the scale of delicacy making finer distinctions until statistically discernible differences appear.[3] The set of discrete and mutually exclusive categories ensures that all alternatives are examined before a given feature is labeled characteristic of the text.

One advantage of representing linguistic information as sets of proportions is that the significance of results can often be assessed by inspection, especially if frequencies are small and if they are based on all instances of a given item in the text. Table 9, for example, shows how often in these two plays Shakespeare used *such* before a content word like a noun as opposed

---

sentence length of Shakespeare (12.39 words) and Bacon (32.59 words), and T. C. Mendenhall, who counted the letters per word in Shakespeare, Bacon, and several other authors and found that the characteristic curves of Shakespeare and Bacon were widely divergent. Hildreth's article, "The Bacon-Shakespeare Controversy," appeared in *University of Nebraska Studies* 2 (1897): 147-162, and Mendenhall's "A Mechanical Solution of a Literary Problem," in *Popular Science Monthly* 60 (1901): 97-105.

[3] According to M. A. K. Halliday, "Delicacy is the scale of differentiation, or depth in detail . . . whose limit at one end is the primary degree in the categories of structure and class. . . .[and] the other limit is the point beyond which no further grammatical relations obtain" ("Categories of the Theory of Grammar," *Word* 17 (1961): 272). For example, one might move from the class determiner to the difference between specific and nonspecific determiners and from there to the difference between specific determiners that are selective or nonselective.

Table 9
Two Classes of Determiner in
Nominal-Group Structure

	Such	*Such a/an*
R2	13	2
Ant.	15	13

to the number of times he placed a determiner after *such*. No test is needed to see that a construction that occurred one out of six times in *Richard II* and increased to a one-to-one proportion in *Antony and Cleopatra* constitutes a quantitatively significant difference in the language of the two plays. Where figures are larger, however, or where there is some doubt about the significance of a set of proportions, the chi-square test is available.

This test ordinarily sets up proportions based on the differences between observed and expected frequencies of an item. Since we do not know the expected frequencies for many grammatical units in English, the chi-square test would appear useless for linguistic study. Moreover, knowing that in any text some constructions will normally occur far more often than others, we cannot create expected frequencies on the assumption that all have an equal possibility of occurrence. Finally, if one is comparing portions of the text, such as two scenes or the lines spoken by two different characters, line length will fluctuate widely. One could obviate the last difficulty by making line length the denominator of all proportions, but, when a word is used rarely in a long text, its possible significance will be lost. For example, when the number of times Antony and Caesar used *shall* was tested against the total lines assigned to each of them, the result was not significant, but, when their uses of *shall* were tested against their uses of *will*, the two sets of proportions were significantly different.[4] One cannot choose words for the bottom line of the proportions arbitrarily, but any systematic opposition recognized by the grammar provides a potential set of proportions.

Grammatical Oppositions

This section shows how the categories of systemic grammar can be used to establish proportions for chi-square testing and thus to reveal quantita-

---

[4] Chi-square for the proportion of *shall* to *will* in the speeches of Caesar and Antony is 7.9200. See Table 32.

tive differences between texts. Normally, one would begin analysis with a theoretical construct, such as a dependent clause, and examine the relevant systems of mood, transitivity, polarity, tense, and so on. To simplify explanation, however, the illustration will be based on an ad hoc study of the *wh-* words in the two plays. These words can be fully tabulated by reference to a concordance; they enter into several different systems of the grammar; and preliminary study of *Antony and Cleopatra* indicates that *wh-* relatives appear in several passages with marked stylistic effect. Although there are more than a dozen of these words in Shakespeare's language, a count of their frequency in the two plays reveals that, compared to *Richard II*, only three of them (*what*, *when*, and *which*) increase noticeably in *Antony* and that, as a group, compounds like *whencesoever*, *whereof*, *whereupon*, and *whoso* decrease by 50 percent in the same play.[5] Since most of these words are either obsolete or archaic today, their decline can be attributed to changes in the language as a whole, whereas the unevenness and the relatively low rate of change in the remaining words suggest that stylistic factors may best explain the differences. In any case, that is the assumption throughout this discussion of *wh-* words.

Each of the words *what*, *when*, and *which* has properties peculiar to itself. Of the three, *what* is subject to the least ambiguity and will therefore provide the data for quantitative analysis here. Table 10 shows how often this word occurs in questions, exclamations, and other types of sentences. The increase observed in the frequency counts is not distributed evenly across all moods but is associated significantly with noninterrogative sentences, a pattern shown also by the words *when* and *which*.[6] When it does not indicate interrogation, the word *what* may be an expletive,

Table 10
Types of Sentences Containing the Word *What*

	Imperative/ Declarative	Interrogative	Exclamatory
R2	53	59	2
Ant.	86	55	2

[5] Table A-8 provides the frequencies of individual *wh-* words.

[6] For the proportion of interrogative to declarative/imperative occurrences of *what* given in Table 10, $\chi^2 = 4.1790$. Table A-9 provides data to show that, in *Antony*, *wh-* words in general occur in declarative/imperative sentences significantly more often than they occur in interrogative sentences. For these proportions of *wh-* words in the two plays, $\chi^2 = 4.6921$.

Table 11
Functions of the Word *What* in Sentence Structure

	Relative	Indirect Question	Indirect Exclamation	Expletive
R2	33	11	2	7
Ant.	64	12	0	10

mark indirect questions and exclamations, or introduce relative clauses. The next question, then, is whether the increased use of *what* in statements occurs consistently through all these functions or whether it concentrates in one of them. Table 11 shows the frequency with which it occurs as an expletive or in various dependent clauses. The fact that an increase in relative clauses explains the higher frequency of the word *what* in *Antony and Cleopatra* narrows the field of inquiry a second time.[7] Even though it may still be argued that relatives as a whole increased in the language or that *what* relatives did so in particular, the case for stylistic difference, as will be seen, rests on increasingly finer distinctions and ultimately on a demonstration of their role in literary structure.

In traditional grammar the relative clauses introduced by *what* are classified as noun clauses, since they occupy all positions of the noun—subject, direct object, object of a preposition. In the latter capacity they may be adjuncts in clause structure or qualifiers in a nominal group. The four nominal uses are exemplified, respectively, by the following sentences:

> Little joy have I
> To breathe this news; yet what I say is true.
> (*R2* 3.4.81-82)

> Think what you will, we seize into our hands
> His plate, his goods, his money, and his lands.
> (*R2* 2.1.209-210)

> To punish me for what you make me do
> Seems much unequal.
> (*Ant.* 2.5.100-101)

> The record of what injuries you did us,
> Though written in our flesh, we shall remember
> As things but done by chance.
> (*Ant.* 5.2.118-120)

[7] The proportion of relatives to indirect questions shown in Table 11 is not significantly different in the two plays.

Table 12
Functions of Clauses Introduced by the Relative Word *What*

	Subject	Complement	Adjunct	Qualifier
R2	2	27	1	3
Ant.	3	37	14	10

Classifying these clauses according to their role in clause structure yields the interesting figures shown in Table 12. That the increase of adjunct and qualifying functions is statistically significant is obvious even from inspection.[8] Moreover, it would be quite valid to combine these functions and to point out that the use of these clauses as prepositional objects accounts for 80 percent of the increase of *what* in *Antony*. Although comment must be postponed until quantitative and linguistic analysis is completed, a few passages exemplifying this feature suggest that it contributes to our sense of difficulty or complexity in the language of the later play:

> Her length of sickness, with what else more serious
> Importeth thee to know, this bears.
> (1.2.124-125)

> And I will boot thee with what gift beside
> Thy modesty can beg.
> (2.5.71-72)

> . . . and by starts
> His fretted fortunes give him hope and fear
> Of what he has and has not.
> (4.12.7-9)

The last structural level at which the word *what* functions is that of nominal group, where it may serve as modifier to the head of the group, as in the first two passages cited above, or as the pronominal head of the group, as shown by the third quotation.[9] Table 13 shows how often *what* has these functions in relative clauses.

Examination of the word *what* has proceeded from the level of sentence, which is the primary degree in the category of structure, through the level of dependent clause, to that of nominal group. This series represents a

---

[8] By combining the figures for subject and complement functions of *what* clauses and those for the adjunct and qualifying functions of these clauses (see Table 12 for data), one obtains proportions where $\chi^2 = 5.7500$. This result shows that the adjunct and qualifying functions of *what* clauses increase significantly in *Antony*.

[9] Data on the modifying function of relative words are provided in Table A-10.

Table 13
Functions of the Relative Word *What* in
Nominal-Group Structure

	Modifier	Head
R2	4	29
Ant.	8	56

move along the scale of delicacy with respect to structure. Another way of establishing sets in the grammar is to ask what systems may be used to describe a sentence, clause, or group. The system of mood has already been examined, but there are many others. The system of theme, for example, "specifies the order of elements in the clause where this is not already fully determined by the transitivity and mood dimensions."[10] When the mood is declarative, the subject of a clause normally occupies initial position, but on occasion a complement or an adjunct may do so. The following passages in which the relative clause assumes first position illustrate, respectively, complement and adjunct theme:

> What you will have, I'll give, and willing too;
> For do we must what force will have us do.
>
> (*R2* 3.3.206-207)

> For what I have conquer'd,
> I grant him part;
>
> (*Ant.* 3.6.34-35)

Although adjunct theme is generally more common than complement theme, there are only three instances of it among these clauses.[11] Probably the preposition-complement structure offers too much intrinsic complexity in this instance (where the complement is a clause) to warrant its being compounded by placing the structure in marked theme position. Table 14 shows how often the *what* clause appears in theme position when used as a complement and when used as an adjunct. All other positions are assumed to be normal.[12] There is obviously a signifi-

[10] Rodney D. Huddleston et al., *Sentence and Clause in Scientific English*, p. 271.
[11] The research undertaken by Huddleston and others suggests that adjunct theme is more frequent than complement theme (*Sentence and Clause*, pp. 272-274). It is difficult to tabulate instances of adjunct theme because they are so numerous and are realized in such a variety of forms, but there is good reason to believe that in Shakespeare's work, especially in *Antony and Cleopatra*, adjunct theme outnumbers complement theme.
[12] In addition to theme, the English language has other ways of calling attention to a constituent by placing it in first position. One of these is to announce a phrase as if

Reflections on Stylistic Analysis

Table 14
Function and Position of Clauses Introduced by Relative *What*

	Complement		Adjunct	
	Theme	Normal	Theme	Normal
R2	11	16	0	1
Ant.	5	32	3	11

cant difference between the two plays with respect to placing these clauses in intital position.[13]

With the study of the various functions of the word *what* enough has been said to exemplify how systemic grammar provides proportions for quantitative analysis. Just as the simple counts in the proportion are readily interpreted by the nonstatistician, so the chi-square test can be easily and quickly applied by someone who lacks sophisticated training or equipment. Its chief drawback is that it tends to be conservative when frequencies are low. One reason why the significance of results can be confidently assessed is the form taken by systemic grammar, namely, that of mutually exclusive categories that exhaust the possible uses of a given element and thus oblige one to examine alternative hypotheses. And, even though results may not be significant at one level of analysis, the scale of delicacy can suggest further hypotheses for testing. For example, had one studied only the proportion of relative uses of *what* to its use in indirect questions, one would have had an important explanation for the increase of this word, but the additional information that in *Antony* these clauses were often governed by a preposition or that in *Richard II* they tended to appear in marked position was not only supplied but also prompted by the grammatical description. Although the basis of comparison changes in each case, the grammar legitimates and controls the shifts by supplying categories that exist independently of the text.

---

it were a topic and then to comment upon it. In the following passage from *Antony*, the *what* clause serves as complement and appears as the topic of the sentence: *What our contempts do often hurl from us, / We wish it ours again* (1.2.127-128). Topic differs from theme in that it places the element outside the clause. In *Richard II* the *what* clause appears twice as topic; in *Antony* there are four occurrences of this relative as topic. In Table 14 all instances of topic positions for *what* clauses are included in the figures for normal position.

[13] When the fourfold table contains figures lower than five, it is impossible to carry out a chi-square test. By combining complements and adjuncts in theme position in the two plays and opposing them to complements and adjuncts in normal position, one can get a significant test result, which indicates that in *Richard II* the *what* clauses tend to occur in first position an unusual number of times.

For purposes of interpretation the focus will be on those relative uses of *what* in which the word serves as a pronoun with homophoric reference.[14] The fact that this construction combines the quality of an indefinite pronoun with the internal structure of a clause (which permits some concreteness through its other constituents) creates a linguistic vehicle whose interplay of the vague and the specific Shakespeare exploits to good effect in *Antony and Cleopatra*. Sometimes it is a circumlocution to avoid naming an unpleasant situation:

> If he mislike
> My speech and what is done, tell him he has
> Hipparchus, my enfranched bondman, . . .
>
> (3.13.147-149)

> She had a prophesying fear
> Of what hath come to pass;
>
> (4.14.120-121)

When the triumvirate meets Pompey to work out a peace treaty, Caesar uses this clause to hint at rewards without committing himself to further obligations:

> *Lep.*   Be pleas'd to tell us
> (For this is from the present) how you take
> The offers we have sent you.
>
> *Caes.*   There's the point.
>
> *Ant.* Which do not be entreated to, but weigh
> What it is worth embrac'd.
>
> *Caes.*   And what may follow,
> To try a larger fortune.
>
> (2.6.29-34)

[14] Homophoric reference with respect to the definite article is defined by M. A. K. Halliday in his "Descriptive Linguistics in Literary Studies," in *English Studies Today*, ed. G. I. Duthie, pp. 26-39. In Huddleston et al., *Sentence and Clause*, the concept is applied to relative clauses (pp. 201-205). Briefly, a word has homophoric reference if it refers to something outside the linguistic context whose identity is regarded by the speaker as self-evident. To speak of *the sun* is normally an instance of homophoric reference with the definite article. The homophoric function of the *what* clause has a frequency of twenty-six in *Richard II* and of fifty-six in *Antony*. Line references to those clauses classified as homophoric are provided in Table B-2. For further examples of homophoric reference, see Chapter Four, note 10.

There seems to be a slight difference between Caesar's use of the relative and Antony's. The line *weigh what it is worth embrac'd* is specified: *it* refers to the *offers* of a few lines earlier; *embrac'd* has *it* for a subject; and *what it is worth*, though technically homophoric, is in fact clarified by Pompey's itemization of the terms of the treaty in lines 34-35. Caesar's line is quite ambiguous. *What may follow*, presumably some benefit other than those already mentioned, has for a possible referent lines 38-39, the peace that will ensue if the treaty is ratified. But this interpretation does not explain *to try a larger fortune*. Is *Pompey* the subject of *to try*? If so, what fortune larger than the claim to Sardinia and Sicily is being offered him? Is there a hint that his territorial power might rival that of the triumvirate or of one of its members? The ambiguity is lost, of course, on the unimaginative Pompey.

Sometimes these clauses are used for sexual innuendo, as in this speech of Cleopatra's eunuch Mardian:

> Not in deed, madam; for I can do nothing
> But what indeed is honest to be done.
> Yet have I fierce affections, and think
> What Venus did with Mars.
>
> (1.5.15-18)

Most often, however, they occur in discourses on fortune, war, and honor:

> Know, worthy Pompey,
> That what they do delay, they not deny.
>
> (2.1.2-3)

> Had our general
> Been what he knew himself, it had gone well.
>
> (3.10.26-27)

> I'll humbly signify what in his name,
> That magical word of war, we have effected;
> How with his banners and his well-paid ranks
> The ne'er-yet-beaten horse of Parthia
> We have jaded out o' th' field.
>
> (3.1.30-34)

These sentences exhibit various kinds of marked word order, such as complement theme, adjuncts wedged between core constituents, and appositional phrases and vocatives interrupting syntax and rhythm. To describe them in quite subjective terms one might note the oblique syntax of the clause when it is the object of a preposition, the slower rhythms, and the harshness of certain sounds, notably, *w* and *th*. All these features appear, together with two relative clauses (one embedded in the other), in this speech of Ventidius:

> He purposeth to Athens; whither, with what haste
> The weight we must convey with 's will permit,
> We shall appear before him.
>
> (3.1.35-37)

The behavior of Ventidius is the most consistently martial and heroic in the play, and one is tempted on the basis of his few speeches to define a heroic style in this play, but the matter is too complex to be so easily isolated.

In general, the major figures in the play employ these clauses in characteristic ways. Lepidus, it develops, has a peculiar fondness for this construction and uses it more often than any other character of his political or dramatic stature.[15] In his speech it can be awkward, suggesting both his eagerness to remain *au courant* of political developments and his failure to do so:

> What you shall know meantime
> Of stirs abroad, I shall beseech you, sir,
> To let me be partaker.
>
> (1.4.81-83)

> To-morrow, Caesar,
> I shall be furnish'd to inform you rightly
> Both what by sea and land I can be able
> To front this present time.
>
> (1.4.76-79)

One notes here other marked stylistic effects: the fact that in the first passage the *what* clause is qualifier to *partaker* and has been detached from its head to be placed in initial position, and the appearance of marginal constituents like *meantime* and *sir* to interrupt *know*, *beseech*, and their complements. In the second quotation there is the odd *can be able* and the displacement of *both* from the expression *by sea and land*. Most of these effects result from deviant word order, but they supply for the

---

[15] Dramatic stature is pragmatically defined in terms of lines per speaker: the higher the number of lines, the higher the dramatic stature. Among speakers with more than twenty lines of blank verse, Lepidus has the highest ratio of *what* clauses.

indefinite *what* clauses a context of convoluted syntax and ponderous rhythm that is marvelously suited to Lepidus's confused diplomacy.

Antony uses *what* relatives to express his feelings of guilt when he learns of Fulvia's death (1.2.127-128), his thoughts of defeat and dishonor, and, above all, his sense of identity:

> See
> How I convey my shame out of thine eyes
> By looking back what I have left behind
> Stroy'd in dishonour.
>
> (3.11.51-55)

> Look thou say
> He makes me angry with him; for he seems
> Proud and disdainful, harping on what I am,
> Not what he knew I was.
>
> (3.13.140-143)

Caesar does not often enhance these clauses by placing them in initial position, and, in terms of words per clause, his are among the shortest in the play. Perhaps their relative simplicity is a function of his subtlety:

> *Ant.*   Will Caesar speak?
>
> *Caes.*   Not till he hears how Antony is touch'd
> With what is spoke already
>
> (2.2.141-143)

His most elaborate use of *what* clauses appears with reference to Cleopatra. When instructing Thyreus about his embassy to her (3.12.27-29), he surrounds them with marked word order; when he wishes to persuade Cleopatra personally of his good intentions, the clauses are doubled, placed in initial position, and arranged in parallel structure:

> Cleopatra,
> Not what you have reserv'd, nor what acknowledg'd,
> Put we i' th' roll of conquest.
>
> (5.2.179-181)

The ability of these relatives to refer to an indeterminate object or event, to surround the reference with considerable embroidery, and still to refrain from naming it precisely may well explain their attraction for a man like Caesar and indeed for the Roman mind generally.

It is therefore necessary to consider the evidence for suggesting that they may be a feature of "Roman" speeches. Content is perhaps a better guide here than speaker. Seventy-nine percent of the speeches that contain these clauses are statements about honor, suicide, warfare, or affairs of state. Among the eighteen characters who use them, two-thirds are Romans or have Roman occupations: they are triumvirs, generals, ambassadors, soldiers, counselors.[16] Hence, while the clauses are not exclusively associated with a Roman context, in an impressive variety of instances they are spoken by Romans about Roman concerns. And if this speaker/ message context should exhibit enough special features to constitute a distinct style within the play, then *what* relatives will certainly be an aspect of that style whether it be labeled formal, heroic, or Roman.

Isolating a distinct style of this kind is complicated by the fact that the possible Roman character of these clauses is subverted by Enobarbus, modified to some extent by Cleopatra, and employed in seriocomic situations by Cleopatra's male servants. Enobarbus subverts the language of warfare and diplomacy by adopting it to convey information that has nothing to do with battles or affairs of state:

> On each side her
> Stood pretty dimpled boys, like smiling Cupids,
> With divers-colour'd fans, whose wind did seem
> To glow the delicate cheeks which they did cool,
> And what they undid did.
>
> (2.2.206-210)
>
> Our courteous Antony,
>
> . . . .
> Being barber'd ten times o'er, goes to the feast,
> And for his ordinary pays his heart
> For what his eyes eat only.
>
> (2.2.227-231)

For this purpose Enobarbus also employs the adverbial relative introduced by *where*:

> Antony will use his affection where it is.
>
> (2.6.139)

[16] Because Roman characters obviously outnumber Egyptian characters in *Antony* and are assigned longer speeches, the fact that Roman speakers have a high frequency of *what* clauses may not be significant from a statistical point of view.

Other women cloy
The appetites they feed, but she makes hungry
Where most she satisfies;

(2.2.241-243)

These adverbial clauses and those governed by *when* may or may not have
an antecedent; when they have none, they function homophorically as
substitutes for place or time, and they refer to some location or event
outside the linguistic context. Enobarbus's choice of *where* rather than
when in the second example tells us that place rather than time is the
source of appetite and satisfaction, a choice of words that is both concrete
and vague enough to be quite suggestive.

There is some mockery of the formal style of *what* clauses by Enobarbus. Behind it one might almost hear Shakespeare himself testing the limits
to which this style might be carried before it degenerates into bombast:

What willingly he did confound he wail'd,
Believe't, till I wept too.

(3.2.58-59)

This speech begins with the rather public rhetorical manner that one might
intuitively associate with a Roman or heroic style assuming that to be
characterized by "difficult" language: the complement realized as a clause
and placed in initial position; the core constituents *what* and *he* separated
by the adjunct *willingly*; the formal use of *did* to express past tense; and
the entire line governed by the *w* alliteration noted in the speeches of
Ventidius (3.1.30-34, 35-37). With *believe't* the tone reverts to the mockery of *That year indeed he was troubled with a rheum*, and by his explicit
protestation of sincerity Enobarbus lets us know that we have been treated
to a parody of the grand manner. This parody might not have been so
effective or so obvious if the grandiloquent context that accompanies
several of these clauses had not been concentrated in and established by
the early scenes of the play—through speeches of Antony and the messenger from Sicyon (1.2.123-124, 127-128, 183-184), through Lepidus, and
especially through Ventidius, who is introduced with all his verbal fanfare
just prior to the conversation between Enobarbus and Agrippa. At the
other extreme is Lepidus, who cannot quite master the trick of it and is
either too earnest in his attempts at diplomatic language, arguing too
sincerely on Antony's behalf (1.4.12-15; 2.2.19-20), or too awkward in his
expression of it (1.4.76-79, 81-83). It may be that Shakespeare himself

sought to control and mitigate the swelling language of the grand manner by gently lampooning it through the unconscious mannerisms of Lepidus or the self-conscious wit of Enobarbus.

Not only does Cleopatra employ these relatives sparingly (the ratio spoken by her is lower than that of every other character in the play), but also, with a single exception (2.5.103), they are concentrated in the latter part of the play. The first of these appears when Thyreus comes from Caesar to win her allegiance from Antony. Like Caesar, Cleopatra can be subtle and ambiguous:

> *Thyr.* He knows that you embrace not Antony
> As you did love, but as you fear'd him.
>
> . . . .
>
> *Cleo.*   He is a god, and knows
> What is most right. Mine honour was not yielded,
> But conquer'd merely.
>
> (3.13.56-57, 60-62)

Thyreus's argument, designed to save Cleopatra's face if she should desert Antony, rests on the semantic distinction between *fear* and *love*. The syntactic parallelism of the sentence that contains these verbs emphasizes by contrast their difference in meaning. Cleopatra seems to confirm the ambassador's statement. Her syntax superficially resembles his: two clauses joined by the conjunction *but* with the same subject, and both verbs in the same tense and voice. However, the verbs *yield* and *conquer* are not contrastive but reciprocal in meaning; one implies the other. We know also from Shakespeare's own *Rape of Lucrece* that in the ancient world whether one yields or is conquered is immaterial, dishonor being equally the result. Converting the verbs to active voice and supplying their logical subjects produces this reading: *I did not yield my honor; Antony merely conquered it.* Where the distinction between *love* and *fear* had been contrasted with the similarity of their syntactic matrix, here the similarity between *yield* and *conquer* is enhanced by the difference in underlying syntax, although that difference is deliberately masked to deceive Thyreus. Finally, the clause *what is most right*, though technically homophoric and placed ambiguously between the two statements, is inclined by the grammatical norm toward Cleopatra's restatement of the case for which it serves as introduction and to which it seems to point. Without flatly contradicting him, Cleopatra tells the ambassador that his argument rests on a distinction without a difference and that, if he would call things by their proper name (*what is most right*), he would realize that he is insulting her. Just after Antony's death Cleopatra employs two of these clauses in a manner that seems rather characteristic of her:

> Good sirs, take heart.
> We'll bury him; and then, what's brave, what's noble,
> Let's do it after the high Roman fashion
> And make death proud to take us.
>
> (4.15.85-88)

The colloquial flavor of ellipsis has already been noted. Its effect here is not unlike that of Charmian's reaction to the death of Cleopatra: *Your crown's awry*. Here there is a similar mingling of light-heartedness and dignity derived in part from combining a formal locution like these relative clauses with colloquial constructions.

If Cleopatra's style of speech and behavior often combines dignity with playfulness, then some explanation can be offered for incidents that tend to compromise her. One of these is the lie she sends to Antony about her death. It is delivered by Mardian:

> What thou wouldst do
> Is done unto thy hand.
>
> (4.14.28-29)

Antony himself calls the man *saucy eunuch* and notes that he wants a tip (*That thou depart'st hence safe | Does pay thy labour richly*). Perhaps Antony was expected to recognize in the mixture of serious speech and sauciness the style of Cleopatra. One recalls her earlier *Not know me yet?* which indeed suggests that she expects him to know when he should or should not take her seriously. And perhaps we, too, by the final scene of the last act are expected to recognize her at work in the Seleucus episode, which also invokes the diplomacy and formality of these clauses:

> *Sel.*   Madam,
>   I had rather seel my lips than to my peril
>   Speak that which is not.
>
> *Cleo.*   What have I kept back?
>
> *Sel.*   Enough to purchase what you have made known.
>
> (5.2.145-148)

It is not unlikely that we should regard this episode as a trick played on

Caesar in view of the seriocomic context of situation where this construction usually appears when used by Cleopatra or her attendants.

Remarks so far have concentrated on *Antony* because the increase of relative noun clauses introduced by *what* was seen to be characteristic of that play, but comparison with *Richard II* is also illuminating. Like Antony's, Richard's concern with his identity and sense of disgrace is expressed by means of these clauses as if there is some indefinable quality in the phenomenon being described:

> O that I were as great
> As is my grief, or lesser than my name!
> Or that I could forget what I have been!
> Or not remember what I must be now!
>
> (3.3.136-139)

> Learn, good soul,
> To think our former state a happy dream;
> From which awak'd, the truth of what we are
> Shows us but this.
>
> (5.1.17-20)

Similarly, they may serve as circumlocutions in a context of subtlety and craft, as in this passage where Aumerle professes friendly interest in his secret enemy, Bolingbroke:

> Cousin, farewell. What presence must not know,
> From where you do remain let paper show.
>
> (1.3.249-250)

The effectiveness of this speech derives mainly from the mystery inherent in the two relative clauses and from their appearance in theme and secondary theme position. Multiple relative clauses also occur in Richard's description of Bolingbroke's departure into exile, considered among the stylistically best passages in the play:

> Ourself and Bushy, Bagot here, and Green
> Observ'd his courtship to the common people;
> How he did seem to dive into their hearts
> With humble and familiar courtesy;
> What reverence he did throw away on slaves,
>
> (1.4.23-27)

Nearly a third of the *what* clauses, however, possess a formulaic character that is reinforced by their use in scenes of challenge and quarreling:

> And mark my greeting well; for what I speak
> My body shall make good upon this earth
>
> (1.1.36-37)
>
> And wish (so please my sovereign), ere I move,
> What my tongue speaks my right-drawn sword may prove.
>
> (1.1.45-46)
>
> By that and all the rites of knighthood else,
> Will I make good against thee, arm to arm,
> What I have spoke or thou canst worse devise.
>
> (1.1.75-77)
>
> Look, what I speak, my life shall prove it true—
>
> (1.1.87)

By explicit reference to utterances in their immediate context, these clauses lose that vague reference which can be so suggestive or so dramatic when carefully evoked. Their rate of occurrence, one in ten lines in this segment of the opening scene, does little to produce the heroic tone that the early use of these clauses helped to create in *Antony*.[17] From one viewpoint, they are appropriate enough to a scene dominated by *a woman's war* of words and to a play where language and ritual have so great a role, but stylistically the clauses are flatulent and self-conscious; they fail to enhance the speaker's stature. The speaker, interestingly, is Bolingbroke, indicating again that the preoccupation with words, words, words in this play is by no means confined to King Richard.

Discussion of these clauses has served a dual purpose: to illustrate a method of quantitative and linguistic analysis that seems quite useful for the formal study of style in literature and to show how results of that analysis can be used to interpret the text. Only adverbial clauses of time match the *what* clauses in the degree of change they exhibit.[18] It may be that their increase indicates a greater preoccupation with time in *Antony*, a possibility that is strengthened by the notable and distinct increase of temporal clauses with antecedents that designate time (*day*, *then*, *pres-*

[17]The possibility that Shakespeare creates a style within a play by repeating a given phrase or construction at certain points (e.g., in the opening scene) or by associating it with a particular character bears further investigation. Such investigation might be rather easily carried out with the aid of an electronic computer.

[18] For an analysis of all relative clauses by function, see Table A-10.

ently, *oft*, etc.). These antecedents intensify and specify the notion of time already present in the clause itself:

> Neglected rather;
> And then when poisoned hours had bound me up
> From mine own knowledge.
>
> (2.2.89-91)

> Of late, when I cried 'Ho!'
> Like boys unto a muss, kings would start forth
> And cry 'Your will?'
>
> (3.13.90-92)

The kinds of time designated by these clauses can be divided into past, future, and a neutral category that includes both present and indefinite

Table 15
Kinds of Time Designated by Temporal
Relative Clauses

	Past	Future	Neutral
R2	12	8	8
Ant.	25	8	28

time in the sense of *whenever*.[19] Table 15 shows that past time doubles in *Antony*, while the neutral category is more than tripled. In *Richard II* the attempts to represent history in heroic terms are few and straightforward:

> His face thou hast, for even so look'd he,
> Accomplish'd with the number of thy hours;
> But when he frown'd, it was against the French
> And not against his friends.
>
> (2.1.176-179)

> Were I but now lord of such hot youth
> As when brave Gaunt thy father and myself
> Rescued the Black Prince, that young Mars of men,
> From forth the ranks of many thousand French,
>
> (2.3.99-102)

Evocation of the past in *Antony*, whether it refers to Roman history or to

---

[19] For a list of textual references to *when* clauses and to the time designations assigned them, see Table B-3.

the achievements of the individual, strikes with greater frequency the antiheroic note that appeared on occasion in the *what* relatives of that play:

> Though I lose
> The praise of it by telling, you must know,
> When Caesar and your brother were at blows,
> Your mother came to Sicily and did find
> Her welcome friendly.
>
>   (2.6.43-47)

> When Antony found Julius Caesar dead,
> He cried almost to roaring; and he wept
> When at Philippi he found Brutus slain.
>
>   (3.2.54-56)

>   Your Caesar's father oft,
> When he hath mus'd of taking kingdoms in,
> Bestow'd his lips on that unworthy place
> As it rain'd kisses.
>
>   (3.13.82-85)

>   For when mine hours
> Were nice and lucky, men did ransom lives
> Of me for jests;
>
>   (3.13.179-181)

To these might be added the reference to Antony's behavior in Alexandria (2.2.73, 90), Enobarbus's wry compliment on Pompey's fighting (2.6.78), Antony's resentment of Caesar's slights to his honor (3.4.6, 9), Scarus's description of Antony's first defeat at sea (3.10.12), and Antony's deliberate attempt to make his soldiers weep by reminding them of his former glory (4.2.22). One could argue that many of these describe the recent past when dishonor had already tarnished Antony's name, but even allusions to Julius Caesar refuse to take that great figure in Roman history quite seriously:

>   Broad-fronted Caesar,
> When thou wast here above the ground, I was
> A morsel for a monarch;
>
>   (1.5.29-31)

References are either to his death or to his affair with Cleopatra. The implications of this attitude toward the past must be pursued in a later chapter; the point to be made here is that temporal clauses increased noticeably in *Antony*, that references to the past were doubled and thus accounted for a substantial amount of that increase, and that the content of these clauses represents a past that is described in terms less heroic than might be expected.

In the group of clauses designated neutral in time, reference can be found to a set where time assumes an abstract philosophical character. In *Richard II* nearly all the clauses in the neutral category have this character, and many are associated with the sun imagery of the play:

> Discomfortable cousin! know'st thou not
> That when the searching eye of heaven is hid
> Behind the globe, that lights the lower world,
> Then thieves and robbers range abroad unseen
> In murthers and in outrage boldly here;
> But when from under this terrestrial ball
> He fires the proud tops of the Eastern pines
> And darts his light through every guilty hole,
> Then murthers, treasons, and detested sins,
> The cloak of night being pluck'd from off their backs,
> Stand bare and naked, trembling at themselves?
>
> (3.2.36-46)

Coupled with the apocalyptic overtones of some temporal clauses of the future, these clauses in the present tense reveal time as avenger:

> Put we our quarrel to the will of heaven,
> Who, when they see the hours ripe on earth,
> Will rain hot vengeance on offenders' heads.
>
> (1.2.6-8)

> And when they from thy bosom pluck a flower,
> Guard it, I pray thee, with a lurking adder
> Whose double tongue may with a mortal touch
> Throw death upon thy sovereign's enemies,
>
> (3.2.19-22)

In *Antony* these philosophical clauses, which can be sometimes identified by the presence of an indefinite pronoun like *one*, *we*, or *he who*, inject a strong note of human responsibility into the temporal reference:

> O, then we bring forth weeds
> When our quick minds lie still, and our ills told us

Is as our earing.
                                                      (1.2.113-115)

But when we in our viciousness grow hard
(O misery on't!) the wise gods seel our eyes,
In our own filth drop our clear judgements, make us
Adore our errors, laugh at's while we strut
To our confusion.
                                                      (3.13.111-115)

When valour preys on reason,
It eats the sword it fights with.
                                                      (3.13.199-200)

Be it known that we, the greatest, are misthought
For things that others do; and, when we fall,
We answer others' merits in our name,
Are therefore to be pitied.
                                                      (5.2.176-179)

Reflective statements of this kind can, of course, be found in constructions other than temporal clauses, but the combination of time, however
indefinite, with philosophical statements about morality is noteworthy,
especially by contrast with temporal statements in *Richard II*. The consequences that pursue men's actions in *Antony* do not occur through the
simple passing of time but operate in time with the inevitability of universal
law: whenever a man behaves in a given way, certain results will follow.[20]

While frequencies are small among the remaining relative clauses, this
fact should only emphasize some rather dramatic changes of proportion
that occur when the clauses are examined in well-defined contexts. A type
of clause that doubles in *Antony* is the nominal function of personal
pronoun relatives, such as one finds in proverbs:

Who tells me true, though in his tale lie death,
I hear him as he flatter'd.
                                                      (1.2.102-103)

[20] Before leaving the subject of *when* clauses, it is worth observing that, while the
number of temporal clause adjuncts nearly doubled in *Antony*, so did the number of
these clauses occurring as theme (in initial position). It is difficult, however, to
ascertain whether this affinity for initial position is a natural consequence of the
increase of temporal clauses or a distinct phenomenon related, e.g., to an increase of
adjunct theme in *Antony*. Owen Thomas observes that placing these clauses in initial
position for both sentence and line was a favorite device used by Shakespeare in the
sonnets (*Transformational Grammar and the Teacher of English*, p. 221).

> Who seeks, and will not take when once 'tis offer'd,
> Shall never find it more.
>
> (2.7.89-90)
>
> Who does i' th' wars more than his captain can
> Becomes his captain's captain;
>
> (3.1.21-22)

The universal reference of *who* imparts a dignity to the construction, which is enhanced by its line-initial position and the strong rhythmic break that marks its syntactic boundary. Nowhere does Cleopatra's tendency to counter the heroic, or Roman, style of the play appear more strongly than in her use of this clause type:

> Who's born that day
> When I forget to send to Antony
> Shall die a beggar.
>
> (1.5.63-65)

Here the clause is moved to the end of the line, all pauses are suppressed until the sentence is completed, and pronoun and verb are elided in a manner that has on other occasions been associated with Cleopatra's language. In passing, the unusual instance of the genitive relative as a noun clause should be noted:

> If Caesar please, our master
> Will leap to be his friend. For us, you know
> Whose he is we are, and that is Caesar's.
>
> (3.13.50-52)

The frequency and function of the personal relative clauses are quite similar in the two plays, the only remarkable point being a change in the type of antecedent taken by the genitive clauses. In *Richard II* antecedents tend to be impersonal, but in *Antony* the number of personal antecedents is four times greater.[21] This change may well owe something to a tendency of the language to restrict *whose* to personal antecedents; nevertheless, the change has stylistic overtones. In both plays these genitive clauses carry a note of power, danger, dread:

[21] Of the fourteen genitive relatives in *Richard II*, three have personal antecedents; in *Antony*, fourteen out of seventeen have personal antecedents.

A thousand flatterers sit within thy crown,
Whose compass is no bigger than thy head;
                        (*R2* 2.1.100-101)

Gaunt am I for the grave, gaunt as a grave,
Whose hollow womb inherits naught but bones.
                        (*R2* 2.1.82-83)

Guard it, I pray thee, with a lurking adder
Whose double tongue may with a mortal touch
Throw death upon thy sovereign's enemies.
                        (*R2* 3.2.20-22)

                . . . creeps apace
Into the hearts of such as have not thriv'd
Upon the present state, whose numbers threaten;
                        (*Ant.* 1.3.50-52)

                And that is it
Hath made me rig my navy, at whose burthen
The anger'd ocean foams;
                        (*Ant.* 2.6.19-21)

                What though you fled
From that great face of war whose several ranges
Frighted each other?
                        (*Ant.* 3.13.4-6)

The danger may assume subtle forms, as in *Richard II* where it is associated with the sensuous and flattering charms that make a man effeminate:

Gaunt.   Though Richard my live's counsel would not hear,
           My death's sad tale may yet undeaf his ear.

  York.   No; it is stopp'd with other flattering sounds,
           As praises, of whose taste the wise are fond,
           Lascivious metres, to whose venom sound
           The open ear of youth doth always listen;
           Report of fashions in proud Italy,
           Whose manners still our tardy apish nation
           Limps after in base imitation.
                        (2.1.15-23)

But most of these antecedents in *Richard II* are impersonal; of the fourteen genitive clauses with personal antecedents in *Antony*, three refer to Octavia and five to Cleopatra. Thus, the clauses that served to describe sensuous charm in the earlier play are here centered on female beauty, and, in their reference to Cleopatra, there is the added note of danger and power:

> O this false soul of Egypt! this grave charm—
> Whose eye beck'd forth my wars and call'd them home,
> Whose bosom was my crownet, my chief end—
>
> (4.12.25-27)
>
> I made these wars for Egypt; and the Queen—
> Whose heart I thought I had, for she had mine,
> Which, whilst it was mine, had annex'd unto't
> A million moe, now lost—
>
> (4.14.15-20)

The relative clauses introduced by *where*, although similar in frequency in the plays, afford insight into the stylistic interaction between grammatical construction and lexical choices. The word *where* in these clauses has an adverbial function designating place, but this locative meaning has little strength in *Richard II*:

> Grief boundeth where it falls,
> Not with the empty hollowness, but weight.
>
> (1.2.58-59)
>
> Woe doth the heavier sit
> Where it perceives it is but faintly borne.
>
> (1.3.280-281)
>
> Where words are scarce, they are seldom spent in vain,
> For they breathe truth that breathe their words in pain.
>
> (2.1.7-8)
>
> Then all too late comes counsel to be heard
> Where will doth mutiny with wit's regard.
>
> (2.1.27-28)
>
> By that fair sun which shows me where thou stand'st,
> I heard thee say, . . .
>
> (4.1.35-36)

Grief, woe, words, and *counsel* are abstractions that, despite the personification and motion supplied by the verbs *fall, sit*, and *come*, dominate the clauses and eliminate any sense of their needing a physical place toward which their motion is directed. The tenuousness of locative meaning is shown by the fact that one could replace *where* by *when* in all but the last of these passages, a substitution impossible in the locative relatives from *Antony* without drastic change of meaning:

> Where souls do couch on flowers, we'll hand in hand
> And with our sprightly port make the ghosts gaze.
> (4.14.51-52)

> Where yond pine does stand
> I shall discover all.
> (4.12.1-2)

> Thou shalt bring him to me
> Where I will write.
> (3.3.49-50)

> I hope well of to-morrow, and will lead you
> Where rather I'll expect victorious life
> Than death and honour.
> (4.2.42-44)

The homophoric character of these relatives, referring, as they must, to the context of situation, is admirably suited to dramatic language, especially when they are couched in imperative statements:

> Good uncle, let this end where it begun;
> We'll calm the Duke of Norfolk, you your son.
> (*R2* 1.1.158-159)

> March on, and mark King Richard how he looks.
> (*R2* 3.3.61)

> Now mark me how I will undo myself.
> (*R2* 4.1.203)

The combination of homophoric relative and imperative matrix occurs less frequently in *Richard II* than in *Antony*, and one notes in these passages from the earlier play the use of *mark* and *how* in a manner that derives perhaps from some commonplace locution. In *Antony* audience and actor alike are directed to see or to imagine the stage action more effectively:

> Look, prithee, Charmian,
> How this Herculean Roman does become
> The carriage of his chafe.
> (1.3.83-85)

> See
> How I convey my shame out of thine eyes
> By looking back what I have left behind
> Stroy'd in dishonour.

> (3.11.51-54)

> Grace grow where those drops fall!

> (4.2.38)

> Bear me, good friends, where Cleopatra bides.

> (4.14.131)

In many plays after *Richard II* Shakespeare replaced or varied the question *But who comes here?* with this construction when he wished to call attention to the entrance of a character or to some business on stage:

> And look where Publius is come to fetch me.

> (*JC* 2.2.108)

> Lo, where he comes!

> (*Oth.* 2.1.183)

> But look where sadly the poor wretch comes reading.

> (*Ham.* 2.2.168)

> Behold where stands
> Th' usurper's cursed head.

> (*Mac.* 5.8.54-55)

That this imperative-with-relative construction may have been peculiar to Shakespeare's style rather than a common manner of speaking is suggested by a difference in the bad and good quartos of *Hamlet*. The pirated quarto of 1603 reads:

> my father, in the habite
> As he liued, looke you how pale he lookes, .
> ... Looke, there he goes.

The good quarto (1604-1605) has

> My father in his habit as he liued,
> Looke where he goes, even now out at the portall.

Minor matters of this kind exhibit the difference between Shakespeare's sensitive response to grammatical elements in the language and that of an untutored ear, and they suggest how deeply his personal style affected even minor aspects of his language.

It would be interesting to discover when Shakespeare began to exploit more fully than he did in *Richard II* the stylistic potential of *wh-* relatives. At least one passage in *Julius Caesar* shows a strong interest in them:

> That you do love me I am nothing jealous.
> What you would work me to, I have some aim.
> How I have thought of this, and of these times,
> I shall recount hereafter.
> . . . .
>   What you have said
> I will consider; what you have to say
> I will with patience hear, . . .
>   (1.2.162-165, 167-169)

Three features noted at various times in the analysis of *Richard II* and *Antony* mark these clauses: high frequency, occurrence in marked theme position, and deliberate suppression of information accompanied by a hint of danger. One is tempted to think that if Shakespeare was indeed experimenting with a new "Roman" style in this play it may have occurred to him that there is something particularly Latin about substituting full clauses for simple nominal groups. The lines are remarkable also for their lexical barrenness. There are nearly four function words for every content word, although in the English language the ratio tends to be one to one. Perhaps Shakespeare wished in this manner to convey Roman austerity, particularly the stoicism of Brutus. Perhaps there is evidence of a new interest in the grammatical skeleton of English. A study of relative clauses in this and other plays written about the same time might well prove an interesting contribution to our knowledge of Shakespeare's stylistic development.

Sampling and Weighting

While it is desirable to have complete counts of linguistic features in a text, when several phenomena are to be observed, when the mode of study requires time-consuming analysis that cannot be easily programmed for a computer, or when a text is epic or novel length, random sampling may be a more practical method of describing a text. In order to determine some basic syntactic properties of the plays, a sample of sentences was taken

Table 16
Measures of Sentence Length

	Word Sample	Line Sample	Sentence Sample	Words per Sentence	Lines per Sentence
R2	3,053	394	121	25.23	3.25
Ant.	2,887	358	160	18.04	2.23

from *Richard II* and *Antony and Cleopatra*.[22] A study of complexity in sentence structure serves also to illustrate some of the problems involved in weighting various factors in order to assign a label like simplicity or complexity to syntax.

As Table 16 shows, the two plays differ with respect to sentence length, whether it be measured in lines or in words per sentence. While the fact that the sentences of *Richard II* are longer than those of *Antony* may not be statistically significant, it may be that a slight difference can assume importance in the work of a single author whose style may be thought fairly stable.[23]

[22] Table B-1 gives a list of line references to the random sample of sentences, and the accompanying notes discuss procedures for drawing the sample.

[23] Sentence length, defined as the "number of words between successive full stops" (C. B. Williams, "A Note on Sentence-Length," in *Statistics and Style*, ed. Lubomír Doležel and Richard W. Bailey, p. 69), is a measure of stylistic variation developed by statisticians, especially by C. B. Williams. A critique of Williams's study points out that over a period of years an author's sentence length may alter so radically that "no proof can with any certainty be established to the effect that the two samples [of an author's sentences] can belong to the same category" (Kai Rander Buch, "A Note on Sentence-Length as Random Variable," in *Statistics and Style*, p. 79). Perhaps one can suggest that, if a single author's work can vary significantly in this respect but that Shakespeare's sentence length does not vary this much, it is an indication of the stability of Shakespeare's style. Some independent indication of such stability comes from Norman Thomas's "Comparative Stylometry in Shakespeare," *Shakespeare Newsletter* 15 (1965): 56. In statistical tests of "filler" words in writings of Shakespeare, Bacon, Marlowe, Nashe, and Scott, Thomas found that "Shakespeare is more noticeably self-consistent than any of the other four authors." But if Shakespeare's style is remarkably stable compared with that of other authors, then slight differences might well be respected. In my own research I have been surprised on several occasions to note virtual identity on certain counts. A case in point is the fact that the expression *the which* occurs five times in *R2*, three times in *Ant.*, and that there are in the later play twenty-three sentences that use a dummy *it* as subject or object (e.g., *It is not Caesar's natural vice to hate | Our great competitor* [*Ant.* 1.4.2-3]) and twenty-two in *R2*. Such constructions tend to be less available to conscious manipulation, and the closeness of the numbers over a thirteen-year period when style was changing rapidly on the levels of rhythm and vocabulary suggests that when changes do appear in the syntax they are worthy of notice, even when they are not statistically significant.

To the extent that sentence length can be a criterion of simplicity/ complexity, it would appear that the syntax of *Antony* is simpler than that of the earlier play. Linguists are understandably reluctant to define the notion of sentence complexity because so many different factors need to be weighed, and their relative weight is not easily assessed. Nevertheless, certain factors can be isolated and considered separately. One of these is sentence length; another is whether the immediate sentence constituents consist of one clause or more than one clause.[24] Among sentences whose immediate constituency is a single clause we may distinguish between minor sentences, so called because they lack a specifiable verb, and the traditional complete sentence, exemplified, respectively, by these pairs:[25]

> What ho, my liege!
> > (*R2* 5.3.74)
>
> Under the earth.
> > (*Ant.* 4.3.12)
>
> How long a time lies in one little word!
> > (*R2* 1.3.213)
>
> The ingratitude of this Seleucus does
> Even make me wild.
> > (*Ant.* 5.2.153-154)

Obviously, these sentences differ with respect to other aspects of syntax. For example, in the second pair of sentences one can see that *time* and *word* are elaborated only by prehead modifiers, while *ingratitude* is elaborated by a posthead qualifier. This level of syntactic structure—technically, the level of nominal and verbal group—is not included in the discussion of sentence complexity and simplicity, which will apply only to the largest constituents in sentence structure.[26]

Sentences whose immediate constituents consist of more than one clause may have as constituents either a paratactic or a hypotactic clause complex. Using a rough gloss from school grammar, parataxis is defined as a

[24] For a discussion of the difficulties involved in stating the relationship of the clause complex to the traditional notions of complex and compound sentences, see Huddleston et al., *Sentence and Clause*, pp. 289-292.

[25] Minor clauses, when they appear as independent sentences, are sometimes called verbless sentences or even nominal sentences.

[26] Systemic grammar distinguishes three levels of syntactic structure: that of the sentence, that of the simple clause (which consists of constituents like subject, predicator, complement, and adjunct), and that of the group, nominal or verbal.

coordinate structure, hypotaxis as a loose type of subordination, such as one finds in a nondefining relative clause. The first pair of sentences illustrates parataxis, the second hypotaxis:

> High-stomach'd are they both and full of ire,
> In rage deaf as the sea, hasty as fire.
>
> (*R2* 1.1.18-19)
>
> These strong Egyptian fetters I must break
> Or lose myself in dotage.
>
> (*Ant.* 1.2.120-121)
>
> Evermore thanks, the exchequer of the poor,
> Which, till my infant fortune comes to years,
> Stands for my bounty.
>
> (*R2* 2.3.65-67)
>
> There,
> My music playing far off, I will betray
> Tawny-finn'd fishes.
>
> (*Ant.* 2.5.10-12)

Table 17 summarizes the quantitative information about the immediate constituents of the sentences in the two samples. The label "Single" includes all sentences that have as their immediate constituency a single

Table 17
Number of Clauses Serving as Immediate
Constituents of Sentences

	Single	Multiple
R2	.49	.51
Ant.	.44	.56

clause (minor or full); "Multiple" includes all sentences that have paratactic or hypotactic complexes as their immediate constituents. The information in Table 17 contradicts the earlier statement, based on sentence length, that the syntax of *Antony* is simpler than that of the earlier play, for it is clear that, looking only at immediate constituents, the syntax of *Richard II* is simpler than that of *Antony*. That these measures of complexity are only minor threads in a network of syntactic levels and relationships becomes obvious when the category "Single" is divided into sentences consisting of one and only one clause and those that contain one clause at the highest level but yield others at lower levels of analysis. An example of the latter is a sentence containing an embedded clause (a tighter kind of subordination exemplified by traditional noun, adjective, and adverb clauses). Another of these sentences with clauses at lower levels contains a clause hypotactically related to a clause constituent rather than to the entire clause. The two types are exemplified, respectively, by the following pairs of sentences (clauses at lower levels are italicized):[27]

> Now put it, God, in the physician's mind
> *To help him to his grave immediately*!
>
> (R2 1.4.59-60)
>
> Look *where they come*!
>
> (Ant. 1.1.10)
>
> What, was I born to this, *that my sad look*
> *Should grace the triumph of great Bolingbroke*?
>
> (R2 3.4.98-99)
>
> O this false soul of Egypt! this grave charm—
> *Whose eye beck'd forth my wars and call'd them home*,
> *Whose bosom was my crownet, my chief end—*
> Like a right gypsy hath at fast and loose
> Beguil'd me to the very heart of loss!
>
> (Ant. 4.12.25-29)

Table 18 divides the category "Single" into sentences consisting of one and only one clause (SØ) and those containing a single clause at top level governing clauses at lower levels (SM). Sentences governed by a clause complex, whether paratactic or hypotactic, are similarly divided into those that contain no further clauses (MØ) and those that govern clauses at lower levels (MM). Despite the over-all increase in *Antony* of sentences consisting of clause complexes, there is no concomitant increase of layer-

Table 18
Immediate and Layered Constituents in Sentence Structure

	SØ	SM	MØ	MM
R2	.19	.29	.09	.42
Ant.	.23	.21	.15	.41

[27] Figures A-1 and A-2 of *Ant.* 1.1.10 and *R2* 3.4.98-99 illustrate, respectively, the difference between the embedded clause and the hypotactic group complex. The method of diagramming used here was first presented by Rodney Huddleston in "Rank and Depth," *Language* 41 (1965): 574-586, and modified somewhat by him in *Sentence and Clause*, pp. 8-17.

ing and embedding at lower levels in the category MM. Moreover, there is an increase of sentences consisting of a single clause (SØ) and a decrease of single clauses dominating lower-level clauses (SM). Finally, the increase of the category "Multiple" in *Antony*, which was shown in Table 17, is due to an increase of parataxis rather than of hypotaxis. Assuming that parataxis is a simpler type of clause relation, this fact represents another tendency toward simplicity in the later play. So far, although the syntax of *Richard II* is simpler than that of *Antony* in that its immediate constituents tend more often to be single clauses, the syntax of *Antony* is simpler on several other counts: sentence length, preference for single-clause sentences, preference for parataxis over hypotaxis, and a decrease in clause structures at lower levels of the sentence.

Below the highest level of constituents, sentences contain further paratactic, hypotactic, and embedded structures, which occur in mixes that defy easy tabulation. Moreover, the lower levels of sentence structure vary in depth and frequency. All these are the multiple factors that make it so difficult to determine sentence complexity. One last attempt to represent this aspect of the syntax of these two plays can be made by determining the ratio of embedding, parataxis, and hypotaxis in all sentences, regardless of the level at which it occurs and regardless of what other factors cooccur. This can be done by determining for each sentence whether there is at any level an instance of an embedded clause or clauses in hypotactic or paratactic relation. The sentence is then marked for the presence of that factor. Thus, a sentence containing hypotaxis and an embedded clause is marked HE, one with parataxis and hypotaxis is PH. The sentences marked in this manner fall into the following categories: S: a single clause (minor or full), no embedding, no complexes; P: one or more paratactic complexes, no embedding, no hypotaxis; H: one or more hypotactic complexes, no embedding, no parataxis; E: embedding, no parataxis, no hypotaxis; PH: parataxis and hypotaxis, no embedding; PE: parataxis and embedding, no hypotaxis; HE: hypotaxis and embedding, no parataxis; and PHE: parataxis, hypotaxis, embedding. To illustrate all these types would be tedious; to name them would require the assistance of Polonius. Suffice it to exemplify those marked PHE, the most complex type, which contain at least one instance each of parataxis, hypotaxis, and embedding:

> Each substance of a grief hath twenty shadows,
> Which shows like grief itself, but is not so;
> For sorrow's eye, glazed with blinding tears,

Divides one thing entire to many objects,
Like perspectives, which rightly gaz'd upon,
Show nothing but confusion—ey'd awry,
Distinguish form.

(*R2* 2.2.14-20)

What was't
That mov'd pale Cassius to conspire? and what
Made the all-honour'd honest Roman, Brutus,
With the arm'd rest, courtiers of beauteous freedom,
To drench the Capitol, but that they would
Have one man but a man?

(*Ant.* 2.6.14-19)

Table 19 gives the ratio of each type of sentence in the sample. The information contained in Table 19 is diffuse, but there is no overlap among the categories.[28] To show the extent to which the sentences in the sample used the three major ways of joining clauses, namely, parataxis, hypotaxis, and embedding, sentences were regrouped so that, for example, all those containing embedding were counted together (E, PE, HE, PHE) and their total was divided by the number of sentences in the sample. The same procedure was followed for all sentences with an instance of hypotaxis (H, PH, HE, PHE) and parataxis (P, PH, PE, PHE). Naturally, there is

Table 19
Sentences Classified by Clause Constituency: Independent Sets

	Simple	Paratactic	Hypotactic	Embedded	Paratactic-Hypotactic	Paratactic-Embedded	Hypotactic-Embedded	Paratactic-Hypotactic-Embedded
R2	.20	.07	.03	.22	.10	.10	.06	.22
Ant.	.23	.08	.06	.14	.05	.17	.11	.16

[28] Those who are more comfortable with the traditional classification of sentences into simple, compound, and complex can easily convert the information in Table 19 to those categories by reading *compound* for P and *complex* for H and E, since one major distinction between the two grammars is that the traditional category "complex" has been subdivided into two kinds of subordination, the looser type being called "hypotaxis" and the other being labeled "embedding." It will be seen that, whereas *Antony* has simple (S) and compound-complex sentences (PH, PE, PHE) in nearly equal proportions, in *Richard II* there are approximately two simple sentences for every three of the compound-complex type. In each play there is roughly one compound sentence (P) for every four complex sentences (H, E, HE).

Table 20
Sentences Classified by Clause Constituency: Overlapping Sets

	Simple	Embedded	Paratactic	Hypotactic
R2	.20	.64	.45	.40
Ant.	.23	.58	.46	.38

a high degree of overlap. No attempt was made to order these factors, to establish their frequency within a sentence, or to distinguish levels on which they occur. For the sake of completeness, the category "Simple" was added in Table 20 to represent the remaining sentences.

The most obvious change shown in Table 20 is the decline of embedding in *Antony*. On the assumption, already invoked, that the looser the relation between clauses the simpler the syntax, parataxis is the simplest construction, hypotaxis second, and embedding the most complex. The decrease in embedding, then, strengthens the information in Table 18 that, to the extent that the presence of embedded clauses is an index of complexity, the lower levels of sentence composition in *Antony* are simpler than those of *Richard II*. On the other hand, the decrease in embedding runs counter to the notion advanced in the discussion of group hypotaxis that the syntax of *Richard II* tends to be more loosely constructed than that of *Antony*. If the decrease in embedding is a valid sign of simpler sentence structure, this tendency toward simplicity in the sentences of the later play may well be related to the data of the preceding chapter. These data revealed the increased violation in *Antony* of selection restrictions. Such a degree of deviance at the point where syntax and semantics meet may have necessitated the simpler mode of sentence composition. Whatever the final explanation, it must depend on the coordination of many disparate pieces of information about the syntax of the plays, a problem that the statistical study of language has not seriously undertaken to solve. The final question for now must be whether the attempt to define complexity and simplicity in these plays can illuminate our understanding of them as works of literature.

"Language in Shakespeare's best plays is dynamic, paralleling the tragic rhythm of action, tracing moral change."[29] Critics generally see this dynamism as a movement from complexity to simplicity. G. W. Knight has cited instances of it in *Hamlet, Antony and Cleopatra, The Winter's*

[29] Herbert Blau, "Language and Structure in Poetic Drama," *Modern Language Quarterly* 18 (1957): 32.

Tale, and *The Tempest*.[30] Harry Levin has pointed out that the leading characters of *Romeo and Juliet* repudiate their early artificial language and the superficial code it represents, replacing frequent rhyme by an "unprecedentedly limpid and passionate" blank verse.[31] Kenneth Muir notes that, "after the highly complex verse spoken by the protagonists in the earlier acts of the play, we are brought to the desperate simplicity of Lady Macbeth's monosyllabic prose."[32] In *The Winter's Tale* Leontes's madness is characterized, according to another critic, by intricate syntax and shifts of diction, but his language "takes on a grave simplicity" when he recovers.[33] These statements are, of course, made about various levels of language (phonology, diction, syntax), and they are generally associated with the language of individuals rather than that of the play as a whole. Nevertheless, it seems useful to ask whether information provided by the random sample of sentences from *Richard II* and *Antony* corroborates critical intuition about the movement from complexity to simplicity in Shakespeare's plays.

One way to answer this question is to compare the frequency of the most simple and the most complex sentence types at the beginning, middle, and end of each play. In the sample from *Richard II* simple sentences (no parataxis, hypotaxis, or embedding at any level) constituted .20 of all sentence types, and there were .22 sentences of the PHE type. These extremes appear rather balanced in the early play; in *Antony* their frequency varies more: .23 for simple sentences and .16 for PHE types. Table 21 gives the ratio of sentences in the first, third, and final acts of each play that are entirely simple and of those that are, presumably, the most complex. The figures in Table 21 indicate that critical intuitions about the movement toward simplicity in Shakespeare's plays are justified by linguistic and statistical data. Such corroboration would be of no particular interest if it were not rather more revealing than the original intuitions. Closer examination of the dynamics of simple and complex sentence types indicates that they do not simply replace each other so much as they constitute a set of proportions that vary throughout the

[30] G. W. Knight, "*Henry VIII* and the Poetry of Conversion," in his *The Crown of Life*, pp. 262-263.

[31] Harry Levin, "Form and Formality in *Romeo and Juliet*," *Shakespeare Quarterly* 11 (1960): 6.

[32] Kenneth Muir, "Shakespeare and Rhetoric," *Shakespeare-Jahrbuch* 90 (1954): 66.

[33] Jonathan Smith, "The Language of Leontes," *Shakespeare Quarterly* 19 (1968): 325.

Table 21
Proportion of Simple to Complex
Sentences per Act

Act	Simple	Complex
R2		
I	.041	.057
III	.024	.082
V	.041	.008
Ant.		
I	.031	.031
III	.031	.025
V	.062	.018

*Sentences containing instances of parataxis, hypotaxis, and embedding (PHE).

plays. Moreover, complexity does not dominate either play at the outset, since the two sentence types appear in relative balance in the opening acts. Both plays manifest a movement toward simplicity in the fifth act, but in *Richard II* it seems to be the result of a remarkable decrease in complex sentences rather than the positive increase of simple sentences that one finds in the last act of *Antony*. The degree of change within the proportions and the direction of that change are distinctly different in the two plays. In *Richard II* the proportions change radically, the simple sentences moving from a moderate amount to low to moderate and the complex sentences moving from moderate to high to low; in *Antony* there is less variation between proportions, and the movement for both types of sentences is in a single direction of increase for simple sentences and decrease for complex sentences. These facts may reflect an aspect of Shakespeare's stylistic development; for example, the less abrupt and less drastic changes in the later play argue a greater control over the material that takes the form of even distribution (perhaps) of sentence types so that sentences other than the obvious PHE type are made to express complexity. Another explanation of these facts is that the direction of change may correspond to real differences in the dramatic action of the two plays, so that the point of greatest contrast coincides with an important confrontation of Bolingbroke and Richard in the third act of *Richard II* and with the first meeting of Caesar and Cleopatra in the final act of *Antony*.

Even this degree of interpretation suggests the need of knowing whether and how these sentence types are associated with certain characters or with the forces represented by those characters. Such a study really requires another sample, but some rough generalizations may be based on the present one. Richard rather decisively favors the PHE sentence, confirming the general critical opinion that his language is quite complex.[34] Bolingbroke's language is balanced between the two types, but, though his simple sentences are evenly distributed throughout the play, the complex types disappear (in the sample) after the third act. Antony's language is balanced with respect to simple and PHE sentence types, and both types are evenly distributed throughout the acts where he appears. While Cleopatra, in the sample, speaks more PHE types than either Antony or Caesar, she prefers the simple sentence, and this preference increases markedly in the final act. The sample allots no simple sentences to Caesar. Although they are necessarily oversimplified, these facts suggest that the changes in proportion at the third and fifth acts of these plays are associated with important changes in the speech of major characters.

Having noted as far as seems feasible the interaction of simplicity and complexity in the two plays, it seems appropriate to conclude by asking why simplicity should dominate the final acts of Shakespeare's plays (especially the later plays) and why this phenomenon should be generally praised by critics. Critics tend to associate the movement toward simplicity with tragedy. Tragic style, writes Elder Olson, is not bombast: "The most affecting passages in the mature Shakespeare are composed in extremely simple language elevated only by what they manifest to us."[35] R. A. Foakes echoes this idea: ". . . the moments of greatest emotional intensity are memorable for such simplicity and directness of language as 'Pray you, undo this button.' "[36] A similarly affecting passage is Charmian's address to her dead mistress, beginning *Your crown's awry.* As

---

[34] It should be remembered that this material is quite simplified, since it does not show other sentence types in their speeches, so that the fact that Antony favors PE sentences is not shown. Moreover, all these generalizations must be quite tentative, since a study of each speaker's language should be based on new samples drawn specifically for that purpose rather than on a sample like this one, which was designed to determine the syntactic properties of the play as a whole. Table A-11 provides figures for S and PHE sentences in the speeches of major characters in each play.

[35] Elder Olson, "Modern Drama and Tragedy," in his *Tragedy and the Theory of Drama*, p. 258.

[36] R. A. Foakes, "Contrasts and Connections: Some Notes on Style in Shakespeare's Comedies and Tragedies," *Shakespeare-Jahrbuch* 90 (1954): 74.

à Kempis said of compunction, it is more important to feel the effect of these sentences then to know how to define it, but it is the business of criticism to do both, even though he who undertakes to "explain" such lines may appear less devout than his brethren.

Certainly, the reason why lines like these affect us is related to our experience of what has preceded in the play, but to compare these sentences as such with something that we call our prior experience is to compare the language of the play (a particular sentence) with an abstraction from that language (our prior experience, however we describe it). If one is going to praise a particular sentence one might ask what earlier sentences he has experienced that makes the experience of these sentences so affecting. Not all simple sentences in the play are associated with the relatively peaceful moments of the tragic conclusion or with the more benign forces of the tragic action. There is also, for example, Goneril's devastating *At your choice, sir*, flung out when Lear refuses to return with her to Albany's palace. She does not allow her father the courtesy of a complete sentence, gives him the lowest possible title of address, and places that in sentence-final position. This choice of final position for the mode of address, in certain circumstances, may be quite neutral; at other times it appears rude.[37] Kent, disguised, addresses Lear for the first time in his borrowed accents:

> *Lear.* How now? What art thou?
>
> *Kent.* A man, sir.
>
> (1.4.10-11)

It is conceivable that Kent here invokes the neutral function of the final position because it implies dialogue between equals. Later in this scene when Lear calls Oswald, his use of the title *sir*, its repetition, and its final position are all deliberately provoking:

> *Lear.* O, you, sir, you! Come you hither, sir.
> Who am I, sir?
>
> *Osw.* My lady's father.
>
> (1.4.85-87)

[37] Compare the use of *sir* in final position (*Lear* 2.1.2,15), where the courtier Curan addresses Edmund in a relatively neutral and businesslike situation, or even of *Thank you, sir*, which Lear uses when his request has been carried out. The final position here is not discourteous, since Lear may be thinking of himself as the other's equal and in any case would be justified in thinking of himself as the superior, whether by rank, age, or experience in suffering.

It is not only the content of Oswald's reply but also its form (minor, no term of address) that infuriates Lear, who echoes and parodies the form: *'My lady's father'? My lord's knave!*

The verbless sentence and the final position of *sir* appear again in these responses of Lear's daughters to their father's unsuccessful attempt to enlist Regan's aid against Goneril:

> *Reg.*   Say you have wrong'd her, sir.
>
> *Gon.*   Why not by th' hand, sir?
>
> *Gon.*   At your choice, sir.
>
> *Reg.*   I dare avouch it, sir. What, fifty followers?
>   (2.4.154, 198, 220, 240)

All these sentences—of Kent, of Lear to Oswald, of the daughters—contrast to some extent with *Pray you, undo this button* where one finds the polite form *pray you*, a term of address, in initial position, which softens the imperative that follows, and a full sentence that has a solemn formality expressive of Lear's inner humility, his respect for those around him, and a courtly dignity lacking in his earlier language.[38]

Charmian's sentence, like Lear's, is simple and effective; but where Lear's simplicity is formal, hers is colloquial. Nor is it the colloquial style of the verbless sentence but an echo of Cleopatra's own language, the colloquial ellipsis found in an earlier, a happier scene:

> *Cleo.*   Let's to billiards. . . .
>
> *Char.*   My arm is sore; best play with Mardian.
>
> *Cleo.*   . . . you'll play with me, sir?
>
> *Cleo.*   I'll none now.
>   Give me mine angle! we'll to th' river.
>   (2.5.3-4, 6, 9-10)

Richard II seems not to afford like passages. As noted, the syntax of this play is more complex, and such simplicity as there is does not increase so

---

[38] The fact that *pray you*, like *prithee*, normally appears in initial position does not alter the argument that Lear's word order adds to the tone of respect, humility, and dignity that permeates this sentence. One can assume a deep grammatical structure where the option is *address, command* as opposed to *command, address*; having chosen the more polite option, the manner in which he realizes *address* is irrelevant.

dramatically in the last act. The few passages in the comparable context of Richard's death are not, technically, simple. Richard's dying speech is

> Mount, mount, my soul! thy seat is up on high;
> Whilst my gross flesh sinks downward, here to die.
>
> (5.5.111-112)

Exton's comment, an attempt at simplicity in that it is a verbless sentence, contains an embedded clause, *As full of valour as of royal blood*; its sequel, *Both have I spilled*, while a single clause, is complicated in another way by its word order.

What was suggested in comparing the final sentences from *Lear* and *Antony* with earlier ones was not that the modern reader of Shakespeare must be sensitized to seventeenth-century forms of address or nuances of informality but that anyone who has experienced certain earlier sentences has been prepared by them for the final modulation of *Pray you, undo this button* and *Your crown's awry*, just as the audience at a concert is prepared for later musical themes by earlier ones.[39] This is not the entire explanation, but part of the explanation for the effect of these sentences must be the notion that the formal features of language from earlier scenes culminate in and are echoed by these simple sentences, whose effect on us is synergistic.

Aspects of Word Order

The phenomenon commonly known as "departure from normal word order" deserves attention in a formal analysis of Shakespeare's syntax. Quantitative studies of word order are generally confined to permutations of subject, verb, and object. When they admit the full variety of permutations of English word order, the data become so fragmented that it is difficult to assess results.[40] The problems addressed in this section, there-

---

[39] This idea is not new, of course, since it is familiar in the work of Susanne Langer, nor is it newly applied to Shakespeare or *Lear*. Ian Milner ("Shakespeare's Climactic Style," in *Charles University on Shakespeare*, ed. Zdněk Stříbrný and Jarmila Emmerová) speaks of passages where simple statements at climactic moments in the play appear in a context that "directly prepares, climaxes, releases, or in some other way expresses the play's primary tension" (p. 152). Of course, he is speaking of the immediate context. Winifred M. T. Nowottny ascribes a technique of montage to the style of *Lear* by which "Shakespeare 'mounts' (and of course places) a passage in such a way that its depth of meaningfulness is *inferred* from something not strictly contained within the passage itself" ("Some Aspects of the Style of *King Lear*," *Shakespeare Survey* 13 [1960]: 53).

[40] Important studies of English word order using traditional grammar are those of P. Fijn van Draat, "Rhythm in English Prose," *Anglia* 36 (1912): 1-58; August West-

fore, are two: formulating adequate categories for statistical analysis, and ensuring that all aspects of word order will be examined.

To discuss departures from normal order, one must first define a norm. For all practical purposes, the norm will be defined here in terms of *constituent* rather than *word* order. Second, the norm will be defined by reference to the syntactic structures of complex, clause, and group. Defining the norm in terms of constituents introduces the high level of generality needed for a statistical study, and the use of different syntactic levels permits a relatively exhaustive study with less overlap and confusion of categories than one usually finds in studies of word order. Normal word order, then, will be defined by the unmarked sequence of constituents in complex, clause, and group. Thus, in a hypotactic complex, alpha, or independent, clauses will occur before beta, or dependent, clauses ($\alpha \cdot \beta$). At clause level, constituents will normally occur in the order subject, predicator, complement, and adjunct (SPCA); and the constituents of a nominal group will be taken to follow the order modifier, head, and qualifier (mhq).

When a sequence is obligatory, even though that sequence is a departure from the general norm of order just outlined, that sequence is regarded as normal. Examples of obligatory departures from the posited norm are the subject-predicator inversion for questions in late modern English or the discontinuity of nominal groups headed by a dummy *it*. There is, however, the further problem of diachrony. It does not seem unreasonable to

---

ern, *On Sentence-Rhythm and Word-Order in Modern English*; and Mats Redin, *Word Order in English Verse from Pope to Sassoon*. Using transformational generative grammar, Irene Fairley has studied word order in the poetry of E. E. Cummings in "Syntax as Style," in *Studies Presented to Roman Jakobson by His Students*, pp. 105-111; and George Landon has proposed some theoretical principles for a study of word order in "The Grammatical Description of Poetic Word-Order in English Verse," *Language and Style* 1 (1969): 194-200.

The traditional studies, especially Redin's, are thorough; but the descriptive categories are not general enough to allow important differences to appear. Moreover, levels of structure are not distinguished, and there is no attempt to type instances of deviance (e.g., inversion *vs.* discontinuity). Thus, Redin proposes half a dozen structures defined by the presence of a direct object (S-O-V-A, objects between auxiliary and verb, object and imperative, etc.) and another half dozen defined by reference to the indirect object (IO-S-V-O, S-IO-V-O, S-IO-V, etc.). In systemic grammar both direct and indirect object would be labeled complements in the description of primary clause structure. Thus, important over-all differences could be noted, while it would still be possible to differentiate further among types of complement. The predominance of complement theme is noted here in *Richard II*, while in both plays special types of complement theme are distinguished—intensive complement theme in *Richard II* and substitute theme in *Antony*.

assume that early and late modern English, sharing as they do the loss of inflectional endings, would also share a large overlap of norms with respect to word order. But to avoid brash assumptions on this basis, no sequence has been labeled deviant in these plays if the texts did not contain some instance of that same sequence in the order that would today be called normal. The sequence *what poor an instrument may do a noble deed* is judged deviant for Shakespeare because in the same play where it occurs we have the sequence *what a wounding shame is this*.

Two types of deviant sequence will be defined, stylistic inversion and stylistic discontinuity. "Stylistic" implies that they are optional rather than obligatory reorderings of constituents. Furthermore, it is assumed that the deviant order of constituents does not affect their meaning, because it does not disturb their deep syntactic relations.[41] "Inversion" means that constituents are permuted ($\alpha \cdot \beta$ becomes $\beta \cdot \alpha$; SPCA becomes CASP, ACSP, etc.; mhq becomes hmq, qh, etc.). "Discontinuity" means that the normal order of constituents is preserved but the constituents have been separated from one another by intervening material ($\alpha \ldots \beta$; S $\ldots$ P, P $\ldots$ C; h $\ldots$ q, etc.). Finally, inversion and discontinuity may occur simultaneously in a structure (PSAC; hmq, etc.), but this phenomenon has no special name.

The possibilities for deviant word order are numerous and are realized in quite startling ways in Shakespeare's language. While this study does not distinguish different types of realization, it is appropriate to note here how an abstract constituent can be realized in a variety of ways that produce varying degrees of deviance. For example, the clause order subject-adjunct-predicator can be more or less remarkable depending on the type of adjunct. The following passages, all containing instances of the sequence SAP, show, respectively, the adjunct realized as a simple adverb, as a prepositional phrase, as a hypotactic clause complex, and as a complex that dominates two further complexes:

> Fulvia *perchance* is angry;
>
> *(Ant.* 1.1.20)

[41] The observation that order inversion does not affect meaning is taken from A. Noam Chomsky, *Aspects of the Theory of Syntax* (pp. 227-228), but systemic grammar is the sole basis for the description of deviant word order, since the norm is derived from structures described by that grammar. Marked theme is discussed in M. A. K. Halliday's "Notes on Transitivity and Theme, Part 2," *Journal of Linguistics* 4 (1968): 179-215, and I am indebted to Halliday for reading and critiquing an early draft of my study of word order. I have also drawn ideas from the coding categories devised by Rodney Huddleston for *Sentence and Clause.* They, of course, are not responsible for my departures from the theory or misunderstandings of it.

But when we *in our viciousness* grow hard
                    (*Ant.* 3.13.111)

Your Caesar's father *oft*,
When he hath mus'd of taking kingdoms in,
Bestow'd his lips on that unworthy place
As it rain'd kisses.
                              (*Ant.* 3.13.82-85)

Yon ribald-rid nag of Egypt
(Whom leprosy o'ertake!) *i' th' midst o' th' fight,*
When vantage like a pair of twins appear'd,
Both as the same, or rather ours the elder—
The breese upon her, like a cow in June,—
Hoists sails, and flies.
                              (*Ant.* 3.10.10-15)

The last example shows an embedded SAP structure in line 12. It also indicates that the subject itself is a hypotactic complex whose alpha (*yon . . . o'ertake*) and beta (*the breese . . . June*) have been separated from each other by the adjunct, and each constituent of this complex dominates a further group complex. It is a small index of the endless variety with which Shakespeare invests a single abstract structure like S . . . P. Possibilities for similar complexity and variety exist at nearly every point of constituent realization, so that any study that sought to define degrees of deviance would be obliged to assess the contribution made by the way in which each constituent is realized.

Because a complete study of constituent order in both plays would be too time-consuming, the random sample of sentences discussed in the previous section was analyzed to obtain some insight into deviant sequences in *Richard II* and *Antony and Cleopatra*.[42] All complexes, clauses, and nominal groups in the sample were parsed, and the sequences were classified as deviant or normal. Deviant sequences were further classified as inverted or discontinuous.

Hypotactic complexes can be either permuted or rendered discontinuous. In the following examples the first passage shows a permuted hypotactic complex. The second shows a beta clause interrupting the alpha clause, making its constituents discontinuous:

---

[42] Line references to the random sample of sentences appear in Table B-1.

> *Prove this a prosp'rous day*, the three-nook'd world
> Shall bear the olive freely.

(Ant. 4.6.6-7)

> A more unhappy lady,
> *If this division chance*, ne'er stood between,
> Praying for both parts.

(Ant. 3.4.12-14)

Discontinuity in a paratactic complex arises when one constituent is enclosed by another:

> Further I say, *and further will maintain*
> *Upon his bad life to make all this good*,
> That he did plot the Duke of Gloucester's death,

(R2 1.1.98-100)

This phenomenon was rare in the sample for *Richard II* and did not appear at all in the sample from *Antony*, although there are instances of it in the later play.[43] It would seem that paratactic complexes cannot be inverted or permuted. Classical rhetoric recognizes the figure *hysteron proton*, in which the logical order of ideas is reversed, as in this passage:

> Th' Antoniad, the Egyptian admiral,
> With all their sixty, *fly and turn the rudder*.

(Ant. 3.10.2-3)

Since this inversion is semantic rather than syntactic, it is not a type of deviance recognized in the present description of marked constituent sequence.

Because it is a more complex issue than can be resolved here, the discussion of inverted clause constituents will be limited to two familiar types. In systemic grammar these are called marked theme and marked mood. Marked theme occurs when any constituent but the subject occupies first place in the declarative clause (ASPC; CSPA; VSPA).[44] If the adjunct

---

[43] See Tables A-12 and A-13 for further observations on deviance in clause complexes.

[44] Binders (*although, if, while*, etc.) and linkers (*and, or*, etc.) are also clause constituents. Excepting that of *if* and *though*, their position is fixed at the beginning of the clause they introduce; hence, no binder can be marked theme. Adjuncts or complements appearing after them may be instances of marked theme. Similarly, *wh*-words do not qualify as theme or prevent another constituent from being themati-

assumes this position, one has adjunct theme; other common types are complement and vocative theme. Predicator theme is a rarer occurrence, but there are instances of it in the two plays. When two such constituents appear in initial position, the result is called double theme and the constituent in second position is known as secondary theme. Triple theme is possible but rare (e.g., *Ant.* 1.4.65-66). Vocative theme, the use of direct address or apostrophe in first position, is a fairly straightforward concept.[45] The variety of realizations assumed by the adjunct has been exemplified, and all these can occur in theme position. The following passages illustrate the more striking complement theme and the unusual predicator theme:[46]

> *My life* thou shalt command, but not my shame.
> > (*R2* 1.1.166)

> *The hopeless word of 'never to return'*
> Breathe I against thee, upon pain of life.
> > (*R2* 1.3.152-153)

> *Fall not a tear*, I say.
> > (*Ant.* 3.11.69)

> *The record of what injuries you did us,*
> *Though written in our flesh*, we shall remember
> As things but done by chance.
> > (*Ant.* 5.2.118-120)

> Wars have not wasted it, for *warr'd* he hath not,
> > (*R2* 2.1.252)

> Whiles we are suitors to their throne, *decays*
> The thing we sue for.
> > (*Ant.* 2.1.4-5)

The following sentences illustrate various types of double theme and serve to introduce instances of adjunct and vocative theme:

> *Then*
> *Three kings* I had newly feasted, . . .
> > (*Ant.* 2.2.75-76)

---

cally marked, because they, too, have an obligatory clause-initial position. A constituent is defined as theme in terms of the predicator of the clause where it occurs. If there is no predicator, the clause does not enter the system of theme.

[45] The assumption is that vocatives normally appear in clause-final position.

[46] See Table B-4 for the line references to complement theme and Table B-7 for the line references to instances of predicator theme.

> *Now, Thomas Mowbray*, do I turn to thee,
> And mark my greeting well;
>
> (R2 1.1.35-36)
>
> *Sir, his chests and treasure*
> He has not with him.
>
> (Ant. 4.5.10-11)
>
> *Now no more*
> The juice of Egypt's grape shall moist this lip.
>
> (Ant. 5.2.284-285)

The second type of clause-constituent inversion is marked mood, which involves the inversion of subject and predicator in declarative clauses. This inversion is possible after marked theme, and it is generally optional.[47] In Shakespeare's English it can occur when the predicator is a simple verb as well as with the auxiliary:

> Three parts of that receipt I had for Calais
> *Disburs'd I* duly to his Highness' soldiers.
>
> (R2 1.1.126-127)
>
> Bring it to that,
> The gold I give thee *will I melt* and pour
> Down thy ill-uttering throat.
>
> (Ant. 2.5.33-35)

According to the sample, these instances of complement and adjunct theme decrease slightly in *Antony*, while vocative theme increases. Marked mood and double theme decrease by a somewhat greater rate in the same play, so that, taken together, the figures in the sample suggest an over-all decline in the permutation of clause constituents.[48] It would seem, then, that in *Antony and Cleopatra* there is a tendency toward more normal sequence with respect to clause constituents.

The permutation of clause constituents by the choices of marked theme and marked mood is the most obvious instance of stylistic inversion at the clause level, but other types may be mentioned briefly. These involve the sequence of complements and adjuncts when two or more occur in the same clause. This sentence illustrates an inversion of the extensive and intensive complements:

---

[47] Marked mood is obligatory after some adjuncts, as in *Never did I see*, etc.

[48] The information about clause deviance in the sample is summarized in Tables A-14 to A-16.

> As nearly as I may,
> I'll play the penitent to you; but mine honesty
> Shall not make *poor my greatness*, nor my power
> Work without it.
>
> (*Ant.* 2.2.91-94)

While adjuncts enjoy great positional mobility, there is at least one rule of sequence that puts adjuncts of place before adjuncts of time. This rule is violated by the following passages:

> Mark Antony is *every hour in Rome*
> Expected.
>
> (*Ant.* 2.1.29-30)

> The beds i' th' East are soft; and thanks to you
> That call'd me *timelier than my purpose hither*;
> For I have gain'd by it.
>
> (*Ant.* 2.6.51-53)

It is obvious that the manner of realizing the adjunct of time in the second passage adds not a little to its degree of deviance. Some adjuncts (termed *nuclear adjuncts*) are more closely tied to the verb than others and behave in a manner more akin to complements than true adjuncts. The result is that, when such adjuncts are moved from their normal position following the verb, the resulting deviant sequence is more striking than usual:

> Yet can I not *of such tame patience* boast
> As to be hush'd and naught at all to say.
>
> (*R2* 1.1.52-53)

> *Of us* must Pompey presently be sought,
> Or else he seeks out us.
>
> (*Ant.* 2.2.161-162)

The second passage shows how adjunct theme can be made more deviant by the type of adjunct chosen. In this case, it is the agentive in passive voice that regularly comes after the verb.

Discontinuity at clause level is posited on two distinctions, that between peripheral and core constituents and that of certain positions in the clause. Subject, predicator, complement, nuclear adjunct, *wh-* words, and most conjunctions are core constituents, whereas vocatives and most adjuncts are considered peripheral. Positions in the clause are defined by reference to the normal order of clause constituents. First position (not to be confused with theme) is that created by subject and predicator, the second by predicator and complement, and the third by two complements. Between the constituents of these positions one may find vocatives or peripheral adjuncts yielding such abstract structures as SVP, SAP; PVC, PAC; CVC, CAC. These structures define discontinuity at clause level. Since several examples of SAP have already been given, discontinuity in the other positions is illustrated in these passages:

Tell her I send *to her* my kind commends;
(*R2* 3.1.38)

Epicurean cooks
Sharpen *with cloyless sauce* his appetite,
(*Ant*. 2.1.24-25)

I'll give thee, *friend,*
An armour all of gold.
(*Ant*. 4.8.26-27)

But let the world rank me *in register*
A master-leaver and a fugitive!
(*Ant*. 4.9.21-22)

It is not unusual to find at clause level discontinuities created by constituents from group level, but these are more appropriately discussed later. Other clause discontinuities, however, may be created when the constituents of a matrix clause are interlaced by the constituents of the embedded clause dominated by the matrix. This type of discontinuity is exemplified by the following passages, where the discontinuous elements are italicized:

I cannot mend it, I must needs confess,
Because my power is weak and all ill left;
(*R2* 2.3.153-154)

Our courteous Antony,
Whom ne'er *the word of 'no'* woman heard *speak*
(*Ant*. 2.2.227-228)

I must needs confess is a clause whose complement is the remainder of the couplet, and this complement is a clause whose final adjunct (*Because . . . left*) is separated from the core constituents *I cannot mend it*. The assumption for the second passage is that the italicized words constitute the complement of the matrix clause *woman ne'er heard* and that this complement is itself an embedded clause, *whom speak the word of 'no'*. Thus, the matrix clause and the embedded clause are interlaced,

Table 22
Varieties of Complement Theme

	Substitute	Secondary	Discontinuous	Intensive	Other	Total Complement Theme*
R2	13	3	13	33	71	124
	.1048	.0242	.1048	.2661	.5726	
Ant.	12	7	9	10	54	88
	.1364	.0795	.1023	.1136	.6136	

*Complements can be simultaneously intensive and discontinuous or substitute and intensive, etc. Hence, the various types will form a total higher than that given in the final column.

making both clauses discontinuous. This type of discontinuity seems most likely to occur with verbs of saying, knowing, and perceiving, since these often dominate embedded clauses.[49]

Because the differences yielded by the sample are slight, it seemed desirable to add some complete studies to the results reported in the sample. At clause level two features were given exhaustive analysis, complement theme (and such instances of marked mood as accompanied it) and PAC structures.[50] Table 22 shows that complement theme decreased by more than 25 percent in *Antony* and that certain aspects of complement theme varied from one play to the other. Substitute theme increased by 3 percent in *Antony*, adding its testimony to the more colloquial character of that play and of the language of Cleopatra, who speaks a higher ratio of this type of complement theme than any other major character:[51]

I have no power upon you; *hers* you are.

(1.3.23)

That you know well. *Something* it is I would—

(1.3.89)

[49] Information about discontinuity of clause constituents is contained in Table A-16.

[50] Line references for complement theme appear in Table B-4, those for PAC structures in Table B-5.

[51] Cleopatra speaks .0568 of the total instances of substitute complement theme, Antony .0227, Caesar .0113, and all others .0454. Total substitute complement theme for the play is .1364 as opposed to .1048 in *Richard II*.

There is a marked increase of the complement in secondary theme position in *Antony*, which may be due to an increase of vocative theme:

> ... and *within three days*
> *You* with your children will he send before.
> (5.2.201-202)

> *O sun, thy uprise* shall I see no more.
> (4.12.18)

Discontinuous complements in theme position occur with equal frequency in each play, but the realization of the complement in *Richard II* reflects a general tendency in that play to favor intensive complements:

> *Quick* is mine ear *to hear of good towards him*.
> (R2 2.1.234)

> *Glad* am I *that your Highness is so arm'd*.
> (R2 3.2.104)

> If you'll patch a quarrel,
> As *matter whole* you have not *to make it with*,
> It must not be with this.
> (*Ant.* 2.2.52-54)

In *Richard II* the marked-mood option is taken significantly more often after complement theme than in *Antony*, but, as Table 23 shows, marked mood assumes different forms depending on the presence or absence of an auxiliary in the verbal group. In the later play marked mood occurs as often with the auxiliary as without it. With respect to the decrease of both complement theme and marked mood, the clauses of *Antony* show a

Table 23
Kinds of Mood Selection after Complement Theme

	Marked Mood* PS	pSP	Marked Mood	Unmarked Mood	Total Complement Theme
R2	38	14	52	72	124
	.7308	.2692	.4194	.5806	
Ant.	4	4	8	80	88
	.5000	.5000	.0909	.9091	

*After complement theme, the mood of declarative sentences is marked if the predicator precedes the subject (*doughty-handed are you*) or if the auxiliary precedes the subject (*nothing can we call our own*).

greater tendency toward normal constituent order. Rhythm doubtless played a large part in determining whether theme and mood would be marked. Marked theme itself changes the normal rhythm of a clause, and the further selection of marked mood appears to sustain that rhythm, whereas reversion to normal order appears to cut it short.[52] The point is best illustrated by examples:

> *Gaunt am I* for the grave, gaunt as a grave,
>   (*R2* 2.1.82)
>
> For *doughty-handed are you*, . . .
>   (*Ant.* 4.8.5)
>
> *The commons hath he pill'd* with grievous taxes
>   (*R2* 2.1.246)
>
> *Our overplus of shipping will we burn,*
>   (*Ant.* 3.7.51
>
>   for *little office*
> *The hateful commons will perform* for us,
>   (*R2* 2.2.136-137)
>
> *These strong Egyptian fetters I must break*
>   (*Ant.* 1.2.120)

The effect of combined marked theme and marked mood can be ascertained by reading the deviant sequences in normal order or the normal sequences in marked order.

The second deviant clause structure to be examined exhaustively was discontinuity in the second clause position, the predicator-complement structure. While the adjunct interrupter occurs with virtually equal frequency in the two plays, a distinction between kinds of adjunct interrupter yields a significant difference. In *Antony* particle adjuncts decrease:

> If then we shall shake *off* our slavish yoke,
> Imp *out* our drooping country's broken wing,
> Redeem *from broking pawn* the blemish'd crown,
> Wipe *off* the dust that hides our sceptre's gilt,
>   (*R2* 2.1.291-294)
>
>   . . . but how the fear of us
> May cement their divisions and bind *up*

---

[52] Halliday discusses the effect of marked theme on sentence prosody in "Notes on Transitivity and Theme, Part 2."

The petty difference we yet not know.
$$(Ant. 2.1.47-49)$$

Other types of adjunct—generally simple adverbs or preposition-complement structures—occur with equal frequency as interrupters in the two plays:

A king of beasts indeed! If aught but beasts,
I had been *still* a happy king of men.
$$(R2 5.1.35-36)$$

Then set *before my face* the Lord Aumerle.
$$(R2 4.1.6)$$

We, ignorant of ourselves,
Beg *often* our own harms, which the wise pow'rs
Deny us for our good.
$$(Ant. 2.1.5-7)$$

. . . but now I'll set my teeth
And send *to darkness* all that stop me.
$$(Ant. 3.13.181-182)$$

The frequency of particle and other adjuncts in second position is recorded in Table 24. This table suggests that Shakespeare in the later style had learned to put as much lexical information as possible into every word and to reduce relatively empty grammatical words.

Table 24
Types of Adjunct Occurring within
Predicator-Complement Structures

	Particle	Lexical	Total PAC
R2	45	57	102
	.4412	.5588	
Ant.	23	58	81
	.2840	.7160	

Instances of nominal-group deviance in the random sample were few, but such differences as appeared were decisive with respect to types of deviance.[53] In *Antony* there were fewer instances of discontinuity in

[53] For the results of nominal-group deviance yielded by the sentence sample, see Table A-17.

nominal groups and a remarkable increase of inversion. Perhaps the most familiar type of nominal-group inversion is that in which the modifier is a postposed adjective:

> More's not seen;
> Or if it be, 'tis with false sorrow's eye,
> Which for *things true* weeps *things imaginary*.
>   (*R2* 2.2.25-27)

> Then put my tires and mantles on him, whilst
> I wore his *sword Philippan*.
>   (*Ant.* 2.5.22-23)

But other types of modifier can also be involved in permutations, including structure words:

> Choose out some secret place, some *reverend* room,
> *More* than thou hast, and with it joy thy life.
>   (*R2* 5.6.25-26)

>   ... but the letters too
> Of *many our* contriving friends in Rome
> Petition us at home.
>   (*Ant.* 1.2.188-190)

The interpretation of these groups is debatable, of course, but it is reasonable to assume that the normal order in the first case is *some room more reverend than thou hast*, and in the second case it might well be *of our many contriving friends*.[54] One of the oddest inversions, not unknown to Angell Day's *Psalter*, is that of the preposition and its complement:

> It stands *your Grace upon* to do him right.
>   (*R2* 2.3.138)

>   It only stands
> *Our lives upon* to use our strongest hands.
>   (*Ant.* 2.1.50-51)

>   Pray you, hasten
> *Your generals after*.
>   (*Ant.* 2.4.1-2)

The first two passages, sharing the same verb and preposition, may have

---

[54] Alternative reconstructions are possible, of course, viz., *of many of our contriving friends*, so that one has an instance of deletion rather than of inversion.

been idiomatic or proverbial. One thinks of the line from one of the Fool's songs in *Lear*: *and go the fools among*. But these daring inversions of structure words are quite rare in both plays. Equally daring though more subtle is the inversion of qualifier and head, whose positions are shown, respectively, by the diagonal lines in the following passages:

> *To safeguard thine own life* /
> *The best way* is to venge my Gloucester's death.
>> (*R2* 1.2.35-36)

> I here importune death awhile, until
> *Of many thousand kisses* / *the poor last*
> I lay upon thy lips.
>> (*Ant.* 4.15.19-21)

As the examples show, the qualifier in a nominal group may vary in structure from a clause to a prepositional phrase. Clauses serving as qualifiers may be nonfinite (the first passage above) or finite.

Qualifying clauses can also follow their heads but may be separated from them by other linguistic units. These separations constitute the most frequent examples of stylistic discontinuity in the nominal group:

> *That hand* shall burn in never-quenching fire
> *That staggers thus my person.*
>> (*R2* 5.5.108-109)

> Yet blessing on *his* heart *that gives it me*!
>> (*R2* 5.5.64)

> Against the blown rose may *they* stop their nose
> *That kneel'd unto the buds.*
>> (*Ant.* 3.13.39-40)

> (As *his* composure must be rare indeed
> *Whom these things cannot blemish*), . . .
>> (*Ant.* 1.4.22-23)

Nonfinite and suppressed clauses serving as qualifiers are harder to detect, and they are more characteristic of *Antony*:

> Next, Cleopatra does confess thy greatness,
> Submits her to thy might, and of thee craves
> *The circle of the Ptolemies* for her heirs,

Now hazarded to thy grace.

(*Ant.* 3.12.16-19)

The odds is gone,
And there is *nothing* left *remarkable*
Beneath the visiting moon.

(*Ant.* 4.15.66-68)

These examples show the richness, variety, and daring with which Shakespeare handled nominal-group constituents.

A complete study of nominal-group deviance confirmed the results of the random sample, as Table 25 shows. The third heading on this table

Table 25
Classes of Deviant Sequence in Nominal-Group Structures: Complete Sets

	Inversion	Discontinuity	Both	Total
R2	15	64	5	84
	.1786	.7619	.0595	
Ant.	20	62	20	102
	.1961	.6078	.1961	

indicates that nominal groups may undergo both inversion and discontinuity. This tendency more than any other single aspect of sequence contributes powerfully to the magic of the style of *Antony*:

Husband, I come!
Now *to that name* my courage prove *my title*!

(5.2.290-291)

Come, thou mortal wretch,
With thy sharp teeth *this knot intrinsicate*
Of life at once untie.

(5.2.306-308)

One reason for the brilliance of these passages is the peculiar rhythm produced by the unusual word order, an effect that can be properly appreciated simply by reading the groups aloud in their normal order. In the first passage the qualifier *to that name* precedes its head (*my title*) and is separated from it by clause constituents. In the second passage the modifier *intrinsicate* has been postposed, making the head (*this knot*) and its quali-

Table 26
Constituents Affected by Nominal-Group Inversion

	Modifiers	Qualifiers	Total
R2	15	5	20
	.7500	.2500	
Ant.	25	15	40
	.6250	.3750	

fier (*of life*) discontinuous. There are four times as many instances of mixed inversion and discontinuity in the later play as one finds in *Richard II*.[55]

Because nominal-group inversion can consist generally of either postposed modifiers or preposed qualifiers, it seemed worthwhile to inquire whether one of these predominated in a given play. Table 26 shows that *Antony* has three times as many preposed qualifiers as the earlier play.

Although it is relatively rare, stylistic inversion can also occur in verbal groups.[56] Here the normal order is assumed to be that auxiliaries precede the main verb, and it is clearly violated in these passages:

> If thou do pardon, whosoever pray,
> More sins for this forgiveness *prosper may*.
> (*R2* 5.3.83-84)

> Where be the sacred vials thou shouldst fill
> With sorrowful water? Now I see, I see,
> In Fulvia's death, how mine *receiv'd shall be*.
> (*Ant.* 1.3.63-65)

The inversion seems motivated by a desire for a rhyming word, but rhyme seems scarcely to have been a concern of Shakespeare in *Antony*. The passage is undoubtedly of a piece with Cleopatra's histrionic behavior in that scene. Negative polarity offers more opportunity for the inversion of verbal-group constituents, and Shakespeare creates many unusual constructions in *Antony* by shifting the negative particle *not* (*never* counts in this description as an adjunct) from its usual position within or adjacent to the verbal group to some other, generally anterior, position:

[55] Line references for nominal-group deviance are given in Table B-6.
[56] Line references for verbal-group inversion appear in Table B-7.

more laugh'd at that I should
Once name you derogately when to sound your name
It *not concern'd* me.

(2.2.33-35)

When the best hint was given him, he *not took't*,
Or did it from his teeth.

(3.4.9-10)

This type of inversion occurs only in *Antony*; negative polarity is quite regular in *Richard II*.

The most common type of discontinuity in the verbal group consists of interrupting the auxiliary and main verbs in much the same fashion that clause constituents were seen to be interrupted earlier. There is little limit to the type or level of constituent that can appear between auxiliary and main verb, as the following passages attest:

Ten thousand bloody crowns of mothers' sons
Shall *ill* become the flower of England's face,
(*R2* 3.3.96-97)

But let us rear
The higher our opinion, that our stirring
Can *from the lap of Egypt's widow* pluck
The ne'er-lust-wearied Antony.
(*Ant.* 2.1.35-38)

I have *from Le Port Blanc, a bay*
In Britain, receiv'd intelligence
(*R2* 2.1.277-278)

And to proclaim it civilly were like
A halter'd neck which does *the hangman* thank
For being yare about him.
(*Ant.* 3.13.129-131)

These verbal groups contain, respectively, a simple adjunct interrupter, an adjunct with a preposition-complement structure, a hypotactic group complex, and a complement.

At other times the constituent that interrupts the verbal group is itself the subject of inversion or discontinuity, as in these examples:

And at this time most easy 'tis to do't,
When my good stars that were my former guides

Have *empty* left their *orbs* and shot their fires
Into th' abysm of hell.

(*Ant.* 3.13.144-147)

and now
Pleas'd fortune does *of Marcus Crassus' death*
Make me *revenger*.

(*Ant.* 3.1.1-3)

Table 27 gives the frequency with which various types of interrupter occur between the constituents of the verbal group. Most of the subject interrupters are the result of marked mood, and the decline in *Antony* of this

Table 27
Varieties of Interrupter in Verbal-Group Structure

	Beta Clause	Subject	Complement	Adjunct	Vocative	Total
R2	5	54	12	70	1	142
	.0352	.3803	.0845	.4930	.0070	
Ant.	0	30	14	92	2	138
	–	.2174	.1014	.6667	.0145	

phenomenon has already been noted. When simple adverbial adjuncts are distinguished from those consisting of a preposition and a complement, it appears that the rise of adjunct interrupters in *Antony* is entirely due to an increase of simple adverbial types.

Inversion and discontinuity can occur simultaneously in the verbal as well as in the nominal group, although it is rarer than it is in the nominal group, and it is similarly characteristic of *Antony and Cleopatra*:

Not Caesar's valour *hath o'erthrown* Antony,
But Antony's hath triumph'd on itself.

(*Ant.* 4.15.14-15)

The phenomenon is virtually restricted to negative verbal groups. Table 28 yields the frequencies for discontinuity and inversion at the level of the verbal group.

Each play affords an example of marked sequence at the level of the word:

. . . *how* heinous *e'er* it be,
To win thy after-love I pardon thee.
(*R2* 5.3.34-35)

Come, thou mortal wretch,
With thy sharp teeth this knot *intrinsicate*
Of life at once untie.
(*Ant.* 5.2.306-308)

Table 28
Classes of Deviant Sequence in Verbal-Group Structure

	Inversion	Discontinuity	Both	Total
R2	1	142	0	143
	.0070	.9930	–	
Ant.	9	138	2	149
	.0604	.9262	.0134	

The first example, which may be termed an instance of discontinuity, was popular enough among the rhetorical features recognized by Shakespeare's contemporaries to have its own name, "tmesis." The second may be a conflation of *intrinsic* and *intricate*. If so, it could also be regarded as a type of discontinuity, assuming that *intricate* is interrupted by the final syllables of *intrinsic*. The two instances of discontinuity are distinguished by the fact that *however* consists of two potentially free, hence easily separated, morphemes, whereas the morphemes involved in the second word are all bound. It is possible that the type found in *Richard II* is more characteristic of an earlier style, while that found in *Antony*, with its daring violation of word structure, is more characteristic of the later style. Such a pattern would reflect the trend toward increasing violation of nominal-group constituents, which characterizes the language of *Antony and Cleopatra*. This trend reaches into the lowest, most closely knit, levels of the language, disturbing constituents normally thought to lie beyond the boundaries even of poetic license. It might be noted in conclusion that the passage containing the word *intrinsicate*, which is often cited for its remarkable style, exhibits marked sequence on three out of three possible levels. There is an instance of double theme (adjunct and complement) at clause level, simultaneous inversion and discontinuity at nominal-group level, and the single instance in the play of word-constituent deviance.

It is now possible to make a general statement about constituent order in the two plays, based on those aspects of clause and group deviance that were studied exhaustively. Frequencies comprising the total instances of clause deviance include complement and predicator theme, marked mood after complement theme, and predicator-complement discontinuity where the interrupter is an adjunct. The frequencies for group deviance contain all instances of nominal- and verbal-group deviance that could be discovered by manual analysis of the text, using the categories described in this section. These frequencies are listed in Table 29. The possibilities for

Table 29
Frequency of Deviant Sequence in Clause and Group Structure

	Complement Theme	Marked Mood	Predicator-Adjunct-Complement	Total Clause	Nominal Group	Verbal Group	Total Group
R2	131	52	102	285	84	143	227
	.4596	.1825	.3579		.3700	.6300	
Ant.	89	8	81	178	102	147	249
	.5000	.0449	.4551		.4096	.5904	

clause deviance are greater than those for group deviance, since there are more clause constituents and the number of constituents per clause tends to be higher than in the nominal group. For this reason the figures that show a decrease in clause deviance for *Antony* may be deceptive. The figures shown in Table 29 indicate a marked decline in clause deviance in the later play, which becomes more remarkable set beside the rise in nominal-group deviance. Hence, it is not unreasonable to suggest that in the later play Shakespeare tended to keep clause-constituent order relatively normal and to indulge in more frequent and more daring types of deviance at the level of the nominal group. Rhythm may have dictated the over-all pattern of change, or it may be that, by keeping the clause relatively simple, he could more easily employ semantic and syntactic deviance elsewhere. Obviously, one needs to study cooccurrences of deviance at different structural levels and to determine formally the exact type of rhythmic change wrought, for example, by marked theme or by nominal-group inversion. Prior to such a complex undertaking one needs more theoretical and methodological knowledge than is now available.

It seems reasonable to propose that Shakespeare's chief purpose for employing these departures from normal constituent order is related to blank-verse rhythm. Renaissance rhetorical theory supports this view. The rhetorician George Puttenham discussed the figures of grammar in terms that anticipate Chomsky's remarks on stylistic inversion: "As your single words may be many waies transfigured to make the meetre or verse more tunable and melodious, so also may your whole and entire clauses be in such sort contrived by the order of their construction as the eare may receive a certaine recreation, although the mind for any noveltie of sence be little or nothing affected. And therefore al your figures of *grammaticall* construction, I accompt them but merely *auricular* in that they reach no furder then the eare."[57]

Puttenham's opinion of the merely auricular figures of grammar doubtless has a modern counterpart in the observation that there are occasions when Shakespeare "merely turns North's eloquent prose into verse," yet it seems a pity to take for granted the witchcraft of Shakespeare's verse rhythms or to ignore the means he used to create them.[58] Mark Van Doren attributed the rhythms of *Antony* in part to the predominance of certain sounds like *i*, short *a*, and *-ing*, but it is interesting to observe in the passages cited by Van Doren that there are also numerous instances of marked word order:[59]

> This common body,
> *Like to a vagabond flag upon the stream,*
> Goes to and back, *lackeying the varying tide,*
> To rot itself with motion.
>
> (1.4.44-47)

> Think on me,
> That am *with Phoebus' amorous pinches* black

[57] George Puttenham, *The Arte of English Poesie*, ed. Gladys Doidge Willcock and Alice Walker, p. 163. Miriam Joseph Rauh notes in *Shakespeare's Use of the Arts of Language* that the figures of grammar increased markedly in the later plays (p. 54).

[58] George Lyman Kittredge, in his Introduction to *Coriolanus* (*Complete Works*, p. 924), intended no slight to Shakespeare, but his remark illustrates the way in which Shakespeare's versification has been underplayed or ignored since the era when it had a major role in establishing the authorship and the chronology of many plays. Recent discussions of Shakespeare's rhythm (as opposed to meter) include John W. Draper's *The Tempo-Patterns of Shakespeare's Plays*; Una Ellis-Fermor's "Some Functions of Verbal Music in Drama," *Shakespeare-Jahrbuch* 90 (1954): 37-48; Julian Markels's final chapter in *The Pillar of the World*; and Georgia S. Dunbar's "The Verse Rhythms of *Antony and Cleopatra*," *Style* 5 (1971): 231-245.

[59] Mark Van Doren, *Shakespeare*, p. 233.

> And wrinkled deep in time?
>
> (1.5.27-29)
>
> Yet, *coming from him*, that great med'cine hath
> *With his tinct* gilded thee.
>
> (1.5.36-37)
>
> She
>
> *In th' habiliments of the goddess Isis |*
> *That day* appear'd;
>
> (3.6.16-18)
>
> *That which is now a horse, | even with a thought*
> The rack dislimns, and makes it indistinct
> As water is in water.
>
> (4.14.9-11)
>
> *With thy sharp teeth | this knot | intrinsicate |*
> *Of life | at once |* untie.
>
> (5.2.307-308)

With the exception of the last two passages, most of these are instances of discontinuity between clause constituents, and the italicized phrases constitute the interrupting elements. Group betas serve as interrupters in the first and third passages; the remaining interrupters are adjuncts. In the second last passage, there is a hypotactic clause complex where the beta clause (*even with a thought*) interrupts its alpha. The last passage exemplifies several types of marked order: triple theme consisting of an initial adjunct (*with . . . teeth*), a complement (*this . . . life*), and another adjunct (*at once*). The complement itself consists of a nominal group whose constituents are simultaneously discontinuous and inverted. In brief, all the passages cited by Mark Van Doren as typical of the rhythms of *Antony* contain, in addition to the features he noted, instances of stylistic discontinuity and inversion.

A full description of the relationship between rhythm and word order cannot be undertaken here, but to mention a few aspects of rhythm may serve as an outline for some future study. The sketch will be highly intuitive and will make no attempt to be rigorous or exhaustive, nor will it be confined only to a discussion of marked word order. Discussion will be limited to *Antony and Cleopatra*. One feature of rhythm is variety of tempo. One senses that the speed of certain lines can be accelerated, slowed, sustained, or cut short. Brief paratactic clauses, for example, create an impression of speed and abruptness that results in the tight-lipped tone of barely controlled anger that Caesar uses to describe Antony's behavior in Egypt:

> he fishes, drinks, and wastes
> The lamps of night in revel;
>
> (1.4.4-5)

The speech of Antony's ambassador, conciliatory and ingratiating, is prolonged by a comparative clause where every constituent is fully explicit:

> I was of late as petty to his ends
> As is the morn-dew on the myrtle leaf
> To his grand sea.
>
> (3.12.8-10)

Both speeds are to be heard in this speech of Caesar's where the initial elements are rather slow (*If . . . voluptuousness; who . . . knowledge*), and the final elements (*full surfeits . . . for't; Pawn . . . judgment*) are rushed as if Caesar can no longer control his anger under the mask of abstraction, analogy, and philosophical aloofness:

> If he fill'd
> His vacancy with his voluptuousness,
> Full surfeits and the dryness of his bones
> Call on him for't! But to confound such time
> That drums him from his sport and speaks as loud
> As his own state and ours—'tis to be chid
> As we rate boys who, being mature in knowledge,
> Pawn their experience to their present pleasure
> And so rebel to judgment.
>
> (1.4.25-33)

In contrast to the abrupt ending of such sentences is a construction like a coda where recursive embedding allows a very gradual slowing of rhythm. Such sentences appear in *Richard II* and are even more typical of *1 Henry IV* and *Henry V*:

> Forthwith a power of English shall we levy,
> *Whose* arms were moulded in their mother's womb
> *To chase* these pagans in those holy fields
> *Over whose* acres walk'd those blessed feet
> *Which* fourteen hundred years ago were nail'd

For our advantage on the bitter cross.

(*1H4* 1.1.22-27)

The *wh-* clauses are embedded rather than hypotactic, so that one does not find the rhythmic suspense found in some of the more Roman speeches of *Antony*.

Allied to the tempo of rhythm, and perhaps a part of it, is the ability to sustain a rhythm at a given point. This can be accomplished by repeating a structure, although there is usually variation within the repetition:

who, *high in name and power,*
Higher than both in blood and life, stands up
For the main soldier;

(1.2.196-198)

The barge *she sat in, like a burnish'd throne,*
Burn'd on the water.

(2.2.196-197)

Her gentlewomen, *like the Nereides,*
So many mermaids, tended her i' th' eyes,

(2.2.211-212)

This rhythm seems to imitate the rocking motion of the barge, and in the following lines, in which one major stress follows the other almost immediately, one can imagine one wave striking before the impetus of its predecessor is spent. One has thus a special kind of recursive stress:

The poop was *beat*en gold;
*Pur*ple the sails, . . .

(2.2.197-198)

In addition to a factor of tempo, the study of rhythm must include a distinction between sentences where all elements belong to the same rhythm pattern and those where beta clauses, vocatives, and appositives break the sentence rhythm and assert a rhythm of their own. When numerous, sentences of the latter type create the open expansive rhythm that one associates with periodic sentences:

Yon ribald-rid nag of Egypt
(*Whom leprosy o'ertake!*) i' th' midst o' th' fight,
When vantage like a pair of twins appear'd,

Both as the same, or rather ours the elder,—
The breese upon her, | like a cow in June,—
Hoists sails, and flies.

(3.10.10-15)

There are other sentences where the basic sentence rhythm is sustained, but where one has an impression of expansion and suspense created by the permutation of clause and group constituents whose position affects but does not break the rhythm. This type combines relative simplicity of syntax with dignity of tone to create that special poignancy of language that one associates with Antony's speeches after defeat:

He *at Philippi* kept
His sword e'en like a dancer, while I struck
The lean and wrinkled Cassius; and 'twas I
That *the mad Brutus* ended. He *alone*
Dealt on lieutenantry and *no practice* had
In the brave squares of war.

(3.11.35-40)

Egypt, thou knew'st too well
My heart was *to thy rudder* tied by th' strings,
And thou shouldst tow me after. *O'er my spirit |*
Thy full supremacy thou knew'st, and that
Thy beck might *from the bidding of the gods*
Command me.

(3.11.56-61)

In most instances the permuted constituents are complements or adjuncts, but one instance of complement theme is further permuted at the level of group (*supremacy o'er my spirit*). The two types of rhythm may well be the components of the phenomenon that Una Ellis-Fermor calls the systole and diastole of a double simultaneous tempo.[60]

Marked theme is related syntactically to this sort of rhythm in that it involves permutation of clause constituents with no break in the rhythm. But, while the former seems designed to prevent stress from falling on the permuted constituent, marked theme seeks to attract emphasis.[61] As is the case with all other features of rhythm, its particular effect will vary

[60] Ellis-Fermor, "Some Functions of Verbal Music," p. 38.
[61] M. A. K. Halliday, reviewing some of these examples of marked word order in an early version of this study, suggested in a private communication that some constit-

with the structure of the constituent that serves as theme. Caesar makes frequent use of elaborate theme constructions in his description of the attempt by Antony and Cleopatra to establish their Eastern empire:

> *I' th' market place | on a tribunal silver'd*
> Cleopatra and himself in chairs of gold
> Were publicly enthron'd. *At the feet* sat
> Caesarion, whom they call my father's son,
> And all the unlawful issue that their lust
> Since then hath made between them. *Unto her*
> He gave the stablishment of Egypt; made her
> *Of lower Syria, Cyprus, Lydia, |*
> *Absolute queen.*
>
> . . . .
>
> *His sons* he there proclaim'd the kings of kings:
> *Great Media, Parthia, and Armenia*
> He gave to Alexander;
>
> (3.6.3-11, 13-16)

The passage proceeds by a dynamic of stresses (the various instances of marked theme), of which the climax is the nonthematic but dramatically inverted nominal group *Of lower Syria, Cyprus, Lydia, | Absolute queen.* In addition to marked theme, monosyllabic adjuncts like *best, most, first,* and *so* offer countless opportunities for manipulating stress, since they fit so easily into any structure:

> Fulvia thy wife first came into the field.
>
> (1.2.92)
>
> Fortune knows
> We scorn her most when most she offers blows.
>
> (3.11.73-74)
>
> Mark Antony I serv'd, who best was worthy
> Best to be serv'd.
>
> (5.1.6-7)

---

uents may have been reordered to prevent the tonic from falling on a given syllable. He defines the tonic syllable as "the one which carries the main pitch movement in the utterance. . . . The tonic syllable is always a strong syllable, and may be, but is not necessarily, longer or louder than the other strong syllables in the utterance" (*A Course in Spoken English, Part Two: Intonation Exercises*, p. iii). See also his article "The Tones of English," *Archivum Linguisticum* 15 (1963): 5-10.

                                    She rend'red life,
          Thy name so buried in her.

                                            (4.14.33-34)

Sometimes these words seem to attract stress; at other times they appear to serve as place fillers allowing stress to fall elsewhere. Since many of them take the form of quantifiers and intensifiers in *Antony*, they add the semantic weight of degree to their stylistic effect and seldom degenerate into simple expediency.

The final point to be made about rhythm involves what might be called dynamics—the way in which rhythm grows to a climax and falls away or the way in which there are transitions from one rhythm to another, similar to a change of key in music. Some aspects of dynamics were mentioned in the discussion of the abrupt or lengthened sentence endings and of Caesar's speech on empire, but among the most effective examples of this phenomenon is Cleopatra's speech as she prepares to meet her lover in death:

          Give me my robe, put on my crown. I have
          Immortal longings in me. Now no more
          The juice of Egypt's grape shall moist this lip.
          Yare, yare, good Iras; quick. Methinks I hear
          Antony call. I see him rouse himself
          To praise my noble act. I hear him mock
          The luck of Caesar, which the gods give men
          To excuse their after wrath. Husband, I come!
          Now to that name my courage prove my title!
          I am fire and air; my other elements
          I give to baser life. So, have you done?
          Come then and take the last warmth of my lips.
          Farewell, kind Charmian. Iras, long farewell.

                                            (5.2.282-295)

Two short, rhythmically balanced clauses are followed by a longer sentence, where *immortal longings* represents a transition from the monosyllabic, rather flat tone of *Give me my robe* to the heightening of the third sentence with its double adjunct theme, its metonymous, structurally full subject, its prophetic *shall*, and the demonstrative of elevation (*this lip*). A second transition to the colloquial *yare, yare* precedes another climactic series beginning with *Methinks I hear*. The rhythm, though not the tone, is broken by the brevity of *Husband, I come*. The next sentence is the rhythmic and semantic climax of the speech with its marked theme (*Now to that name*; *my other elements*) and its aspiration to a realm beyond change. The passage then diminishes gradually to the final line, with its own internal transitions from colloquial to lofty, where the vocatives, one normal, the other marked, create special rhythmic complexes on either side of the caesura.

A comparison of Cleopatra's speeches in the final lines of the play with those she speaks in the last scene of Act One suggests that stylistic features of diction are equally remarkable in both scenes, but that marked word order and a particular kind of rhythm distinguish the marvelous conclusion of the play from the language that precedes it.[62] That rhythm is created chiefly by means of marked theme and by permutation of nominal-group constituents. It dominates the passage analyzed above and appears as well in two other important speeches from the final scene:

> My resolution's plac'd, and I have nothing
> Of woman in me. *Now* | *from head to foot*
> I am marble-constant. *Now* the fleeting moon
> *No planet is of mine*.
>
> > (5.2.238-241)
>
> *Now* boast thee, death, *in thy possession* | *lies*
> A lass unparallel'd. *Downy windows*, close;
> And golden Phoebus never be beheld
> Of eyes *again* so royal!
>
> > (5.2.318-321)

If one were to rewrite these lines in their normal order and read them aloud, one would need no further proof that Shakespeare's use of marked word order to create the rhythms of *Antony and Cleopatra* is not merely but magically auricular.

---

[62] See pp. 208-209. Arranged in normal order, *Ant.* 5.2.238-241 reads *I am marble-constant from head to foot now. The fleeting moon is no planet of mine now.* The tonic still falls on *now* but coincides with the fading/falling pattern of sentence-final intonation, whereas placing *now* in theme position attracted the tonic and suspended the finality of the constituents at the end of the sentence. To place *Ant.* 5.2.318-321 in normal order is almost sacrilegious: *Boast thee now death; an unparallel'd lass lies in thy possession. Close, downy windows, and golden Phoebus never again be beheld of eyes so royal.* The diction, the figures, the imagery remain unchanged, but few would dispute the signal contribution made to the beauty of this passage by marked word order and its attendant rhythm.

This chapter has examined some methods for the formal analysis of style. The first section proposed that style can be viewed as a set of proportions and suggested that the chi-square test offers a useful statistic for determining whether two proportions are significantly different, while systemic grammar provides exhaustive and mutually exclusive categories for chi-square testing and for ensuring that all hypotheses are examined within a given segment of the grammar. This point was illustrated by reference to *wh-* words, which revealed that relative clauses introduced by *what*, *when*, and *which* increase significantly in *Antony and Cleopatra*. The section on sampling and weighting discussed the difficulty of defining a notion like sentence complexity. Remarks were exemplified by analyzing the immediate constituents of sentences and by determining the relative amount of parataxis, hypotaxis, and embedding in a sample of sentences drawn from the two plays. Finally, the section on word order sought to establish an exhaustively and formally defined set of categories for the tabulation of departures from normal word order. The notion of normal word order was redefined as the unmarked sequence of constituents in the syntactic structures of clause complex, clause, and group. Two types of marked sequence were distinguished, inversion and discontinuity; these were exemplified and tabulated at all syntactic levels.

Such tables and figures as have been provided are offered as a certain kind of evidence for accepting or rejecting a particular linguistic item as a distinctive feature of the text, but there is no claim that they constitute conclusive "proof" or indeed that this type of evidence is intrinsically superior to any other type of evidence that manifests a similar sense of responsibility to the entire text and to the complex properties of language. Certainly, there is no claim that the differences between plays discerned as a result of quantitative analysis will in themselves explain the aesthetic effect of either play or the fact that the language of *Antony* is considered superior to that of *Richard II*. All statements made have a very tentative basis, depending as they do on the comparison of two plays, on particular decisions about the classification of linguistic data, and on many other contingencies that are subject to change. The real value of quantification is that it pushes one to explicate intuitions about style in an effort to sub-stantiate them. Often this can be done only by being disappointed by frequency counts, by a subsequent refinement of the hypothesis, and by the formulation of a statement that has very specific constraints. For example, the possibility that group beta clauses made a special contribu-tion to the style of *Antony and Cleopatra* was an early and persistent intuition. It would have been convenient had this contribution been simply a matter of high frequency, but a study of the sentence sample exploded this hypothesis and suggested instead that the position, length, and context of these clauses in *Antony* caused them to stand out more than those of *Richard II*, even though they were no more frequent. This information in turn could be generalized to a statement about left-branching sentences and periodic rhythm. Since style seems to be created by just these sorts of relational and narrowly defined phenomena, intuition need not suffer greatly in a formal and quantitative study of style.

CHAPTER FOUR

Grammar as Meaning

Meaning in the Grammatical Mode

The previous two chapters have shown how the constraints of grammatically defined and statistically significant structural units operate in the analysis of a literary text. The third constraint on the method of stylistic analysis requires that the results of formal analysis be used to interpret the text. While the third constraint has been illustrated in both these chapters, it is now necessary to discuss the basis for this practice. Theoretically, one needs a hypothesis to explain the data.[1] Formulating a hypothesis of any kind must always involve an intuitive leap of the mind from concrete data to abstract explanation, and there is no reason why those who undertake the formal study of literary texts should be deterred from using their intuition by a false "scientism," which is never exhibited by the best research in the physical sciences. Solid ground from which to make the intuitive leap is often provided by the results of formal linguistic analysis. Meaning in literature derives not only from the semantic content of a lexical word like *noble* but also from the grammatical features

---

[1] The difficulty of taking this step has been noted by Richard W. Bailey in "Current Trends in the Analysis of Style," *Style* 1 (1967): 5. A more detailed discussion appears in Louis T. Milic's "Against the Typology of Styles," in *Essays on the Language of Literature*, ed. Seymour Chatman and Samuel R. Levin, p. 447.

of that word—for example, in *Antony* its frequent use with vocatives, its collocation with the quantifier *most*, its formal scatter into variants like *unnoble, nobleness,* and *nobility*. These environments give it the meaning associated with person and direct address, with superlative and hyperbole, and with abstract qualities. Hence, any text may be said to possess whatever formal meaning resides in those grammatical features that are characteristic of it.

The semantic theory of J. R. Firth emphasized the fact that every grammatical feature of a language has meaning: "Normal grammatical markers such as *the, their, -ing, -er, -s* make possible a statement of meaning in the grammatical mode."[2] This meaning is often so subtle that its force appears only when a text is translated into another language. Roman Jakobson has noted the difficulty of translating Heine's poem about the love of a pine tree for a palm tree from the German where the words for these trees are, respectively, masculine and feminine gender, into French where they are both masculine, into Russian where they are both feminine, or into English where there is no gender at all.[3] Another way of assessing the impact of formal meaning in a text is to make a slight change in some feature, as is done in this passage from *Coriolanus*:

> See here these movers that do prize their honours
> At a crack'd drachma!
>
>   (1.5.5-6)
>
> See here the movers that do prize their honours
> At a crack'd drachma!
>
> See here these movers; they do prize their honours
> At a crack'd drachma!

In the original passage the demonstrative (*these*) and the imperative combine with the context of situation to produce the remarkable effect of these lines. There is heavy pointing to the business on stage where Marcius watches the Roman soldiers carrying their spoils from the besieged city of Corioles when they should still be fighting. The speaker's language, with its demonstrative and the reinforcement of *movers* by the relative clause,

[2] J. R. Firth, "Modes of Meaning," *Essays and Studies by Members of the English Association* 4 (1951): 127. See also Firth's "Techniques of Semantics," in his *Papers in Linguistics*, pp. 7-33.

[3] Roman Jakobson, "Grammatical and Lexical Meaning," lecture delivered during the Linguistic Institute at UCLA on July 6, 1966.

points to the activity and underscores it. The demonstrative also suggests the alienation of the speaker, who points verbally to men who are near enough to be visible (*see here*). Replacing the demonstrative with the definite article weakens specification and pointing. Attention that had been entirely concentrated on *movers* is now divided, by implication, between the movers in question and some other movers. The second change, from *that* to *they* varies the rhythm. In the original it was compressed until it exploded on *drachma* because it had a single tone group and a single tonic syllable, which fell on that final word. In the altered version there are two sentences, two tone groups, two tonic syllables, and, consequently, a more diffuse rhythm.[4] Phonological meaning made the speaker of the original lines a more impetuous and angry person than is the man who takes the pauses necessitated by the changed rhythm of the substitute version.

Determiners and the Fictional World

On the basis of such formal meaning as is demonstrably present in syntax and phonology, one is justified in forming hypotheses to interpret the text. When literature is the object of stylistic analysis, it is logical that the formulation of hypotheses should be related to an attempt to specify the content and application of critical terms like *tone*, *theme*, and *narrative structure*.[5] These terms are themselves hypothetical constructs derived from the study of literature, particularly from patterns formed by lexical items, but, as this study has indicated, function words (e.g., *what*, *whose*, *when*) can contribute to the formation of these patterns.

A concept like *fictional world* can be defined in part by a study of the determiners that modify words designating aspects of that world in a given work of literature. Determiners like *the*, *this*, *my*, and *a* carry a meaning of modification that dictates the angle from which the referent of a given noun is viewed. Thus, an examination of nouns referring to the physical universe in *Richard II* and *Antony and Cleopatra* revealed that *earth*, *world*, *fire*, *sea*, and so on were modified by possessives and demonstrative

---

[4] For a discussion of tone group and tonic syllable, see M. A. K. Halliday's Introduction to his *A Course in Spoken English, Part Two: Intonation Exercises*, p. iii.

[5] For attempts to define "narrative structure" in formal linguistic terms, see Vladímir I. Propp's *Morphology of the Folktale*; Eugene Dorfman's "The Structure of Narrative: A Linguistic Approach," *The History of Ideas Newsletter* 2 (1956): 63-67, and *The Narreme in the Medieval Romance Epic*; and Thomas Klammer's "Multihierarchical Structure in a Middle English Breton Lay—A Tagmemic Analysis," *Language and Style* 4 (1971): 3-23.

determiners to a significantly higher degree in *Richard II* than in *Antony*, which relies more on the definite article as a modifier for such words.[6] The favoring of possessive determiners for words like *earth* and *land* in the earlier play reinforces the picture of a feudal society where concern for land ownership is primary, and it is understandable that one finds here many phrases like *our territories, your fearful land, my gentle earth, our sea-walled garden, my forest woods, fair King Richard's land*.[7] The higher frequency of demonstratives to describe the physical universe is harder to explain. It may be that the intrinsically dramatic, pointing nature of such words was used for creating verbal scenery:

> These high wild hills and rough uneven ways
> Draws out our miles and makes them wearisome;
> >   (2.3.4-5)

> King Richard lies
> Within the limits of yon lime and stone;
> >   (3.3.25-26)

> What sport shall we devise here in this garden
> To drive away the heavy thought of care?
> >   (3.4.1-2)

> Go bind thou up yon dangling apricocks,
> Which, like unruly children, make their sire
> Stoop with oppression of their prodigal weight.
> >   (3.4.29-31)

It may also be that speakers other than the King were unwilling to speak so possessively of land and chose diplomatically to use the demonstrative. The richest source of demonstratives in *Richard II* is Gaunt's famous speech:

> This royal throne of kings, this scept'red isle,
> This earth of majesty, this seat of Mars,
> This other Eden, demi-paradise,
>
> . . . .

---

[6] Table A-18 provides the statistical data for the discussion of the determiners modifying references to the physical universe of the two plays. The notes that discuss this table illustrate the kinds of grammatical meaning derived from each determiner.

[7] Caroline F. E. Spurgeon, in *Shakespeare's Imagery and What It Tells Us*, first pointed out the high incidence of garden imagery in *Richard II* (pp. 220-224) and of *world* as a dominant note in *Antony and Cleopatra* (pp. 352-353).

> This blessed plot, this earth, this realm, this England,
>
> . . . .
>
> This land of such dear souls, this dear dear land,
>
> . . . .
>
> Is now leas'd out (I die pronouncing it)
> Like to a tenement or pelting farm.
>
> . . . .
>
> That England that was wont to conquer others
> Hath made a shameful conquest of itself.
>   (2.1.40-42, 50, 57, 59-60, 65-66)

Here Gaunt's use of the demonstrative creates the elevation required for the declamatory style of his language; it strikes a note of detachment appropriate for the speech of a dying prophet and perhaps a note of alienation that prepares the way for the concluding condemnation. Finally, the demonstrative portrays a stable universe that provides security for its inhabitants:

> This earth shall have a feeling, and these stones
> Prove armed soldiers ere her native king
> Shall falter under foul rebellion's arms.
>   (3.2.24-26)

This sense of security derives from a close connection between the world (in a general sense) and the land that one owns:

> Why, cousin, wert thou regent of the world,
> It were a shame to let this land by lease;
> But, for thy world enjoying but this land,
> Is it not more than shame to shame it so?
>   (2.1.109-112)

Twenty percent of the instances of *world* in this play occur in Richard's final soliloquy, where it is compared to and equated with his prison: *this hard world, my ragged prison walls*. In both comparisons, of the world to land and to a prison, its normal global extension is reduced to a narrow compass that can be easily grasped. Expressions like *this new world*, *the lower world*, and *a new world's crown* distinguish between the worlds of man and of God, of time and of eternity. If one is unsuccessful in the first, there is still a chance of achieving status in the other:

> Our holy lives must win a new world's crown,
> Which our profane hours here have stricken down.
>
> (5.1.24-25)

A quarter of the references to *world* are modified by the demonstrative, as shown in Table 30. The demonstrative creates an impression that one can

Table 30
Determiners Modifying the Word *World*

	Definite	Demonstrative	Possessive	Other	Total
R2	11	7	1	2	21
	.5238	.3333	.0476	.0952	
Ant.	37	4	0	1	42
	.8810	.0952	–	.0238	

point to it with the certitude that it is always there and always the same, just as the land that constitutes the world of this play is a stable commodity obtained by legal title. One does not need to fight for it; one claims it by right, an attitude that is ultimately as characteristic of the usurper Bolingbroke as it is of the deposed Richard.

In *Antony* the word *world* occurs with a frequency that is double that of *Richard II* and indeed of most other plays.[8] It is typically modified by the various functions of the definite article, although one occasionally finds the demonstrative with its other meaning, alienation, especially toward the close of the play:[9]

> It were for me
> To throw my sceptre at the injurious gods,
> To tell them that this world did equal theirs
> Till they had stol'n our jewel.
>
> (4.15.75-77)

[8] According to Marvin Spevack's *Complete and Systematic Concordance*, *world* occurs with these frequencies in some of the major plays: *R2*, twenty-one; *1H4*, twenty-four; *2H4*, sixteen; *H5*, seventeen; *JC*, eighteen; *Ham.*, twenty-six; *Oth.*, twenty-nine; *Lear*, twenty-one; *Mac.*, six; *Ant.*, forty-four; *Cor.*, twenty-one. These figures include both verse and prose, and variants like *world's*, but they do not include variants like *worldly*, *world-sharers*, *worldling*, etc.

[9] As the notes to Table A-18 explain, the demonstrative is viewed as having two opposite meanings—elevation and alienation.

> Shall I abide
> In this dull world, which in thy absence is
> No better than a sty?
>
>   (4.15.60-62)
>
> *Cleo.*   What should I stay—
> *Char.*   In this wild world?
>   (5.2.316)

That the world is a self-evident object is clear from the fact that it is generally specified by the homophoric function of the definite article. Men move across it with an ease that contrasts remarkably with the attitudes of Mowbray and Bolingbroke, who find the whole world inadequate compensation for the loss of England:

> Then thus I turn me from my country's light
> To dwell in solemn shades of endless night.
>
> .   .   .   .
> Farewell, my liege. Now no way can I stray.
> Save back to England, all the world's my way.
>   (*R2* 1.3.176-177, 206-207)
>
> The third o' th' world is yours, which with a snaffle
> You may pace easy, . . .
>
>   (*Ant.* 2.2.63-64)
>
>   Yet if I knew
> What hoop should hold us staunch, from edge to edge
> O' th' world I would pursue it.
>   (*Ant.* 2.2.116-118)

A man must move rapidly about in this world if he is to demonstrate or to preserve his claim to dominion over it. The world of *Antony* is constantly in motion, a point made rather tellingly in the revel aboard Pompey's boat where a servant carries off a third part of it in the person of Lepidus, where it is potentially changing hands from the triumvirate to Pompey, where Menas wishes it might go on wheels, and where the boy sings, *Cup us till the world go round*. It is this world that Cleopatra commands to stand still when Antony dies. Perhaps the most interesting source of its mobility is its variable size and shape. Grammatically this variety is expressed by the fact that a quarter of the references to it occur in phrases introduced by a quantitative expression: *the triple pillar of the world*; *the third o' th' world; the whole world; the third part of the world; the greater cantle of the world; half the bulk o' th' world; the three-nook'd world; a moiety of the world; I, that with my sword/Quarter'd the world.*

The individual is measured against the backdrop of the world, which is the source of his status, and the status sought is always superlative and singular: *the greatest soldier of the world, senators alone of this great world, the greatest prince of the world, sole sir o' th' world.* But in a world that is in motion this ground of comparison is hardly dependable, and a man's status changes quite literally with the size and the shape of the world. Thus, it is at once a source of higher status and of greater anxiety in *Antony and Cleopatra* than it was in *Richard II.*

Another dimension of the fictional world can be measured by examining nouns introduced by the homophoric function of the definite article. This function yields a formal index to the objects, persons, values, and symbols that are seen as common knowledge by the characters in a work of literature and indeed by its author.[10] It is not so difficult to determine what nouns are self-specifying as it is to classify these nouns into categories designating components of the fictional world. Since no fully developed semantic theory exists, ad hoc categories have been derived for this purpose from the nouns modified by homophoric *the*. These categories include the physical universe of space and time, the four elements, and general references to the world; the social universe of references to the individual by name, part of the body, or faculty of soul, and to the individual by rank, occupation, nationality, and so on; and the cultural universe of artifacts, places, events, language, values, and ideas. To the first universe belong words like *the hill, the stars, the East*; to the second are assigned such terms as *the mind, the poor, the champion, the wise*; and to the last belong *the dice, the feast, the fancy, the gods.*[11]

When the self-evident objects in the fictional world of the two plays are examined, one finds, not unexpectedly, a significant emphasis on status in

[10] Since the definite article does not explain the noun it modifies, one can distinguish three ways in which it is specified by other means: anaphorically, if the head refers to a preceding explanatory word (*Lep.* "But *small* to greater matters must give way." *Eno.* "Not if *the small* come first" [*Ant.* 2.2.11-12]); homophorically, if the head is common knowledge ("To-night we'll wander through *the streets*" [*Ant.* 1.1.53]); and cataphorically, if the head is specified by a phrase or a clause that follows it ("and note *the qualities of people*" [*Ant.* 1.1.53-54]). See also M. A. K. Halliday, "Descriptive Linguistics in Literary Studies," in *English Studies Today*, ed. G. I. Duthie, pp. 26-39.

[11] For a complete list of the lexical items in each of these categories, see Tables A-20 through A-22. For a set of frequencies, see Table A-19.

Richard II with its plethora of dukes, earls, nobles, bishops, and duchesses. Although *Antony* does not lack its share of emperors, superfluous kings, and triumvirs, people are more often defined in economic and moral terms: *the seedsman, the hangman, the comedians; the fool, the liar, the discontents.* The self-evident physical universe differs from that revealed by the earlier study of all the determiners modifying nouns referring to the four elements and the world. The fact that the category *earth* is not well represented by homophoric *the* in *Richard II* complements the characteristic attitude toward land in this play; one does not readily speak of *the earth* as if it were common knowledge and common property. *Water*, a category as important as *world* in *Antony*, is similarly obscured in this survey confined to the definite article because a third of its occurrences are in expressions like *by sea, at sea, by sea and land.* Perhaps this ablative emphasis suggests that the sea not only is an aspect of the universe but also has important instrumental uses for the inhabitants of this fictional world. Among categories of culture, nouns designating place in *Richard II* tend to be enclosed areas like *the lists* or to imply indoor gatherings:

> Inquire at London, 'mongst the taverns there,
> For there, they say, he daily doth frequent,
> With unrestrained loose companions,
> Even such, they say, as stand in narrow lanes
>
> (5.3.5-8)

In *Antony* there are places large enough to accommodate the Egyptian populace, the shouting varletry, and the Roman legions:

> *Caes.*   Here's the manner of 't:
> I' th' market place on a tribunal silver'd
> Cleopatra and himself in chairs of gold
> Were publicly enthron'd.
>
> . . . .
>
> *Maec.*   This in the public eye?
>
> *Caes.* I' th' common show-place, where they exercise.
>
> (3.6.2-5, 11-12)

The reference to events, a time-oriented category, is four times greater in *Antony* than in *Richard II*. Half of the events in *Antony* are associated with battles and warfare. This study of the homophoric function of the definite article with its emphasis on ascribed status and enclosed place in *Richard II* fills out the earlier picture of the stable land-oriented world of that play, while the stress on achieved status and on time in *Antony* provides further evidence of its mobile and shifting world.

Time and change are major motifs in *Antony*, and the fact that they appeared so clearly in a study based on formal categories like determiners in general and the definite article in particular suggests that grammatical meaning can contribute as much to a specification of a critical term like *theme* as it did to the definition of the fictional world. Of course, the content words modified by the determiners contributed a great deal to the emergence of these themes, but the theme of time can be deduced from other, more formal, aspects of grammatical meaning, such as the temporal relative clauses discussed as characteristic of *Antony* in Chapter 3. The formal meanings of time and change can also be derived from verbs that have an obvious temporal meaning because they are inflected for tense. The verb system of these plays will not be examined in this study, but verbalized nouns, which presumably retain some temporal meaning, offer an interesting substitute. The text of *Antony and Cleopatra* has a high frequency of agent nouns, many of them coined: *world-sharers, reapers, dancer, haters, wishers, rhymers, boggler, jailer, teller, wearer, feeders, homager, breather, deserver, partaker, plighter, revenger* (2), *sworder, reconciler, runner, bringer, armourer, sleeper, master-leaver, surfeiter.*[12] These words seem to have all the activity popularly associated with verbs, although many of them as verbs are not particularly "active" (*wear, deserve, sleep, surfeit*) and a few are not derived from verbs at all (*sword, homage, armour*). But when these words are glossed in terms of their common feature, *agent*, they have the meaning of *one who wears, deserves, pays homage, wields a sword, dons armour,* and so on. Since an agent is one who *acts*, this feature is the source of the verbal and active character of these nouns. There is, in addition, an implication of present tense, for it is unlikely that one could gloss these words as *one who has jailed* or *one who will jail*. The agent morpheme, then, adds to its stems the verbal meaning of action in the present.

Gerunds, the most common type of verbal noun, do not increase significantly in *Antony*, but they are used with determiners to a significantly higher degree in that play than in *Richard II:*[13]

---

[12] For a complete list of nouns classified as agent nouns, see pp. 296 and 300.

[13] Table A-23 provides the evidence for an increase of specific determiners before gerunds. A list of words classified as gerunds or verbal nouns appears in Appendix A, p. 279.

But, sir, forgive me;
Since my becomings kill me when they do not
Eye well to you.

(1.3.95-97)

Have I my pillow left unpress'd in Rome,
Forborne the getting of a lawful race,
And by a gem of women, to be abus'd
By one that looks on feeders?

(3.13.106-109)

In the first passage from *Antony* the word *eye*, itself a noun turned verb, and the agent noun *feeders* in the second passage are, like the gerunds *getting* and *becomings*, functionally ambivalent. The context thus reinforces the verbal character of the nominalized form, while the use of determiners (*my* and *the*) reinforces their nominal character. Both types of reinforcement heighten the tension created by the double function of these constructions. In *Richard II*, on the other hand, there are elements that distract attention from the verbal noun:

Watching breeds leanness, leanness is all gaunt.
The pleasure that some fathers feed upon
Is my strict fast—I mean my children's looks—
And therein fasting hast thou made me gaunt.

(2.1.78-81)

How brooks your Grace the air
After your late tossing on the breaking seas?

(3.2.2-3)

After the gerund *watching*, attention is distracted by the repetition of *leanness* and the pun on *Gaunt*. *Fasting* in the same passage may be a gerund but it may also be a gerundive modifying *me* or even *thou*, which is physically closer to it. The participial use of *breaking* seems similarly to detract from the nominal force of *tossing* because it follows so soon upon it. The force of these verbal nouns in the passages from *Richard II* is thus weakened by competing devices. That Shakespeare later learned the value of space and position as well as of reinforcement by similar forms is evident in this striking use of the gerund:

Rather on Nilus' mud
Lay me stark-nak'd and let the waterflies

                    Blow me into abhorring!
                                    (5.2.58-60)

What might be termed Shakespeare's new awareness of the possibilities in the
gerund, especially of its use with a determiner, is clear from the following
passages, where the phrasing is nearly identical and where repetition not only
conveys the careful tone of controlled anger in the speakers but also suggests
on the part of the playwright a simple fascination with the construction:

> *Ant.*   My being in Egypt, Caesar,
>   What was't to you?
>
> *Caes.* No more than my residing here at Rome
>   Might be to you in Egypt. Yet if you there
>   Did practise on my state, your being in Egypt
>   Might be my question.
>   (2.2.35-40)
>
>   Thou hast forspoke my being in these wars,
>   And say'st it is not fit.
>   (3.7.3-4)

Another source of verbalized nouns in *Antony* is functional shift. While
the exact number of conversions in this or in any other play is debatable,
about half the agent nouns just cited are probably genuine instances, as are
the following: *ass unpolicied, discandying, pelleted, spaniel'd, boy my greatness, safed the bringer, paragon my man of men.* In several instances there is a
conflation of different functions. To use *safe* as a verb in place of the usual
make safe is not simply to make a verb of an adjective but to collapse the
predicator-complement relation into a single word. The same is true of *homager* (*to pay homage*) and *sworder* (*brandish a sword*) or of *spaniel'd* (*fawn
like a spaniel*) and *unpolicied* (*to outwit in the matter of policy*). Functional
shift, even more than the other verbalized nouns, has an internal tension born
of the conflation of functions. The predicator/complement composition
invites and challenges the reader or hearer to dissolve the construction into
its original components, and the fact that it is a nonce form gives it an ephem-
eral quality. These hints of imminent dissolution and transitoriness in functional shift, together with its relative abundance in *Antony*, make an important contribution to the theme of time and change in this play.[14]

[14] For a tentative list of instances of functional shift or conversion in *Antony and
Cleopatra*, see Appendix A, p. 300. Some time ago Donald W. Lee challenged the idea
that there is much functional shift in Shakespeare (*Functional Change in Early En-*

Formal features of the language of *Richard II* yield the meaning of stability associated with aspects of that play. The high frequency of adjectives is one of its most striking characteristics. Since adjectives describe properties of nouns, they tend, like nouns, to be associated with the static universe of objects and essences in contrast to the dynamic verbal world of action and time.[15] F. E. Halliday noted that phrases like *revengement and a scourge* were characteristic of the historical plays and romantic comedies written about the same time as *Richard II*: "This linking of words, phrases, and clauses by means of the conjunction 'and' is perhaps the most obvious characteristic of the middle style, a parallelism that contributes to the spaciousness of the verse, and gives to the long Lancastrian recitatives a pronounced epic flavour."[16] One might add that the sense of mass and balance created by these compounds adds to one's sense of stability in the play. The frequent use of rhyming couplets and of end-stopped lines creates a phonology appropriate to the enclosed places and snug universe of this play, where the lower world is sheltered and a man's ambitions are limited by an almost palpable firmament:[17]

> *York.*   Take not, good cousin, further than you should,
>   Lest you mistake. The heavens are over our heads.
>
> *Boling.* I know it, uncle, and oppose not myself
>   Against their will.
>
>   (3.3.16-19)

Another feature that may contribute to the formal meaning of changelessness is the presence of archaic phrases, which are especially noticeable in the ritual scenes of Act One: *a recreant and most degenerate traitor, on pain to be found false and recreant, this outdar'd dastard, so base a parle.* Some of these phrases are reminiscent of a time when French had a

---

glish). Hereward T. Price takes exception to Lee's contention in "Shakespeare's Parts of Speech," *San Francisco Quarterly* 18 (1952): 19.

[15] Bernard Groom, *The Diction of Poetry from Spenser to Bridges*, finds in the Spenserian diction of middle-period plays like *Richard II* a note of stability and universal order (p. 38).

[16] F. E. Halliday, *The Poetry of Shakespeare's Plays*, p. 106. For quantitative evidence supporting Halliday's remarks on linked words, see Table A-24.

[17] That *Richard II* employs end-stopped lines and rhymed couplet to a marked degree scarcely requires documentation, but evidence may be found in E. K. Chambers, *William Shakespeare: A Study of Facts and Problems*, I, 243-274, and in William A. Neilson and Ashley H. Thorndike, *The Facts about Shakespeare*, pp. 69-77. One of the Neilson and Thorndike tables appears in James V. Cunningham (ed.), *The Problem of Style*, p. 234.

stronger hold on English than it had in Shakespeare's day. French survived especially in legal language. It is not surprising, therefore, to find French locutions with postposed adjectives in speeches arguing for the legal rights of Bolingbroke:

> If you do wrongfully seize Hereford's rights,
> Call in the letters patents that he hath
> By his attorneys general to sue
> His livery, and deny his off'red homage,
> You pluck a thousand dangers on your head,
>   (2.1.201-205)

The legal expression *letters patents* appears again in 2.3.130, and the tendency to make the adjective agree in number with the noun is reflected also in *lords appellants* (4.1.104). One occasionally has the impression that the verbal character of certain suffixes was still alive for Shakespeare, especially in these lines where the verbal implication of *passage* and *manage* seems quite pronounced:

> See, see, King Richard doth himself appear,
> As doth the blushing discontented sun
> From out the fiery portal of the East
> When he perceives the envious clouds are bent
> To dim his glory and to stain the track
> Of his bright passage to the Occident.
>   (3.3.62-67)
>
> Down, down I come, like glist'ring Phaëton,
> Wanting the manage of unruly jades.
>   (3.3.178-179)

Here, incidentally, one finds that confluence of person, context, and image and the similar grammatical construction (*his bright passage to*, *the manage of*) which was noted earlier in the cooccurrence of Pompey, images of fortune and the sea, and constructions like *the ebb'd man, thy wan'd lip*.[18] Clearly, *Richard II* does not lack effective passages containing verbalized nouns.

It would be of some interest for a study of Shakespeare's developing sense of style and decorum to learn whether he deliberately created

[18] See pp. 71-72.

archaic overtones in the early scenes of *Richard II*. In any case, this evocation of the past contributes some formal features to the meaning of stability in this play because the past, being dead, lies beyond change:

> In that dead time when Gloucester's death was plotted,
> I heard you say, 'Is not my arm of length,
> That reacheth from the restful English court
> As far as Calais to mine uncle's head?'
>
> (4.1.10-13)

Although this scene where Aumerle is called to judgment by Bolingbroke does not lack obvious formulas, it is noteworthy that one does not sense in it the same degree of archaizing as one finds in the early scenes. This lack may indicate, among other things, that Bolingbroke threatens the stability of this world.

Verbal Emblems and Point of View

Point of view, the angle from which a character or a situation is described, can also be formalized in part by examining determiners. In the opening lines of *Antony and Cleopatra* the sentence *this dotage o'erflows the measure* has a particular subject governing a universal object. The determiners suggest that the issue raised does not lie in the existence of a vice called *dotage* but in the fact that a private vice has become a public threat. A certain indulgence in folly can be tolerated to a commonly accepted limit, but Antony, who has apparently been excused on other occasions, has now exceeded that limit. That his behavior threatens the social order is expressed by *the measure*, where the homophoric function of the definite article reveals the speaker's assumption of common knowledge, shared values, and moral consensus. Everyone is aware of *the measure* as everyone is aware of *the sun*. In the next lines the specific determiners that refer to Antony are contrasted with the nonspecific determiner used to describe Cleopatra:

> Those his goodly eyes
> That o'er the files and musters of the war
> Have glow'd like plated Mars, now bend, now turn
> The office and devotion of their view
> Upon a tawny front. His captain's heart,
> Which in the scuffles of great fights hath burst
> The buckles on his breast, reneges all temper
> And is become the bellows and the fan

              To cool a gypsy's lust.

                              (1.1.2-10)

The proportion of specific to nonspecific determiners in these lines is
twice that of the play as a whole.[19] Antony's heroic stature is built up by
the strong emphasis of possessives, demonstratives, and definites and also
by comparison with the contempt shown for Cleopatra in *a tawny front, a
gypsy's lust*, and (later) *a strumpet's fool*. All three of these nonspecific
groups occur in sentence-final position and just before the metrical caesura
so that they receive emphasis from the fading/falling intonation and the
marked pause. Even their internal phonological shape is the same (a word
of two syllables followed by a monosyllable). Philo's attitude toward
Cleopatra is apparent not only from the nouns *gypsy's lust* and *strumpet*
but also from his choice of the nonspecific determiner. Had he called
Cleopatra *the tawny front* or *the gypsy* he would have ascribed to her a
unique status in the social consciousness, such as he had assigned to *the
measure* or such as Roderigo accords Othello when he calls him *the thick-
lips* (1.1.66).
    Philo's view of Cleopatra is shared by other Roman speakers, and it is
similarly expressed by nonspecific determiners. Pompey refers to her as *a
certain queen* brought to Caesar in a mattress (with overtones of
quean/whore).[20] Caesar calls her *a whore*, Maecenas *a trull / That noises it
against us*. In his anger Antony speaks of her as *a right gypsy, a boggler, a
morsel cold upon / Dead Caesar's trencher*, and *a fragment of Gneius
Pompey's*. Enobarbus reminds Antony that she is *a wonderful piece of
work*. Cleopatra appears to share this opinion of herself because she too
favors the nonspecific determiner. But the indefinite article is often used
by other speakers to describe themselves, and, more important, Cleopatra's
use of this determiner is coupled with strikingly different nouns as the
play progresses:[21]

[19] In *Antony and Cleopatra* specific determiners (definite article, demonstratives,
possessives) outnumber nonspecific determiners (indefinite article, *any, some*, etc.)
by approximately four and a half to one, whereas in the first six lines of *Antony*
there are nine specific to one nonspecific determiner.
[20] Maurice Charney in *Shakespeare's Roman Plays* (p. 20) points out a possible pun
on *queen / quean* (whore) in 1.2.121. This pun may occur in *a certain queen*, as
well.
[21] With the exception of Caesar, the major characters in both plays use the indefinite article to describe themselves more often than they use any other determiner
except the possessive. For statistical information on the determiners used by Cleopatra, Antony, Caesar, Richard, and Bolingbroke, see Tables A-25 through A-29. For

Broad-fronted Caesar,
When thou wast here above the ground, I was
A morsel for a monarch;

(1.5.29-31)

A charge we bear i' th' war
And, as the president of my kingdom, will
Appear there for a man.

(3.7.17-19)

No more but e'en a woman, and commanded
By such poor passion as the maid that milks
And does the meanest chares.

(4.15.72-74)

The position of these speeches in the beginning, middle, and end of the
play suggests that Cleopatra moves from the Roman view of herself as
partial (*morsel, piece, fragment*) to a view of herself as a figure of power
(*president of my kingdom; a man*). The second stage asserts her dignity in
terms that have Roman overtones. After Antony's death, as Manfred
Weidhorn points out, she denies the privileged titles by which her servants
seek to rouse her from her swoon—*lady, madam, royal Egypt, Empress* and
affirms simply that she is a woman.[22] Her self-presentation progresses
from the deviant roles of *whore* and *man* to acceptance of her womanhood
and humanity. The third stage is a purgation that paves the way for the
final assertion of dignity through her inherited title of *queen* and her
achieved title of wife to Antony:

If your master
Would have a queen his beggar, you must tell him
That majesty, to keep decorum, must
No less beg than a kingdom.

(5.2.15-18)

Where art thou, death?
Come hither, come! Come, come, and take a queen
Worth many babes and beggars!

(5.2.46-48)

---

line references to the determiners used by each of these characters, see Tables B-8
through B-12.
[22] Manfred Weidhorn, "The Relation of Title and Name to Identity in Shakespearean Tragedy," *Studies in English Literature* 9 (1969): 303-319.

> Show me, my women, like a queen. Go fetch
> My best attires. I am again for Cydnus,
> To meet Mark Antony.
>
> (5.2.227-229)

> Husband, I come!
> Now to that name my courage prove my title!
>
> (5.2.290-291)

Further evidence of Cleopatra's emphasis on personal worth in the final act comes from her use of the demonstrative of exaltation:

> This mortal house I'll ruin,
> Do Caesar what he can.
>
> (5.2.51-52)

> Now no more
> The juice of Egypt's grape shall moist this lip.
>
> (5.2.284-285)

> Come, thou mortal wretch,
> With thy sharp teeth this knot intrinsicate
> Of life at once untie.
>
> (5.2.306-308)

Charmian's apostrophe to the dead Queen evokes her femininity, her eternal youth, and that curious blend of formality and informality which marks Cleopatra's personal style:

> Now boast thee, death, in thy possession lies
> A lass unparallel'd.
>
> (5.2.318-319)

The suggestion of nonentity and contempt that has so often accompanied the description of Cleopatra by the nonspecific determiner is at last canceled by the remarkable adjective that asserts forever her uniqueness.

While Antony addresses Cleopatra by a variety of affectionate terms that require no determiner—*chuck, love, lady, dame, girl, gentle, thou day o' th' world*—the most characteristic of these seems to be *Egypt*, which is reserved for moments of the greatest poignancy:

> O, whither hast thou led me, Egypt?
>
> . . . .

> Egypt, thou knew'st too well
> My heart was to thy rudder tied by th' strings,
> And thou shouldst tow me after.
>
> (3.11.51, 56-58)

> I am dying, Egypt, dying; only
> I here importune death awhile, until
> Of many thousand kisses the poor last
> I lay upon thy lips.
>
> (4.15.18-21)

Egypt combines the sense of power and mystery, of queen and gypsy, that informs a good portion of Antony's address and reference to Cleopatra. He is the only person other than herself to use the demonstrative of her, and it is generally to gain distance from her. That the attempt is foredoomed to failure is clear from the fact that half of the demonstratives modify nouns referring to Egypt or to terms designating its magical power: *these strong Egyptian fetters, this enchanting queen, this foul Egyptian, this false soul of Egypt, this grave charm.*

Caesar's view of Cleopatra is appropriately political. He generally refers to her by name or by title: *the Queen of Ptolemy, the Queen, the Queen of Egypt.* He addresses her as *good Queen, dear Queen,* and he calls her *Egypt* when they meet. Once he forgets his manners and his dignity and refers to her as a whore, but he is never capable of seeing in her that combined charm and dignity which fascinates Antony and which enables even Agrippa to call her *royal wench* and *rare Egyptian.*

Possessive determiners (*my, your, her,* etc.) furnish a clue to those objects, characteristics, and interpersonal relations that a speaker sees as his own or that are seen by others to belong particularly to him. When they modify objects or parts of the body, they acquire an emblematic function that serves to identify and to stabilize the character amid the changing points of view. Thus, there is no special distinction between Cleopatra's view of her person and the way in which other characters see her. Her femininity, fertility, and royalty are captured in expressions like *my breast, the memory of my womb,* and *my bluest veins.* Her possessions are symbols of her queenly power: *my/our crown* (4), *my sceptre, my country, my kingdom, my Egypt, my brave Egyptians all; my tires and mantles, my best attires, my robe.* These are emblems of the ruler and several of them appear in the speeches of King Richard.

An examination of moral qualities ascribed to Cleopatra and introduced by possessive determiners yields material more closely related to the thematic and dramatic facets of her personality. Other speakers ascribe no faults to Cleopatra, although she herself acknowledges some; these are mentioned early in the play, whereas reference to the better traits clusters in the later scenes. Thus, she speaks of *my becomings, my unpitied folly* (1.3); *my former sharpness* (3.3); *mine honour* (3.13); *my resolution* (4.15); *my resolution, my greatness, my noble act, my courage* (5.2). Thyreus first mentions *your honour* (3.13) and Antony repeats it (4.15); Caesar speaks of *her greatness* (5.1) and *your wisdom* (5.2). The movement toward nobility parallels that already noted with respect to the nonspecific determiner and suggests that the view of Cleopatra changes in the course of the dramatic action and also that the change is deliberately created. Many possessive determiners modify nouns referring directly or metaphorically to aspects of time, change, and fortune: *my oblivion, my salad days, my music, my birthday, my chance, my death, my life, my heaven, my baby . . .that sucks the nurse asleep; thy sovereign leisure, her fortunes, her death* (2), *her life in Rome.* To these might be added a few references to the sea: *mine angle, my bended hook, my fearful sails, thy rudder, your angling.* These quick verbal strokes introduced by the possessive determiner reveal the ruler, the woman, and the human being subject to time and change. Like so much in Shakespeare's art they are representational rather than realistic or naturalistic. The dramatic reality of Cleopatra, of course, is not exhausted by a list of her possessions or even of all nouns that refer to her. She emerges as a living person only in the total action and dialogue and movement of the entire play.

Among the nouns modified by possessive determiners and used to describe Antony's physical appearance one finds emblems that yield insight into his personality. His neck is *arm'd*, indicating his martial disposition. His references to *my blood, sides*, and *stomach* imply the passions of which these physical elements are the source. *Hair*, mentioned several times, has associated with it the physical property of grayness, but it is really a symbol of Antony's age and folly. Just as bodily parts serve to represent states of soul, so the facets of his personality are expressed by the material objects he possesses. In terms of such objects one sees the Antony of *Julius Caesar* who games with cocks and quails, who is the seasoned warrior in *armour, helmet,* and *sword*, and whose wealth is summed up by *my fleet* and *my treasure.* He is the night reveler and, notwithstanding, the shrewd leader of men:

Well, my good fellows, wait on me tonight.
Scant not my cups, and make as much of me
As when mine empire was your fellow too
And suffer'd my command.

(4.2.20-23)

He is the doting lover who speaks to Cleopatra of *my playfellow, your hand* and the faithful lover/faithless husband who talks of leaving *my pillow unpress'd in Rome*. With one exception, whenever Antony speaks of his heart it is seen as subject to Cleopatra, a love/honor ambivalence that appears in the words that he uses most often with the possessive determiner—*queen* (8), *heart* (7), and *sword* (6).

Antony's concept of himself is relatively interiorized. He speaks of *my idleness, despair, shame, baseness, greatness, honour, honesty,* and *glory,* and, in his own eyes, at least, such generous acknowledgment of faults carries an implied request for pardon and consequent extenuation of them:

Sir,
He fell upon me ere admitted. Then
Three kings I had newly feasted, and did want
Of what I was i' th' morning; but next day
I told him of myself, which was as much
As to have ask'd him pardon.

(2.2.74-79)

One perceives in Antony's catalogue of his qualities a balance of good and bad traits detectable also in those attributed to him by his fellow Romans: *this dotage, his captain's heart* (Philo); *his faults, all his goodness, the noble Antony* (Lepidus); *his honour, his soldiership, this amorous sur feiter, the libertine, the ne'er-lust-wearied Antony* (Pompey); *the best of men, his insolence* (Agrippa); *his offence, his well-paid ranks, that magical word of war* (Ventidius); *his abominations, one so great* (Maecenas); *the noble ruin, a doting mallard* (Scarus); *a sworder, a fall'n lord, mine of bounty, nobler than my revolt is infamous* (Enobarbus). This citation of phrases out of context ignores the fact that many speakers see Antony's bad qualities as subduing and vitiating the good, and it fails to recognize the ironic remarks made of Antony, particularly by Ventidius, who alone casts aspersions on his military prowess, and by the schoolmaster, who suggests in Antony a less than large-hearted tendency to honor men according to his convenience (3.12.8-10). Nevertheless, the list has some force in suggesting that men cannot mention Antony's faults without admitting his virtues.

If anyone tips the balance against Antony, it is Caesar, who describes him as *a man who is the abstract of all faults | That all men follow* (1.4.9-10), yet names only faults of sensuality: *his foils, his lightness, his vacancy, his voluptuousness, his sport, his shames, his flaw; thy wassails; your excuses; the old ruffian.* As Enobarbus is later to discover from observing Caesar himself, there are worse faults than passion in a leader (4.6.12-20), though no one in the play attributes these worse traits to Antony. The few compliments that Caesar allows Antony—*thine honour, so like a soldier; so great a thing, his glory*—are clearly tinged with the political myopia that makes Caesar first mention Antony as *our great competitor* (partner) and that makes it impossible for him to praise Antony objectively even when he is safely dead:

> But we do lanch
> Diseases in our bodies. I must perforce
> Have shown to thee such a declining day
> Or look on thine: we could not stall together
> In the whole world.
>
> (5.1.36-40)

Cleopatra is the natural counter to Caesar, not only because she is less inclined than he to list Antony's faults, but also because she does not anatomize him after the fashion of Caesar and the other Roman speakers. Her view of Antony shifts from the early mockery of *thy cheek, that blood of thine, that same eye, his chafe* to terms that designate the whole man—personal pronouns (*he, him*), titles (*my lord*), and, above all, his name (*my brave Mark Antony, the curled Antony*). If one compares the speeches of Cleopatra and of Caesar, one finds that Cleopatra's mention of the whole man Antony is three times more frequent than her reference to aspects of his personality, whereas whole and part are closer together in Caesar's references to him. Table 31 provides evidence for this statement.[23] Even when Cleopatra distinguishes facets of Antony's personality, it is in a context of completeness:

[23] In Table 31, references to the whole Antony by Caesar and Cleopatra include their use of his name, as well as nouns introduced by zero determiner and by the definite article. References to the part include nouns preceded by the possessive determiner. The totals are smaller than their total reference to Antony, since some of these include irrelevant material. The proportions are not significantly different, but Cleopatra's reference to the whole man is some 14 percent higher than Caesar's.

> O well-divided disposition! Note him,
> Note him, good Charmian; 'tis the man; but note him!
> He was not sad, for he would shine on those
> That make their looks by his; he was not merry,
> Which seem'd to tell them his remembrance lay
> In Egypt with his joy; but between both.
>
> (1.5.53-58)

Table 31
Modes of Reference to Antony

Speaker	Part	Whole
Cleopatra	20	70
Caesar	15	27

Her most thorough analysis of Antony occurs in her dream vision (5.2.82-92), yet here again the mention of so many parts together adds up to a complete man.

And this finally is the point to be made about the balance of qualities in Antony: He is a total human being, one whose qualities, good or bad, deserve equal mention. This impression is not only a product of Cleopatra's bias in his favor but also the final Roman judgment of Antony expressed by Maecenas and Agrippa, whose statements are unhampered by Caesar's special concerns:

> *Maec.*   His taints and honours
>   Wag'd equal with him.
>
> *Agr.*   A rarer spirit never
>   Did steer humanity; but you gods will give us
>   Some faults to make us men.
>
>   (5.1.30-33)

This tribute bears comparison with Antony's own apostrophe to the dead Brutus in a much earlier play:

> His life was gentle, and the elements
> So mix'd in him that Nature might stand up
> And say to all the world, 'This was a man!'
>   (*JC* 5.5.73-75)

Though the four elements were intimately connected with personality in the psychology of Shakespeare's day, one feels there is an important distinction (apart from what we know of Brutus and Antony in the two plays) between the man who consists of the four elements and the man of taints and honors. The latter indeed seems the more admirable for his human frailty, but the point, for the present, is not whether Brutus is a nobler man than Antony or whether Antony's role of hero in the later play falls to him by default, but that both men are judged to be men on the basis of a certain integrity or harmony of being and that their very manhood suffices to win approbation. One may recall in this context Hamlet's eulogy of his father: *He was a man, take him for all in all. / I shall not look upon his like again* (1.2.187-188).

Would you praise Caesar, says Enobarbus as he and Agrippa comment ironically on relations among the triumvirs, *say 'Caesar'–go no further*. Whether through intention to praise, through fascination with the name, or through some dramatic motive, Shakespeare has identified Caesar by his name. Not only does the mention of it outnumber that of other characters—[Octavius] Caesar (150), Antony (141), Cleopatra (31)—but it also is almost an exclusive mode of reference and address to him. Fifty percent of the total references to Caesar are by name, compared with 22 percent for Antony and 7 percent for Cleopatra. Where Antony's name is varied with forms like *Antonius, Antonio, Mark Antony, Marcus Antonius*, he is always *Caesar*. Such variety as is offered to the mention of Caesar comes chiefly from slurs cast by Antony on *our Caesar* or by Cleopatra on the *ass unpolicied*. Phrases introduced by *the*, used elsewhere to praise Antony (*the firm Roman, the triple pillar of the world, the best of men*), are applied to Caesar ironically: *the scarce-bearded Caesar, the young Roman boy, the boy Caesar*.

In the possessions that Caesar ascribes to himself one finds none of the imperial opulence characteristic of Antony and of Cleopatra. There is instead some rather ascetic reference to *my tent, my letters, my missive, my writings*, which agrees well with the mention of such parts of the body as *my tongue, my brain, my hand, my body, our will, our flesh* and of these inner dispositions: *my intent, my business, my bond, my state, my band, my purposes, my thinking, my question; thy biddings, your business, your cause, your ends, his power* (3), *his mandate*. Even Caesar's feelings are rendered hollow by the imperial possessive that precedes them: *our love, our care and pity, our triumph*. The one human title accorded him is *brother*, yet even his feeling for *my sister* is vitiated by his willingness to regard her as a hoop to mend his shaky political alliance with

Antony (2.2.116-118) and to treat her as his *alter ego*: *You come not* / *Like Caesar's sister* (3.6.42-43).

If there is one word in addition to his name that identifies Caesar, it is his use of the auxiliary that Shakespeare calls the *absolute shall* (*Cor.* 3.1.89-90). *Shall* occurs four times as often in his speech as the modal *will*. The overbalance of *shall* can be further appreciated from Table 32, which

Table 32
Proportion of *Shall* to *Will* in the Speeches
of Major Characters

Speaker	*Shall/Shalt*	*Will/Wilt*
Antony	29	28
Cleopatra	24	29
Caesar	23	4
Richard	38	20
Bolingbroke	25	15

shows that in the language of Antony and of Cleopatra the proportion of *shall* to *will* is one to one.[24] *Shall* appears to have several functions in the speech of all three characters: those of solemn promise, of prophesy, and of command:

> No, sweet Octavia,
> You shall hear from me still. The time shall not
> Outgo my thinking on you.
>
> (3.2.59-61)
>
> The time of universal peace is near.
> Prove this a prosp'rous day, the three-nook'd world
> Shall bear the olive freely.
>
> (4.6.5-7)
>
> Arise! You shall not kneel.
> I pray you rise. Rise, Egypt.
>
> (5.2.114-115)

[24] Table 32 provides the frequencies with which the major characters in the two plays use the modal auxiliaries *shall* and *will*. The variants *shalt* and *wilt* but not *should, would,* etc. are included. *Will* as a noun and a main verb *(read his will, think what you will)* have been omitted. The proportion of *shall* to *will* is significantly different in the speeches of Caesar and Antony (χ^2 = 7.9200), but not in those of Richard and Bolingbroke.

There seem to be no explicit criteria by which the three functions can be distinguished, but the use of *shall* can at least be termed a marker of formality in Caesar's style. With his name as subject and this modal as predicate, one has a fairly complete picture of Caesar, *kaiser* and *imperator*: *Caesar shall.*[25]

Caesar's presentation of himself as a man who relies on native shrewdness and who is devoted to his sister, the chaste Roman matron, and the general view of him as the archetypal ruler are given a further dimension by Antony, Cleopatra, and Enobarbus. Antony mocks his soldiership in terms often used by Shakespeare's plain blunt soldiers to describe effeminate courtiers (*a dancer, his gay comparisons, his points*), but he recognizes in Caesar the soldier of fortune whose cocks and quails beat his own against odds. His awareness of Caesar's youth is akin to his perception of him as a man of waxing fortune: *blossoming Caesar, the approaching Caesar*. These epithets accord well with a set of possessives that are as characteristic of him as the cerebral attributes cited above: *his chance, his vantage, his fortunes, his fate, his happiness*. Cleopatra, who confers on him some of his best titles (*thy greatness, thy might, thy grace, thy lordliness*), also recognizes that it is paltry to be Caesar, since he is only *Fortune's knave, a minister of her will*.

The technique of fashioning characters through verbal emblems is as skilled in *Richard II* as it is in *Antony and Cleopatra*. The presentation of King Richard (to the extent that determiners can reveal it) moves from a generalized picture of him as *the King* to greater specification in Act Three, some degree of interiorization in the fourth act, and the final insight that

> Nor I, nor any man that but man is,
> With nothing shall be pleas'd till he be eas'd
> With being nothing.
>
> (5.5.39-41)

Although Richard is always conscious of his royal office, in the acts prior to his return from Ireland his frequent use of the royal *we* suggests he is more concerned with playing the role of king than with thinking about it.

[25] R. A. Foakes first called attention to the high frequency of proper names in *Julius Caesar* ("An Approach to *Julius Caesar*," *Shakespeare Quarterly* 5 [1954]: 259-270) where he notes that the name *Caesar* had "long been in use to signify an all-conquering, absolute monarch" (p. 266).

He uses the plural possessive not only in the self-conscious ritual scenes
(e.g., 1.3.119-143) but also in moments of brisker business:

> And we create, in absence of ourself,
> Our uncle York Lord Governor of England;
> For he is just and always lov'd us well.
> Come on, our queen. To-morrow must we part.
> Be merry, for our time of stay is short.
>
> (2.1.219-223)

Upon his return to England, even before the extent of Bolingbroke's
strength and the weakness of his position are reported to him, Richard is
psychologically the individual rather than the king. His first speech is
uttered in the first person singular:

> I weep for joy
> To stand upon my kingdom once again.
> Dear earth, I do salute thee with my hand,
> Though rebels wound thee with their horses' hoofs.
>
> (3.2.4-7)

This shift in language suggests that the least threat to his power suffices to
fill him with self-doubt. Reminded that he is king, he reverts momentarily
to the royal pronoun:

> Are we not high?
> High be our thoughts.
>
> (3.2.88-89)

But the interrogative and imperative modes of this reflection lack conviction. His last use of the royal pronoun refers to his kingship in hypotheti-
cal-statement and indirect-discourse constructions:

> We are amaz'd; and thus long have we stood
> To watch the fearful bending of thy knee,
> Because we thought ourself thy lawful king.
> And if we be, how dare thy joints forget
> To pay their awful duty to our presence?
> If we be not, show us the hand of God
> That hath dismiss'd us from our stewardship;
> For well we know no hand of blood and bone

> Can gripe the sacred handle of our sceptre,
> Unless he do profane, steal, or usurp.
>
> (3.3.72-81)

When Richard begins to reflect upon the fact that he is king, he uses a syntax of doubt that expresses the degree to which his conviction has been shaken. In this act where Richard discards the imperial *we*, the verbal symbol of privilege and the prerogative of the few, he takes up the inclusive *we* in the speech beginning *Let's talk of graves, of worms, and epitaphs*. This new function of the pronoun *we/our* in his speech acknowledges his common humanity as clearly as the tenor of the speech itself.

Together with the shift from *our* to *my* and from imperial to inclusive *we/our*, the notion of *a king* appears for the first time in Richard's language:[26]

> Look not to the ground,
> Ye favourites of a king.
>
> (3.2.87-88)

> for within the hollow crown
> That rounds the mortal temples of a king
> Keeps Death his court;
>
> (3.2.160-162)

> Subjected thus,
> How can you say to me I am a king?
>
> (3.2.176-177)

> A king, woe's slave, shall kingly woe obey.
>
> (3.2.210)

The nonspecific determiner *a/an*, contrasted with the definite article or proper names (*the King, King Richard*), implies one of several kings, and Richard's increasing use of it represents a further expression of his growing

---

[26] The figures in Table 33 include all references to King Richard by himself and all other characters. If the figures for *the King, King Richard*, and *Our* were totaled and labeled "Formal" or "Impersonal," while all others were added and labeled "Informal" or "Personal," the evidence would be still more striking. In the deposition scene alone, Richard uses *a king* eight times as if to impress upon Bolingbroke the transitory, nonunique character of this status. The introduction of this phrase is by the Duke of York, who reminds Richard that his office depends upon due succession (2.1.198); its second use is by Bolingbroke (3.1.8) in a passage describing both himself and Richard in terms of the nonspecific determiner. This usage may suggest a tendency on his part to emphasize their equality.

awareness of the split between role and person and of the fact that he is not *the King* but *a king*. The use of his given name contributes another factor to the verbal process by which Richard is presented as the king in early scenes and emerges as an individual at the end of the play. Reference to him as *the King* is nearly four times as numerous in the first two acts as the combined mention of him as *King Richard* and *Richard*. By the third act, however, these last two designations outnumber *the King*; and in the last two acts *Richard*, the most personal of the three terms, outnumbers the other two.[27] These changes are summarized in Table 33.

Table 33
Modes of Reference to King Richard

Act	a King	the King	King Richard	Richard	Our(sg.)	My/Mine
I	0	8	3	0	38	8
II	1	22	0	5	9	1
III	8	11	10	5	12	40
IV	8	2	0	7	0	43
V	4	4	3	6	0	23
Total	21	47	16	23	59	115

A final means of tracing Richard's progress from generalized king to the man of the last soliloquy is to examine the kinds of nouns modified by the first person possessives. In the first two acts, reference to himself or to his family is infrequent compared with mention of his political concerns: *our leisure, presence, subject, doctors, officers-at-arms; law, Council, kingdom's earth, peace, dominions, sentence, part, state, subjects, land, justice; England, coffers, royal realm, subjects, affairs, substitutes, wants, soldiers; Irish wars, pilgrimage, assistance, time of stay; my seat, my sceptre's awe.* These nouns, all introduced by possessive determiners in Richard's speeches, refer to affairs of state and may be termed impersonal compared with mention of parts of the body or of his relationship to other people (*cousin, eyes and ears, blood, cheek, hands, Uncle Gaunt, father's brother's son*, etc.). Impersonal possessions (34) outnumber personal possessions (22) in all the speeches of Richard in Acts One and Two, as

[27] It is important to observe in Table 33 that the totals do not reflect important dynamic developments in the play. A study of the language in each act of the play would doubtless be rewarding.

Table 34
Personal and Impersonal Possessives in King Richard's Speeches

Act	Personal		Impersonal		Total	
	My/Mine	*Our*	*My/Mine*	*Our*	Personal	Impersonal
I	4	11	4	27	15	31
II	0	7	1	2	7	3
III	20	2	20	10	22	30
IV	28	0	15	0	28	15
V	18	0	5	0	18	5
Total	70	20	45	39	90	84

Table 34 shows.[28] This point might not be so remarkable if both Boling-broke and Mowbray did not present themselves in highly personal terms (as a perusal of their possessive determiners shows) or if there were no early attempts by Mowbray, Gaunt, and York to ascribe to Richard attri-butes of a more personal character. Clearly, personal pronouns, proper names, titles, and possessions combine to present Richard with the reserve, courtesy, and distance befitting his kingly role in the first two acts of the play. This presentation is shared by Richard and by other characters with the exception of Mowbray (1.1.111-114, 126-131, 165-169) and of Gaunt and York in the second act.

In the remaining acts Richard's mention of personal nouns increases, and among the lists of nouns modified by the possessive determiner one can distinguish further between personal nouns that designate external objects (goods, persons) and those that manifest interior dispositions (emotions and those parts of the body that symbolize them). A third of the posses-sives used by Richard in Act Four refer to his inner dispositions and another third to parts of the body. He speaks of *my griefs* (4), *glories*, *cares* (2), *folly*, *wretchedness*, *cross*, *sins*, *sorrow* (2); of *my limbs*, *hand*

[28] Table 34 supplies the evidence for the statement that in the speeches of King Richard the first person possessive determiner reveals in the nouns that it modifies a preference for personal nouns over impersonal nouns as the play progresses. Personal nouns are defined as parts of the body (*my heart*, *my head*), feelings (*my griefs*), and designations of kinship (*my wife*, *my uncle*), while impersonal nouns are defined as affairs of state (*our Irish wars*), possessions (*my kingdom*, *my goblets*), and designa-tions of people from a political or a social point of view (*our doctors*, *mine enemy*). Possessive determiners include *my*, *mine*, and *our* (sg.). In compounds and in series like *My manors, rents, revenues I forgo* (4.1.212) each noun is counted as a possessive even if it is not directly modified by a determiner.

(3), *head, heart, tears, tongue, breath, eyes* (2), *soul*, and *face*. Thus, by the fourth act, when the deposition has been accomplished, there is a marked increase of the name *Richard*, the phrase *a king*, reference to personal possessions, the exclusive use of *my* rather than *our* (sg.), and, among personal possessions, a high frequency of reference to inner dispositions.

While this analysis of Richard's character is necessarily incomplete, it does represent a real dimension of the language in the play and it reveals a changing pattern of reference to King Richard by himself and others. Hence, it is worth noting that, when he consciously mentions his inner dispositions, he names feelings of grief, sorrow, and care. Pride, jealousy, anger, ambition—the emotional and moral stuff of Shakespeare's later tragic heroes—are absent. Richard is not so much aware of faults as he is of misery. Even reflections on name and language, which many critics view as central to his tragedy, are subordinated to the emotion of grief.[29] To the extent that a study of possessive determiners and of the nouns they modify can yield insight into Richard's tragic development, it reveals an early preoccupation with kingship and the later expressions of sadness. It does not suggest, however, that his sorrow necessarily stems from the loss of his kingdom. On the contrary, Richard's sorrow is quite generalized, and it seems to proceed rather from the realization that to be simply human and without power is to be unhappy.

As might be expected, the presentation of Bolingbroke pursues a course opposite to Richard's—from particularized individual to generalized king. His early role of knight and noble is pictured with greater detail than that of Richard's kingship. Though vilified by Mowbray, he first appears as a man of epic qualities. The Duchess of Gloucester views him as her champion against the injustice of Woodstock's death, his father as the heir to his fabled title, and the nobles as a check on the king's power. Considering that he speaks nearly half as many lines as Richard, his presentation of himself through the use of possessive determiners exceeds that of Richard.[30] These possessives abound in the first act whether they be mentioned through Bolingbroke's own heroic boasts, Mowbray's insults, or Gaunt's encouragement: *my speech, prince, greeting, body, divine soul,*

[29] See Tables A-33 and A-34 for data on references to language and grief in the speeches of King Richard and Bolingbroke.

[30] Bolingbroke's presentation of himself in terms of possessive determiners exceeds that of Richard by 12 percent. Richard's total use of the first possessive is 174 of his total references (236), yielding .7330. Bolingbroke's is 109 of 128, yielding .8515.

sovereign (2), *tongue* (2), *blood* (2), *honour, life, descent, father, height, teeth, knee, lord, cousin, head, innocency, comfort, banishment, enemy, heart, freedom, mother, nurse*; *thy heart, throat, good cause, blows, words, friends, grief, youth, cause,* etc.; *his throat, blood, bosom, heartblood.* The rather intimate detail provided by these material and spiritual possessions, especially when it is contrasted with the impersonalized attributes of Richard noted above, enlists one's sympathy for Bolingbroke as a fellow human being.

Critics have questioned the extent to which Bolingbroke aspired to the crown or had it thrust upon him by Richard's incompetence and the barons' restlessness.[31] Although Richard's view of his cousin may well be prejudiced by his own part in Woodstock's death (1.2.37-41) and his consequent fear of exposure, a study of possessives as emblematic of character lends some credence to Richard's opinion that Bolingbroke is an ambitious schemer from the outset. If any bodily part, for example, serves as an emblem of the future King Henry the Fourth, it is the knee, symbol of courtesy and flattery; and this fact forms an appropriate contrast with Richard's emblem, the ear ever open to flattery (2.1.4, 16-26, etc.). In no other English history play are *knee* and *ear* so firmly balanced in frequency.[32] Half the references to knees in this play are to Bolingbroke, the remainder being associated with Aumerle and the Duchess of York, who beg his mercy in the final act. The readiness with which Bolingbroke crooks his supple knee not only is noted through Richard's eyes (1.4.32-33) but also is witnessed by the audience on three separate occasions:

> Lord Marshal, let me kiss my sovereign's hand
> And bow my knee before his Majesty;
> For Mowbray and myself are like two men
> That vow a long and weary pilgrimage.
>
> (1.3.46-49)

> Fair cousin, you debase your princely knee
> To make the base earth proud with kissing it.
> Me rather had my heart might feel your love
> Than my unpleas'd eye see your courtesy.
> Up, cousin, up! Your heart is up, I know,

[31] Brents Stirling, for example, argues that deposing Richard does not become an issue for Bolingbroke before their meeting at Flint Castle ("Bolingbroke's 'Decision,' " *Shakespeare Quarterly* 2 [1951]: 27-34).

[32] See Tables A-31 and A-32.

Thus high at least, although your knee be low.

(3.3.190-195)

Boling. I shall not need transport my words by you;
Here comes his Grace in person. My noble uncle!

[*Kneels.*]

York. Show me thy humble heart, and not thy knee,
Whose duty is deceivable and false.

(2.3.81-84)

The last of these shows that Richard is not the only person to suspect the sincerity of this gesture, and there is further evidence of Bolingbroke's specious humility in the rudeness of his speech to Berkeley and his ready curtsy to his uncle. The distinction between this sign of submission and the intention of the signmaker is most apparent when Northumberland delivers Bolingbroke's message and must be reminded by Richard to kneel, even though Bolingbroke has enjoined humble behavior and gracious words (3.3.32-38, 72-76, 114-115).

Perhaps it is significant of something more than Richard's weakness that Bolingbroke's message results in the King's capitulation. Sometimes seen as a man of action and a foil to Richard's reliance on wordplay, Bolingbroke in fact makes good use of that second vehicle of flattery, speech. His fondness for talk is noted by enemy and friend alike. Mowbray first accuses him of waging a *woman's war* of words (1.1.47-50); Northumberland praises his *fair discourse* (2.3.6-7); and he himself makes much of returning favors with thanks, *the exchequer of the poor* (2.3.65). If one looks at the evidence provided by possessive determiners, there is as much reference to Bolingbroke's use of language as to Richard's. The latter speaks of *my name, conjuration, word, breath, tongue*; others speak to Richard of *thy/your word, sentence* and refer to *his title.* Bolingbroke exceeds this list with *my speech, greeting* (2), *leave* (2), *words* (2), *commends, breath, tongue* (2); others mention *thy/your speech, words, discourse, quarrel, tongue* (2), *mouth,* and refer to *his demands, words.*[33]

It may be that, despite his show of power, Bolingbroke, even in *Richard II*, is portrayed not so much as a man of action but as a diplomat and a politician, a feature that he shares with Caesar, whom he resembles in several other respects. In general, Bolingbroke is correct and courteous in

---

[33] The hypothesis that preoccupation with language characterizes Bolingbroke as much as Richard is advanced with great tentativeness; the evidence is presented in Tables A-33 and A-34.

his mention of King Richard (although his mention of Richard moves from great formality to the familiar *Richard* and *cousin* of the later acts). But, just as Caesar's decorous reference to Cleopatra once slips into calling her *a whore* (when he is strongly provoked by Octavia's return), so Bolingbroke speaks finally of *this living fear* and *this terror*, and the effectiveness of such lapses is enhanced by the general decorum usually exhibited in the language of both Caesar and Bolingbroke. Bolingbroke also shares with Caesar the fact that his name occurs with an extraordinarily high frequency. The names of *Hereford* and *Bolingbroke* taken together appear a total of eighty times, and there are half a dozen other references to *Lancaster* and *Harry*. But Bolingbroke shares traits with Antony as well—his knighthood, his wealth and easy promise of bounty to followers, his democratic courtship of the common man, his sense of fortune, and the ascription to himself of similar virtues (*honour* [2], *bounty* [2], *duty*, *service*, *courtesy*, *valour*). With Caesar he shares a great emphasis on name, a sense of political decorum in language, and a preference for diplomacy rather than force. That this study of determiners should reveal features in a single character that are later more sharply divided between the verbal portraits of Antony and Caesar may be a reflection of his ambiguous role (usurper yet finally king).

Emphasis and Elevation: The Nominal Group

The determiners that have been the focus of Chapter Four constitute only one aspect of nominal-group structure. The final section of this chapter will be devoted to a consideration of other aspects of the nominal group, especially those elements that serve to heighten the diction of the two plays and to give it point and emphasis. Among these must be proper names and noble titles, which constitute a substantial 10 percent of the content words and 5 percent of all words in each play.[34] In this respect the plays are similar, but the proportion of name to title differs significantly. There are twice as many names as titles in *Antony* and almost as many titles as names in *Richard II*.[35] Although there is only a 2 percent

[34] Assuming that content words constitute roughly half of most texts, the total verse words in each play were divided by 2 and the reduced figure used to obtain the ratio of names and titles among content words. In *R2* 1,060 of 10,904 and in *Ant.* 1,152 of 10,888 yield, respectively, .0972 and .1058, or roughly 10 percent of the content words. For other procedures used in the analysis of names and titles, see the notes that accompany Tables A-35 to A-37.

[35] The proportion of names to titles in the two plays, as listed in Table 35, is significantly different: $\chi^2 = 40.9779$.

increase of names in the later play, those mentioned most often occur with much higher frequencies than the highest-ranking names in *Richard II*. Thus *God*, which ranks first in *Richard II*, occurs 67 times, and *Boling-broke*, which holds next place, occurs 49 times. In the later play, *Caesar* ranks first with 150 occurrences and *Antony* (135) is a close second.[36] But the most important differences between names in the two plays are inspired by phonology.

Monosyllables like *Gaunt* and *York* are five times more frequent in *Richard II* than monosyllabic names in the later play, while in *Antony* polysyllables like *Ventidius* and *Enobarbus* are six times more frequent than they are in *Richard II*. There are also twice as many names of three syllables in *Antony*, so that it would be reasonable to assume that names of three or more syllables are a stylistic feature of that play. By their polysyllabic phonology, names like *Charmian*, *Cleopatra*, and *Enobarbus* invoke the classical world where Latin and Greek were dominant languages.[37] Allied to this pattern of phonology in the internal composition of proper names is the use of names in reference or in direct address. Normally, reference to a name effects no change in rhythm unless there is apposition, but direct adress creates one or two pauses, depending on its position in the sentence:

> Ink and paper, Charmian.
> Welcome, my good Alexas. Did I, Charmian,
> Ever love Caesar so?
>
> *(Ant.* 1.5.65-67)

Table 35 shows that direct address doubles in *Antony*, and this preference for vocatives is reflected in its use of titles as well.[38] The change undoubtedly increases the dramatic character of the language, since vocatives are markers of inclusion, but the combination of internal phonology and of increased direct address makes a major contribution to the sound pattern of *Antony and Cleopatra*. The stylistic difference between the two plays can be appreciated from these passages, where the

---

[36] See Table A-36 for the rank of high-frequency names in the two plays.

[37] See Table A-37 for syllables per name in the plays, together with procedural notes.

[38] See the totals in Table 35, which show how often names and titles are used in reference or in direct address. The proportion of vocatives to reference among names yields $\chi^2 = 39.4210$; for this set of proportions among titles, $\chi^2 = 4.9756$. Both results show significant differences between the plays.

Table 35
Vocative and Referential Functions of Names and Titles

	Names			Titles		
	Vocative	Reference	Total	Vocative	Reference	Total
R2	74	539	613	167	280	447
Ant.	209	608	817	223	112	335

count of lines and of names per line is similar but where the effect of names is remarkably dissimilar:

> Many a time hath banish'd Norfolk fought
> For Jesu Christ in glorious Christian field,
> Streaming the ensign of the Christian cross
> Against black pagans, Turks, and Saracens;
> And, toil'd with works of war, retir'd himself
> To Italy; and there, at Venice, gave
> His body to that pleasant country's earth
> And his pure soul unto his captain, Christ,
>
> (*R2* 4.1.92-99)

Ven. Now, darting Parthia, art thou stroke, and now
> Pleas'd fortune does of Marcus Crassus' death
> Make me revenger. Bear the King's son's body
> Before our army. Thy Pacorus, Orodes,
> Pays this for Marcus Crassus.

Sil.   Noble Ventidius,
> Whilst yet with Parthian blood thy sword is warm,
> The fugitive Parthians follow. Spur through Media,
> Mesopotamia, and the shelters whither
> The routed fly.
>
> (*Ant.* 3.1.1-9)

A final way of determining the difference between the uses of proper names in the two plays is to consider references to persons as opposed to places and objects.[39] The number of place/object names is slightly higher in *Richard II* because it was necessary to count names like *York* and

---

[39] Each name was marked once as designating a person or an object/place; in some cases the name was marked for both person and object/place. Of the 138 names in *Richard II*, 95 were persons, 54 were places or objects; in *Antony*, the 174 names were distributed between 121 persons and 53 others. Hence, there are .6884 persons in *R2*, .3913 others; in *Ant.* it is .6956 and .3103. For other procedures, see Table A-35 and accompanying notes.

Lancaster both as persons and places. This last point brings up the question of the thematic significance of names and titles in the two plays.

The heroes in both plays are preoccupied with their identity, but the difference between them is obvious from the fact that in *Richard II* the emphasis on name is balanced by an equal concern for title, while in *Antony* the mention of names is double that of titles. A title can be gained or lost while its possessor remains unchanged. Hereford becomes Lancaster, then king, although there is no discernible change in his behavior. Aumerle is reduced to the title Rutland because he is what he has always been, Richard's friend. The title does not proclaim the man nor does the individual confer worth on the title, since the same title can be assumed by individuals of widely differing characters: *And long live Henry, fourth of that name*. The name is virtually a title.

King Richard struggles to discover the human being masked by his royal title. The name he invokes in moments of crisis is not *Richard* but *King*:

> I had forgot myself. Am I not king?
> Awake, thou coward majesty! thou sleepest.
> Is not the King's name twenty thousand names?
> Arm, arm, my name! A puny subject strikes
> At thy great glory.
> *(R2 3.2.83-87)*

> No lord of thine, thou haught insulting man,
> Nor no man's lord. I have no name, no title—
> No, not that name was given me at the font—
> But 'tis usurp'd. Alack the heavy day,
> That I have worn so many winters out
> And know not now what name to call myself!
> *(R2 4.1.254-259)*

In the second of these speeches no less than in the first, the context (*no man's lord, usurp'd, a mockery king of snow, majesty*) suggests that title rather than name is foremost in Richard's mind. Even his complaint about losing his baptismal name is, according to Kittredge, part of the logic of succession: If he is not king, he is not Richard, since Richard should be king.

Identity, like status, is derived from the power to claim sovereignty over land, and a title is valuable chiefly as the link between land and its owner. What is at stake in *Richard II* is not personal identity (associated with name) or honor (good name) but rank (title) and power (claim to land).

The question of personal identity may be implicit in the play, but it is not central to it. The hero must learn what it is to be a man rather than a king before he can discover what it means to be one man rather than another.

In *Antony and Cleopatra* identity comes from the reputation given to the name by the achievements of its possessor. This concern for name brooks no alternatives; if a person fails to live up to it, there is no other:

> Moon and stars!
> Whip him. Were't twenty of the greatest tributaries
> That do acknowledge Caesar, should I find them
> So saucy with the hand of she here—what's her name
> Since she was Cleopatra?
> . . . .
> This Jack of Caesar's shall
> Bear us an errand to him.
>
> (3.13.95-99, 103-104)

A change in behavior entails a loss of name, but once earned the name itself is a source of stability. Like a title, it begins to assume the characteristics of a common noun: *an Antony, another Antony, my Antony*. Fortunately, Antony's loss of power makes it possible for him to preserve his unique name, whereas Caesar's triumph changes his name into a common title signifying not the individual but the role:

> My desolation does begin to make
> A better life. 'Tis paltry to be Caesar.
> Not being Fortune, he's but Fortune's knave,
> A minister of her will.
>
> (5.2.1-4)

To be Caesar is to have only the identity that comes from such power as Fortune sees fit to confer.

The name/title proportions in the two plays suggest different sources of identity and different views of stability. In *Richard II* to be a man rather than a king means to feel the pull toward the nothingness inherent in creaturehood and consequent upon mortality. Hence the speeches on death in Act Three and the final soliloquy on being pleased with being nothing; hence the feelings of sadness that predominate in the deposition scene over any conscious preoccupation in Richard's speeches with the inadequacy of language. In *Antony* the movement of the hero is toward reintegration and immortality, and this change is accomplished through the unique, irreducible, nontransferable identity of the individual called *Mark Antony*.

Names, particularly those with a polysyllabic shape and a vocative function, seem to be a means of heightening the diction of *Antony*. A study of nominal groups introduced by the first singular possessive determiner (*my/mine*) revealed that synecdoche is more frequent in *Richard II* than in *Antony and Cleopatra*.[40] Its effect is similarly to elevate the language of the play. The substitution of part for whole, especially when a part of the body is made responsible for a significant human action, creates a curious disjunction between agent and instrument:

> Desolate, desolate will I hence and die!
> The last leave of thee takes my weeping eye.
>
> *(R2* 1.2.73-74)
>
> What my tongue speaks my right-drawn sword may prove.
>
> *(R2* 1.1.46)
>
> My heart this covenant makes, my hand thus seals it.
>
> *(R2* 2.3.50)
>
> What my tongue dares not, that my heart shall say.
>
> *(R2* 5.5.97)

In *Antony and Cleopatra* synecdoche is less often expressed by parallelism, and one finds fewer distinctions between body and soul. Indeed, the part that is substituted for the whole tends to be some moral quality rather than a limb or a bodily organ:

> . . . —she, Eros, has
> Pack'd cards with Caesar and false-play'd my glory
> Unto an enemy's triumph.
>
> *(Ant.* 4.14.18-20)
>
> Since Cleopatra died
> I have liv'd in such dishonour that the gods
> Detest my baseness.
>
> (4.14.55-57)

In both plays where one might normally expect *I take my last leave* or *she*

---

[40] See Tables A-38 for statistical data on synecdoche and B-13 for line references.

played me false, one finds that some aspect of body or spirit has been substituted for the total human being.

Allied to the instances of synecdoche created by nominal groups introduced by the first singular possessives are the phenomena represented by certain adjective-noun collocations in *Richard II*: *eager tongues, daring tongue, joyful tongue*; *sacred blood, old blood, youthful blood, faithful blood*; *noble eye, unpleas'd eye*; *banish'd hands, royal hands, revengeful hand*; *slanderous lips*; *treacherous ear*; *princely knee*; *greedy looks*. When these are compared with the frequency of metaphoric adjective-noun collocations, as they are in Table 36, the importance of synecdoche to the style of *Richard II* becomes still more apparent.[41] Such expressions abound among the numerous adjective-noun collocations of the earlier play, and they do not strike the same note of incongruity that one experiences in *R2* 1.2.73-74. These dichotomies, which compress the malice and

Table 36
Rhetorical Figures Created by Adjective-Noun Collocations

	Synecdochic	Metaphoric	Total
R2	104	264	368
Ant.	30	159	189

[41] The study of adjective-noun collocations in Chapter Two suggested that a substantial group of these collocations did not violate the restrictions defined for the classification of metaphor, but that these phrases, consisting of adjectives and nouns that could be labeled both human or both animate, violated other conditions, namely, restrictions on the collocation of adjectives designating a part with nouns designating a whole. Thus, in an expression like *youthful blood* the words are both animate, but, since the language is clearly figurative, it seems best to account for the phenomenon by invoking the idea that one is ascribing to a part of an animate being (*blood*) a quality normally associated with the whole being (*youthfulness*).
The idea that some part/whole relation has been violated is obvious, and the traditional word *synecdoche* exists to express it, but there seem to be no formalisms in terms of which the violation can be stated explicitly. The dominance relations that describe the body and its parts are based on sentences like *the arm has a hand*, but the adjective-noun collocations in question tend to be copula sentences. Only one type of copula, the generic (*a boy is human*), involves a hierarchy of dominance and, again, it does not seem to comprise the adjective-noun collocations under consideration here. Perhaps the violation consists in some crossing of lines between the two hierarchies of dominance.
Discussion might be less awkward if one could see the collocations as a type of personification, but there are few adjectives in the set that can be restricted to human beings. Animals have *tongues, blood, eyes*, and *ears*, and sentences like *the dog is eager, joyful, faithful, old*, etc. are commonplace enough. Hence, a sentence like *the tongue is eager* need not be an instance of personification.

the goodness of the human spirit into a physical emblem, seem to epitomize what is best in the diction of this play.

It is not easy to say why synecdoche should seem more successful in the adjective-noun collocations of *Richard II* than in the subject-predicator relations cited earlier from that play, but here is one possible explanation: In instances of synecdoche involving body-spirit dichotomies, the part is rendered independent of its possessor by the ascription to it of activities that are normally performed only by an animate agent.

At one syntactic level, the figure is created by violating selection restrictions on the concatenation of part with whole, but the type of restriction may be defined more narrowly by invoking the broad difference between attribution and action. When the syntax involves attribution (*tongues are eager*; *hand is revengeful*) the activity ascribed to the physical organ (the part) continues to operate within the agent (the whole), but when the syntax assumes a more active form (*eye takes leave*; *heart makes covenant*), the activity passes outside the agent and is externalized. Semantically, the difference is equivalent to Aristotle's distinction between immanent and transient activity. With transient activity the measure of independence from the true agent that is accorded the physical organ is greater; hence, its behavior is more incongruous. Confining the synecdochic relation to attributes (as in the adjective-noun relations of *Richard II* and in the moral qualities of *Antony*) keeps the behavior of the part more clearly under the control of the true agent. Perhaps the difference can be appreciated by examination of this passage where both types of synecdoche appear:

> Me rather had my heart might feel your love
> Than my unpleas'd eye see your courtesy.
>   (*R2* 3.3.192-193)

In the first line *my heart* governs the verb *feel*, which is normally predicated of the entire person. In the second line one finds not only the synecdochic parallel *than my eye see your courtesy* but also an additional figure, *my unpleas'd eye*. This phrase seems a more adequate subject for *see your courtesy* because it has been made more representative of the whole by the adjective *unpleas'd*.

But perhaps the major key to preserving the sense of wholeness and adequacy in these instances of synecdoche is the possessive determiner, whose presence implies personality and animacy. When this determiner is absent from phrases designating parts of the body, the element of incongruity increases sharply, as in this passage from *Hamlet*:

> No, let the candied tongue lick absurd pomp,
> And crook the pregnant hinges of the knee
> Where thrift may follow fawning.

$$(3.2.65-67)$$

Here the part is completely independent of the whole, and the notion of a normal human possessor is further canceled by the violation of selection restrictions in *candied tongue* and *pregnant hinges*. To determine whether such figures increase in the later style would require a separate study. If so, they may represent a further development of an aspect of style that reached its own kind of perfection in the synecdochic adjective-noun relations of *Richard II*.

The concrete character of the possessive determiner, coupled with the abstractness of certain nouns, adds to the dynamic tension of opposites that has often been perceived as characteristic of *Antony* and of other plays belonging to Shakespeare's mature style. Despite the fact that possessive determiners decrease in *Antony and Cleopatra*, they increase before certain types of nouns in this play, namely, verbal nouns in *-ing* and abstract nouns in *-ion*.[42] The latter type of noun (*conjuration, ostentation, oppression*, etc.) appears with nearly equal frequency in the two plays. In *Richard II* they are modified by specific determiners and zero in roughly equal proportions, and, within the category of specific determiners, by the definite and the possessive with equal frequency. In *Antony*, however, specific determiners are more than double the instances of zero before nouns in *-ion*, and the possessive is clearly the reason for the increase of specific determiners.[43] Table 37 records this information. Assuming that a specific determiner detracts from the abstract character of a noun, whereas

[42] See Table A-23 for specific determiners before verbal nouns in *-ing*.

[43] Possessive determiners in *Richard II* (1,239) outnumber those of *Antony* (1,073). The count, undertaken for a separate study, includes the prose of *Antony*. In Table 38 the category "Possessive" (determiner) includes nominal possessives like *night's blackness*.

The abstract nouns ending in *-ion* and *-ness* were first drawn from the reverse word list in Spevack's *Concordance*. Individual concordances to the two plays were then searched to see whether a given noun was present and to study its context. The following nouns were present in one or both plays but rejected from the final study because they were judged to be concrete rather than abstract: *champions, companion, pinion, legions,* and *fashion. Faction (R2 2.2.57)* was construed as an adjective.

Table 37
Types of Determiner before Abstract Nouns

	Nouns in *-ion*				Nouns in *-ness*			
	Nonspecific	Specific	Zero	Total	Nonspecific	Specific	Zero	Total
R2	5	28	33	66	4	26	7	37
	.0757	.4242	.5000		.1081	.7027	.1891	
Ant.	7	47	17	71	4	38	23	65
	.0985	.6619	.2394		.0615	.5846	.3538	

the omission of a determiner emphasizes its abstractness, one can suggest that Latinate abstractions (represented by words in *-ion*) tend to be concretized in *Antony and Cleopatra*:

> *Our separation* so abides and flies
> (1.3.102)
> *Her motion* and *her station* are as one.
> (3.3.22)
> ... Antony, most large
> In *his abominations*, ...
> (3.6.93-94)
> *My resolution* and my hands I'll trust;
> (4.15.49)

The person referred to by the possessive determiner in these instances is to some extent enhanced by the philosophical and universal character of the abstract noun.

Another type of abstract noun, ending in *-ness*, increases markedly though not significantly in the later play (*sharpness, nobleness, lightness*, etc.). With these nouns the distribution of determiners changes, as shown in Table 38. In *Richard II* specific determiners triple before such words compared to zero; in the later play there is a marked increase of zero before words in *-ness* compared to instances of zero before these words in *Richard II*. Some examples may illustrate the different effects of determiners upon *-ness* nouns in the two plays:

> Such neighbour nearness to our sacred blood
> Should nothing privilege him nor partialize

The unstooping firmness of my upright soul.

(*R2* 1.1.119-121)

Which, I protest, hath very much beguil'd
The tediousness and process of my travel;

(*R2* 2.3.11-12)

But that your royalty
Holds idleness your subject, I should take you
For idleness itself.

(*Ant.* 1.3.91-93)

The soul and body rive not more in parting
Than greatness going off.

(*Ant.* 4.13.5-6)

Table 38
Types of Specific Determiners before Abstract Nouns

	Abstract Nouns in *-ion*				Abstract Nouns in *-ness*			
	Defi-nite	Demon-strative	Posses-sive	Total	Defi-nite	Demon-strative	Posses-sive	Total
R2	10 .1515	9 .1363	9 .1363	28	4 .1081	6 .1621	16 .4324	26
Ant.	7 .0985	2 .0281	38 .5352	47	8 .1230	6 .0923	24 .3692	38

In sum, abstract nouns in *-ness* increase in *Antony* compared to nouns in *-ion*; in *Richard II* nouns in *-ness* are often specified, whereas in *Antony* there is a significant increase of zero before such nouns; and, while in *Richard II* nouns in *-ion* may or may not have a modifier, in *Antony* they are specified twice as often as they are left unspecified.

The last two points reveal most about the differing character of the diction in these plays. The nouns in *-ness* belong to what is called the native English portion of Shakespeare's vocabulary, which is often deemed concrete in comparison with the more abstract Latinate nouns formed by the suffix *-ion*. The adjectival base of *sharpness, lightness, blackness*, and so on seems more concrete than the verbal base of *conjuration, oppression, occupation*, and so on. Perhaps the reason is that adjectives are properties thought to inhere in concrete objects. Whatever the basis for it, the popular assumption is that words like *blackness* are more concrete than words like *suspicion*, even though morphologically both fall into the category of abstract nouns. In *Richard II* the more "concrete" noun in -*ness* occurs with a determiner that reinforces its concreteness. The tendency in *Antony* to leave the "concrete" nouns in -*ness* undetermined emphasizes their abstract character; conversely, the fact that in this same play the "abstract" type in -*ion* takes a determiner underplays its abstract character. In both instances one finds a tension between abstract and concrete in the diction of nominal groups containing nouns in -*ness* or -*ion*. This tension is already present, of course, in nouns of the -*ness* type, since the abstract suffix is added to the concrete adjectival base.

On the whole, there seems to be an increase of specification in the nominal-group structures of *Antony and Cleopatra*. This increase manifests itself in groups introduced by nonspecific determiners but specified by a clause or phrase following the head of the nominal group:

> I' th' market place on *a tribunal silver'd*
>
> (3.6.3)
>
> And gives his potent regiment to *a trull*
> *That noises it against us.*
>
> (3.6.95-96)

Occasionally, a substitute head will be qualified although it would be possible to eliminate the need for qualification:

> Fall not a tear, I say. *One of them* rates
> *All that is won and lost.*
>
> (3.11.69-70)
>
> 'Tis better playing with a lion's whelp
> Than with *an old one dying.*
>
> (3.13.94-95)

This tendency to specify the nonspecific or the substitute head of a nominal group increases significantly in the later play.[44]

Another type of nominal-group structure manifests intensification rather than specification but serves similarly to focus attention on the nominal group where it occurs. This structure is one in which the head is introduced by a modifier that demands a qualifier. There are several structures

[44] As shown in Table A-40, one in five nominal groups introduced by the indefinite article is followed by a qualifier in *Richard II*; in *Antony* the rate is one in three. The qualification of substitute heads occurs one in eleven times in *Richard II*; one in three substitute heads are qualified in the later play.

of this kind and the type of qualifier they demand will vary with the modifier, but only one type has been tabulated in this study, namely, groups introduced by a word like *such* or *so* and qualified by a *that* clause:

> Purple the sails, and *so* perfumed *that*
> *The winds were lovesick with them*;
> > (*Ant.* 2.2.198-199)

> Sir, sir, thou art *so* leaky
> *That we must leave thee to thy sinking*, for
> Thy dearest quit thee.
> > (*Ant.* 3.13.63-65)

> Since Cleopatra died
> I have liv'd in *such* dishonour *that the gods*
> *Detest my baseness.*
> > (*Ant.* 4.14.55-57)

There are four of these constructions in *Richard II*, eleven in *Antony and Cleopatra*.[45]

More interesting than either of these phenomena are nominal groups where specification is redundant. Proper names, which need no specification at all, may nevertheless appear with a determiner or with a determiner and an adjective. The remarkable increase in *Antony* of determiners before proper names is demonstrated by the figures in Table 39. The stylistically marked flavor of these nominal groups is due in part to the fact that most of them occur in reference rather than in address. It is obviously not so remarkable to say *Welcome, my good Alexas* as it is to say *How goes it with my brave Mark Antony*, and neither of these is as unusual as proper

Table 39
Frequency of Modifiers before Proper Names

	Determiner+Name	Determiner+Adjective/Noun+Name	Total
R2	1	5	6
Ant.	10	23	33

[45] A complete study of comparatives might reveal other differences between the plays. One thinks in *Antony* of these comparatives, which seem typical of its language: *as petty to his ends / As is the morn-dew*, etc. or *their story is / No less in pity than his glory*, etc., but there are many instances of comparatives with *more than* in *Richard II*, and one might need to make some finer distinctions before real differences would emerge.

names introduced by the definite article: *The banish'd Norfolk, the mounting Bolingbroke; the curled Antony, the valiant Caesar, the lean and wrinkled Cassius, the strong-wing'd Mercury.* The tone created by this construction can vary depending on the type of determiner or adjective employed: *my Richard; our Caesar, this Seleucus; a noble Lepidus, some squeaking Cleopatra, this traitor Bolingbroke.* Since the great majority of these constructions occur in reference and with the definite article, the over-all tone is one of elevation.[46] It is interesting to observe that with respect to proper names that are simply modified by adjectives, the plays appear to be equal: *false Mowbray, glist'ring Phaëton, plume-pluck'd Richard; plated Mars, noble Ventidius, fortunate Caesar.* There are forty-nine of these in *Richard II* and forty-nine in *Antony and Cleopatra*, but, given the high frequency of adjectives in one play and of proper names in the other, it is difficult to judge the significance of these figures.

A similar heightening occurs in certain constructions introduced by the demonstrative determiner. One of these is constituted by the fact that there is a higher than average frequency of monosyllabic adjectives after the demonstrative determiner. Moreover, half of these are the single word *great*: *that great med'cine, that great property, this great world, this great fairy, that great face of war, this great solemnity*, and so on. In fact a fifth of the total instances of *great* in *Antony and Cleopatra* appear after the demonstrative determiner.[47]

It might be noted in passing that the study of point of view undertaken earlier in this chapter showed that the use of demonstrative determiners for persons increased slightly in *Antony*. They are used with reference to King Richard and Bolingbroke .0238 and .0219, respectively; to Antony .0353 and to Cleopatra .0340. Whether used for praise or for blame their presence indicates heightened tone, and their higher frequency with the major characters of the later play is not surprising.

The second marked construction introduced by the demonstrative appears in the opening lines of *Antony* and helps to establish the special tone of this play: *Those his goodly eyes / That o'er the files and musters of the war* (1.1.2-3). Nominal groups introduced by both a demonstrative

[46] A complete list of names introduced by a determiner is provided in Appendix A on p. 307.

[47] The notes that accompany Tables A-41 and A-42 provide information about nominal groups introduced by the demonstrative determiner. The tables themselves provide quantitative evidence for the increase of monosyllabic adjectives after the demonstrative determiner. They also provide procedures for obtaining the data in Table 40.

Table 40
Types of Nominal Groups Introduced by Demonstrative Determiners

	Head	Adjective + Head	Head + Qualifier	Adjective + Head + Qualifier/Beta Clause	Total
R2	113	66	39	16	234
	.4829	.2820	.1666	.0683	
Ant.	70	33	21	15	139
	.5035	.2374	.1510	.1079	

and a possessive are striking and relatively rare in both plays. There are three of them in *Richard II* and five in *Antony*, but, whereas in the earlier play only one has posthead qualification, in the later play four have clauses following the noun.[48] Table 40 shows that, in terms of ratios, the presence of qualifying or beta clauses after nominal groups introduced by a demonstrative and an adjective increase markedly. Even without a possessive determiner, groups consisting of a demonstrative, an adjective, a noun, and a following clause are impressive. To exemplify them is to cite some of the most striking passages in *Antony and Cleopatra*:

> ... *this* great gap *of time*
> *My Antony is away.*
>   (1.5.5-6)

> ... *that* noble countenance
> *Wherein the worship of the whole world lies.*
>   (4.14.85-86)

> ... *those* flower-soft hands
> *That yarely frame the office.*
>   (2.2.215-216)

> ... *this* knot intrinsicate
> *Of life* ...
>   (5.2.307-308)

These constructions, in addition to being very specific, have a high degree of cohesion. The demonstrative, so to speak, points to the following noun (cataphoric reference) and the qualifying/beta clause points back to the same noun (anaphoric reference). Hence, despite their length

---

[48] In *Richard II* these appear in 1.3.22-24, 145-147; 4.1.18-19. The remaining four in *Antony* are 2.3.19-20; 3.5.19-20; 4.5.2-3; 4.15.52-55.

and grammatical weight, these nominal groups have a compactness and a coherence that make them readily understood.

This phenomenon of modifiers referring forward or backward to the head of the nominal group might be provisionally labeled "pointing."[49] In the earlier play the pointing appears to be in one direction, cataphoric— from modifier forward to the head of the nominal group. Later the pointing was more balanced, as a comparison of these two passages suggests:

> Why have those banish'd and forbidden legs
> Dar'd once to touch a dust of England's ground?
> But then more why?—why have they dar'd to march
> So many miles upon her peaceful bosom,
> Frighting her pale-fac'd villages with war
> And ostentation of despised arms?
>
> (*R2* 2.3.90-95)

> Caesar, I bring thee word
> Menecrates and Menas, famous pirates,
> Make the sea serve them, which they ear and wound
> With keels of every kind. Many hot inroads
> They make in Italy; the borders maritime
> Lack blood to think on't, and flush youth revolt.
> No vessel can peep forth but 'tis as soon
> Taken as seen; for Pompey's name strikes more
> Than could his war resisted.
>
> (*Ant.* 1.4.47-55)

In the first passage the nominal groups, viewed as images, are more than adequate; *pale-fac'd villages*, with its anticipation of Picasso's *Guernica*, ranks among the best phrases in the play, but a careful study of the surrounding syntax reveals some flaws. *A dust* undoubtedly means *a grain of dust*, but this phrase would not suit the meter and *the dust* would not convey the proper meaning. Syntax is sacrificed for meter and meaning, and it hardly seems to matter. The *banish'd and forbidden legs* that march on England's bosom are far enough removed from *despised arms* so that no

---

[49] In an early pilot study, nominal groups were studied with a view to tabulating differences in the frequency of anaphoric specification, but only groups introduced by determiners were examined, and there seemed to be no appreciable difference between the plays in this respect. However, the tendency to posthead qualification may be greater in one play or the other when the group has no determiner, and such groups were not examined.

one seriously wonders how the arms are to be displayed by these trunkless appendages, yet, had Shakespeare been as concerned here to specify abstract nouns as he was later, the difficulty of supplying, for example, a possessive determiner for *ostentation* might have prevented the incongruity. The crucial difference between the passages, however, lies in the internal syntax of the nominal groups. Only two groups in the first quotation are provided with qualifying clauses: *dust* and *ostentation*. They are also two of the three groups that have little or no prehead modification. All others are heavily supplied with determiners and adjectives. In fact, modification before the nouns is so strong and qualification after them so generally absent that one might say that the nominal groups are top-heavy.

Despite occasional compression, the passage from *Antony* is clear and syntactically smooth. New names are introduced and identified, comparisons are fully explicit, and nominal groups are virtually welded to the context. *Word* is specified by the rest of the sentence in which it occurs; *Menecrates and Menas*, subjects in the clause that specifies *word*, are further specified by apposition; *sea*, the subject of a second embedded clause, is specified by *which they ear . . . kind.* In the remaining sentences, *the borders maritime* is specified by *to think on't* and *no vessel* by *but 'tis . . . seen.* The one-directional, front-heavy specification of groups in *Richard II* seems to have been exchanged for a balance of both types of specification, cataphoric and anaphoric.

This fourth chapter has been devoted, in one form or another, to a consideration of the nominal group—to the grammatical meaning inherent in determiners and to the formal patterns created by certain types of noun and by particular nominal-group structures. One section gave an exhaustive and systematic account of the references to the main characters of *Richard II* and of *Antony and Cleopatra*. All references to five characters were examined according to the type of determiner that governed them. Determiners were selected as the basis of analysis because they subtly control one's attitude toward the nouns they modify and thus serve as an index to point of view, while possessive determiners in particular modify nouns that yield emblematic sketches of a character's status and personality. The method of analysis revealed stylistic differences within each play with respect to characterization and to the changes a character undergoes in the course of the play.

While grammatical meaning seems to have been equally exploited in each play, there are important differences in the patterning of nominal groups.

The final section of the chapter has suggested that some patterns that have unnecessary, unusual, or redundant specification are employed increasingly in *Antony and Cleopatra* to create an elevated tone. Heightening is achieved also through proper names in *Antony* and synecdoche in *Richard II*. Doubtless these and other aspects of language discussed in earlier chapters might be pursued further, but to do so might be to make life *the slave of thought. Time, that takes survey of all the world, must have a stop* and so must the pursuit of Shakespeare's infinite and elusive variety.

CHAPTER FIVE

Charting the Dimensions of Style

Dimensions for the Future

In the preceding chapters the language of *Richard II* and of *Antony and Cleopatra* has been analyzed in order to illustrate the theory that style is a propositional function and to exemplify some methods of describing objects in the domain of the style function. The first chapter outlined the general theory of style, and the second suggested that style can be located in any segment of a literary work, since it is a function of the entire work. In the third chapter some formal techniques for a structural description of literary texts were proposed, and in the fourth a rationale was presented for relating the results of formal analysis to traditional categories of literary theory. One purpose of this study has thus been achieved, but much remains to be said about the language of these two plays and about other aspects of stylistic analysis. The analysis of the plays is incomplete not only because traditional features of imagery, rhetoric, and dramatic structure have been deliberately excluded but also because limitations of time have precluded even a complete and formal description of syntax, the major focus of study. Systems of the verb and of transitivity are among the most obvious omissions.[1] Similarly, certain aspects of methodology

---

[1] Robert D. Eagleson has conducted an exhaustive computer-aided investigation into the nonfinite verbal group in all the plays of Shakespeare. Results are reported in

have been neglected. Before the final summary and evaluation, therefore, it seems desirable to consider some directions for further study of these plays and of style in general.

One syntactic feature that appears to play an important role in Shakespeare's style is that of deletion, especially deletion that is the result of stylistic choice rather than of an obligatory grammatical rule. It is obviously more difficult to tabulate deleted constituents than it is to study overt markers of syntax, but deleted constituents can usually be retrieved from a study of context or by an application of syntactic rules, as in this passage where the omitted words are supplied in brackets:

> . . . none [of] our parts [was] so poor
> But [that it] was a race of heaven.
>
> (*Ant.* 1.3.36-37)

There are numerous passages like this in *Antony* and they deserve consideration in any complete statement about the style of this play, since they help to create the compression and complexity that one senses in its language despite an over-all increase of simple sentences. Caesar's indictment of the Roman people, notable for its alternation of compressed and expanded syntax, yields some insight into Shakespeare's use of deletion:

> It hath been taught us from the primal state
> That he which is was wish'd until he were;
> And the ebb'd man, ne'er lov'd till ne'er worth love,
> Comes dear'd by being lack'd. This common body,
> Like to a vagabond flag upon the stream,
> Goes to and back, lackeying the varying tide,
> To rot itself with motion.
>
> (1.4.41-47)

The first two lines are quite explicit in their syntax, although the fact that the pronouns lack a referent and the verb *to be* a complement creates a sense of missing elements. Relatively empty of information, these lines contrast sharply with the compressed content of *ebb'd man* where several

---

his doctoral thesis for the University of London, which is entitled "A Linguistic, Stylistic Analysis of the Non-Finite Verb Clause in Shakespeare's Plays." For an application of transitivity to stylistic studies, see M. A. K. Halliday's "Linguistic Function and Literary Style," in *Literary Style*, ed. Seymour Chatman, pp. 330-365.

pieces of information have been suppressed.[2] Subjects and predicators are left out of the beta clauses (*who is* ne'er lov'd till *he is* ne'er worth love), and syllables are deleted from words (*be*comes, *un*til, ne*ver*, and possibly *en*deared). Adding to the compression is the high frequency of past tense verb forms (*ebb'd, lov'd, dear'd, lack'd*), all clipped to create consonant clusters that offer some difficulty to pronunciation.

Beginning with *This common body* the tension is released. Ideas and syntax are expanded to the point of redundancy. Expressions like *to and back, vagabond, tide, varying,* and *lackeying* repeat the same idea of unceasing motion. In the phrase *like to a vagabond flag* one finds two prepositions, although they could have been omitted (cf. *life, a very rebel to my will* [4.9.14]). Some measure of compression and expansion can be obtained by comparing the frequency of prepositions and determiners in the twenty-four words from *that he* to *lack'd* and in the same number of words from *this common* to *motion.* The first set contains only one of each (*the, by*) and the second has four of each (*this, a, the* [2] ; *like, to, upon, with*). Finally, only two words in the first group are not monosyllabic, while fully a third of the words in the second contain more than one syllable.

The reduction of determiners and prepositions decreases the semantic and phonological breathing space that such words permit between fully lexical items and thus contributes to the effect of compression. The alternation of compression and expansion in this passage may be an aspect of rhythm, particularly of modulation. In any case, a complete description of deletion would have to distinguish obligatory from optional deletions, describe syntactic and semantic deletions, and show how the compression that results serves an artistic purpose.

With respect to diction, one finds still other features that have yet to be described. Using a statistic like Yule's K, which measures the repeat rate of words, one could determine the richness of vocabulary in each play. One recognizes intuitively that the vocabulary of *Richard II* is more repetitive than that of *Antony,* but knowledge of the richness of vocabulary in the two plays might help validate other intuitions. For example, agent nouns in *-er* may seem characteristic of *Antony* but they increase only slightly in

[2] The assumption is that some suppressed information includes a deep syntactic structure, *the man has ebbed,* and a semantic structure implied by such other sentences in the play as *the full Caesar, the fullest man, his emptiness,* etc., which refer to the rise and fall of tides and fortune.

that play. However, three out of twenty-two agent nouns in *Richard II* were repeated (*rider* [2], *flatterer* [4], *beggar* [3]), while only one in twenty-six of *Antony* was repeated (*revenger* [2]). A related phenomenon is the fact that words of similar frequency seem to differ greatly in quality. Nouns in *-ing* occur fifty-two times in *Richard II* and fifty times in *Antony*, yet one resists giving equal weight to *his writing, his coming, my greeting* and *the discandying, thy deserving, our earing.*

This latter point may be related to the rarity rather than the richness of vocabulary. One hopes that the existence of computer-generated concordances of old-spelling and edited texts will make possible a systematic and complete study of unique, rare, coined, and difficult words in Shakespeare. Such knowledge would provide a basis for resolving questions about the relative complexity of style. There are sentences in *Antony* where the vocabulary seems commonplace and the syntax carries the burden of complexity:

> By this marriage
> All little jealousies, which now seem great,
> And all great fears, which now import their dangers,
> Would then be nothing.
>
> (2.2.133-136)

The entire force of the sentence derives from its periodic structure, its word order, and its rhythm. Group betas create suspense, and the monosyllabic adjuncts *now* and *then* appear in strategic positions; but the vocabulary is undistinguished, there is little figurative language, and no imagery is used. In the following sentences, however, one finds simple syntax supporting heightened diction:

> His legs bestrid the ocean: his rear'd arm
> Crested the world.
>
> (5.2.82-83)

> Saucy lictors
> Will catch at us like strumpets, and scald rhymers
> Ballad us out o' tune.
>
> (5.2.214-216)

Here the syntax is chiefly paratactic, all clause and group constituents appear in normal order, and each clause has a simple rhythm. But the vocabulary is richer and more striking. One finds functional shift in *ballad*, a violation of selection retrictions in *bestrid ocean, arm crested world*, and so on. More to the point, one feels that apart from these phenomena (which can be syntactically defined) the vocabulary is more unusual than that of Agrippa's speech even though there are no coinages, inkhorn terms, or polysyllables in the lot. The result is that despite the simple syntax one can hardly call these simple sentences, but just now there are no formal means for deciding when or how vocabulary as such adds to sentence complexity.

The morphological variants to which a given word is subject and the syntactic functions that it serves may well be clues to its stylistic impact. The word *noble*, for example, appears thirty-one times in *Richard II* and thirty-three times in *Antony and Cleopatra*. In *Richard II*, however, the word has what J. R. Firth would call a formal scatter of three: *noble*, *nobles*, and *noblesse*.[3] In *Antony*, it has seven morphological forms, six of them new (*nobles* and *noblesse* have disappeared): *nobly, nobler, noblest, unnoble, nobility*, and *nobleness*. These variants increase the totals to thirty-five in the English and forty-six in the Roman history play, but the formal scatter itself is more than doubled in *Antony*. In both plays the word *noble* functions most often as an adjective modifying a title, a proper name, or a part of the body. As an adjective it is intensified by *most* once in *Richard II* and five times in *Antony*. Predictably, proper names modified by *noble* increase in *Antony*, but it also modifies in this play abstract nouns like *pleasure, weakness, deed*, and *act*. These factors—its increasing appearance with proper names, its use before abstract nouns, and its intensification by *most*—suggest that the word *noble* in *Antony* implies a moral quality, whereas in *Richard II* it was a conventional designation accorded anyone with a peerage.

The syntactic frames where *noble* occurs are more varied in *Antony* than in *Richard II*, and some of them constitute stylistic features in their own right. The word appears with the reflexive in *that I should not be noble to myself* and serves in the colloquial topic/comment structure *what's brave, what's noble*. Its presence in *'Tis a noble Lepidus* creates an ironic contrast with *Here comes/The noble Antony*. These varied syntactic functions, together with the increased formal scatter of the word, enhance the importance of the word *noble* in Shakespeare's lexicon. It would be interesting to know whether these phenomena are simply the result of Shakespeare's syntax growing more varied in time or whether

---

[3] J. R. Firth, "Technique of Semantics," in his *Papers in Linguistics*, p. 25.

particular words are placed by him in special formal settings to show them off to best advantage.

In addition to the complete statement about features of syntax and diction needed to round out the analysis of style, it is necessary to describe phenomena that are perceived intuitively but for which no formalism now exists. Since semantic theory is still rudimentary, it is difficult to formalize the study of imagery, but current research in computational stylistics has made possible some real advances in this area. Sally Sedelow used *Hamlet* to show how the computer can construct from the text a thesaurus that will establish groups of images and indicate how one group is related to or derived from another.[4] John B. Smith, working with Joyce's *A Portrait of the Artist as a Young Man*, devised a method of charting the relative frequency of images in each chapter of the novel.[5] This procedure, which could easily be adapted to Shakespeare's work, reveals the dynamic interaction of images as the literary work unfolds.

Image study of this sort depends chiefly on vocabulary, but some images are created by other means and one would like also to formalize these. In *Antony* there are many expressions that suggest that an extreme limit has been reached or exceeded, but it is not easy to specify what creates the impression. Undoubtedly, superlatives and quantifying adjectives convey some of this information, but it would be interesting to formalize the syntactic forms or grammatical features assumed by expressions of this kind:

> Though you in swearing shake the throned gods,
>
> (1.3.28)
>
> He cried almost to roaring;
>
> (3.2.55)
>
> Thy beck might from the bidding of the gods
> Command me.
>
> (3.11.60-61)

---

[4] The most generally available report of this study is Sally Y. Sedelow and Walter A. Sedelow, "Categories and Procedures for Content Analysis in the Humanities," in *The Analysis of Communication Content*, ed. George Gerbner et al., esp. pp. 487-499.

[5] John B. Smith, "A Computer-Assisted Analysis of Imagery in Joyce's *A Portrait of the Artist*," Ph.D. thesis, University of North Carolina.

> ... and let the waterflies
> Blow me into abhorring!
>
> (5.2.59-60)
>
> You lie, up to the hearing of the gods!
>
> (5.2.95)
>
> It's past the size of dreaming.
>
> (5.2.97)

These lines have a common grammatical construction in the verbal noun and in the fact that the verbal noun appears as complement to a preposition, but neither of these facts suffices to explain the notion of extremity and excess conveyed by each line. That notion sometimes appears in the preposition (*into, up to*), sometimes in words like *past* and *almost*, and sometimes simply in the lexical word *gods*, which refers to beings whose abode in the heavens and whose superhuman powers make them one limit of existence. The verbal noun seems to contribute nothing as such, yet its presence is intriguing.

Some of the features in the lines cited above can be found in other constructions conveying the same note of limit or excess of limit:

> This speed of Caesar's
> Carries beyond belief.
>
> (3.7.75-76)
>
> That sleep and feeding may prorogue his honour
> Even till a Lethe'd dulness!
>
> (2.1.26-27)
>
> Round even to faultiness.
>
> (3.3.33)
>
> It smites me
> Beneath the fall I have.
>
> (5.2.171)

The verbal noun is no longer present, and the prepositions carry most of the meaning one wishes to document. Three of the nouns governed by the prepositions are abstract, and even *fall* has a nonphysical sense that might allow it to be classified as an abstract noun.

In another group of lines, the abstract noun continues to occur, but the prepositional phrase has disappeared and seems to have been replaced by intensifiers of degree (*so*, *such*) and negatives implying absolute denial:

> ... yet must Antony
> *No way* excuse his foils when we do bear
> *So* great *weight* in his *lightness*.
>
> (1.4.23-25)

> I *never* saw an action of *such* shame.
> Experience, manhood, honour, *ne'er* before
> Did violate *so* itself.
>
> (3.10.22-24)

The presence of *such* and the absolute modifier *no* in the above passages invites the consideration that other lines containing words of this kind but lacking a negative might also be included in the set:

> For her own person,
> It beggar'd *all description*.
>
> (2.2.202-203)

> His power went out in *such distractions* as
> Beguil'd all spies.
>
> (3.7.77-78)

The passages now have little in common, although the idea of relating the semantic content of limit/excess to a formal feature might be preserved by noting that a great many passages contain abstract nouns and all have some formal marker of degree, such as a preposition, submodifiers, intensifiers, and negatives, but granting even this point one has to consider passages like these:

> Wash the congealment from your wounds and kiss
> The honour'd gashes whole.
>
> (4.8.10-11)

> Prithee go hence!
> Or I shall show the cinders of my spirits
> Through th' ashes of my chance.
>
> (5.2.172-174)

> and their story is
> No less in pity than his glory which
> Brought them to be lamented.
>
> (5.2.364-366)

In the first passage extremes appear to meet, and one is brought in two successive words (*gashes whole*) from one sort of extreme to another. In the second *cinders* and *ashes* are opposites, and the leap from one extreme to the other is conveyed by *through*. Finally, lowliness (*pity*) and loftiness (*glory*) are defined as extreme limits by reference to each other. But this analysis depends rather more on semantics than on syntax, although it is possible to argue that the double complement of the first passage, the preposition *through* in the second, or the comparative in the third are as responsible for our interpretation as the meaning of the individual words. All these lines, with their common semantic content of limit and excess of limit, are an important aspect of the style of *Antony*. Neither imagery nor syntax will wholly explain them, yet no completely formal description of style is possible until some means of assigning expressions to this category has been devised.

Some of the more abstract relationships in a text cannot easily be stated by reference to language. An earlier comparison of passages describing a civil uprising revealed that the figure of Bolingbroke was overshadowed by the syntax, whereas that of Pompey had been magnified by it.[6] The same difference in presenting a heroic figure can be discerned in these descriptions of King Richard and Antony:

> *Boling.* See, see, King Richard doth himself appear,
> As doth the blushing discontented sun
> From out the fiery portal of the East
> When he perceives the envious clouds are bent
> To dim his glory and to stain the track
> Of his bright passage to the Occident.
>
> *York.* Yet looks he like a king. Behold, his eye,
> As bright as is the eagle's, lightens forth
> Controlling majesty. Alack, alack, for woe,
> That any harm should stain so fair a show!
> (*R2* 3.3.62-71)
>
> Nay, but this dotage of our general's
> O'erflows the measure. Those his goodly eyes
> That o'er the files and musters of the war
> Have glow'd like plated Mars, now bend, now turn
> The office and devotion of their view
> Upon a tawny front. His captain's heart,

[6] See pp. 59-60.

Which in the scuffles of great fights hath burst
The buckles on his breast, reneges all temper
And is become the bellows and the fan
To cool a gypsy's lust.

(*Ant*. 1.1.1-10)

In each passage the hero is described by another character in terms that
elevate him above his fellows, and in both instances he is in danger of
losing the power and preeminence ascribed to him. Particular attention is
paid in each to the eyes and to the fact that objects can be controlled by a
glance. The language of the earlier passage is as impressive as that of the
later one, but King Richard is quickly lost in the elaborate comparison of
his person to the sun and of his eye to the eagle's. His is a borrowed glory
visible only by comparison to objects that are, after all, inferior to him on
the scale of being. Antony is anatomized, it is true, by reference to *this
dotage*, *his goodly eyes*, and *his captain's heart*, but each of these controls
every statement made about him.[7] His person, nevertheless, is the source
of the greatness described; even when he is compared to another being,
that other is a god and the comparison is admitted only after Antony's
importance has been clearly established and only in a brief phrase, not in a
series of elaborate clauses.

Bolingbroke's triumphant entry into London followed by the deposed
Richard (5.2.7-36) is paralleled by Antony's recital of the humiliation he
must endure if Eros refuses to kill him (4.14.72-77). In the first of these
one is distracted by a long epic simile comparing the mob to a theater
audience and Bolingbroke to a popular actor whom Richard has the mis-
fortune to follow. All mention of Bolingbroke is completed before Richard is described; Richard's disgrace comes from the mob, not from Bolingbroke or from his own sense of shame. In *Antony* there are no comparisons. The disgraced hero is presented first, then the conqueror, and once
again the vanquished rival. The interlaced syntax describes a scene in
which the disgrace of one man is due to the triumph of the other and the
triumph of one to the presence of the other. To these might be added the
scenes where Richard breaks the mirror (4.1.276-291) and where Antony
compares himself to the shifting clouds (4.14.1-14). In both, the hero's
perception of his dissolution coincides with the unraveling of the dramatic
action. But, just as epic similes served in other passages from *Richard II* to

[7] For further discussion of this point see p. 219.

divert one's attention from the main figure, in the mirror scene the echoes from Marlowe and the device of anaphora are similarly distracting. Antony's cloud speech might be as distracting as the comparison of Richard to the sun but for Shakespeare's handling of markers of inclusion. Antony's remarks to Eros—*Sometime we see; thou hast seen these signs*—and Eros's corroboration—*It does, my lord*—make it clear that we are witnessing, not two men comparing their king to the sun or an eagle, but two men talking to each other about the fantastic shapes that clouds assume.

In the scenes from *Richard II*, then, the character is described by reference to objects and events outside the dramatic action—Bolingbroke is compared to a river, Richard to an eagle, the sun, an actor, and, by implication, Marlowe's ill-fated Dr. Faustus. In *Antony*, the sources of enlargement all lie within the world of the drama itself—Pompey is defined by reference to the Roman mob, Antony by his personal qualities and by natural objects that are perceived by the characters as part of their environment. It is difficult to formalize these remarks, yet they constitute important differences in the style of the two plays. One might therefore invoke Roman Jakobson's observation that poetic language calls attention to itself and suggest that, in some sense to be further defined, the language of *Richard II* is more poetic than dramatic, while that of *Antony and Cleopatra* is somehow perfectly poetic yet admirably subordinated to dramatic purposes because it calls attention, not to itself, but to the context of situation.

A complete study of style must certainly take cognizance of the speech distinctive of different characters in a play. The language of Caesar and of Cleopatra differ markedly, while Antony's style resembles Cleopatra's in most respects, especially in colloquial features like ellipsis and substitution. Table 41 gives ratios for some features in the speech of Antony, Cleopatra, and Caesar.[8] The data in Table 41 will be discussed in a later section of this chapter, "Defining the Style Function."

---

[8] The criteria for most of the categories listed in Table 41 have all been discussed elsewhere, with the exception of ellipsis and substitution. Substitution includes all pronouns (personal, demonstrative, indefinite) with the exception of *wh-* and *that* relatives, all pronominal determiners, and the *thee* of *prithee*. It also includes substitute forms like the adverbs *thus, so,* and *therein* and the nominals *the first, both, one, thing,* etc., but no substitute verbs like *do*. While this information could have been obtained from concordances, for the limited purposes of this section of the study the count was undertaken manually from the text. Ellipsis is defined as the contraction of pronominal and verbal forms as in *we'll, there's, th'art, 'tis, to't, from's,* etc., but not contractions of individual words like *call'd, i' th' midst, o'ertake,* etc. Clause and group deviance here refers to all instances of group deviance but only

Table 41
Dimensions of the Language of Antony, Cleopatra, and Caesar

Dimension*	Antony	Cleopatra	Çaesar
Ellipsis	.1155	.1373	.0669
Substitution	.9571	.9597	.8157
Interrogatives	.0737	.1373	.0287
Imperatives	.3083	.3179	.2224
Clause deviance	.0258	.0268	.0191
Group deviance	.0294	.0298	.0334
Group betas	.0602	.0134	.0622
What relatives	.0147	.0089	.0263
When relatives	.0233	.0194	.0143

*The data in this table were obtained by counting each linguistic feature for each speaker and dividing the speaker's total blank-verse lines into the frequency thus obtained. The data are represented as a set of ratios because the total line length varies.

To distinguish the speech of one character from another's is one type of intratextual variation that should be part of a complete description; to note the manner in which a character's speech changes in the course of the play is another. In *Richard II*, King Richard's total use of personal references was balanced by impersonal references, but the proportions changed from act to act and shifted radically in favor of personal reference toward the end of the play. Similarly, a study of early and late scenes revealed important changes in Cleopatra's language. The final scene of Act One was compared to the final scene of Act Five beginning with *He words me*, omitting the interview with the Clown (*Avoid and leave him* to *Well, get thee gone*), and concluding with *What should I stay*.

Two major groups of features were examined in these scenes. One consisted of items that were known to be characteristic of the play as a whole and that could be identified in a single word: vocatives, proper names, polysyllabic names, names preceded by a determiner, abstract nouns in *-ness*, quantifiers, monosyllabic adjectives, past participial adjectives, *let* optatives and *wh-* clauses. The second group consisted of group betas and all instances of marked constituent order. The first set of features appears with roughly equal ratios in both scenes, but the second set clearly differ-

---

to complement theme in the case of clause deviance; these were not previously tabulated for individual characters.

entiates Cleopatra's language in the first act from that of her final speeches.[9] Marked word order is 22 percent higher in these last lines.

Extending the study of marked sequence to the entire act shows that over 50 percent of the total instances of complement theme and of nominal-group deviance occur in Cleopatra's speeches. These constitute 40 percent of her total instances of complement theme in the entire play and 50 percent of her total instances of group deviance. Hence, a study of Cleopatra's use of marked sequence in Act Five reveals two things: her language changes radically in this act and her use of marked sequence dominates the act. And, as noted earlier, the rhythms created by marked sequence contribute in no small measure to the beauty of this act.

An allied but largely unexplored topic is the fact that certain features may be quite prominent in a given passage whether or not they characterize the text as a whole. *Wh-* relatives in *Antony* are an interesting example of this phenomenon, for only three types (*what*, *when*, and *which*) occur with significant frequency, yet in some passages these and other, nonstylistic, relatives (*whose*, *where*, etc.), taken together, create the impression that relative clauses in general are characteristic of the play. Overall, there is one relative clause in every eleven lines of *Antony*, excluding prose as usual. In Caesar's praise of Antony's soldiership (1.4.55-71) and in Antony's report to Enobarbus of political conditions in Rome (1.2.183-203), the rate is one in three lines. In one speech of Ventidius's (3.1.30-38), the rate is one in two. For Enobarbus's description of Cleopatra's appearance upon the river of Cydnus (2.2.196-231), there is one *wh-* relative for every four lines, but in the first fifteen lines alone the ratio is one in three:[10]

> The barge she sat in, like a burnish'd throne,
> Burn'd on the water. The poop was beaten gold;
> Purple the sails, and so perfumed that
> The winds were lovesick with them; the oars were silver
> Which to the tune of flutes kept stroke, and made
> The water which they beat to follow faster,

[9] Features of the first set, divided by the total lines examined, yield 115.25 for 1.5 and 120.00 for 5.2.191ff.; features of the second set yield, for each scene respectively, 28.81 and 50.66.

[10] The raw frequency of all *wh-* words increases by eighty-two in *Antony*, that of all relative clauses by eighty-five. See Table A-8 and Table A-9.

As amorous of their strokes. For her own person,
It beggar'd all description. She did lie
In her pavilion, cloth-of-gold of tissue,
O'erpicturing that Venus where we see
The fancy outwork nature. On each side her
Stood pretty dimpled boys, like smiling Cupids,
With divers-colour'd fans, whose wind did seem
To glow the delicate cheeks which they did cool,
And what they undid did. . . .
Her gentlewomen, like the Nereides,
So many mermaids, tended her i' th' eyes,
And made their bends adornings.

(2.2.196-213)

Naturally, the beauty of this speech does not derive simply from the high frequency of relative clauses, but they are an important element in its effectiveness. In some instances they modify nouns in a way that makes the nouns highly specific: *the water which they beat*, *the delicate cheeks which they did cool*. The information supplied by these two clauses is hardly necessary, but the redundancy gives verbal emphasis as if the speaker is pointing to details in a picture lest the beholder overlook or fail to appreciate them.

Some relatives clearly affect the rhythm. In *the oars were silver / Which to the tune of flutes kept stroke*, there is a pause after *silver*, but the continuative character of the relative requires that it should not be too great. It is not just a question of a run-on line but of a delicate balance between the pause required after *silver* and the need to keep the relative close to the antecedent from which it has been separated. Within that relative clause there is further rhythmic control by the thematic adjunct *to the tune of flutes*, which, by delaying the tonic until the word *stroke*, lightens, accelerates, and expands the rhythm of the clause in a manner that would be completely destroyed if the clause read *which kept stroke to the tune of flutes*.[11] It should be added, of course, that other rhythms are created by other group beta clauses, particularly by recursive group betas, and by other instances of marked sequence.

Because this passage is frequently cited as an example of the fidelity with which Shakespeare followed his source, it is instructive to compare

---

[11] The alternative to this discontinuity would be *the oars, which to the / Tune of flutes kept stroke, were silver*, an entirely different rhythm.

his use of relatives with North's.[12] North employs sixteen relative clauses, and seven of these are introduced by explicit *wh-* words; Shakespeare uses fourteen relative clauses, of which ten are introduced by explicit *wh-* words. More impressive than this increase of *wh-* relatives is the fact that seven of the ten in Shakespeare's version contain *new* information, as shown by the italicized relatives in the following passages:

> . . . and made
> The water *which* they beat to follow faster
> As amorous of their strokes.

> . . . *whose* wind did seem
> To glow the delicate cheeks / *which* they did cool,
> And *what* they undid did.

> . . . did sit alone,
> Whistling to th' air; *which*, but for vacancy,
> Had gone to gaze on Cleopatra too,

> Our courteous Antony,
> *Whom* ne'er the word of 'no' woman heard speak,
> Being barber'd ten times o'er, goes to the feast,
> And for his ordinary pays his heart
> For *what* his eyes eat only.

A dominant new image in the description is that of the perfumed air that floats from the barge and that is itself enamored of Cleopatra's beauty. It receives its verbal expression in four of these relative clauses, recalling a point made earlier that some relatives seem to be associated with sensuous beauty.

The clustering of a generally characteristic feature like the *wh-* relatives of *Antony* in the passage cited should be distinguished from the fact that a feature that is not considered stylistic for the text as a whole may nevertheless appear with extraordinary frequency in a particular passage. The adjectives of the barge scene are a case in point. There one finds an extraordinary ratio: one adjective for every eleven words.[13] All but one of the fourteen

---

[12] The barge scene in Shakespeare, for the purposes of this discussion, includes *Ant.* 2.2.196-231, except for Agrippa's two brief interjections. The relevant passage from North occurs on pp. 201-202 of *Shakespeare's Plutarch*, ed. T. J. B. Spencer. It commences with *she disdained* and concludes with *no tongue can express it*. The two passages are compared in Appendix A, pp. 315-317.

[13] In *Richard II* there is one adjective for every twenty-two words; in *Antony*, one adjective for thirty-four words. Hence, there are twice as many adjectives in this passage as one finds in *Richard II* on the whole and almost three times the over-all ratio of adjectives to total blank-verse words in *Antony*.

adjectives in the passage is Shakespeare's own addition to his source. These adjectives clearly include and as clearly exclude certain properties of adjectives in both plays. One finds the doubling of adjectives noted in *Richard II* (*pretty dimpled boys, strange invisible perfume*), but with the single exception of the adjective borrowed from North there is a conspicuous absence of Spenserian suffixes. Over a quarter of the adjectives are cast in the past participial form typical of *Antony* (*burnish'd, beaten, dimpled, divers-colour'd*), but there is only one monosyllable in the lot. More than any other aspect of the passage, the adjectives convey the impression that this passage is particularly poetic and that it constitutes a remarkable departure from the usual manner of the blunt, ironic Enobarbus. This sudden dominance of a feature that has before been more or less underplayed has been termed "foregrounding," and there are those who see this phenomenon as the essence of style.[14]

Dimensions of the Present

The review of subjects to be included in a complete description of the style of these plays does not exhaust the possibilities, but it must suffice. The following summary of what has been said about the style of *Richard II* and of *Antony and Cleopatra* in the three methodological chapters of this study will proceed in the order dictated by linguistic theory—from the syntax of the sentence to that of the clause, the group, and the word.

The sentences of *Antony* are shorter than those of *Richard II* whether one measures them by words, clauses, or lines per sentence. Exclamatory sentences were more frequent in the earlier play, but imperatives increased significantly in the later play. There was no difference between the plays in the frequency of interrogatives, but *Richard II* showed a high number of *who* questions, while verbless questions and questions in declarative form marked the interrogatives of *Antony*. The imperatives of *Antony* were further distinguished by *let* optatives and by verbless forms. The increase of verbless interrogatives and imperatives is doubtless related to the fact that minor and simple sentences increase in *Antony*, while embedding,

---

[14] "Foregrounding" is "the use of the devices of the language in such a way that this use itself attracts attention and is perceived as uncommon" (Bohuslav Havranek, "The Functional Differentiation of the Standard Language," in *A Prague School Reader on Esthetics, Literary Structure, and Style*, ed. and trans. Paul L. Garvin, p. 10). According to Jan Mukařovský, the architect of Czech structuralist aesthetics, the aesthetic function of language consists in the systematic and maximum foregrounding of some elements against a background of automatized language. See his "Standard Language and Poetic Language," in the same collection.

more characteristic of *Richard II*, decreases. An attempt to define sentence complexity showed that the immediate constituents of sentences in *Antony* tend to be a single clause and in *Richard II* a clause complex. Left-branching sentences created by group hypotaxis increased in *Antony*, producing symmetrical structures and periodic rhythms in contrast to the asymmetrical right-branching sentences of *Richard II*. With the exception of the study of mood, the analysis of sentences is based on a random sample rather than on the entire text.

The single attempt to measure clause length, undertaken in the discussion of group betas, suggested that in *Antony* clauses were shorter than in *Richard II* and that a decrease of adjuncts may explain the shorter clause. Group beta clauses in *Richard II* tended to have ambiguous antecedents and to attach themselves to clause- or sentence-final constituents; in *Antony* ambiguity was controlled by reducing embedded clauses in the immediate context of the group beta and by observing normal constituent sequence. The affinity of group betas for clause- and sentence-initial constituents creates the left-branching sentences of *Antony* associated with Roman speakers.

Relative clauses increased in *Antony*, although compound relative words like *whereto*, typical of *Richard II*, were sharply reduced. In the later play the favored relative words were the nominal *what*, the adverbial *when*, and the qualifying *which*. The homophoric, or self-specifying, function of the nominal and adverbial relatives was conspicuous in *Antony*. *What* clauses occurred frequently in preposition-complement structures and *when* clauses in initial position, and these constitute further characteristics of the style of *Antony*. Temporal relatives often took an expression of time as their antecedent, a fact that reinforced the meaning of time in the play, as did the fact that past-time reference doubled in these clauses.

It is convenient to summarize what has been said about nominal-group structure by reference to the primary group constituents of modifier, head, and qualifier. The high frequency of adjectives is a marked feature of modification in *Richard II*, but in *Antony* grammatical modifiers, especially determiners, are used to create special types of nominal groups. Highly characteristic of *Antony* are groups consisting of a determiner and a proper name (*an Antony, her Antony*) or of the definite article, an adjective, and a proper name (*the valiant Caesar*). Demonstrative determiners appear to a marked degree with monosyllabic adjectives in the same play, particularly with *great* (*that great property, this great world*). Similarly, the occurrence of demonstrative and possessive determiners before words like *land*, *earth*, and *world* is characteristic of *Richard II* and appears to be independent of the high frequency of such lexical words. *Antony*, on the other hand, favors words like *sea* with zero determiner and *world* with quantifiers and the homophoric function of the definite article. Other modifying structures peculiar to each play are groups like *such gentle sorrow* in *Richard II* and *such another emphasis* in *Antony*. Nouns in *-ing* and *-ion* occurred with similar frequency in both plays, but they become, together with the increase of nouns in *-ness*, a distinctive mark of *Antony* because they appear so often with possessive determiners.

Among types of head, titles abound in *Richard II*, pronouns and proper names in *Antony*. It may also be the case that functional shift, especially of nouns to verbs (*boy*, *ballad*), is more characteristic of *Antony*. There is a higher proportion of paratactic nominal groups in *Richard II* to occurrences of *and* than one finds in *Antony*, and two or three adjectives will modify a noun in this play though such multiplicity is rare in the later play.

It is also characteristic of the later play to qualify nominal groups introduced by a nonspecific determiner or groups consisting of a substitute head. Qualification is carried a step further in *Antony* when groups introduced by a specific determiner like the demonstrative are completed by a qualifying clause (*this good purpose that so fairly shows*). Modifier and qualifier work together in structures like *so lated. . . that I | Have lost my way*, where the intensifier *so* demands a qualifier. Such groups are characteristic of *Antony*, and it seems reasonable to conclude that, where Shakespeare relied on adjectives to lend interest and point to nominal groups in *Richard II*, he tends more often in *Antony* to invoke grammatical determiners and qualifiers to make his language highly specific and concrete even to the point of providing further specification to groups that are already specified.

To the syntax of the word belong many features traditionally associated with diction—syllables per word, types of affix, and the provenance of words. The study of diction here was confined to preposed adjectives and a limited number of nouns. The nouns studied were agent nouns in *-er*, verbal nouns in *-ing*, and abstract nouns in *-ion* and *-ness*. Abstract nouns in *-ness* increased noticeably in *Antony*, and a large number of the agent nouns in this play appear to be coinages. Adjectives of two syllables were preferred to monosyllabic adjectives in *Richard II*, whereas in *Antony* the ratio of these types was equal because monosyllabic adjectives increased as two-syllabled adjectives decreased. Proper names, however, reveal quite another set of proportions. In *Richard II* monosyllabic names are slightly more frequent than polysyllabic names, but in *Antony* polysyllabic names are ten times as frequent as monosyllabic names. At a rough estimate, three-quarters of the proper names and preposed adjectives in *Richard II* are words of one and two syllables, while a third of the names and adjectives in *Antony* are polysyllabic.[15] Although it is not strictly a matter of diction, it is convenient to note here that colloquial contractions of pronouns before verbs or after prepositions characterize the style of the later play and, more particularly, the language of the two major characters.

Analysis of affixes indicated that the adjectives in *Richard II* were characterized by a higher frequency of prefixes. The ratio of suffixes to adjectives in these two plays was virtually the same, but the type of suffix differed. English suffixes like *-y* and *-less* were favored in the earlier play; later there was an over-all increase of Latinate suffixes with *-(i)an* a special favorite. As is well known, superlatives characterize the adjectives of *Antony*; furthermore, the combination of inflected adjectives, numerals, and intensifiers like *more* and *most* can be subsumed under the heading "quantifier," so that quantification is as distinctive of *Antony* as qualification is of *Richard II*. Finally, the two plays differed in participial adjectives, with present tense marking those of the English play and past tense the Roman.

What has been traditionally called unusual word order was redefined as marked constituent sequence and was examined, either by sample or by exhaustive analysis, at the levels of sentence, clause, and group. Two types of marked sequence were distinguished, inversion and discontinuity. A study of the random sentence sample showed that in the paratactic complexes of *Richard II* one clause tends to include the other, while the separation of alpha and beta in hypotactic group complexes is more characteristic of *Antony*. In both plays, therefore, discontinuity rather than inversion seems to be the preferred type of marked sequence at sentence level.

The sequence of clause constituents in *Richard II* is distinguished by complement theme, especially by intensive complements in theme position, and by the frequent choice of marked mood, especially of the PS variety, after complement theme. While complement theme and marked mood are both reduced in *Antony*, when they do occur the former is notable for the high frequency of pronouns in theme position and a

---

[15] For the frequencies of syllables per adjective, see Table 6, for proper names, Table A-37.

tendency to assume secondary theme position, and marked mood tends to be of the pSP variety. The increase of complements in secondary theme position in *Antony* may be related to the fact that double theme increases in this play, as does vocative theme. All these are types of inverted sequence at the clause level, and they are based on exhaustive analysis, not on a sample.

A complete study of discontinuity at clause level was confined to structures where the predicator and complement are interrupted by an adjunct (PAC). The intervening adjunct tends to be a particle in *Richard II* and a fully lexical word or phrase in *Antony*. The sentence sample from *Antony* indicated that clauses with two complements may have increased in this play and that such clauses are subject to both types of marked sequence; that is, the complements may be inverted (*make poor my greatness*) or rendered discontinuous by the presence of some other constituent (*rank me in register / A master-leaver*).

The handling of sequence at group level is among the most attractive features of *Antony*. Only in this play does one find such daring liberties taken with verbal-group structure (*Not Caesar's valour hath o'erthrown Antony*) or such combinations of inversion and discontinuity in nominal-group structure as *conclusions infinite / Of easy ways to die*. Another salient type of marked group sequence in *Antony* is the inversion of qualifier and head (*Of many thousand kisses the poor last*). Discontinuities like *They love not poison that do poison need* are the most characteristic form of nominal-group deviance in *Richard II*.

To this survey of stylistic features that are deemed characteristic of the plays by virtue of formal analysis may be added the results of attempts to interpret data in the light of rhetorical and literary theory. Thus, the figures of metaphor and synecdoche were discussed as violations of certain restrictions on adjective-noun relations. Fictional world and point of view were examined chiefly through a study of determiners and the lexical content of the nouns they modify. Finally, interrogatives were seen to be associated with women or strong emotion, the personal relative clauses (*whom, whose*, etc.) with women or sensuous pleasure, colloquial language (contractions, verbless sentences) with Cleopatra and Antony rather than with Caesar, and group beta clauses with Antony and Caesar.

By way of a more concrete summary, several features ascribed to the style of each play can be shown to cluster in passages that are reasonably representative of their respective plays:

Then, as I said, the Duke, great Bolingbroke,
Mounted upon a hot and fiery steed
Which his aspiring rider seem'd to know,
With slow but stately pace kept on his course,
Whilst all tongues cried 'God save thee, Bolingbroke!'
You would have thought the very windows spake,
So many greedy looks of young and old
Through casements darted their desiring eyes
Upon his visage; and that all the walls
With painted imagery had said at once
'Jesu preserve thee! Welcome, Bolingbroke!'
                                    (*R2* 5.2.7-17)

          Ah, dear, if I be so,
From my cold heart let heaven engender hail,
And poison it in the source, and the first stone
Drop in my neck; as it determines, so
Dissolve my life! The next Caesarion smite!
Till by degrees the memory of my womb,
Together with my brave Egyptians all,
By the discandying of this pelleted storm,
Lie graveless, till the flies and gnats of Nile
Have buried them for prey!
                                    (*Ant.* 3.13.158-167)

In the first passage one observes the paratactic nominal group *young and old* and the doubling of adjectives in *hot and fiery* and *slow but stately*. There is one adjective for every nine words. The suffixes *-y* and *-ly* are characteristic, as are the two present participial adjectives. The use of *so* in the second sentence is typical in two respects, and in both respects it is clearly contrastive with the style of *Antony*. As a modifier it assumes the form *so* X Y. whereas in the later play it would be more likely to occur as *so* X *a* Y, and it does not demand, so to speak, its qualifiers. The more likely structure in *Antony* would be *so greedy that you would have thought* and so on. The consequent looseness of structure that one finds in this sentence occurs also in the previous sentence where the subject of *to know* in the third line can be either *which* or *rider*. *Which* is the more likely choice, and in that case *aspiring rider* is an instance of complement theme, another characteristic of the play. Both sentences have elaborate subjects and manifest a tendency toward left-branching structure, but all other constituents are so simple that the result is not structurally symmetrical. In sum, there are nine or ten aspects of syntax in these lines that were found to be stylistic features of *Richard II*.

Cleopatra's speech is one where syntax and vocabulary are both complex. Indeed the sentence structure belies the contention that the syntax of this play is simpler than that of *Richard II*, but it is undeniably rich in other stylistic features. There is the vocative *dear*, the three proper names (two of them polysyllabic), and the verbal noun *discandying*. This verbal and the word *pelleted* are probably both instances of functional shift and may even be coinages. For every eighteen words there is one adjective, half the proportion found in the passage from *Richard II*. The adjectives include the monosyllabic *cold* and *brave*, the past participle *pelleted*, and the quantifier *first*. An optative imperative introduced by *let* governs the mood of the entire speech, and the nominal-group constituents *my brave Egyptians all* are assumed to be inverted. Though the study of constituent sequence was not complete enough to determine whether they are significant, one finds several other examples of marked sequence—the SCP in *The next Caesarion smite* and at least three instances of adjunct theme (*from . . . heart, so, by degrees*). Depending on how one weights them, one could say that there are some ten to fifteen stylistic features in this passage.

Before reviewing questions of methodology, it is useful to consider what this study has added to our knowledge of Shakespeare's style. Every new insight into Shakespeare's language is valuable in itself, but new insights have the further use of justifying formal analysis. One can always argue that the documentation of intuition is sufficient justification for formal stylistic analysis, yet it is also desirable that linguistic and quantitative methods of study be revealing and productive.

In many cases, particularly with respect to diction, this study has restated features of style that have been noted by others. That adjectives decrease as Shakespeare's style develops is common knowledge. F. E. Halliday noted that paratactic nominal groups were typical of Shakespeare's middle style, although he did not use that name for the phenomenon and he did not exemplify it by citations from *Richard II*. Bernard Groom analyzed the Spenserian elements in the diction of the middle-period plays, and Maurice Charney documented, among other things, the abundance of superlatives in *Antony*. Vivian Salmon pointed out that agent nouns in *-er* are a general characteristic of Shakespeare's language, and A. C. Partridge has shown that contractions increase markedly in the later plays. In this study each of these isolated statements has been gathered together by a comprehensive framework; their specific dimensions have been charted; and certain relationships among them pointed out. One hopes that the contrastive method of viewing these features in the light of two plays has shed new light on old knowledge.

At other times popular ideas have been modified. It is a common opinion that compound adjectives are a mark of the middle style. They are undoubtedly more frequent in *Richard II* than in *Antony*, but, since adjectives are also more frequent, the proportion of compound to total adjectives is virtually the same for both plays and compounds are in this sense as characteristic of one play as they are of the other. What may be characteristic of the middle style is the tendency in *Richard II* to place two or three adjectives before a noun, a phenomenon doubtless allied to the frequency of paratactic nominal groups. One tends to associate Latinate words with aspects of the later style, yet one of the most typically Latinate words, the abstract noun in *-ion*, is of similar frequency in both plays. The tension between abstract and concrete, often remarked only with respect to the juxtaposition of Latinate and Saxon words in the later style, was observed also in *Antony* in the characteristic use of the concrete possessive determiner to modify abstract nouns, in the addition of the abstract suffix *-ness* to concrete adjectives, and in the kinds of selection restrictions that are violated in adjective-noun relations. The latter is, of course, a question of imagery. Wolfgang Clemen, in his study of Shakespeare's stylistic development, noted a growing tendency toward the mingling of abstract and concrete images in the middle period (to which *Richard II* may be assigned). It is to be noted, however, that (at least where adjective-noun relations are concerned) the mingling of abstract and concrete is more characteristic of *Antony* than of *Richard II*. In one sense this trait is obvious, but a more complete knowledge of how imagery operates in texts can be tantamount to new knowledge. For example, Julian Markels sees synecdoche as a characteristic of style in *Antony and Cleopatra*. Synecdoche is indeed present in the play, but the data in this study suggest further that the figure is not so typical of *Antony* as it is of *Richard II*, that Antony is not presented so indirectly in these opening lines as King Richard in 3.3.62-71 or as Bolingbroke in 3.2.106-111, and that the synecdochic presentation of Antony in the speeches of Caesar contrasts with that of Cleopatra, who tends to see him as a total human being.[16]

[16] Julian Markels (*The Pillar of the World*, p. 156) uses the term *metonymy* (change of name) to describe the mode of reference to Antony in 1.1.1-11, but *synecdoche* (part/whole relations) is more accurate. For earlier discussion of this material, see pp. 166-169.

Several features may be intuitively obvious to many readers of Shakespeare. The preference for titles in one play and for names in the other, or the increase of simple and verbless sentences in *Antony*, or the high frequency in the later play of optative imperatives governed by *let* have been mentioned by critics in their discussion of nonstylistic aspects of these plays.[17] Most statements made about characters, themes, and the fictional world of the two plays are common knowledge, but the method of documenting these intuitions by reference to determiners is new and provides fresh perspectives on old topics. For example, identity is not the same sort of problem in *Richard II* that it is in *Antony* if the analysis of point of view or the proportion of title to name has any significance.

Of course, some results may be regarded by unsympathetic critics as trivial. The count of syllables per adjective or proper name is certainly liable to this charge, yet information of this kind can have important implications. The first is methodological—a simple over-all count of syllables per content word in the two plays will probably not reveal any appreciable difference between them with respect to the frequency of polysyllabic and shorter words. Yet one need not abandon hypotheses, for example, about the prominence of polysyllabic words in *Antony* if the frequency study is based, as it has been here, on word classes rather than on total words. A second implication is the fact that the high frequency of polysyllabic names in *Antony* may affect meter and will certainly affect rhythm, since vocatives also increase in this play, often affect its rhythm, and will often consist of polysyllabic names. Finally, it is possible to discover a third stylistic feature by combining two others. In *Antony and Cleopatra*, for example, a third of the names modified by adjectives consist of a monosyllabic adjective before a polysyllabic name.[18] Few would

---

[17] R. A. Foakes first called attention to the importance of proper names in Shakespeare's work, and his observations are more than intuitive, since he lists the frequencies of important names in half a dozen plays. See Note 14 of his "An Approach to *Julius Caesar*," *Shakespeare Quarterly* 5 (1954): 259-270. Reuben A. Brower discusses optative imperatives as "heroic oaths" in his *Hero and Saint*, p. 321.

[18] The exact figure is sixteen monosyllabic adjectives before polysyllabic names out of forty-nine names preceded by adjectives in *Antony*. In *Richard II* ten out of forty-six modified names take this phonological shape: *high Hereford* (2), *old Lancaster*, *poor Bolingbroke*, *proud Bolingbroke* (2), *great Bolingbroke* (2), *proud Hereford*, *grim Necessity*. As usual there is a great deal of repetition, and the combination centers on *Bolingbroke*, one of the few polysyllabic names in the play and a name with a very high frequency. Still, there is reason to believe that this phonological combination is a small strand in Shakespeare's presentation of Bolingbroke as a heroic figure.

dispute the effectiveness of the combination: *dull Octavia, strong Eno-barb, pale Cassius, good Diomed, kind Charmian, salt Cleopatra*, and so on. What one chooses to regard as important or insignificant is usually a matter of one's ulterior objectives and interests. Those who contend with J. R. Firth that it is part of the meaning of a Frenchman to sound like a Frenchman will agree that the high frequency of polysyllabic proper names and the relative increase of monosyllabic adjectives is part of the meaning of *Antony and Cleopatra*.[19]

Shakespeare's word order and its possible relationship to verse rhythm seem not to have been explored previously, although Sr. Miriam Joseph noted the increase of the figures of grammar, and some of these are labels for unusual word order. Particular observations' about the increase of nouns in *-ness*, vocatives, past participial adjectives, quantifiers, relative clauses, various types of nominal-group structure, and the role played by group beta clauses in left-branching sentences are all new and are all stylistic properties of *Antony and Cleopatra*. Finally, the idea of concentrating in a study of Shakespeare's style on blank-verse syntax, of including in it syntactic structures below the level of the sentence, and of undertaking a formal and exhaustive analysis of many stylistic features in two plays is new. *Richard II* and *Antony and Cleopatra* were chosen for study because they represent distinct periods of Shakespeare's stylistic development, and it seems reasonable to assume that features found to be characteristic of these two plays belong as well to other plays of their respective periods. Thus, what has been said of *Antony* may apply also to *Macbeth*, *Lear*, and *Coriolanus*; and features of *Richard II* will perhaps be found in *Romeo*, *A Midsummer Night's Dream*, and other English history plays.[20]

Defining the Style Function

Style has been defined as a propositional function $S(A)$; the style of a given object as $S(a)$. Because a function can exist only between two well-defined sets, the first step in the study of style must be to specify the

[19] J. R. Firth's well-known remark has been recorded in various forms; one version appears in "Modes of Meaning," *Essays and Studies by Members of the English Association* 4 (1951): 120.

[20] G. W. Knight rightly contends that each play has a unique style ("The *Othello* Music," in his *The Wheel of Fire*, p. 97), but such remarks must refer to the total style. There is no reason why some of the features that contribute to the unique style of one play should not appear as features in the unique style of other plays. This is particularly true when the features in question are derived from grammatical rather than lexical categories.

structural components of objects in the domain of the function. When the theory is applied, the method of specifying the structural components of a given object will vary depending on the type of object to be described. One cannot define paintings by reference to language, but language might reasonably supply the basis for a study of style in literature. In this study of style in *Richard II* and *Antony and Cleopatra*, the method of specifying structural components has been to identify and to count certain linguistic units, such as relative clauses, kinds of deviant sequence, and proper names. These units had been previously defined and organized by linguistic theory, but the fact that they could be shown to contribute to an understanding of the texts as literature was taken to be sufficient reason for viewing them as valid components of literary works rather than as purely linguistic entities. Given the present state of linguistic theory, many aspects of literary structure cannot be formalized; hence, the complex task of describing these plays cannot be completed here and no definitive statement about their style can be made.

It is possible, however, to illustrate how the theory of style as a function can be applied and to define provisionally some aspects of style in the two plays by reference to the data of this study. The formula for applying the theory of the style function has its origin in the Pythagorean theorem, which states that the square of the hypotenuse of a right triangle is equal to the sum of the squares of its two sides. In analytic geometry this theorem provides the basis for measuring the distance, d, between two points on a flat surface by means of the formula $d = \sqrt{(a - c)^2 + (b - d)^2}$, where a, b, c, and d are the coordinates of the two points. When two points are defined by many dimensions, the formula can be generalized to yield a measure of the distance between them.[21] For example, one can state one difference in style between *Richard II* and *Antony and Cleopatra* with respect to sentence mood by specifying the frequencies (coordinates) of each type of sentence in the two plays. Since the length of these plays is equal when prose is omitted, the coordinates of sentence mood can be specified by the simple frequencies for exclamatory, interrogative, and

---

[21] The formula $d = \sqrt{(a - c)^2 + (b - d)^2}$ measures the distance between two points where the distance is a straight line and where all coordinates used to define the points are plotted in an orthogonal system, independent of one another. In a study of style encompassing all of Shakespeare's plays, the line drawn through the points that define the components of each play would undoubtedly be a curved line. By an extension of analytic geometry, it would be possible to calculate the equation of a curve representing the locus of many plays.

imperative sentences recorded in Table 1.[22] The structural components of *Richard II* can thus be represented as a point whose coordinates with respect to sentence mood are (12, 236, 460); similarly the structural components of *Antony and Cleopatra* for the corresponding choices in the system of mood are (8, 261, 780). The difference in the styles of the two plays can thus be calculated as the distance between (12, 236, 460) and (8, 261, 780) by expanding and applying the formula given above:

$$d = \sqrt{(12\text{-}8)^2 + (236\text{-}261)^2 + (460\text{-}780)^2}$$

$$d = \sqrt{103{,}041}$$

$$d = 321$$

The number 321 represents the difference in the styles of *Richard II* and *Antony and Cleopatra* with respect to sentence mood.

The notion that certain texts have similar styles or that the styles of two texts differ can thus be redefined as observations about the closeness or distance of points in the domain of the style function.[23] It is virtually certain that a complete specification of the structural components of literary texts will yield a set of uniquely defined points. In this sense all styles are different, but the points associated with some styles are closer to one another than the points associated with other styles. When two points are close together, this fact can be explained on the basis of dimensions that have been specified by similar coordinates; when they are at a great distance from each other, their dimensions have been specified by markedly different coordinates.

The more complete the description of the object in the domain of style, the more accurate will be the statement about similarities and differences between the styles associated with those objects. Since an exhaustive description of a long text is time-consuming, there is a tendency on the part of analysts of style to select and emphasize dimensions of a text whose specifications are likely to differ widely, but such selectivity can

[22] Where texts are not of the same length, ratios could be substituted for simple frequencies. A complete statement about the system of mood must, of course, include the frequency of declarative sentences.

[23] The style-function theory would require the use of statistical measures to establish sets in the style space, to determine what dimensions explain a given distance between two literary works, or to decide what distance between points will be deemed significant so that two texts may be assigned to different authors or to different periods within the career of a single author.

introduce serious distortion. In Table 41, for example, there is a set of coordinates that might be said to define provisionally the styles of the three major characters in *Antony and Cleopatra*. Applying the formula for the distance between points to the data in Table 41, one finds that the distance between the styles of Antony and Cleopatra is .0828; that between Antony and Caesar is .1789; and the distance between Cleopatra and Caesar is .2222. As one might expect intuitively, Cleopatra and Caesar are far apart. Antony is comparatively near both these figures, but he is closer to Cleopatra. These results confirm one's impression of an Antony who shares Cleopatra's preference for colloquial language (defined here by ellipsis and substitution) but who can rival Caesar's oratory (defined by group beta complexes) when he chooses to do so.

Assuming for the sake of example that these results reflect real and complete differences among these three speakers, it follows that any sampling of dimensions that purports to represent the characteristic styles of each speaker should reflect this pattern. If one should decide, however, that Antony and Caesar are typically Roman speakers and that the characteristic mark of a Roman speaker is a high frequency of group beta clauses, he might obtain a very different set of results from those recorded in the preceding paragraph. To illustrate this example Figure 2 shows that the proportion of group beta clauses to instances of nominal-group deviance in the speeches of all three characters has been plotted as a set of points in two-dimensional space. In Figure 2 the points associated with the styles of Antony and Caesar are remarkably close together, but they lie at some

Group betas : Group deviance

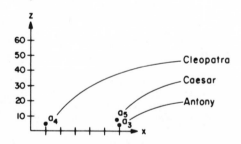

Fig. 2. The effect of selectivity on the style function

remove from the point that represents the style of Cleopatra. The pattern revealed by Figure 2 is quite dissimilar to that shown when several dimensions are used to define the points associated with the styles of these speakers. When one seeks only to specify the source of felt differences between the styles of two texts, such bias in the presentation of the data may be allowed, but the dimensions that explain the distance between two styles are not to be confused with style itself. The style of any object is associated with a point specified by many dimensions, namely, all the dimensions of the total work. When several works are compared, they will be identical with respect to some dimensions (*Richard II* and *Antony and Cleopatra* are identical in the frequency of echo questions, for example); they will be similar along other dimensions; and they will be markedly different from one another in still other dimensions. The theory that style is a function of the total work does not restrict or reduce style to those dimensions that account for differences but requires that all dimensions be specified before the style of an object can be finally defined. Despite the multiplicity of dimensions and the complexity of the task, the theory of the style function gives coherence to the work of stylistic analysis by postulating the view that style is not a collection of features but a single point defined by many dimensions.

The mathematical formula used to apply the theory of the style function in the preceding paragraphs requires that the dimensions used to define the structural components of an object must be independent of one another. The data on sentence mood in Table 1, for example, are independent of one another because they are based on the mutually exclusive categories of the system of mood, but the data in Table 2, which yield the frequencies and classes of interrogative sentences, are not independent of the data on interrogatives in Table 1. Table 1 shows that all interrogatives increase by a frequency of 25 in *Antony*, while Table 2 shows that a particular type of interrogative, variant questions, increases by a frequency of 32. Hence, in specifying the dimensions of the two plays, one must choose either the over-all frequency of interrogatives or the frequencies of the classes of interrogatives. The categories of systemic grammar are organized in such a way that choosing independent dimensions need never create a problem. Indeed, the scale of delicacy, where grammatical units are arranged from the primary degree of structure (e.g., clauses) to the point beyond which no further grammatical relations obtain (e.g., embedded relative clauses introduced by *when*) allows one to take several cross-sectional views of the multidimensional literary object. One may wish to examine the primary degree of delicacy when comparing texts that are quite dissimilar (Chaucer's poems and Dickens's novels) and to invoke the greatest degree of delicacy when texts are quite similar (sections of the same literary work).

The fact that categories are independent of one another in the language does not necessarily mean that they will be independent in a given text. Some grammatical categories seem to dominate certain texts.[24] If these categories can be identified and their relationship to others charted, dependent categories can be eliminated or modified when the dimensions for describing the text are stated in their final form. It would seem, for example, that adjectives are dominant in *Richard II*. The significant presence of intensive complements in theme position in this play may be related to the high frequency of adjectives, since intensive complements are often adjectival. If this hypothesis proved true, then the high frequency of marked mood, especially of the predicator-subject variety, might also be related to the high frequency of adjectives, since this type of marked mood usually follows intensive complement theme in *Richard II*. Thus, at least two stylistic features may be related to the high frequency of adjectives in this play. Ironically, one can simplify the data only by increasing and extending them.

In order to state relations of dependence among textual features, the description of linguistic features must be conducted with greater rigor than was possible in this study, where the aim was to establish a comprehensive framework for the study of style rather than to concentrate on a particular task. A more rigorous description of features would seek to determine the factors that condition the presence and frequency of stylistic features.

Suppose that one wished to know how often the auxiliary and the head of a verbal group were interrupted by another constituent, as happens in this example:

> But let us rear
> The higher our opinion, that our stirring
> *Can* from the lap of Egypt's widow *pluck*
> The ne'er-lust-wearied Antony.
> (*Ant.* 2.1.35-38)

[24] In "A Framework for the Statistical Analysis of Style," Lubomír Doležel discusses the need for examining text characteristics to see which ones are highly correlated and to eliminate the dependent characteristics (*Statistics and Style*, ed. Lubomír Doležel and Richard W. Bailey, p. 19).

One would need to know the frequency of auxiliary verbs, since this information constitutes the fundamental condition that makes it possible for the verbal group to include other constituents and would set an upper limit on the number of times such discontinuity was possible. Since interrogatives make subject inclusion in the verbal group obligatory, these must not be counted among the instances of stylistic discontinuity of verbal-group constituents. This much information can be obtained from a concordance by a perusal of all tense and modal auxiliary verbs (*have*, *do*, *may*, etc.).

The possibility of interrupting a verbal group is further conditioned by whether or not there is a clause constituent available to serve as a nested item. In the following clauses there are none:

> There's beggary in the love that *can be reckon'd*
> > (*Ant.* 1.1.15)
>
> And such a twain *can do't*, in which I bind,
> > (*Ant.* 1.1.38)
>
> It does from childishness. *Can Fulvia die*?
> > (*Ant.* 1.3.58)

These conditions may be defined by rules of grammar, but there are others that can be defined only by probability or appropriateness. To define such rules is an important goal of stylistic analysis. A study of verbal-group discontinuity is only one thread in the complex phenomenon of marked sequence, yet it is staggering to consider what must be undertaken by a linguistically and quantitatively sophisticated study of this single feature. Among other things, it would be necessary to determine whether certain types of interrupter are more likely to occur than others, since it is possible that relatively common words like *never* could explain the discontinuities in one play, while in another nested items might assume complex forms, as in this interlacing of nominal- and verbal-group constituents:

> Now, darting Parthia, art thou stroke, and now
> Pleas'd fortune does *of Marcus Crassus' death*
> Make me *revenger*.
> > (*Ant.* 3.1.1-3)

This example raises the question of the probability of verbal-group interruption occurring when other departures from normal word order occur in the immediate context. The above example shows that multiple discontinuity can occur, but one would not expect it to happen too often. Similarly, if another set of stylistic oppositions is operating, then nesting may be suppressed in its favor:

> That jade hath eat bread from my royal hand;
> This hand hath made him proud with clapping him.
>   (*R2* 5.5.85-86)

Assuming that the desire for parallelism is dominant stylistically, verbal-group interruption in one line would spoil it; in two lines, it might create excessive ornamentation.

The likelihood of discontinuous negatives, commands, negative questions, and negative commands must also be considered. The interruption of verbal groups in questions by elements other than the obligatorily included subject is possible and occurs, but, if one could assess the general probability of its happening, it would not be so great as that of interrupting a verbal group in a declarative sentence. It seems most unlikely that nesting would occur in the verbal group of an interpolated clause:

> Write to him
> (I *will subscribe*) gentle adieus and greetings.
>   (*Ant.* 4.5.13-14)

Then there are semantic considerations. Meaning sometimes depends on the position an item assumes in the verbal group:

> Our holy lives must win a new world's crown,
> Which our profane hours here have stricken down.
>   (*R2* 5.1.24-25)

If these lines were altered so that *here* interrupted the verbal group, the meaning of *here* could change from signifying *here in this life* or *in this world*, to the more specifically locative meaning, *in this spot*. A major consideration would be whether obscurity in the semantic component would tolerate the additional abnormality of verbal-group discontinuity. This obscurity could occur with a particularly difficult metaphor, or it might be produced by a fairly unusual word occurring as head of the verbal group:

> Epicurean cooks
> Sharpen with cloyless sauce his appetite,
> That sleep and feeding may prorogue his honour

Even till a Lethe'd dulness!

(Ant. 2.1.24-27)

One can think of several other reasons why Shakespeare did not include *his honour* within the verbal group; for example, he may have wanted a light ending, but this may serve to exemplify the main point.

Phonology undoubtedly plays a major part in determining whether or not a verbal group will be rendered discontinuous. Rhyme, meter, and placement of the tonic syllable are all affected by constituent order; or constituent order may be changed to accommodate them. All these factors must be sorted out, not only for the study of verbal-group sequence but also for all types of marked sequence and indeed for all other aspects of style.

From Grammatical Style to Rhetorical Style

The method used here for specifying the structural components of two literary texts has fulfilled certain minimal requirements for stylistic analysis. It has formalized the data in order to define some sources of felt differences between two plays of Shakespeare and in order to establish an explicit basis for comparing these and any other group of texts. The method was not invoked with a view to making a final and definitive statement about the style of these plays, but with the intention of answering certain questions about the location of style, the usefulness of linguistic and quantitative techniques for stylistic analysis, and the possibility of relating concepts like "fictional world" and "point of view" to formal stylistic studies. It is by no means certain that the simple linguistic categories adopted here supply the best possible dimensions for the study of style. If traditional stylistic labels like "colloquial," "heroic," and "dramatic" could be defined in a precise manner, such labels might constitute a set of dimensions for specifying the structural components of a literary work. What has been said about the need of determining the factors that condition the presence of a linguistic feature in a text applies all the more strongly to the attempt to define stylistic labels.

It is impossible, for example, to state categorically that the syntax of *Antony and Cleopatra* is more or less complex than that of *Richard II*. Certainly there are many ways in which the syntax of the later play seems more complex. Left-branching sentences are a case in point, but, since they tend to consist of clauses whose constituents appear in normal sequence, the tendency toward normal sequence may be construed as a simplifying feature that cancels the complexity created by left-branching sentences. Moreover, other aspects of sentence structure in *Antony* show a tendency toward simplicity in that sentences on the whole are shorter, sentences consisting of a single clause increase in frequency, and embedding decreases. Verbless sentences, ellipsis, and the higher frequency of pronouns all testify to an increase of colloquial language whose presence in *Antony* may argue a greater simplicity of syntax. On the other hand, the sequence of nominal-group constituents tends toward greater deviance in the later play, a circumstance that may contribute to sentence complexity, since it operates at a more rigidly controlled level of the language and thus constitutes a more serious violation of rules.

If nominal groups are more complex with respect to sequence, however, their structure may in some ways have grown simpler in *Antony and Cleopatra*. Prehead modification has been reduced by the decrease of adjectives, and the tendency to add qualifiers to nominal groups introduced by nonspecific determiners or governed by substitute heads has resulted in a more cohesive group structure. Increased cohesion in nominal-group structure is matched by greater cohesion in hypotactic group complexes. Whereas the syntax of *Richard II* manifested a tendency toward ambiguity that made it difficult to determine the antecedents of certain clauses, this tendency was corrected in the later play by reducing the number and length of embedded clauses in the matrix of the hypotactic complex. Cohesion thus increases clarity, and clarity may create an impression of greater simplicity in nominal-group structure. The cohesion gained by reducing clause constituents, however, could lead to compression, and compression may be a factor that complicates syntax. Similarly, the reduction of adjectives may simplify nominal-group structure, but the figures of speech created by adjective-noun collocations in *Antony* grow more complex, assuming that reification is a more complex figure than personification.

Finally, rhythm, an aspect of style that has not been investigated formally in this study, is probably related to the changes in syntax observed in *Antony and Cleopatra*. The fact that the rhythms of this play seem more varied, subtle, and dynamic than those of *Richard II* may point toward greater complexity in sentence prosody. Indeed it is tempting to suggest that whatever changes Shakespeare made in his syntax were made with a view to rhythmic effect. In *Richard II* he seems to have ignored or wrenched certain rules of syntax in order to maintain a single rhythm—a rather sonorous and expansive rhythm. In *Antony* he seems to have realized that he could manipulate and vary rhythm by changing syntactic structures and the sequence of constituents within them. These changes entailed greater attention to the rules of syntax, if only to break them in the most effective manner.

One might summarize these remarks by suggesting that the bare syntactic structures, especially the clauses, of *Antony and Cleopatra* are simpler than those of *Richard II*, even though one might easily find half a dozen sentences in *Antony* that are altogether more complex than any half dozen sentences taken from the earlier play. This increased simplicity in *Antony* centers in the clause, the linguistic unit that appears to carry the greatest amount of information. The fact that clauses are simpler in themselves while their external nexes (e.g., in hypotactic group complexes) and their internal constituents (e.g., nominal groups) are more cohesive makes it possible for Shakespeare to complicate other levels of syntax without too great a loss of clarity. Thus, rhythm can be complicated by left-branching sentences and by deviant nominal-group sequence, and meaning can be complicated by more striking figures of speech because the syntax of the clause remains simple enough to convey the information needed to interpret these more complex rhythms and meanings.

This summary statement about the relative complexity of syntax in *Richard II* and *Antony and Cleopatra* illustrates the difficulty of defining stylistic labels with the kind of precision required to use such labels as the dimensions of a coordinate system in a quantitative study of style. When students of style have learned as much about the rules that govern the behavior of language in a literary text as linguists have learned about grammar, it is conceivable that they could devise a set of well-defined labels that would serve as the dimensions of a coordinate system. The result might be a rhetoric with the same theoretical status now accorded to grammar. Until such a rhetoric exists, however, grammar supplies the most comprehensive, formal, and systematic categories for the description of style in literary texts. It is to be hoped that the careful study of texts by reference to grammar will prepare the ground for a formal theory of rhetoric.

It may not be amiss in concluding this evaluative discussion of stylistic theory and methodology to suggest some intermediate steps that might be taken in order to achieve the goal of a formal theory of rhetoric. One of the greatest needs is that of formalizing aspects of literature that cannot now be included in the study of style because they cannot be clearly defined. Second, special statistics could be created to measure the complex and refined data yielded by a sophisticated study of literary texts. There is also a particular need for automatic parsers and other programs that make it possible to analyze many long texts by computer. Texts of different authors, periods, and genres could be completely described so that more can be learned about the operation of language in literature. Similarly, efforts must be made to determine what constraints set limits on the operation of language in the special context of literature and what special correlations among language features exist so that the amount of data can be reduced. Formalisms for defining traditional stylistic labels might be devised or conventions adopted for specifying their content. Finally, wherever possible, the study of style should be conducted on similar linguistic and statistical bases so that enough information becomes available for comparative studies of the sort that make it possible to define universal rules of style in literature.

Chapter Five has been devoted to a discussion of those dimensions of style that have not been exhaustively treated in this study. Some of these dimensions, especially those dealing with the semantic component of the language or with the relationship between language and the context of situation, were omitted because there is no theoretical apparatus for describing them formally. Other dimensions, such as vocabulary, imagery, and certain aspects of syntax, were omitted for lack of time and space and because charting them would not yield any new theoretical or methodological knowledge to the present study. The dimensions described in earlier chapters were summarized and related to existing discussions of Shakespeare's language. Finally, the theory of the style function was illustrated by a provisional application, and possible further developments of the theory were discussed briefly.

CHAPTER SIX

From Stylistics to Poetics

History and Poetry

A brief discussion of Shakespeare's poetics—the artistic creed that explains in part the development of his style from the elegiac lyricism of *Richard II* to the epic brilliance of *Antony and Cleopatra*—might appropriately supplement this detailed investigation of Shakespeare's stylistic practice. Shakespeare's views about the poet's role, like his opinions on love, society, and politics, must be deduced from his works and the deductions eked out by more explicit statements on the subject made by his contemporaries. One aspect of Shakespeare's poetics, his view of the relationship between history and poetry, can be gleaned from a consideration of some structural similarities between *Richard II* and *Antony and Cleopatra* as well as from statements in these plays about fortune and imagination.

Several similarities between the plays have been pointed out by Peter Alexander: "The duel between Antony and Octavius repeats in a more spacious theatre that between Richard and Bolingbroke. Richard throws away a kingdom, while Antony squanders an empire, and as Antony has the capacity for rule and affairs that Richard had not, the Roman's conduct might be judged the more heinous, especially when such an aggravation as his liaison with Cleopatra is put in the balance."[1] Alexander observes, however, that the nationalism that permeates *Richard II* and injects a strong note of moral feeling into that play is absent from the Roman history with the result that Antony emerges as a man of heroic stature to whose preeminence Cleopatra bears witness.

The remarkable effect gained by involving a figure like Cleopatra in the dramatization of history can be best appreciated by comparing the discussions of fortune that occur toward the close of each play. One is initiated by King Richard, the other by Cleopatra. Both are addressed to the men who now stand high in fortune's favor. Early in the deposition scene Richard persuades Bolingbroke to enact with him a tableau:

> Give me the crown. Here, cousin, seize the crown.
> Here, cousin,
> On this side my hand, and on that side yours.
> Now is this golden crown like a deep well
> That owes two buckets, filling one another,
> The emptier ever dancing in the air,
> The other down, unseen, and full of water.
> That bucket down and full of tears am I,
> Drinking my griefs whilst you mount up on high.
>
> (4.1.181-189)

The buckets in the well are a familiar variant of the image of fortune's wheel. While Richard's commentary reveals great preoccupation with his own psychological state, the lesson in history is there for Bolingbroke to read. For the second time in this scene Richard engages his cousin in behavior that jars the latter's self-possession and gives the deposed king a measure of control over his adversary.[2] This tableau is followed by another in which Richard divests himself, actually or symbolically, of the insignia of office. The speech *Now mark me how I will undo myself* contains a further lesson in history, which is directed as much to the theater audience as to members of the onstage court. With the benefit of hindsight the audience realizes that the prayer *God keep all vows unbroke that swear to thee* will not be answered, since Northumberland will rebel

---

[1] Peter Alexander, *Alexander's Introductions to Shakespeare*, p. 169.
[2] Like the interrogatives in the closing lines of this scene (4.1.302-318), Richard's syntax here acquires the force of reality. His questions are answered and his commands are obeyed; moreover, they become instruments for revealing important truths, as was argued earlier (see pp. 30-34).

against King Henry IV. Richard here and elsewhere (5.1.55-68) assumes a prophetic role. He manifests an insight into history and human conduct that renders him superior to Bolingbroke, who has yet to experience the vicissitudes of kingship. More important, this insight places Richard above fortune, since it assures him that fortune can do no more harm to him than she has now done.

The lessons on fortune in the deposition scene of *Richard II* resemble events that occur during the meeting of Caesar and Cleopatra in the last act of *Antony*. Just as Richard engages Bolingbroke in activities and dialogue that unmask his pretensions and reveal the impermanence of his present position, so Cleopatra embroils Caesar in the Seleucus episode.[3] Like the ritual of the crown, it is an object lesson in the fate of the powerful, and, like the analogy of the buckets in the well, Cleopatra's commentary describes the turn of fortune's wheel:

> See, Caesar! O, behold,
> How pomp is followed! Mine will now be yours;
> And should we shift estates, yours would be mine.
> (5.2.150-152)

Several factors suggest that Cleopatra has engineered this incident. It recalls earlier scenes between Cleopatra and the messenger who brought word of Antony's marriage. Seleucus is threatened with physical violence, as the messenger had been, and he is questioned in order to elicit an answer that Cleopatra wants to hear. That this is the case seems obvious from the fact that Cleopatra need not have asked any question at all and had complete control over the type of question she would ask. Had she in fact kept something back that she wished to conceal, she would never have allowed the messenger this opportunity:

Cleo.   What have I kept back?

Sel.   Enough to purchase what you have made known.
(5.2.147-148)

Her response to Seleucus's apparent betrayal alludes only incidentally to

---

[3] Although it may be argued that Cleopatra could have chosen an object lesson on fortune that would be less damaging than the Seleucus episode, she could not have chosen one more indicative of Caesar's intentions. He is not alarmed by the news that Cleopatra has apparently kept in reserve a second fortune equal to the one she has shown him. Cleopatra concludes from his patronizing and conciliatory tone (*Feed and sleep* are words more appropriately used of an animal being fattened for a feast) that Caesar intends to lead her in triumph (*He words me, girls*).

the matter of the treasure, elaborates her own humiliation and Caesar's power, and concludes with a hint that Caesar, who shares her greatness, may one day share her defeat:

> Be it known that we, the greatest, are misthought
> For things that others do; and, when we fall,
> We answer others' merits in our name,
> Are therefore to be pitied.

(5.2.176-179)

One could argue that the discussion of fortune is a red herring intended to distract Caesar's attention from the question of Cleopatra's treasure, but that is to ignore the speech on fortune that opens and sets the tone for this final scene of the play:

> My desolation does begin to make
> A better life. 'Tis paltry to be Caesar.
> Not being Fortune, he's but Fortune's knave,
> A minister of her will. And it is great
> To do that thing that ends all other deeds,
> Which shackles accidents and bolts up change,
> Which sleeps, and never palates more the dung,
> The beggar's nurse and Caesar's.

(5.2.1-8)

With these words Cleopatra describes Caesar's submission to fortune and her determination to resist its sway as well as Caesar's. Prior to her meeting with him, she sends him messages that are carefully phrased to clarify their relative positions:

> If your master
> Would have a queen his beggar, you must tell him
> That majesty, to keep decorum, must
> No less beg than a kingdom. If he please
> To give me conquer'd Egypt for my son,
> He gives me so much of mine own as I
> Will kneel to him with thanks.

(5.2.15-21)

This speech denies Caesar's pretensions to sovereignty. She refers to him as *your master*, clearly implying that he is not hers. She herself is *majesty*. In asking to keep her own kingdom for her heir, she could scarcely ask for more. Caesar will be granting her what is hers by right, and for his generosity will receive a curtsy. The next speech continues to align Caesar with fortune and to disassociate Cleopatra from any hint of submission to his power:

> Pray you tell him
> I am his fortune's vassal and I send him
> The greatness he has got. I hourly learn
> A doctrine of obedience, and would gladly
> Look him i' th' face.
>
> (5.2.28-32)

Cleopatra will acknowledge only that she is subject to fortune as Caesar himself is; they are equally fortune's slaves. That she would gladly look Caesar in the face is no great sign of obedience but a statement that she is neither ashamed nor afraid to confront him.

The dignity that marks this confrontation is an important departure from Shakespeare's source, for Plutarch describes Cleopatra in terms suggesting a complete moral and physical breakdown: ". . . her voice was small and trembling, her eyes sunk into her head with continual blubbering, and moreover they might see the most part of her stomach torn in sunder. To be short, her body was not much better than her mind."[4] In Shakespeare's play Cleopatra not only is in command of herself but also asserts her authority over Caesar's. She defies him by insisting upon kneeling when he wishes her to rise and exposes the spurious character of his magnanimity by her equally false humility:

> *Caes.* Arise! You shall not kneel.
> I pray you rise. Rise, Egypt.
>
> *Cleo.* Sir, the gods
> Will have it thus. My master and my lord
> I must obey.
>
> (5.2.114-117)

Her refusal to rise is a gestural assertion of control over her own behavior, and her words remind Caesar that he is subject to forces beyond his control. Her own defeat is thus explained as obedience to the gods and not to Caesar.

---

[4]T. J. B. Spencer, ed., *Shakespeare's Plutarch*, pp. 286-287.

Caesar enters into the game and with a further show of magnanimity
cancels all of Cleopatra's past triumphs over him (through Antony) by
attributing them to fortune:

> Take to you no hard thoughts.
> The record of what injuries you did us,
> Though written in our flesh, we shall remember
> As things but done by chance.
>
> (5.2.117-120)

Cleopatra's reply, at first blush, seems to be a capitulaticn to Caesar's
charges and an acceptance of his pardon:

> Sole sir o' th' world,
> I cannot project mine own cause so well
> To make it clear; but do confess I have
> Been laden with like frailties which before
> Have often sham'd our sex.
>
> (5.2.120-124)

These words present some difficulty.[5] They may be Cleopatra's version of
the diplomatic jargon that Thyreus had affected on his earlier embassy
from Caesar, or they may mean that Cleopatra has accepted Caesar's statement of the case and is willing to attribute her past victories to fortune.
The phrase *like frailties* may refer to those of chance. If so, they are also
the frailties of women. By associating herself with the frailties of women,
she aligns herself with fortune, a female deity, and by this alliance she
reasserts her sway over Caesar, who is *fortune's knave, a minister of her
will*. By using Cleopatra to voice the reflections on fortune that had been
assigned to the hero in *Richard II*, Shakespeare divides the roles of actor
and commentator, which had been united in the person of King Richard.
The significance of this division for *Antony and Cleopatra* will become
apparent as the discussion of imagination is developed.

In one of the most popular and influential statements of Renaissance
literary theory, Sir Philip Sidney spells out the connection between history
and fortune, on the one hand, and between history and poetry, on the
other: ". . . the Historian in his bare *Was* hath many times that which wee

---

[5] In the Variorum discussion of this passage, Benjamin Heath et al. agree that
project means to represent or to plead a cause. There is no commentary on *like
frailties* (*The Tragedie of Anthonie, and Cleopatra*, ed. Horace Howard Furness,
p. 349).

call fortune to ouer-rule the best wisdome. Manie times he must tell euents whereof he can yeelde no cause: or, if hee doe, it must be poeticall."[6] By attributing the power of Bolingbroke and Caesar to fortune, Shakespeare adopts the historian's explanation of the past. Both heroes lose power and are blamed for doing so, yet they emerge morally and dramatically victorious over their successful rivals. From this general point of view, the differences between the type and degree of guilt attaching to the heroes' behavior are irrelevant. The important point is that their carelessness and irresponsibility not only detract from their own stature but make it impossible to accord admiration to their successors. Bolingbroke and Caesar, because they gain ascendancy through the weakness of their opponents rather than through military prowess or moral worth, emerge as opportunists. They owe their place in history to a fluke of fortune.

If the poet seeks an explanation other than fortune to account for the fall of heroes and the rise of lesser men, he must "be poeticall"; that is, he must exercise his imagination. Assuming that statements about fortune in these plays yield the historian's viewpoint, one might reasonably expect that imaginative explanations and statements about imagination itself will offer a glimpse of the poet's view of his material. Whether a given explanation derives wholly from Shakespeare's imagination or from his source is immaterial to the theory that explanation is poetical, since one of Shakespeare's sources, at least, was considered a good poet. Plutarch, who is mentioned several times in Sidney's *Apologie*, is commended as a writer of history and moral philosophy who *trymmeth both theyr garments with gards of Poesie.*

Imagination is a second theme common to these plays, and in both it is related to the theme of fortune, for it is imagination that renders men superior to the vicissitudes of fortune. In *Richard II* Gaunt advises his son to use his imagination to sweeten the harshness of exile:

> Look, what thy soul holds dear, imagine it
> To lie that way thou goest, not whence thou com'st.
> Suppose the singing birds musicians,
> The grass whereon thou tread'st the presence strow'd,
> The flowers fair ladies, and thy steps no more
> Than a delightful measure or a dance;
> For gnarling sorrow hath less power to bite

[6] Philip Sidney's "An Apology for Poesie," in *English Literary Criticism: The Renaissance*, ed. O. B. Hardison, p. 114. All future citations of Renaissance rhetoricians will be to this collection.

> The man that mocks at it and sets it light.
>
> (1.3.286-293)

Bolingbroke's reply might be regarded as the triumph of common sense and experience over Platonism and rationalism:

> O, who can hold a fire in his hand
> By thinking on the frosty Caucasus?
> Or cloy the hungry edge of appetite
> By bare imagination of a feast?
> Or wallow naked in December snow
> By thinking on fantastic summer's heat?
> O, no! The apprehension of the good
> Gives but the greater feeling to the worse.
>
> (1.3.294-301)

Nevertheless, it is instructive to compare the kinds of objects on which Gaunt counsels exercise of the imagination with those mentioned by his son. The latter maintains that imagination cannot feed hunger, overcome pain, or relieve cold. This view of imagination is not unlike Falstaff's concept of honor. It cannot bring a man any material benefit and is therefore useless. On a later occasion Bolingbroke again shows his need of the material when he seeks tangible evidence of his gentle birth:

> Whilst you have fed upon my signories,
> Dispark'd my parks and fell'd my forest woods,
> From my own windows torn my household coat,
> Ras'd out my imprese, leaving me no sign,
> Save men's opinions and my living blood,
> To show the world I am a gentleman.
>
> (3.1.22-27)

Gaunt, however, had not claimed that imagination had power over the physical and material world. He suggested only that certain aspects of reality could be enhanced by its power. Moreover, the preface to his counsel, that one must make a virtue of necessity, indicates that Gaunt does not advocate an ostrichlike refusal to see reality but a practical way of dealing with a problem that offers no other solution. Bolingbroke's reply that to apprehend good when suffering evil increases one's unhappiness may be seen as a crushing counterargument or it may indicate the complete bankruptcy of his imaginative powers.

The latter hypothesis is supported by the conclusion of the play, where the peace of mind achieved by Richard is in marked contrast with Bolingbroke's sense of guilt. Imagination does not enable Richard to escape confinement or ultimate death, but it ameliorates circumstances from which he can derive no other consolation because it offers him insight into his essential humanity. It is King Richard who follows Gaunt's advice to make the best of a bad situation by using his imagination and who transmits it to his queen:

> Learn, good soul,
> To think our former state a happy dream;
> From which awak'd, the truth of what we are
> Shows us but this. I am sworn brother, sweet,
> To grim Necessity, and he and I
> Will keep a league till death.
>
> . . . .
> Think I am dead, and that even here thou takest,
> As from my deathbed, thy last living leave.
>
> (5.1.17-22, 38-39)

Richard had previously abused imagination by dreaming that the spiritual forces of heaven would be used to protect his temporal power, but by the final act he has come to realize the folly of using a spiritual faculty to achieve material goals. Thus, in his prison soliloquy he invokes imagination to achieve moral resignation to a situation dictated by necessity:

> I have been studying how I may compare
> This prison where I live unto the world;
> And, for because the world is populous,
> And here is not a creature but myself,
> I cannot do it. Yet I'll hammer it out.
> My brain I'll prove the female to my soul,
> My soul the father; and these two beget
> A generation of still-breeding thoughts;
> And these same thoughts people this little world,
> In humours like the people of this world,
> For no thought is contented.
>
> . . . .
> Thus play I in one person many people,
> And none contented.
>
> . . . .

But whate'er I be,
Nor I, nor any man that but man is,
With nothing shall be pleas'd till he be eas'd
With being nothing.

(5.5.1-11, 31-32, 38-41)

Richard uses role-playing in an effort to achieve self-knowledge. This ability to cast oneself in various roles is a function of the imagination, as the analogy of generation indicates.

Because he attaches no value to faculties like imagination, King Henry can never resolve his guilt. His hope to allay the pangs of conscience is quite as absurd as the attempt to cloy the edge of appetite by imagining a feast, for it seeks to resolve a spiritual problem by material means:

I'll make a voyage to the Holy Land
To wash this blood off from my guilty hand.

(5.6.49-50)

Physical activity will no more absolve moral guilt than imaginative activity will assuage physical pain.[7] Bolingbroke errs by confusing the material and the spiritual realm; Richard had once erred by confusing spiritual and temporal power but is granted insight and consequent peace of mind precisely because he is an imaginative man whose poetic gifts finally lead him to truth.

In certain passages of Shakespeare's work, taken from plays whose dates and dramatic aims differ widely, one finds statements that yield further insights into Shakespeare's view of imagination. As Richard's soliloquy suggests, this faculty is needed for role-playing, and role-playing is an instrument of self-knowledge, a way of getting at truths that would otherwise remain hidden. Shakespeare's use of role-playing or of the play within a play to arrive at truth in both *Hamlet* and *1 Henry IV* is well documented. The link between role-playing and imagination is also explicit in *2 Henry IV* when Prince Hal rebukes the Lord Chief Justice for having once sent him to prison. The Justice defends himself by inviting the Prince to exchange roles:

---

[7] There are implications here for a Protestant view of the relationship between the mind and the material world, and they make *Richard II* a less medieval play than one might normally suppose it to be.

Just. Question your royal thoughts, make the case yours;
      Be now the father and propose a son;
      Hear your own dignity so much profan'd,
      See your most dreadful laws so loosely slighted,
      Behold yourself so by a son disdain'd,
      And then imagine me taking your part
      And, in your power, so silencing your son.
      . . . .
Prince. You are right, Justice, and you weigh this well.
      Therefore still bear the balance and the sword;
                 (*2H4* 5.2.91-97, 102-103)

The parts assigned to imagination in role-playing and to role-playing in the attainment of self-knowledge can be derived from other passages where Shakespeare discusses the means of achieving self-knowledge. For example, when Cassius tempts Brutus to join the conspiracy against Caesar, he speaks of the impossibility of seeing oneself except by reflection in a glass or through the eyes of another person who serves as a looking glass (*JC* 1.2.51-70). In *Troilus* this argument is repeated in terms that suggest a relationship between the looking glass and role-playing:

          . . . nor doth the eye itself,
      That most pure spirit of sense, behold itself,
      Not going from itself;
      . . . .
      For speculation turns not to itself
      Till it hath travell'd, and is mirror'd there
      Where it may see itself.
             (3.3.105-107, 109-111)

Achilles here stresses the fact that the eye needs to move beyond itself in order to view itself. Role-playing, too, involves going out of the self. Imagination is required for role-playing and serves in this capacity as a glass, or reflector. It is invoked for this purpose in the conversation between the Lord Chief Justice and Prince Hal and in Richard's prison soliloquy.

The comparison of the imagination to a glass was probably common enough in the poetic theory of Shakespeare's day, but this detailed statement by Puttenham suggests that imagination is a special type of glass:

And this phantasie may be resembled to a glasse, as hath bene sayd,

whereof there be many tempers and manner of makinges, as the *perspec-
tiues* doe acknowledge, for some be false glasses and shew thinges otherwise than they be in deede, and others right as they be in deede, neither
fairer nor fouler, nor greater nor smaller. There be againe of these glasses
that shew thinges exceeding faire and comely; others that shew figures
very monstruous & illfauored. Euen so is the phantasticall part of man (if
it be not disordered) a representer of the best, most comely, and bewtifull
images or appearances of thinges to the soule and according to their very
truth.[8]

In *Henry V*, a play that expresses in its prologues no little concern with
the power of imagination, one finds a reference to perspectives that are
further associated with the power of love to transform what it sees:

> *King, H.*   . . . and you may, some of you, thank love for my blind-
>   ness, who cannot see many a fair French city for one fair
>   French maid that stands in my way.
>
> *France.*   Yes, my lord, you see them perspectively—the cities
>   turn'd into a maid; for they are all girdled with maiden
>   walls that war hath never ent'red.
>
> (*H5* 5.2.343-350)

Hence, while there seems to be no explicit comparison by Shakespeare of
imagination to a perspective glass, the association here between perspectives and the mind transformed by love and the association elsewhere
between the mind transformed by love and the imagination (e.g., *MND*
1.1.232-235) supply evidence for suggesting that Shakespeare, together
with Puttenham, might have viewed imagination as a perspective glass.
   Interestingly enough, the idea of perspectives appears in both *Richard II*
and *Antony and Cleopatra*. In the former, at least, there is some hint of its
relationship to the power of imagination. When Bushy attempts to allay
the Queen's presentiment of sorrow, his counsel is not unlike Gaunt's
attempt to console Bolingbroke by advising him to look upon the events
and objects of his exile with an imaginative rather than a realistic eye:

> Each substance of a grief hath twenty shadows,
> Which shows like grief itself, but is not so;
> For sorrow's eye, glazed with blinding tears,
> Divides one thing entire to many objects,

[8] Hardison, *English Literary Criticism*, pp. 156-157.

> Like perspectives, which rightly gaz'd upon,
> Show nothing but confusion—ey'd awry,
> Distinguish form.

> (*R2* 2.2.14-20)

John Dover Wilson observes in these lines some confusion between perspective pictures and a perspective glass, and he remarks that the point of Bushy's conceit lies in the fact that the perspective is *rightly gaz'd upon* when *ey'd awry*. In other words, to see the picture properly one must view it from the side rather than directly.[9]

In *Antony* there is a reference to the type of perspective picture that showed contrasted figures of a lion or a lamb depending on how one viewed them. This element of contrast seems to be a regular feature of these pictures. After the messenger has delivered the news of Antony's marriage to Octavia and has been roundly scolded, Cleopatra continues to debate what course of action she must now pursue with respect to Antony:

> Let him for ever go!—let him not!—Charmian,
> Though he be painted one way like a Gorgon,
> The other way's a Mars.

> (2.5.115-117)

These lines demonstrate further Cleopatra's ability to see the whole Antony rather than to adopt a partial Roman view of him. They also place her among those lovers who look not with the eyes but with the mind, since she is able to observe more than is evident at this time in Antony's behavior.

One can observe, therefore, a train of associations between imagination and role-playing, between role-playing and self-knowledge, between self-knowledge and looking-glasses, between perspective glasses and imagination, and between both of the latter and the power of love to transform objects beheld by the eye. As its function in role-playing suggests, imagination, like a perspective glass, gives the viewer a knowledge of himself that can be achieved only by reflection and by indirection. The idea that perspectives yield various shapes relates them further to Shakespeare's descriptions of imagination. Worcester, for example, remarks that Hot-

---

[9] In their editions of *Richard II*, both Irving Ribner and John Dover Wilson comment on perspectives with reference to 2.2.14-20.

spur's imagination allows him to apprehend *a world of figures (1H4 1.3.209)*, and Orsino states that fancy is *full of shapes (TN 1.1.14)*. Finally, imagination, being a more intuitive type of knowledge than reason, might well resemble the perspective glass, or picture, that shows confusion when looked at directly but yields form when viewed obliquely. Like role-playing, it is an indirect way of finding out directions.

To serve as a reflector limits the activity of imagination to objects and events that in fact exist. In the famous speech of Theseus, the imaginations of the lunatic and the lover are similarly tied to reality, the one magnifying a horde of devils, the other investing a dark beloved with Helen's beauty (*MND* 5.1.4-22). The poet's imagination alone is genuinely creative, since it *bodies forth | The forms of things unknown . . . and gives to airy nothing | A local habitation and a name*. Like Bolingbroke's speech, the remarks of Theseus can be regarded as a denigration of imagination, but critics have warned against construing this speech apart from the dramatic context. R. W. Dent notes that the audience has been doubly obliged to exercise its imagination upon hearing that *this green plot shall be our stage, this hawthorn brake our tiring house*, since they must first imagine a green plot and then imagine it turned into a stage.[10] Edward Dowden had earlier maintained that Shakespeare does not identify with Theseus but presents him as a worldly man of action who would naturally make light of imagination.[11] Whatever Theseus's attitude toward the imaginative types he describes, the functions he ascribes to imagination are not false as they had been with Bolingbroke. They are all mental activities that transform, not matter, but mind.

Perspectives on Imagination

The views of imagination presented in *Antony and Cleopatra* seem more varied and more complex in their relationship to other thematic motifs than those presented in *Richard II*. Here imagination, fortune, power, honor, and permanence are interwoven in various patterns, which emerge as different characters reveal their attitude toward imagination. Each of them seeks power and the honor attached to it; each hopes that the honor sought will be permanent; but they differ in that some seek it through imagination while others wait upon fortune, failing to realize that only imagination can guarantee the permanence of honor.

[10] R. W. Dent, "Imagination in *A Midsummer Night's Dream*," in *Shakespeare 400*, ed. James G. McManaway, p. 126.
[11] Edward Dowden, *Shakspere: A Critical Study of His Mind and Art*, pp. 68-69.

Pompey, associated with fortune through his reliance on the sea and his characterization as *the ebb'd man*, cannot recognize an opportunity to seize power, because he lacks imagination. When Menas asks *Wilt thou be lord of the whole world*, he replies *How should that be*? It is interesting to compare Pompey's response to the words *lord of the whole world* with that of Marlowe's Tamburlaine to a chance phrase in Menaphon's report to King Cosroe:

Menaphon.	Your majesty shall shortly have your wish,
	And ride in triumph through Persepolis.
Tamburlaine.	And ride in triumph through Persepolis!
	Is it not brave to be a king, Techelles?
	Usumcasane and Theridamas,
	Is it not passing brave to be a king,
	And ride in triumph through Persepolis?
	(2.5.48-54)

Tamburlaine's imagination is fired not only by the concept of kingship but also by the words, which he repeats twice; his thirst for power is confirmed at this moment. This response and his admiration of Zenocrate's beauty suggest a strong link between imagination and power in Marlowe's hero. By contrast, Pompey appears not only as a man who lacks the ruthlessness requisite for the true Machiavel but also as a pretender to power who lacks the inspiration needed to seize the moment and means placed before him.

Pompey's failure is repeated on a smaller scale by others in the course of the play. Labienus and Ventidius are courageous soldiers, and the latter observes that Antony has won more in his lieutenants than in his own person. Ventidius realizes that a subordinate has power potentially equal to that of his general. If he were an imaginative man like Tamburlaine, he would become discontented and seek to gain the power that lies within his reach. Iago is such a man. Ventidius reveals his lack of imagination when he contents himself with a lower place instead of challenging Antony's power. He will cross no Rubicons. The same holds true for all the kings who desert Antony to follow Caesar. They are reprehensible less for desertion than for the fact that not one thinks to seize an opportunity for greater honor when the field lies open to him.

Caesar's surprise at discovering that the world remains unchanged by events of significance to him would appear to place him with imaginative men like King Richard, who expected the land to protect him from the consequences of rebellion. When Octavia returns to Rome, he is disappointed that nature has given him no advance notice:

> The trees by th' way
> Should have borne men, and expectation fainted,
> Longing for what it had not. Nay, the dust
> Should have ascended to the roof of heaven,
> Rais'd by your populous troops.
>
> (3.6.46-50)

He is similarly disappointed by the quiet announcement of Antony's death:

> The breaking of so great a thing should make
> A greater crack. The round world
> Should have shook lions into civil streets
> And citizens to their dens.
>
> (5.1.14-17)

Granting that such sentiments link Caesar with the imaginative King Richard, it should be noted that these expectations on the part of both men constitute an abuse of imagination, which is a nonmaterial faculty that cannot effect changes in the material world. Furthermore, King Richard is the more imaginative because he uses the language of prophecy and command when he calls for a transformation of the world around him (3.2.12-26), whereas Caesar's tone is one of petulant frustration that betrays his sense of powerlessness to carry out his wishes. Caesar's imagination appears all the more impoverished because his reception of the news that Antony is dead appears in immediate contrast with Cleopatra's. In the preceding scene, when the dying Antony is carried to her monument, Cleopatra decrees that the world should be destroyed:

> O sun,
> Burn the great sphere thou mov'st in! Darkling stand
> The varying shore o' th' world!
>
> (4.15.9-11)

There is no subsequent occasion on which she observes, like Caesar, that these events should have occurred but did not. In her mind the world *has* come to an end.

Nevertheless, one may wonder why Shakespeare, who had described through the literal-minded Casca the portents surrounding the assassination of Julius Caesar, should take pains in the later Roman history to deny their existence on the occasion of Antony's death. To an audience familiar with *Julius Caesar*, Octavius's statement might convey the impression that the earlier play was indeed a work of fiction, whereas the spectacle now presented to them is sober fact. This device flatters us into thinking that we can distinguish fact from fancy at the precise moment when Shakespeare has most successfully deceived us through Cleopatra's words at Antony's death. The images of darkness and desolation that dominate the play from this scene to its close convince us that *there is nothing left remarkable | Beneath the visiting moon*. Cleopatra, as will be shown, is the one major character in the play who is richly endowed with imagination and who, on this account, is the key to our understanding of it.

The attitude of Antony toward imagination is revealed indirectly by his love for Cleopatra and by his preoccupation with honor. His ability to appreciate Cleopatra's greatness places him, on the one hand, in the tradition of Tamburlaine as a hero whose imagination is stirred by beauty to achieve power and honor and, on the other, places him in clear contrast with Caesar, who cannot distinguish the Queen of Egypt from her maids in waiting, because he lacks the intuitive knowledge to sense the presence of true nobility. Antony's concern for reputation is quite conventional. His dying request that those around him should *please your thoughts | In feeding them with those my former fortunes* (4.15.52-53) has parallels in *Hamlet, Othello*, and *Coriolanus*.[12] The hero's search for honor provides a meeting ground for hero and poet because the fame acquired by the hero is enhanced and preserved by the latter's imagination. This theme can best be developed in a history play, which enables the audience to compare the inadequacy of a chronicle that purports to be true with the more universal truth revealed through poetry.

Although the theme of honor is not so fully developed in *Richard II* as in the Roman play, there are hints of its presence in the final act, where the damage that has been wrought by fortune threatens to become permanently written into the pages of history. After advising Queen Isabel to imagine that he is dead, Richard enjoins upon her the duty of safeguarding his reputation:

> In winter's tedious nights sit by the fire
> With good old folks, and let them tell thee tales

---

[12]Compare, for example, *Oth.* 5.2.340-343, *Ham.* 5.2.355-360, and *Cor.* 5.6.113-116. I am indebted for this interpretation of *Ant.* 4.15.52-55 to Reuben A. Brower's *Hero and Saint*, p. 336.

Of woful ages long ago betid;
And ere thou bid good-night, to quite their griefs
Tell thou the lamentable tale of me,
And send the hearers weeping to their beds.
For why, the senseless brands will sympathize
The heavy accent of thy moving tongue
And in compassion weep the fire out;
And some will mourn in ashes, some coal-black,
For the deposing of a rightful king.

                                              (5.1.40-50)

While Richard's reference to reputation is not explicit, it can be inferred from the word *rightful*. He asserts the legitimacy of his kingship lest it be obscured by history and lest his lawful claim to the throne be viewed with Bolingbroke's succession as equally the work of fortune rather than of honorable right.

Richard's farewell to his queen is entirely the work of Shakespeare's imagination. One might almost regard this scene in which the hero's reputation is entrusted to a woman, a loving wife, and a royal personage as an early sketch for the last act of *Antony and Cleopatra*. Queen Isabel's capacity to carry out the task entrusted to her is demonstrated in the opening lines. Her references to the deposed king have an epic quality: *Julius Caesar's ill-erected tower*; *the model where old Troy did stand*. These allusions to the juncture of English history and classical antiquity project Richard into a fabled past that belongs more to the realm of imagination than to that of fact. In the final act of *Antony*, Cleopatra, through her dream vision of Antony and her prophetic insight into the future, becomes the champion of imagination and transforms simple witness into a panegyric of the poet's role.

Cleopatra's consciousness is more perceptive than that of Enobarbus, who is usually viewed as the official commentator in this play; and her greater insight is best demonstrated by comparing their statements on nature and fancy. When Enobarbus describes Cleopatra's progress along the river of Cydnus, he insists that the reality of what he has seen exceeds all that his listeners have imagined from the reports they have heard (2.2.183-189). He stresses the difference between his eyewitness account and hearsay:

> *Eno.*   When she first met Mark Antony, she purs'd
> up his heart, upon the river of Cydnus.

> *Agr.* There she appear'd indeed; or my
> reporter devis'd well for her.
>
> *Eno.* I will tell you.
>
> (2.2.191-195)

The implication is that the "true" version surpasses any that reporters can devise. It is important to have Enobarbus emphasize the factual nature of his account and to imply that beside it all others must pale into insignificance, for Shakespeare is preparing to undercut his statement here and in the lines that follow:

> She did lie
> In her pavilion, cloth-of-gold of tissue,
> O'erpicturing that Venus where we see
> The fancy outwork nature.
>
> (2.2.203-206)

The last of these lines does not appear in North's Plutarch, which reads *apparelled and attired like the goddess Venus commonly drawn in picture* and goes on immediately to describe the young boys.[13] This addition creates one of those multiple regressions that remind the audience that this is, after all, a play. It begins with the statement that the picture of Venus shows imagination superior to nature; qualifies this by adding that the reality of Cleopatra, being a work of nature, surpasses the picture of Venus; but obliges one finally to reflect that Enobarbus's description of Cleopatra is itself the product of Shakespeare's (or Plutarch's) imagination. Enobarbus stops before the last stage is reached and the poet does not force the final reflection upon us, because it is more appropriately placed in the mouth of Cleopatra, who can best interpret it for us at the conclusion of the play:

> Nature wants stuff
> To vie strange forms with fancy; yet, t'imagine
> An Antony were nature's piece 'gainst fancy,
> Condemning shadows quite.
>
> (5.2.97-100)

Here the multiple regression must come to a halt, for the conflict between nature and fancy has been resolved and imagination has been accorded its

---

[13] T. J. B. Spencer, *Shakespeare's Plutarch*, p. 201.

proper role. That role, as defined by Renaissance poetics, is summed up by Sir Philip Sidney in his *Apologie for Poetrie*: "Neyther let it be deemed too sawcie a comparison to ballance the highest poynt of mans wit with the efficacie of Nature: but rather giue right honor to the heauenly Maker of that maker, who, hauing made man to his owne likenes, set him beyond and ouer all the workes of that second nature, which in nothing hee sheweth so much as in Poetrie, when with the force of a diuine breath he bringeth things forth far surpassing her dooings . . ."[14] Enobarbus and Cleopatra both recognize that they are part of a story, but Enobarbus thinks that the story belongs to the brazen world of history, while Cleopatra realizes that it is the golden product of the poet's imagination.

The imperfect character of Enobarbus's judgments is revealed elsewhere by Shakespeare's account of his death. Here is dramatic proof that poetry preserves truths that history obscures. The uninterpreted fact is that Enobarbus left Antony, joined Caesar, and died a short time later. To this fact Plutarch added the "poeticall" idea that Enobarbus repented his desertion: ". . . and the same Domitius, as though he gave him to understand that he repented his open treason, he died immediately after."[15] Shakespeare brings to Plutarch's simple hint a dramatist's awareness of the audience. In a soliloquy he develops the touch of self-consciousness found earlier in Enobarbus's resolve to find a place in the story by continued allegiance to his fallen lord:

> Be witness to me, O thou blessed moon,
> When men revolted shall upon record
> Bear hateful memory, poor Enobarbus did
> Before thy face repent!
>
> . . . .
>   O Antony,
> Nobler than my revolt is infamous,
> Forgive me in thine own particular,
> But let the world rank me in register

---

[14] Hardison, *English Literary Criticism*, p. 105. Sidney's alliance of man's imagination with divine creative power appears also in Puttenham (ibid., p. 148), and Ben Jonson, who, though anxious that nature should be trained by exercise and imitation, admits that poets are born not made and that the poet speaks "somewhat above a mortall mouth" (ibid., pp. 281-283). These ideas were common enough in Shakespeare's time; hence, there is no attempt here to prove sources, only to cite a convenient and popular expression of them in Sidney's work.

[15] T. J. B. Spencer, *Shakespeare's Plutarch*, p. 253.

A master-leaver and a fugitive!
(4.9.7-10, 18-22)

Enobarbus's repentance alters the judgment of history on Antony. If we have credited him that Antony was wrong to make his will lord of his reason, we must now believe his reaffirmation of Antony's nobility. The judgments of Enobarbus are subject to the limitations ascribed by Sidney to the moral philosopher, who cannot see beyond the particular instance, and to the historian, who cannot interpret what he sees. The imperfection of Enobarbus's rational interpretation of events is nowhere more evident than in the fact that he dies unaware that his repentance has been given a witness more sympathetic than the melancholy moon. That imagination attains a more truthful and perfect vision than reason is shown by the poet's ability to save Enobarbus from the adverse opinion of history and to assure him of an honorable place in Antony's story. It will be argued later that Enobarbus's sense of disgrace at death and our knowledge that he has been saved from it is paralleled, with some variations, in the death of Antony.

The apparent contradictions in *Antony and Cleopatra* can be said to arise from the distinct modes of apprehension embodied in Enobarbus and Cleopatra. One mode of apprehension belongs to the world of the moral philosopher, who judges events in the light of reason, and to the historian, who attributes them to chance when no reason for them is apparent. The moral philosopher and the historian, described by Sidney as the poet's chief rivals, may be said to share a single, literal, way of viewing the world. Theirs is the viewpoint ascribed not only to Enobarbus but also to Antony and to most of the Roman figures in the play. Cleopatra can be said to share the poet's viewpoint, an intuitive vision of a golden world. The two modes of apprehension are in conflict only in the sense that one is incomplete while the other is complete. This hypothesis acknowledges the contrarieties in the play without finding them ultimately problematic and without suggesting that they can be reconciled only as a dynamic tension of opposites. It solves the problem for those who regard Antony's decision for Cleopatra as a choice of sensuality over reason and who see this choice as unsuited to the stature befitting a tragic hero. It gives the lie to the thesis that the special beauty of the language in the play obscures the lovers' essential tawdriness, and it makes it possible to read Antony's story as a tragedy without losing sight of the fact that the total effect of the play is not tragic.

The two modes of apprehension present Antony's story to us as a per-spective picture. As shown by Bushy's speech to the Queen in *Richard II* (2.2.16-20), perspectives can be viewed awry to show nothing but confu-sion, or they can be viewed rightly to distinguish form. Ironically, to view the picture directly is to view it awry. Viewed on the literal level of moral philosophy and history, Antony's story is a confused set of events in which folly and fortune produce the tragic downfall of the hero. Viewed obliquely, through the eyes of imagination, it is an epic in which love redeems the hero's honor and translates the lovers beyond time and change.

More Lasting than Bronze

To view Antony's story imaginatively is to see it through the eyes of Cleopatra. Since she is entrusted with the poet's task of conferring im-mortal honor upon Antony, it is important to explore the sources of honor in the play and to show that Cleopatra can appreciate their worth. Rome has often been seen as the major source of honor in this play; Roman values of duty, control, and patriotism supply the standards by which honor is judged. Yet Rome has its unattractive aspects.[16] It is difficult to find any Roman besides Antony with a genuine sense of honor. Pompey talks of it in the same breath with which he condones treachery by his lieutenant. Agrippa and Maecenas are admirers of Antony but followers of Caesar. At best they are ambassadors and counsellors rather than men of heroic stature; at worst they are gossips who listen to the common liars and talebearers of Rome. As indicated in an earlier chapter, Caesar has little sense of himself. His parts and possessions are those of an automaton governed by intellect but lacking passion and will. He seeks to control others rather than himself and in his drive for power he relies on ideas of fortune and destiny rather than on his own imagination and ability. Thus, he lacks any real sense of honor.

Honor is valued to the extent that it is permanent in a world where fortune threatens continually to destroy it. Rome cannot confer lasting reputation, for Rome is nothing in Shakespeare's imagination if not fickle. Both Caesar and Antony denounce its slippery people, while Demetrius and Agrippa comment on the dishonest character of its judgments. Rome is the city of fortune whose opinions ebb and flow with the tide, and the world that Rome seeks to dominate is itself an unstable element in the play.

[16] Norman Rabkin, for example, argues in *Shakespeare and the Common Under-standing* that there are in this play two pictures of Rome, one where honor is the watchword, and another where Rome becomes a vicious political arena (p. 186).

If an ideal of honor exists in the Roman world of the play, it is due to Antony himself. The ideas of honor expressed by Philo and Demetrius or by Agrippa and Maecenas are inspired by Antony's behavior. Caesar's speeches on honor are specific encomia of Antony. All that these men know about honor they have learned from Antony; honor is not to be found in some abstract Roman ideal but embodied in Antony's own exploits and standards.

Cleopatra is aware of the spurious quality in the demands made of Antony in the name of honor defined as an abstract Roman ideal. From the outset of the play her assessment of the issues at stake if Antony accedes to these demands is more clearheaded than his. When Caesar's ambassadors arrive in Alexandria, she uses her power over Antony to unmask the situation in Rome and to point out the choices open to him:

> Nay, hear them, Antony.
> Fulvia perchance is angry; or who knows
> If the scarce-bearded Caesar have not sent
> His pow'rful mandate to you: 'Do this, or this;
> Take in this kingdom, and enfranchise that.
> Perform't, or else we damn thee.'
>
> (1.1.19-24)

Her words depict the attitude of Fulvia and the arrogant demands of Caesar accurately enough. As we later learn, Fulvia's motive for waging war was not duty or patriotism but a desire to bring Antony out of Egypt, an action that served only to humiliate Antony before Caesar (2.2.94-98). The contempt that Cleopatra ascribes to Caesar is verified by the first words we hear him speak (1.4.1-10) and by his attitude in the quarrel scene. Her assumption of Caesar's voice and her use of the phrase *we damn thee* exposes Caesar's aspiration to supreme power. For a moment he appears supreme because he is seen to command an Antony powerful enough to free and conquer kingdoms at will, but beyond his commands is the voice of Cleopatra, who has called him into being, has allowed him to strut for a while, silences him, and proves her ability to control the commander of the commander. By her mockery she wins the contest between them for Antony's allegiance. Her fleeting and ironic deification of Caesar in this opening scene anticipates her final and triumphant glorification of Antony and demonstrates her power to confer or to withhold honor. Cleopatra's words on this occasion can be seen as selfish, but they can also be construed as an attempt to liberate Antony from the unworthy de-

mands of Rome and from a vain attempt to gain honor where no honor is
to be had. Her role-playing and her use of indirection are exercises of
imagination, designed to reveal the truth.

Cleopatra's demonstration of the bankruptcy of Roman sources of
honor inspires Antony to stake his reputation on a new source of honor
and to redefine nobility:

> Let Rome in Tiber melt and the wide arch
> Of the rang'd empire fall!
> . . . .
>   The nobleness of life
> Is to do thus [*embracing*] ; when such a mutual pair
> And such a twain can do't, in which I bind,
> On pain of punishment, the world to weet
> We stand up peerless.
>
> (1.1.33-34, 36-40)

From the moment when Cleopatra challenges Antony's claim to honor as a
peerless lover, ideas of martial honor alternate with the view that military
glory is not an end in itself but a means of honoring the beloved. Antony's
decision to leave Cleopatra and return to Rome seems to be motivated by
a sense of duty and a refusal to allow his love for her to interfere:

> These strong Egyptian fetters I must break
> Or lose myself in dotage.
>
> (1.2.120-121)
>
> I must from this enchanting queen break off.
>
> (1.2.132)

Must implies an obligation to be honored, but it says nothing of the
speaker's intention. That Antony does not intend a complete break seems
clear from the later expression of his decision:

> I shall break
> The cause of our expedience to the Queen
> And get her leave to part.
>
> (1.2.184-186)

Antony's submission to Cleopatra is as complete as if he had never reflected that he must break with her. His language, indeed, suggests that

chivalric fidelity to her motivates his departure for Rome, his aspirations while he is in Rome, and the final decisive battles of his career:

> By the fire
> That quickens Nilus' slime, I go from hence
> Thy soldier, servant, making peace or war
> As thou affect'st.
>
> (1.3.68-71)

> 'Say the firm Roman to great Egypt sends
> This treasure of an oyster; at whose foot,
> To mend the petty present, I will piece
> Her opulent throne with kingdoms. All the East,
> Say thou, shall call her mistress.'
>
> (1.5.43-47)

> I made these wars for Egypt; and the Queen—
> Whose heart I thought I had, for she had mine,
> Which, whilst it was mine, had annex'd unto't
> A million moe, now lost—she, Eros, has
> Pack'd cards with Caesar and false-play'd my glory
> Unto an enemy's triumph.
>
> (4.14.15-20)

To the extent that he submits his martial deeds to Cleopatra's pleasure, Antony resembles the hero of medieval legend rather than the hero of classical epic. His behavior, unworthy of a classical hero, is altogether admirable in the hero of legend and romance.

Antony's candidacy for the title of romantic hero would appear to be weakened by Cleopatra's skepticism about his claim to stand before the world as the peerless lover:

> Excellent falsehood!
> Why did he marry Fulvia, and not love her?
> I'll seem the fool I am not. Antony
> Will be himself.
>
> (1.1.40-43)

Many commentators construe the last of these lines in a general sense as *the fool he is*, yet in view of Antony's protestation and Cleopatra's own mention of Fulvia, Kittredge's more specific interpretation seems more likely: Cleopatra will pretend to be foolish enough to believe Antony, while he will continue to be the deceiver he has always been to her and to Fulvia. To Cleopatra, it is unthinkable that a man can claim preeminence as a lover while he is married to another woman.

A remark in Shakespeare's source sheds some light both on Cleopatra's jealousy of Antony's marriage and on her fear of separation from him. Cleopatra's friends noted that Octavia had the honor of the title "wife," while she, the queen of many nations, had only the name of "mistress": "... and yet that she disdained not so to be called, if it might please him she might enjoy his company and live with him;..."[17] The title of mistress has no meaning when the lover is absent; hence, as Enobarbus notes, Cleopatra's business wholly depends on Antony's abode. The bawdy remark emphasizes her sensuality, but sensual evidence is the only proof she has of any title to Antony.

Antony's marriage to Octavia, which manifests some insensitivity to Cleopatra's feelings and suggests callousness toward Octavia by marrying her only for reasons of policy, also requires explanation before his claim to honor in love can be justified. In judging Antony's behavior, it is necessary to consider carefully the sequence of events surrounding his marriage. Having made the agreement, he meets Octavia, apologizes for his past behavior, and promises that *that to come | Shall all be done by th' rule.* Octavia leaves; the Soothsayer appears immediately and warns Antony against Caesar. The reconciliation with Caesar and the agreement to marry Octavia manifest the strength of Caesar's control over Antony: *Thy lustre thickens | When he shines by.* Antony is struck by the truth of these words and after the Soothsayer's departure makes a clear-cut decision for Cleopatra and against martial honor:

> I will to Egypt;
> And though I make this marriage for my peace,
> I' th' East my pleasure lies. O, come Ventidius,
> You must to Parthia.

>   (2.3.38-41)

This command to Ventidius, which seems merely to conclude the scene, in fact underscores the division between the old source of honor and the new. Parthia represents the monumental challenge to Roman military prowess, and Ventidius becomes the only Roman ever to rout *the ne'er-yet-beaten horse of Parthia.* Antony's explicit rejection of a unique oppor-

---

[17] T. J. B. Spencer, *Shakespeare's Plutarch*, p. 241.

tunity to achieve martial honor is dramatized by his relegating to Ventidius his sense of obligation and by stating his own intention as a simple expression of will: *You must to Parthia*; *I will to Egypt*. Once these alternatives might have struggled within him, but such conflicts appear now to be ended. These lines serve also as a transition to the comedy of Act Two, Scene Five. Having learned of Antony's decision to return to Cleopatra, the audience has greater liberty to enjoy her discomfiture at the news of his marriage, knowing that all will be well. In the next scene Antony has no sooner contracted the marriage than he is on his way to Mount Misenum to negotiate with Pompey:

> Sir, Mark Antony
> Will e'en but kiss Octavia, and we'll follow.
> (2.4.2-3)

This passage hints that the marriage has not been consummated, and a later speech of Antony's suggests that it never was:

> Have I my pillow left unpress'd in Rome,
> Forborne the getting of a lawful race,
> And by a gem of women, to be abus'd
> By one that looks on feeders?
> (3.13.106-109)

Plutarch, however, makes it abundantly clear that Octavia had several children by Antony.[18] Such fidelity to Cleopatra helps to explain the degree of jealousy and the vision of himself as cuckolded when Cleopatra allows Thyreus to kiss her hand:

> O that I were
> Upon the hill of Basan to outroar

[18] Events in Shakespeare's source explain how he might have entertained a credible fiction that Antony could be married to Octavia, spend some time with her, and yet fail to consummate the marriage. The departure of Octavia in Act Three, Scene Four, on an embassy of reconciliation in fact conflates two such journeys. To the first of these belongs her sense of dilemma at the prospect of war between her husband and her brother. The second brings her to Athens only to find that Antony has departed, whereupon she returns permanently to Rome. Since the interim between marriage and the final break might be largely occupied with such travels, it would not be difficult to imagine that Antony could be depicted as faithful to Cleopatra during his marriage to Octavia (see Plutarch's account, T. J. B. Spencer, *Shakespeare's Plutarch*, pp. 240-242).

> The horned herd! for I have savage cause,
>   (3.13.126-128)

If one accepts the argument that the marriage was never consummated and observes further that it is Octavia's own idea to leave Antony, one cannot accuse him of being dishonorable in his treatment of Octavia or disloyal to Cleopatra.

Cleopatra's persistent interest in marriage is more than petty jealousy or a manifestation of shrewishness. It is related to the theme of honor. In the second scene of the play, when Charmian and Iras talk of marriage, they mention the need of decorum in the choice of partners. Fulvia and Octavia are unsuitable wives for Antony because they tarnish his honor, the first by involving him in a war that hurts his reputation with Caesar and the second by returning to Rome in a manner that elicits sympathy for herself and blame for Antony.[19] Because marriage symbolizes indissoluble union, it is a type of the immutability that should accompany perfect honor. While Cleopatra's maids discuss marriage, the Soothsayer predicts death. To marry before death is to be subject to separation by the death of one partner (Fulvia) or by desertion (Octavia). Cleopatra, who opens the play by seeking tangible evidence of Antony's love, closes it by offering incontrovertible proof of her own:

> If it be love indeed, tell me how much.
>   (1.1.14)

> Husband, I come!
> Now to that name my courage prove my title!
>   (5.2.290-291)

Her death is the final demonstration of Antony's claim to honor in love because it proves that she is worthy of the sacrifice of martial honor made by Antony for her sake and because, by assuming the form of marriage, it signifies the permanence of that honor.

Because Antony's honor is bound up with Cleopatra's, his apparently dishonorable defeat at Actium is transmuted into the most striking evidence that he deserves honor as the greatest lover of the world. The

---

[19] Ibid. Plutarch here observes that Octavia's continued regard for Antony after her return to Rome caused the Romans to hate Antony and thus did him great harm. Fulvia's damage to Antony's reputation consisted in her waging war with Caesar, thus making it appear that Antony had broken his oath of partnership with him (see ibid., pp. 207-208; *Ant.* 2.2.94-98).

perspectives of common sense and imagination are nowhere more evident than in the dramatization of this event. To Enobarbus, the moral philosopher, Antony's behavior during the first battle is an irrational course for whose consequences Antony is wholly to blame:

> *Cleo.* Is Antony or we in fault for this?
>
> *Eno.* Antony only, that would make his will
> Lord of his reason.
>
> (3.13.2-4)

While Antony concurs in this judgment after his first defeat, he later presents us with the historian's explanation in a striking image of the turns of fortune's wheel:

> Fortune and Antony part here; even here
> Do we shake hands. All come to this? The hearts
> That spaniel'd me at heels, to whom I gave
> Their wishes, do discandy, melt their sweets
> On blossoming Caesar; and this pine is bark'd,
> That overtopp'd them all.
>
> (4.12.19-24)

Caesar, too, invokes the judgment of reason and of history when he asks his friends to see

> How hardly I was drawn into this war,
> How calm and gentle I proceeded still
> In all my writings.
>
> (5.1.74-76)

These judgments are final only if reason and fortune are the ultimate explanations of human events. Fortune is ultimate only when all other explanation fails; that is, when imagination is lacking. Reason is ultimate only if it is possible or desirable to belong wholly to oneself. Antony's loss at Actium is like the loss of himself, not in an absolute sense but in his sense of the changed relationship with Caesar, which appears uppermost in his mind after the shock of defeat:

> He at Philippi kept
> His sword e'en like a dancer, while I struck
> The lean and wrinkled Cassius; and 'twas I
> That the mad Brutus ended.

. . . .
           Now I must
To the young man send humble treaties, dodge
And palter in the shifts of lowness, who
With half the bulk o' th' world play'd as I pleas'd,
Making and marring fortunes.
                 (3.11.35-38, 61-65)

Because Caesar's victory is a gift from fortune, Antony remains the greatest soldier of the world, but it no longer appears that way in his own eyes, because the fact is no longer recognized by Caesar or by those who take their cue from Caesar's opinion. Since honor and reputation are intimately related, Antony cannot be the greatest soldier of the world if no one else acknowledges this fact. Self-approbation does not suffice, because self-knowledge cannot be complete without the aid of reflection:

       . . . no man is the lord of anything,
       Though in and of him there be much consisting,
       Till he communicate his parts to others;
       Nor doth he of himself know them for aught
       Till he behold them formed in th' applause
       Where th' are extended, who, like an arch, reverb'rate
       The voice again; or, like a gate of steel
       Fronting the sun, receives and renders back
       His figure and his heat.
                 (*Tro.* 3.3.115-123)

Ulysses's argument is a radical version of the theory that self-knowledge can be complete only with the aid of another, for it implies that even full control of the self is impossible without recognition of that self by others. Hence, the rational explanation of Antony's tragedy—that it stems from the loss of himself and can be redeemed only by regaining some measure of control over the self—is as incomplete as the view that his defeat must be attributed to fortune.[20] To blame the passions of men or the fortunes of war for Actium is to accept the explanation of the moral philosopher or of the historian.

    Before he can fully know himself to be a man of honor, Antony must be

[20] Brower, in *Hero and Saint* argues on these grounds that Antony is a tragic hero (pp. 328-377), but he also acknowledges that "the tragedy of the heroic" is presented together with "the heroism of love" (p. 318).

formed in the applause of others, and the honor thus gained must be established beyond threat of loss. Only poetry can perform this office for Antony, and the more successful the poet, the greater the honor to be gained by both hero and poet. To view Antony's defeat at Actium as a marvelous change wrought by Cleopatra, the spokesman for imagination, is to recognize the hand of the poet, who builds monuments more lasting than bronze.

Antony's desertion of the battle represents the nadir of his control over self. It is also one of the greatest proofs of love that he can offer. The same action that deprives him of one kind of honor confers on him the title of peerless lover. He does not see it this way, for he judges his behavior from the standpoint of reason, but the spectacle of his desertion is offered to the audience as such a proof. They first view his sense of loss and humiliation before Caesar and then witness his confession to Cleopatra:

> Egypt, thou knew'st too well
> My heart was to thy rudder tied by th' strings,
> And thou shouldst tow me after. O'er my spirit
> Thy full supremacy thou knew'st, and that
> Thy beck might from the bidding of the gods
> Command me.
>
> (3.11.56-61)

Caesar's victory must be attributed neither to his own soldiership nor to Antony's lack of it. That Antony should have been subdued by Cleopatra is part of Caesar's luck. If Antony makes his will lord of his reason, it is because he loves Cleopatra. She is the ultimate cause of both Caesar's luck and Antony's loss, and the fact that she is so is the poet's explanation for the battle of Actium and the source of Antony's subsequent reputation.

A second reason why Antony alone cannot be the perfect measure of honor is the fact that he cannot ensure its permanence, and the thought that the man he knows himself to be is subject to mutability, whether from his own passions or from time and fortune, is uppermost in his mind as he contemplates his defeat:

> Here I am Antony;
> Yet cannot hold this visible shape, my knave.
>
> (4.14.13-14)

Nowhere is there a more convincing argument that honor cannot come from the self alone. Antony is staggered by the realization that he can never be totally sure again what it is to be Antony.

Antony's soliloquy after his first defeat stresses his sense of loss; after the second, he voices his sense of impermanence and metamorphosis. Cleopatra has lured him to fight at sea, and the sea has been his undoing; yet it has also conspired with the magic of Cleopatra to transform Antony from the earthbound warrior who seeks honor with his sword to the legendary lover whose honor is derived from the beloved. The fact that Rome is fickle and the world mutable suggests that the earth, the traditional symbol of stability, is no longer to be trusted.[21] Hence, it was appropriate that the god Hercules should have left Antony and that Cleopatra should have congratulated him on his escape from the world's great snare when he comes victorious from his battle on land. Although he is not conscious of it, because he thinks within history and the story told by history is tragic, Antony's honor is finally dependent on Cleopatra's recognition of his greatness rather than on his own deeds. Water, which is consistently associated with Cleopatra until the moment of her death, becomes a means of restoring Antony's honor. It is suggested that the sea where Antony suffers defeat is less a symbol of instability than a power able to convert the frail mortality of flesh to objects of lasting beauty:

> Full fadom five thy father lies;
>   Of his bones are coral made;
> Those are pearls that were his eyes;
>   Nothing of him that doth fade
> But doth suffer a sea-change
> Into something rich and strange;
>   (*Tmp.* 1.2.396-401)

After Antony's first defeat at sea, Scarus had called him the noble ruin of Cleopatra's magic. On that occasion Antony for the first time calls her *Egypt*, a title that summons up, at least for Shakespeare's audience, the mysterious gypsy of preternatural powers. Earlier, Pompey had coupled Cleopatra and magic:

>   But all the charms of love,
>   Salt Cleopatra, soften thy wan'd lip!

[21] For justification of the view that the world is unstable in *Antony*, see pp. 151-153.

> Let witchcraft join with beauty, lust with both!
>
>   (2.1.20-22)

There is even a hint in *charms*, *salt*, and *wan'd* that Cleopatra and magic are associated with the sea. But nowhere else in the play do so many terms of magic cluster as appear in Antony's speech after his second and decisive defeat at sea:

>   All is lost!
> This foul Egyptian hath betrayed me!
>
> . . . .
>   Bid them all fly!
> For when I am reveng'd upon my charm,
> I have done all.
>
> . . . .
> O this false soul of Egypt! this grave charm—
> Whose eye beck'd forth my wars and call'd them home,
> Whose bosom was my crownet, my chief end—
> Like a right gypsy hath at fast and loose
> Beguil'd me to the very heart of loss!
>
> . . . .
>   The witch shall die.
>   (4.12.9-10, 15-17, 25-29, 47)

These terms of magic, coupled in various places with Cleopatra and the sea and occurring during Antony's two defeats at sea, suggest that Antony undergoes a metamorphosis for which Cleopatra is responsible. In the same way she will later be responsible for ensuring by her dream vision that the honor lost by defeat will be converted permanently to the honor conferred by love.

   Like the lovers of *A Midsummer Night's Dream* Antony is never fully aware of the magical forces at work upon him, although his metamorphosis, like theirs, grows to something of great constancy. The hand of fancy is concealed from his consciousness with the result that from his own point of view his story is genuinely tragic, but the same irony surrounds his death that was present at the death of Enobarbus. Antony dies thinking that he himself has redeemed his honor, yet he cannot ensure that posterity will recall him as *the greatest prince o' th' world | The noblest*. It becomes immediately evident that Caesar cancels these superlatives by claiming equality with him and pronounces the judgment of history by attributing the outcome of their rivalry to their stars (5.1.35-48). Agrippa, speaking as the moral philosopher, sees him, finally, as a man. These encomia are not sufficient to satisfy Antony's own view of himself, and they prove that Antony's own deeds do not suffice to bring him the honor he expects. Cleopatra's final vision, which lifts him above the earth and transforms the Antony who could not keep his visible shape into a demigod, pronounces the poet's judgment upon him and thus brings him lasting honor.

Cleopatra: Spokesman for the Imagination

When the dramatic function of Cleopatra as spokesman for the imagination is recognized, some of the apparent inconsistencies in her character disappear. Shakespeare describes Cleopatra and the country she rules in terms appropriate to one who inspires poetry and defends the power of imagination. The reference to Antony's fascination by *a tawny front* and *a gypsy's lust* recalls the fact that Shakespeare had stated many years earlier that to see Helen's beauty in a brow of Egypt was a function of imagination. The fact that the Roman mind mistrusts such beauty recalls the puritanical mind that sees poetry, the product of imagination, as a tissue of lies. Egypt's serpents, symbols of cunning and wisdom, and her soothsayers, who predict the future and discern daemons, show Cleopatra's land as a world of intuitive knowledge. In such a world imagination resides. References to abundance, feasting, drinking, and other aspects of sensuality not only are symbols of wantonness but also can be associated with the teeming life of imagination, itself a faculty of the sensitive powers of the soul. Cleopatra's infinite variety is not mere fickleness but a property of fancy, which is *so full of shapes*. The mercurial and contradictory figures that it bodies forth resemble the *wrangling queen*, whose charm is enhanced by every passion, who is *quickly ill, and well*, and who cannot be staled by custom or withered by age. Like poetry, the oldest of the arts, she is wrinkled deep in time yet conquers its mutability. All of the poet's traditional roles are affirmed of Cleopatra. Her fifth act vision of *some squeaking Cleopatra* is a prediction fulfilled before the eyes of the audience, thus making her eligible for the oldest of poetic titles, that of prophet. On the authority of Antony, we learn that she is *cunning past man's thought*, while Enobarbus, pretending to misunderstand him, replies with a quibble that bestows on her the additional poetic titles of maker and feigner:

Alack, sir, no! Her passions are made of nothing but the finest part

of pure love. We cannot call her winds and waters sighs and tears.
They are greater storms and tempests than almanacs can report.
This cannot be cunning in her; if it be, she makes a show'r of rain
as well as Jove.

(1.2.151-157)

Cleopatra is not merely cunning; her ability to dissemble and her power to
evoke belief in her dissembling are divine skills equal to those possessed by
the king of the gods.[22]

When Enobarbus speaks of Cleopatra's sighs and tears, he adds to the
imagery of water familiarly associated with her that of wind. This image
reappears in his later description of her progress on the river Cydnus where
the winds that fill the sails of the barge are lovesick, and wind from the
fans seems to *glow the delicate cheeks which they did cool*; where invisible
perfume hits the city's wharves and the air, *but for vacancy | Had gone to
gaze on Cleopatra too | And made a gap in nature.*[23] The lovesick winds
and the air that sought a glimpse of Cleopatra are both additions to his
source by Shakespeare, as is this odd anecdote with which Enobarbus
concludes his description:

> I saw her once
> Hop forty paces through the public street;
> And having lost her breath, she spoke, and panted,
> That she did make defect perfection
> And, breathless, pow'r breathe forth.

(2.2.233-237)

It seems an irrelevant rejoinder to Agrippa's comment on Cleopatra's affair
with Julius Caesar, which is couched in terms of husbandry and farming.
Perhaps Enobarbus, still held captive to his memory, has not heard the
remark; perhaps he wishes to correct Agrippa's earthy vision, suggesting
that the source of Cleopatra's fascination is as intangible as air. It may be
that, entranced by her power over such strong men as Antony and Julius

---

[22] In Hardison, *English Literary Criticism*, Sidney (p. 103), Puttenham (p. 148),
and Jonson (p. 279) all mention the etymology of *poet* as the Greek word for *maker*.
The poet's ability to counterfeit is mentioned by Puttenham (p. 148); Jonson (p.
279), who uses *fainer* as a synonym to *maker*; and Sidney, who says the poet brings
forth "formes such as neuer were in Nature" (p. 104).
[23] For a discussion of the imagery of air and winds in the barge scene, see p. 211.

Caesar, he begins to ponder the possible sources of it but can only produce an anecdote that seems, for reasons he cannot make clear, to explain that power. In any case, the anecdote suggests that Cleopatra's power has the quality of breath and that its source lies beyond normal human means. Poetic inspiration, of course, takes its name from the word *spiritus*, or *breath*, and the very notion of inspiration implies a source transcending human nature.

Two of the major images associated with Cleopatra, the serpent and the Nile, are symbols not only of fertility but also fertility of a specific sort. Serpent and river are often seen with reference to spontaneous generation. The earliest serpent reference is to the courser's hair (1.2.185), which was supposed to come to life as a worm or a small serpent when it fell into water. There is also Lepidus's observation that the serpent of Egypt is bred from mud by the operation of the sun. Both posit the generation of life from nonliving matter, and in this respect they recall the poet's ability to bring something from nothing. The Nile, whose slime is quickened by the sun, is another important image of spontaneous generation. Cleopatra, "the serpent of old Nile," is doubly related to the concept of spontaneous generation. While water is generally regarded as a symbol of Cleopatra's fickleness and a malign factor in Antony's defeat, it can also be and often is, in the later plays of Shakespeare like *Pericles* or *The Tempest* a source of regeneration.

While it is not an image, Cleopatra's awareness of language deserves mention. Plutarch observes that delightful conversation was among the charms that most attracted Antony to Cleopatra. Shakespeare's Cleopatra is familiar with terms of rhetoric. When Charmian praises *that brave Caesar*, Cleopatra tells her to *be chok'd with such another emphasis*. She delivers a grammar lesson on the semantics of *but yet*. Like Hamlet she cannot resist the opportunity to give the conventional phrase *I'll take my leave* an ironic twist (5.2.134). The famous metaphor of *salad days* is too explicit to be unself-conscious. Above all, Cleopatra understands an important tenet of Renaissance poetics, the idea of decorum that she expresses first when she asks her messenger why he wears *so tart a favour / To trumpet such good tidings* and that she voices magnificently in her message to Caesar:

> If your master
> Would have a queen his beggar, you must tell him
> That majesty, to keep decorum, must

No less beg than a kingdom.

(5.2.15-18)

It would be most indecorous to view this spokesman for imagination at any point in the play as a shrill-voiced strumpet who bears little resemblance to the witty queen of Plutarch.

This analysis of images that surround Cleopatra and that can be construed as properties of the poet or of imagination is not intended to imply that she is an allegorical figure or a symbol, but to suggest that her behavior, her words, and her world of Egypt have properties in which imagination is at home. She moves the prosaic Enobarbus to poetry, transfixes Pompey the Great, and inspires his son to invoke her aid in his wars against Rome. She outlives all these great conquerors and outwits Octavius, leaving him to such hollow triumph as fortune sees fit to bestow upon him. Her self-consciousness as a character has already been explored with reference to her vision of the Roman triumph and her defense of imagination.[24] With Hamlet and Prospero she shares an awareness of theater that manifests itself also in her direct participation in the playwright's role. She manipulates Antony, traps Caesar with the Seleucus episode, and plays one against the other (1.1.19-32) to achieve her own ends. She controls the interpretation of history, rewriting the chronicle of Caesar's Egyptian campaign so that he is remembered as one who paid her homage while he planned future conquests.

The scene in which she obliges the messenger to describe Octavia in terms agreeable to her and the use of Seleucus to deceive Caesar are minidramas designed to control the actions of others. That she is aware of her power to manage Antony is abundantly clear from her early speech *If you find him sad, / Say I am dancing* (1.3.3-5). Charmian warns her against such contrariness lest she lose Antony, but Cleopatra's policy would seem to be proven sound by the event because, no matter how great the provocation, she never loses Antony. There is no radical discontinuity between her behavior in the earlier and later parts of the play. The Thyreus episode is a playlet she designs to deceive Octavius. At the conclusion of his embassy, although she has already controverted his view of her honor, she appears to reward his embassy by her message to Caesar:

Most kind messenger,
Say to great Caesar this: in deputation

[24] For a discussion of Cleopatra's speech on the Roman triumph, see pp. 60-61.

> I kiss his conqu'ring hand. Tell him I am prompt
> To lay my crown at's feet, and there to kneel.
> Tell him, from his all-obeying breath I hear
> The doom of Egypt.
>
> (3.13.73-78)

For Cleopatra to kiss Caesar's hand *in deputation*, that is, by means of his messenger, is, in effect, to acknowledge his mastery over her.[25] But the episode concludes with Thyreus kissing Cleopatra's hand. Thus, Caesar's deputy pays her Caesar's homage and the total effect of her sending obedience to Caesar is thereby canceled. She makes this point clear when she reminds Thyreus that a mightier Caesar than Octavius had paid her homage:

> Your Caesar's father oft,
> When he hath mus'd of taking kingdoms in,
> Bestow'd his lips on that unworthy place
> As it rain'd kisses.
>
> (3.13.82-85)

These lines recall her earlier remark that hers is *a hand that kings / Have lipp'd, and trembled kissing*. Antony's outraged interpretation of this action is accurate; Cleopatra is bestowing a favor on Thyreus and through him upon Octavius. But to bestow favors in this manner is hardly a gesture of submission or humility.

If Cleopatra's meeting with Caesar served to suggest Caesar's potential position at the bottom of fortune's wheel, the vision of Antony in which he appears above the world of change would seem to place him at the top of fortune's wheel, except that he can never again lose his position of preeminence. This dream, the key to the entire play, has the function of forming Antony through its applause and of asserting the supremacy of imagination over reason and history:

> I dreamt there was an Emperor Antony—
> O, such another sleep, that I might see
> But such another man! . . .
> His face was as the heav'ns, and therein stuck
> A sun and moon, which kept their course and lighted
> The little O, the earth. . . .

[25]The First Folio reads *disputation*, but Kittredge emends this to *deputation*, a reading preserved by Irving Ribner and used also by John Dover Wilson and G. B. Evans in their editions of this play.

> His legs bestrid the ocean: his rear'd arm
> Crested the world. His voice was propertied
> As all the tuned spheres, and that to friends;
> But when he meant to quail and shake the orb,
> He was as rattling thunder. For his bounty,
> There was no winter in't; an autumn 'twas
> That grew the more by reaping. His delights
> Were dolphin-like: they show'd his back above
> The element they liv'd in. In his livery
> Walk'd crowns and crownets. Realms and islands were
> As plates dropp'd from his pocket. . . .
> Think you there was or might be such a man
> As this I dreamt of?

(5.2.76-94)

Cleopatra's vision gives permanence to instability and final form to Antony's visible shape. Derek Traversi has stated that this deification of Antony is, after all, an illusion, yet there is no phrase in it that does not summon up the Antony who has been revealed in the preceding acts.[26] The man whose *legs bestrid the ocean* is the man who *o'er green Neptune's back with ships made cities*. The face that *lighted the little O* once shone on *those that make their looks by his*. The arm that *crested the world* belonged to *the demi-Atlas* and *burgonet of men*. The voice of *rattling thunder* sought to *outroar the horned herd* on Basan. His bounty was attested by offering his defeated followers all his treasure and by his treatment of Enobarbus. *Realms and islands* might well drop from the pockets of one who promised to piece Cleopatra's throne with kingdoms and who at last kissed away kingdoms and provinces. The testimony of our eyes and ears during the first four acts obliges us to answer that there was once such a man as this. It is the final perspective of Antony, anatomizing him only to complete his picture and to reveal the Mars of men. If Cleopatra's dream is an illusion, then so is the play; but, if we have until now believed in the play, then we are bound to believe in the dream.

Cleopatra has a greater claim upon our belief than Enobarbus, who dies before the story ends. She has seen the story from all perspectives and has been given the final reflection upon it. Nor does Caesar's concluding speech give the lie to her vision:

---

[26] Derek Traversi, *Shakespeare: The Roman Plays*, pp. 194-195.

> She shall be buried by her Antony.
> No grave upon the earth shall clip in it
> A pair so famous.
>
> (5.2.361-363)

This statement negates the idea that the magnitude of these lovers can be constrained by a narrow grave.

Since Cleopatra herself can never be excluded from Antony's story, it is appropriate that the one occasion when Antony's consciousness transcends the limits of history should include both lovers in a reference that leaves little doubt of Shakespeare's final view of his characters:

> Where souls do couch on flowers, we'll hand in hand
> And with our sprightly port make the ghosts gaze.
> Dido and her Aeneas shall want troops,
> And all the haunt be ours.—Come, Eros, Eros!
>
> (4.14.51-54)

The Elysian future that Antony envisions is a reality created by poetry. Significantly, the lovers who will be shunted aside are the lovers of Vergil's great literary epic. There is more than a hint of poetic rivalry in these words; they are a challenge. The immortality, the life with Cleopatra that Antony pictures for himself, is no illusion but a reality created by Shakespeare's poetry. Shakespeare challenges Vergil by choosing for his classical play a hero whose behavior is antithetical to that of *pius Aeneas*. Unlike Aeneas, who deserted his love from a sense of duty and patriotism, Antony deserts country and duty for love of Cleopatra. *Antony and Cleopatra* is a play not about tawdry middle-aged lovers but about the power of imagination to place an Egyptian puppet and a drunken Antony on the stage and, by poetry, to make the audience forget their smaller-than-life reality. If Helen's beauty was a theme for honor's tongue, to see her beauty in a brow of Egypt and to communicate that vision was a theme for honor that would spur any poet of the Renaissance to emulate the ancients by creating a drama whose verbal opulence might wrest the laurel from the great classical master and give the story of Antony and Cleopatra its most felicitous expression.

APPENDIX A

Supplementary Tables and Notes on Procedure

Interrogatives and Imperatives

Like all other frequencies in this study, those for interrogatives and imperatives were assembled manually, but, whereas many counts are aided by the study of structure words in a concordance, this assistance was available only to a limited degree for sentence types. The concordance has the value of establishing the total frequency for a word like *what*, which can then be analyzed into its interrogative, exclamatory, and relative functions. Thus, the concordance provides some measure of certitude that all instances of these sentences and clause types have been found, even though the analysis itself might not have the consistency one would achieve with an automatic parsing program. The assistance of the concordance here was limited to *wh-* interrogatives, exclamatory sentences, and optative imperatives with an overt auxiliary. All other question types and jussive imperatives were counted from the text, and, though location, speaker, and other pieces of information were recorded separately for each of these, it is always possible to overlook an item. Such oversights should not be numerous enough to substantially affect statistical results, especially when frequencies are high or when tests have a high level of significance. That is generally the case with the data of this section whenever quantitative criteria are invoked.

Shakespeare's use of traditional sentence types (declarative, interrogative, etc.) has been systematically studied by Vivian Salmon, who has described their structure, their structural variants, and the factors that might lead an Elizabethan to choose one variant over another. The mood system of late modern English has been described in *Sentence and Clause in Scientific English* by Rodney D. Huddleston et al. (pp. 95-119). Both these studies have furnished useful information for the analysis and interpretation of mood in these two plays, but the results recorded here are not so detailed as theirs. The types of question distinguished are *yes/no*, *wh-*, and a group of variants exemplified as follows:

1. Echo questions

   Aum.   It is no more
                Than my poor life must answer.
   Duch.   Thy life answer?
                       (*R2* 5.2.82-83)

2. Disjunctive questions

                Is she shrill-tongu'd or low?
                       (*Ant.* 3.3.15)

3. Tags

                        He spake it twice
             And urg'd it twice together, did he not?
                       (*R2* 5.4.4-5)

4. Declaratives

                Why, it contains no king?
                       (*R2* 3.3.24)

5. Verbless

                The manner of their deaths?
                       (*Ant.* 5.2.340)

Terms of address like *Madam?* were included among minor interrogatives. These variants were not sorted out for each character, but it is clear that they occur most often in the speech of Antony and Cleopatra and their followers. Their increase in *Antony* is significant, and the difference they make in the plays can be appreciated from the figures in Table A-1.

Table A-1
Frequency and Types of Variant Questions

	Echo	Disjunctive	Tags	Declarative	Verbless	Total
R2	9	1	2	1	0	13
Ant.	9	4	5	8	19	45

Imperatives are classified into jussives, such as *go* or *come*, the volitive optative with *may* or with the *NP + VN* structure described by Vivian Salmon, the optative with *let*, and verbless imperatives. The jussive need not be exemplified, but it should be noted that expressions like *go muster* were counted as two separate imperatives. The second type of imperative, now restricted to expressions like *God help us* or to very formal contexts, can easily be recognized. It is sometimes marked by the auxiliary *may*, by the deletion of inflectional *-s* when the subject is third person singular, or by the presence of lexical items like *God* or *Heaven*:

> And when I mount, alive may I not light
> If I be traitor or unjustly fight!
> (*R2* 1.1.82-83)

> *Boling.* Many years of happy days befall
> My gracious sovereign, my most loving liege!

> *Mowb.* Each day still better other's happiness
> Until the heavens, envying earth's good hap,
> Add an immortal title to your crown!
> (*R2* 1.1.20-24)

Let is present in the other form of the optative unless it is deleted by branching in a paratactic construction, such as the following:

> Let him take thee
> And hoist thee up to the shouting plebeians.
> (*Ant.* 4.12.33-34)

When this occurs, two instances of *let* are counted. This procedure explains why the frequency of *let* optatives is higher than that yielded by consulting the word in a concordance.

The verbless imperatives are not a category generally recognized by grammatical description, since there are no formal recognition criteria for determining when a verbless sentence is or is not imperative. Those expressions counted as verbless imperatives are often adverbial expressions of motion, such as these:

> To horse, to horse! Urge doubts to them that fear.
> (*R2* 2.1.299)

> To the vales,
> And hold our best advantage.
> (*Ant.* 4.11.3-4)

As can be seen, these occur in the context of other imperatives; often they close a scene. Nominal expressions can be more problematic, but the context often suggests their imperative function:

> Comfort, my liege. Remember who you are.
> (*R2* 3.2.82)

> *Cleo.* Give me some music! music, moody food
> Of us that trade in love.

Omnes.   The music, ho!
                                            (*Ant.* 2.5.1-2)

In the second passage *The music, ho!* is counted as a verbless imperative, but not Cleopatra's *music, moody food | Of us that trade in love,* which is in apposition with her previous statement.

Because, however, such decisions must be far more subjective than the tabulation of regular imperatives, verbless imperatives have not been included in the count of terms of address. Terms of address were counted (although *pray you* and *prithee* were excluded) because an additional measure of formality was wanted, and, since the verbless imperatives are seen as a sign of informality, the two categories serve as independent measures of formality and informality. In all totals provided in Tables A-2

Table A-2
Proportion of Interrogatives to Imperatives Used by Main Speakers

Speaker	Interrogatives	Imperatives
R2		
King Richard	84	137
Bolingbroke	27	82
York	32	55
Gaunt	7	29
Northumberland	5	16
Mowbray	1	14
Queen	19	22
Duchess of York	20	26
Aumerle	9	17
Carlisle	3	7
Duchess of Gloucester	7	10
Ant.		
Antony	60	251
Cleopatra	92	213
Caesar	12	93
Enobarbus	20	27
Charmian	7	24
Agrippa	3	7
Lepidus	0	10
Dolabella	4	8
Pompey	15	36
Octavia	2	9
Menas	3	13

Table A-3
Ratio of Interrogatives to Imperatives Used by Main Speakers

Speaker	Interrogatives	Imperatives
R2		
King Richard	.1112	.1814
Bolingbroke	.0653	.1985
York	.1111	.1909
Gaunt	.0364	.1510
Northumberland	.0349	.2027
Mowbray	.0074	.1037
Queen	.1652	.1913
Aumerle	.1058	.2000
Carlisle	.0441	.1029
Duchess of Gloucester	.1206	.1724
Ant.		
Antony	.0737	.3083
Cleopatra	.1373	.3179
Caesar	.0287	.2224
Enobarbus	.0793	.1071
Charmian	.1029	.3529
Agrippa	.0526	.1228
Lepidus	–	.1785
Dolabella	.0833	.1666
Pompey	.3750	.9000
Octavius	.0540	.2432
Menas	.1500	.6500

and A-3, however, terms of address are not counted though verbless imperatives are.

One type of imperative (presumably volitive) recognized by Salmon was overlooked at the time of this study, namely, the construction with *that* and *that ever*:

> O that I were a mockery king of snow,
> Standing before the sun of Bolingbroke
> To melt myself away in water drops!
> (*R2* 4.1.260-262)
>
> That ever I should call thee castaway!
> (*Ant.* 3.6.40)

There were three of these imperatives in *Richard II*, all spoken by King Richard. In *Antony* there were five, two spoken by Antony and one apiece by Cleopatra, Caesar, and Enobarbus. Although these imperatives are not included among the frequencies listed in the tables where imperatives are mentioned, they are too few to alter the general trends.

As with so many forms of address in the courtly society for which Shakespeare wrote, to issue an order was an exercise in diplomacy. Naturally such orders will assume linguistic forms other than the imperative, and, often, the more solemn the command the less likely it is to take that form, as happens when Richard sentences Bolingbroke:

> You, cousin Hereford, upon pain of life,
> Till twice five summers have enrich'd our fields
> Shall not regreet our fair dominions
> But tread the stranger paths of banishment.
>   (*R2* 1.3.140-143)

These and similar commands cannot be easily tabulated, and what is said about the imperative style of different speakers in this study must be considered with this fact in mind.

Adjectives

The study of adjective-noun relations includes only adjectives like *blue, noble, great*, which in systemic grammar are called epithets as opposed to prenoun modifiers like *other* and *usual*, to noun modifiers like *traitor* in *traitor coward*, to limiting adjectives, such as numerals, and to possessive determiners like that in *woman's war*. Only preposed adjectives were examined; traditional predicate adjectives and participial adjectives introducing subordinate clauses were excluded.

For the data in Table 6, the number of syllables per adjective was counted on the basis of Kittredge's text. Thus, *wan'd* is one syllable but *forked* is two; *burnish'd* and *prosp'rous* are two but *prepared* and *poisonous* are three; and so on. There were very few adjectives of five syllables, none with six. The syllables in compound adjectives (*sky-aspiring*) are not included in the figures, but, since in each play approximately half of these consisted of two monosyllables (1-1) and the other half of combinations that added up to three or more syllables in proportions similar to the ordinary adjectives, including or excluding them does not alter the trends shown here.

Participial adjectives can be easily distinguished from those that merely end in *-ing* or *-en* by transposing adjective and noun to form a meaningful sentence. Thus, one can transpose *a lurking adder* to *an adder that lurks*, but this cannot be done with *a dining room* or *a cunning instrument*. *Gilded earth* will easily read *X gilded the earth* but *golden crown* cannot be rewritten in the same way. All the participial adjectives listed in Table 7 are capable of transposition to a meaningful phrase or sentence.

At times one of the multiple adjectives may be a compound, which happens four times in *Richard II* and once in *Antony and Cleopatra*, but no adjustment was made for this fact in recording the figures in Table 8; hence, the figures for "Multiple/Triple" include those phrases in which there is a compound and an ordinary adjective, as in *sky-aspiring and ambitious thoughts*, and the figures for "Compound" include this instance of *sky-aspiring*.

The following lists contain the *-ing* words counted as gerunds, or verbal nouns, in this study. In *Richard II*, Act One: *giving, letting, suff'ring, defending, breathing, plaining, thinking* (2), *parting, underbearing*; Act Two: *feeding, being, watching, fasting, spilling, robbing, suffering, departing, parting, thinking, numb'ring, drinking, braving, coming*; Act Three: *urging, tossing, meeting* (2), *dying, fearing, bending, turning, coming, hearing, kissing, dancing, weeping, eating, speaking, telling*; Act Four: *breathing, confessing, deposing*; Act Five: *resting, deposing, wooing, coming, being* (2), *pardoning, cleansing, clapping, taking, weeping*.

The following were counted as verbal nouns in *Antony*, Act One: *earing, breathing, swearing* (2), *going* (3), *dissembling, becomings, tippling, looking*; Act Two: *stirring, stomaching, being* (2), *residing, learning, adornings, landing, angling, feasting*; Act Three: *roaring, going, shipping* (2), *being, refusing, yielding, doting, swerving, sinking, taking, playing, getting, following, discandying*; Act Four: *deserving, parting, kissing, feeding*; Act Five: *breaking, trusting, undoing, abhorring, reaping, hearing, dreaming, taking, leave-taking, swelling*.

These words were excluded from the list of verbal nouns in *Richard II*: *greeting* (3), *lendings, lodgings, blessings* (2), *lightning, feeling* (3), *lining, tidings* (4), *writing* (4), *mournings*. These words were excluded from *Antony*: *biddings* (2), *greeting* (3), *meanings, holding, writings*.

Table A-4 requires little comment beyond the note that the figures for suffixes include the inflected morphemes *-er*, *-est* for the comparison of

Table A-4
Kinds of Adjectival Suffixes

	English Suffixes					Latinate Suffixes					
	-ful	*-less*	*-ly*	*-y*	Total	*-ate*	*-ent*	*-(i)an*	*-able -ible*	*-ous*	Total
R2	27	15	18	34	94	2	5	1	7	27	42
	.2872	.1595	.1914	.3617		.0476	.1190	.0238	.1666	.6428	
Ant.	12	2	8	14	36	1	2	18	8	22	51
	.3333	.0555	.2220	.3888		.0196	.0392	.3529	.1568	.4313	

adjectives and the endings *-ing* and *-ed/-en* on participial adjectives. Separate figures for these endings are given in Table 7 of the text and Table A-5 below. Only genuine suffixes are recognized, so that *heavy* and *merry* are not included in the count of adjectives ending in *-y*; neither is *happy/unhappy*, though it could be argued that *hap* was a free base in Shakespeare's day. Bound bases in Latinate words like *inveterate*, *immaculate*, and *degenerate* were recognized in the count of prefixes and suffixes.

There are 400 suffixes in *Richard II* and their ratio to total adjectives is .4012; in *Antony* the ratio of the 259 suffixes to total adjectives is .4003. While there is no difference between the ratio of suffixes in the two plays, prefixes decrease in *Antony*. There are 37 prefixes in *Richard II* whose ratio to the total adjectives is .0371; in *Antony* the ratio of 13 prefixes to total adjectives is .0200.

The proportion of the total English to the total Latinate suffixes given in Table A-4 indicates a significant decrease in English suffixes and a significant increase in Latinate suffixes. For this proportion, $\chi^2 = 15.6804$. The change in the proportion of types of suffix is interesting in view of the over-all stability of suffixes in the two plays.

The proportion of inflected comparatives to inflected superlatives shown in the first panel of Table A-5 has a significant result: $\chi^2 = 4.9704$. *More* and *most* were included in the figures of the second panel only when they preceded a preposed adjective. For the third panel, numbers that preceded a noun were counted whether or not they also preceded an adjective. Thus, both *six years* and *six frozen winters* were counted although the number in the first expression precedes a noun. *One* was not counted unless the context clearly indicates that it is intended to be a numerical adjective, as in *twenty men to one*. Ordinals and cardinals are both included, as well as the *twice* of *twice five*, the *triple* of *triple-turn'd* (which is also counted as a compound adjective elsewhere), and expressions like *sevenfold*. *Ten thousand* as a single figure is counted once. The last panel of figures in Table A-5 is derived as follows: *quantifying* adjectives consist of the inflected comparatives and superlatives tallied in the first panel, the *more* and *most* of the second panel, and the numerals of the third panel; the figure for *qualifying* adjectives was obtained by subtracting the data in

Table A-5
Kinds of Quantifying Adjectives

	Comparative	Superlative	*More*	*Most*	Numerals	Quanti-fying	Quali-fying
R2	17	9	1	4	75	106	971
Ant.	17	31	14	21	52	135	599

Table A-6
Categories of Nouns Modified by Present Participial Adjectives

	Abstract	Concrete	Human	Proper Name	Total Present Participial Adjectives
R2	13	46	33	6	98
	.1326	.4693	.3367	.1428	
Ant.	5	20	5	5	35
	.1428	.5714	.1428	.1428	

the first panel only from the total adjectives in each play. The proportion of quantifying to qualifying adjectives in the two plays is significantly different: $\chi^2 = 26.9251$.

Table A-6 classifies the types of noun modified by present participial adjectives and provides the data for the statement that these participles occurred more frequently before concrete nouns in *Antony* than in *Richard II* in proportion to the total number of adjectives in each play.

Certain problems occurred in preparing the figures for Table A-7. The first, which arose from the number of synecdoches in both plays (e.g., *conqu'ring hand*), was solved by excluding these from the table and treating them separately in Chapter Four. The second problem was created by

Table A-7
Classes of Metaphoric Adjective-Noun Collocations

Text	Total Collocations		Metaphoric		Reification		Animation		Personification	
	No.	Percent	No.	Ratio	No.	Ratio	No.	Ratio	No.	Ratio
R2	997	100	264	.2647	52	.1969	34	.1287	178	.6742
Ant.	647	100	159	.2457	46	.2893	12	.0754	101	.6352
Owen	947	100	50	.0527	18	.3600	10	.2000	22	.4400

expressions like *cold words*, which are quite figurative but from a formal point of view do not violate selection restrictions, since both adjective and noun are concrete. Expressions of speech, time, and relation, which are grammatically concrete but appear intuitively abstract because they are not perceptible by the senses, were classified as abstract.

If this procedure does not wholly invalidate the comparison between the metaphors of Shakespeare and of Wilfred Owen, it may be of some interest to compare the figures for the three sets of data. The data for Wilfred Owen adapted from George Landon's study of metaphor, specifically from

Table III of his work (p. 174). An attempt was made to follow the system of classification devised by Landon, where "reification is exhibited by a collocation containing one lexical item specified as concrete, the other as abstract; animation . . . where one lexical item is marked as animate, the other as concrete or abstract; personification where one form is marked human, the other animate, concrete, or abstract" (p. 172). As noted in the discussion of the figures in *Antony*, in some half dozen collocations of human/concrete the movement of thought was from human to concrete; hence, these collocations were classified as reification rather than personification.

While there are too many factors like time, culture, and genre lying between Shakespeare and Wilfred Owen to invite intelligent comment, one similarity is noteworthy, namely, the fact that the rank for the different figures is the same in all three texts, with personification first, reification second, and animation last. This similarity may be especially interesting in view of Landon's data, which show that reification is strongly favored over the other figures when object relations were examined.

The ratios given in the last three columns of Table A-7 were obtained by dividing the number of metaphoric (not total) collocations into the instances of reification, animation, and personification.

Wh- Words

The figures in Table A-8 give the frequency in *Richard II* and *Antony and Cleopatra* of the *wh-* words. Contractions like *what's* are included in these figures. Counts are based on a computer-generated concordance of the 1936 Kittredge edition of the *Complete Words* and show a few differences from the Spevack concordance of the G. B. Evans texts. For example, Kittredge emends F_1 to *Die where thou hast liv'd!* (*Ant.* 4.15.38), thereby affecting the count of *when* and *where*, since Evans retains the Folio *when*. Similarly, Kittredge in *Ant.* 1.2.117 reads *ho* where Evans, following F_1, has *how*.

The *wh-* words in English are related to one another by the fact that they can have relative and interrogative functions. They do not, of course, comprise the full set of relative words, since *that* and *as* are not included among them. Furthermore, a full study of relatives must include many clauses that lack an overt introductory word. Since it is less likely to have an antecedent, *how* may have only a marginal relative function; nevertheless, it is traditionally included among these words and there are some instances of its taking an antecedent in these plays.

Although these words in Shakespeare have several uses that are now obsolete, this fact did not create any serious difficulty for the analysis of relative clauses, since classification in this instance depended chiefly on

Table A-8
Frequency of *Wh-* Words

	Richard II	*Antony and Cleopatra*
How	47	53
What	114	144
When	38	68
Where	40	48
Which	72	99
Who	33	25
Whom	9	13
Whose	14	19
Why	30	24
Whence	3	1
Whencesoever	1	0
Wherefore	3	4
Wherein	4	3
Whereof	5	0
Whereon	1	1
Whereto	3	0
Whereupon	1	0
Wherewith	1	0
Whither	3	4
Whoso	1	0
Whosoever	1	0
Total	424	506

whether or not a clause had an antecedent and whether or not it functioned in clause or group structure. Nevertheless, some mention of the obsolete constructions is in order here. Noun clauses may occur as the direct object of a verb that already has a direct object, as in these instances:

> March on, and mark King Richard how he looks.
> (*R2* 3.3.61)

> We'll hear him what he says.
> (*Ant.* 5.1.51)

These constructions were treated as clause constituents, the first as a noun clause with *how* having adverbial function, the second as a noun clause with *what* as a pronoun. On four occasions in *Richard II* (1.2.39; 3.3.45; 1.1.90; 1.1.172) and twice in *Antony* (3.1.28 and below), *which* is preceded by the definite article:

> To lend me arms and aid when I requir'd them,
> The which you both denied.
>
> > (*Ant.* 2.2.88-89)

These constructions can be clause betas or group betas, depending on the nature of their antecedents. At other times relative *which* serves as modifier to a noun, a construction not fully obsolete:

> Further I say, and further will maintain
> . . . .
> That he did plot the Duke of Gloucester's death,
> . . . .
> Sluic'd out his innocent soul through streams of blood;
> Which blood, like sacrificing Abel's, cries,
> . . . .
> To me for justice and rough chastisement;
>
> > (*R2* 1.1.98-106)

These constructions presented some difficulty, but except for this passage (a group beta), they were classified as adjunct clauses because the relative word served as the object of a preposition and the whole functioned in clause structure (see *R2* 2.2.87; *Ant.* 1.4.79; 2.3.3-5; 3.9.2). The use of personal pronoun relatives as noun clauses is discussed on p. 79. A peculiarity of *what* clauses is mentioned in the discussion of Table B-2.

Other unusual instances of these words may belong to the language or they may be due to poetic license:

> . . . I thank thee, king,
> For thy great bounty that not only giv'st
> Me cause to wail, but teachest me the way
> How to lament the cause.
>
> > (*R2* 4.1.299-302)
>
> Then let it do at once
> The thing why thou has drawn it.
>
> > (*Ant.* 4.14.88-89)

In the first passage either *the way* or *how* is redundant; in the second *why* appears where we would use *for which*. At other times—for example, in the phrase *have notice what we purpose* (*Ant.* 1.2.184)—there is no preposition where one might be expected. One suspects that in these and similar cases poetic license or rhetorical practice is responsible for the apparent peculiarities, but poets today might not exercise these particular liberties and there is in any case a strong tie between the state of the language and the degree and type of poetic license.

Innovating tendencies in Shakespeare's use of the *wh-* words are less obvious. The single instance of interrogative *which* in *Antony* (5.2.112) may be one; the decline in compound relatives like *whereon, whoso* is undoubtedly another. Whether the latter is related to the increase of prep-osition-complement structures among *what* clauses is not a possibility that was investigated, although a quick glance at the latter suggests that it is not.

Table A-9 analyzes the *wh-* words by mood at sentence and clause levels. The headings at sentence level are "Declarative/Imperative," "Interroga-tive," and "Exclamatory." At clause level the headings are "Relative," "Question" (for indirect interrogatives), and "Other," which varies with the word. "Other" includes the use of *how, what,* and *why* as expletives,

Table A-9
Types of Sentences and Clauses Containing *Wh-*Words

		Sentences			Clauses		
		Declarative/ Imperative	Inter-rogative	Excla-matory	Relative	Question	Other
How	*R2*	21	18	8	16	3	2
	Ant.	40	8	5	19	9	12
What	*R2*	53	59	2	33	11	9
	Ant.	86	55	3	64	12	10
When	*R2*	36	2	–	28	2	6
	Ant.	67	1	–	61	0	6
Where	*R2*	29	11	–	23	3	3
	Ant.	25	23	–	20	1	4
Which	*R2*	72	0	–	70	2	0
	Ant.	98	1	–	97	1	0
Who	*R2*	21	12	–	16	5	0
	Ant.	20	5	–	17	3	0
Whom	*R2*	8	1	–	8	0	0
	Ant.	13	0	–	12	1	0
Whose	*R2*	14	0	–	14	0	0
	Ant.	19	0	–	18	1	0
Why	*R2*	18	12	–	2	3	13
	Ant.	10	14	–	1	0	9
Others	*R2*	22	5	–	21	1	0
	Ant.	8	5	–	7	1	0
Total	*R2*	294	120	10	231	30	33
	Ant.	386	112	8	316	29	41

the conditioning uses of *when* and *where* (e.g., with the meanings *since* and *whereas*), and the two uses of *what* as indirect exclamation.

There was little difficulty in recognizing the question types. Analysis was entirely guided by the punctuation of Kittredge's text. Thus, in the line *How? not dead? not dead? (Ant.* 4.14.103) one *wh-* and two *yes/no* questions were counted. In Shakespeare's English, it would be possible occasionally to mistake questions for imperatives, as in *Think on me, | That am with Phoebus' amorous pinches black (Ant.* 1.5.27-28). Since Kittredge punctuates this as a question, it was so recorded. This practice accounts for the fact that there are two more *wh-* questions recorded for *Richard II* than there are interrogative uses for *wh-* words in Table A-9.

> O, who can hold a fire in his hand
> By thinking on the frosty Caucasus?
> Or cloy the hungry edge of appetite
> By bare imagination of a feast?
> Or wallow naked in December snow
> By thinking on fantastic summer's heat?
> (*R2* 1.3.294-299)

These lines were counted as three *wh-* questions, even though the word *who* appears only once. A related, though nontextual, problem arises with the expression *how now*, which was recorded as an expletive in Table A-9 and (when justified) as an interrogative in Table 2. This duplication accounts for the fact that there are ten more *wh-* interrogatives listed for *Antony* in Table 2 than in Table A-9.

Table A-10 records the frequency with which the *wh-* words function as relative pronouns in complexes, clauses, and nominal groups. Following Huddleston (p. 465), adverbial relatives introduced by *when*, *where*, *why* (and in this case *how*) were classified as adjuncts if they had no antecedent, as beta clauses if the antecedent was a clause or a clause constituent, and as qualifiers if the antecedent was a dummy *it* (e.g., *When it appears to you where this begins, Ant.* 3.4.33). In terms of rhythm, however, most of the beta clauses were closely tied to their antecedents, with a few exceptions where the relative clause seemed to have an appositional relation to its antecedent:

> For God's sake let us sit upon the ground
> And tell sad stories of the death of kings!
> How some have been depos'd, some slain in war,
> Some haunted by the ghosts they have depos'd,
> (*R2* 3.2.155-158)

Maec.	This in the public eye?
Caes.	I' th' common show-place, where they exercise.
	(*Ant.* 3.6.11-12)

Table A-10
Types of Relative Structures Introduced by *Wh-* Words

		Clause Beta	Group Beta	Subject or Complement	Adjunct	Modifier	Qualifier
How	*R2*	–	5	11	–	(4)	–
	Ant.	–	1	18	–	(8)	–
What	*R2*	–	–	29	1	(4)	3
	Ant.	–	–	40	14	(8)	10
When	*R2*	–	3	–	24	–	1
	Ant.	–	13	–	45	–	3
Where	*R2*	–	6	–	17	–	0
	Ant.	–	7	–	12	–	1
Which	*R2*	7	36	–	1	(2)	26
	Ant.	14	38	–	4	(3)	41
Who	*R2*	–	12	2	–	–	2
	Ant.	–	13	4	–	–	0
Whom	*R2*	–	6	–	–	–	2
	Ant.	–	9	–	–	–	3
Whose	*R2*	–	13	0	–	(14)	1
	Ant.	–	16	1	–	(17)	1
Why	*R2*	–	1	–	1	–	–
	Ant.	–	1	–	0	–	–
Others	*R2*	0	8	2	3	–	8
	Ant.	1	1	0	1	–	4
Total	*R2*	7	90	44	47	(10)	43
	Ant.	15	99	63	76	(19)	63

There are not many of these in either play (*R2* 1.1.195; 2.2.79; 4.1.291; *Ant.* 1.4.57; 3.13.168), and the rhythmic break is probably a function of meter.

The increase in *Antony* of modifying functions of the relative, noted with respect to *what*, is seen also in *how* and *which*. *Whose*, of course, has an obligatory modifying function. Figures for modifiers are in parentheses to indicate that they overlap other categories and are not to be counted in the total relative uses of a given word.

In Table A-10 the first column (Kβ) indicates the frequency with which the relative word occurred in a beta clause whose alpha was another full clause, and the second column (Gβ) gives the frequency of relative words in group beta clauses. The next column (S,C) indicates how often a relative word occurred in a clause that was embedded as subject or complement in a matrix clause, and the fourth (A) shows how often the relative word appeared in a clause that was embedded as an adjunct in a matrix clause. The last two columns give the frequency with which these words served as modifiers in a nominal group or in a clause that was embedded as qualifier to a nominal group.

Sentence Structure

Table A-11 gives the proportion of simple to PHE sentences in the speeches of major characters in each play. PHE represents sentences containing at least one instance each of parataxis, hypotaxis, and embedding. The data are based on the random sample of sentences (Table B-1).

Table A-11
Proportion of Simple to Complex Sentences Used by Major Characters

	Richard	Bolingbroke	Antony	Cleopatra	Caesar
Simple	.10	.26	.16	.26	–
Complex*	.23	.26	.18	.20	.15

*Those sentences containing instances of parataxis, hypotaxis, and embedding.

Figure A-1 shows that the relative clause *where they come* is dominated by an adjunct; that is, it is embedded in clause structure. Figure A-2 has four levels: the clause *what was I born*, which is the immediate constituent

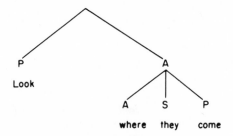

Ant. I.I.I0

Fig. A-1. Tree diagram of an embedded clause.
P, predicator; *A*, adjunct; *S*, subject.

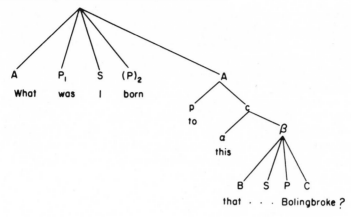

R2 3.4.98−99

Fig. A-2. Tree diagram of a hypotactic group complex. A, adjunct; P_1, first part of predicator; S, subject; P_2, second part of predicator; p, preposition; c, complement to preposition; α, group element in complex; β, hypotactic clause in complex; B, binder; S, subject; P, predicator; C, clause complement.

of the sentence; a preposition-complement structure (*to this*); the hypotactic group complex (*this that . . . Bolingbroke*); and the beta clause (*that . . . Bolingbroke*).

Constituent Sequence

Tables A-12 through A-17 provide data for the study of marked constituent order, based on the random sample of sentences (see Table B-1). At

Table A-12
Proportion of Normal to Deviant Sequence in Clause and Group Complexes

	Normal		Deviant		Total
	Paratactic	Hypotactic	Paratactic	Hypotactic	
R2	95	72	3	37	207
	.4589	.3478	.0144	.1787	
Ant.	113	57	0	36	206
	.5485	.2766	−	.1748	

the level of the clause complex, Table A-12 shows little difference between the two plays as far as deviance is concerned. The interesting phenomenon is the fact that the ratio of normal hypotactic complexes decreases by seven in *Antony*, which may cause the instances of hypotactic deviance in that play to stand out more sharply even though they do not decrease. Because the figures in Table A-12 revealed little variation from play to play, two further attempts were made to distinguish the plays on the basis of constituent order in the hypotactic complex. The first distinction showed a slight decrease of stylistic inversion ($\beta \cdot \alpha$) in *Antony* and a slight increase of discontinuity in the same play. Results are recorded in the first panel of Table A-13. The second distinction involves two types of dis-

Table A-13
Types of Deviant Sequence in Hypotactic Complexes

	Classes of Deviant Sequence			Types of Discontinuity		
	Inversion	Discontinuity	Total	Inclusion	Separation	Total
R2	16	21	37	19	2	21
	.4324	.5675		.9047	.0952	
Ant.	15	21	36	16	5	21
	.4166	.5832		.7619	.2380	

continuity in the complex, one in which the alpha and beta constituents are completely separated and one in which one of these constituents is included in the other. On the basis of the distinction between separation and inclusion, it appears that inclusion is more characteristic of *Richard II* and separation of *Antony and Cleopatra*. These data appear in the second panel of Table A-13.

As with the complexes, the instances of deviance in clause structure seem to vary little from play to play (Table A-14), but the distinction between inverted and discontinuous types of deviance produces notably different results when types of inversion are studied (Table A-15) and when types of discontinuity are distinguished (Table A-16). Table A-17 supplies the data yielded by the sample for the study of nominal-group deviance.

Determiners

These notes explain and exemplify the criteria used to define the formal meaning ascribed to determiners in Chapter Four. The nonspecific determiner—confined here to *a, an, another, some,* and *any*—is often used in a

Table A-14
Types of Deviant Sequence in Clause Structure

	Total Clauses			Instances of Deviance		
	Normal	Deviances	Total*	Inversion	Discontinuity	Total
R2	386	130	514	101	29	130
	.7509	.2529		.7769	.2230	
Ant.	417	137	546	111	26	137
	.7637	.2509		.8102	.1897	

*Because a clause can have more than one instance of deviance, the totals for the first panel signify the total number of clauses examined, not the total of the figures in the panel.

Table A-15
Types of Inversion in Clause Structure

	Complement Theme	Adjunct Theme	Vocative Theme	Total Theme	Marked Mood	Double Theme*	Total Inversions
R2	15	62	12	89	12	13	101
	.1685	.6966	.1348	.8811	.1188	.1287	
Ant.	16	68	17	101	10	10	111
	.1584	.6733	.1532	.9099	.0900	.0900	

*The figures for double theme are not included in the total instances of inverted clause structures, because any instances of double theme must contain instances of complement, adjunct, or vocative theme, each of which were separately totaled.

Table A-16
Types of Discontinuity in Clause Structure

	SXP*	PXC	CXC	. . .	Total
R2	14	10	0	1	25
	.5600	.4000	—	.0400	
Ant.	14	9	1	2	26
	.5385	.3461	.0384	.0769	

*Headings define the basic clause positions where interrupting elements can occur, namely, subject-predicator, predicator-complement, complement-complement. X symbolizes the interrupting element. The ellipsis signifies that a single clause constituent, such as a complement, may be interrupted.

Table A-17
Classes of Deviant Sequence in Nominal-Group Structure: Sample

	Normal Groups	Deviances	Group Total*	Inversion	Discontinuity	Total
R2	958	12	970	2	10	12
	.9876	.0124		.1667	.8333	
Ant.	965	16	978	8	8	16
	.9867	.0164		.5000	.5000	

*Because a group can have more than one instance of deviance, the totals for the first panel signify the number of groups examined, not the sum of the figures in the second panel.

neutral sense in these plays, especially when the speaker is describing the roles that he plays. Thus, Antony speaks of himself as *a workman*, *a soldier*, and *a man of steel* (4.4.18, 30, 33). Other instances of the neutral function with implications of role are contained in these passages from *Antony*:

> Broad-fronted Caesar,
> When thou wast here above the ground, I was
> A morsel for a monarch;
>   (1.5.29-31)

> Who's born that day
> When I forget to send to Antony
> Shall die a beggar.
>   (1.5.63-65)

> O, that his fault should make a knave of thee,
> That art not what th' art sure of!
>   (2.5.102-103)

On several occasions, however, the nonspecific determiner suggests a belittling function that can be identified if the word *some* can replace *a*, as in the modern English expression *some fool* or *some idiot*:

> The breese upon her, like a cow in June,—
>   (3.10.14)

For other examples of the use of *a/an* to express contempt, consider the distinction between *a noble Lepidus* and *the noble Antony* and the discussion of Cleopatra on pages 160-163.

The demonstrative (*this, that, these, those*) can have a general function of indicating some distance, physical or psychological, between speaker and referent, but the motives for creating this verbal distance can vary.

Sometimes the demonstrative is used in passages where high praise is added to the natural meaning of emphasis and pointing, and Gaunt's speech on England seems generally to use it for praise (*R2* 2.1.40-66). But it can also imply strong disassociation from the term it modifies: *this amorous surfeiter, this grave charm, these three world-sharers* (*Ant.* 2.1.33; 4.12.25; 2.7.76). These functions have been labeled the demonstrative of elevation and of alienation. The two determiners *a* and *this* combine to emphasize Caesar's disgust with the fickleness of the Roman populace:

> This common body,
> Like to a vagabond flag upon the stream,
> (1.4.44-45)

Unfortunately, no test can be provided for distinguishing the two functions of the demonstrative other than intuition, and it must be acknowledged here and throughout the discussion of determiner functions that the noun and its other modifiers (adjectives, posthead qualifiers) certainly contribute much to our interpretation of the modifying function of the determiner.

Possessive determiners carry certain meanings over and above those of ownership. The most obvious examples are those associated with the royal *we* and the distinction between familiar *thou* and formal *you*. The latter distinction has been greatly refined by the studies of Roger Brown and Albert Gilman in "The Pronouns of Power and Solidarity" (*Style in Language*, ed. Sebeok), and Angus McIntosh has applied their refinements to a study of Shakespeare ("King Lear, Act I, Scene i: A Stylistic Note"). Abbott notes that certain uses of *your* can indicate vulgarity and cites this passage from *Antony*:

> Your serpent of Egypt is bred now of
> your mud by the operation of your sun; so is your crocodile.
> (2.7.29-31)

One might also cite *Hamlet* 4.3.22-26 and *Othello* 2.3.78-88. Finally, because of their direct association with personal pronouns, possessive determiners can acquire the expressive, conative, and referential functions described by Roman Jakobson ("Closing Statement," in *Style in Language*, p. 357).

The definite article can have a function of self-evident reference, as has been pointed out. Two further categories used to classify determiners in the tables of this appendix are "Zero" and "Other." The "Zero" category accounts for the fact that nouns are not always modified by determiners, as these examples show:

O, but they say the tongues of dying men
Enforce attention like deep harmony.
                                                    (*R2* 2.1.5-6)
                         Truths would be tales,
Where now half-tales be truths.
                                                    (*Ant.* 2.2.136-137)

In Tables A-18 and A-19 the category "Other" was created chiefly to take account of vocatives where no determiner is possible: *Forgiveness, horse! Why do I rail on thee* (*R2* 5.5.90), where *horse* in Table A-18 is assigned to the general label *earth*. Similarly, *sun* is assigned to the label *fire* in *O sun, / Burn the great sphere thou mov'st in!* (*Ant.* 4.15.9-10).

The information in Table A-18 summarizes the frequency of references to aspects of the physical universe. The words in the first column (*world, earth*, etc.) are labels designating those aspects. Hence, under the label *earth* come words like *land, trees, adder, garden, apricots*. Table A-18 shows thirty-seven more references to the physical universe in *Antony* than in *Richard II*. Hence, when a determiner like the demonstrative or the possessive occurs with double or quadruple frequency in *Richard II*, its importance for that play is obvious. The greater frequency of the definite article in *Antony* becomes apparent only when one resorts to percents and sees that in *Richard II* (79/181) aspects of the physical universe are modified by the definite article 44 percent of the time, and in *Antony* (135/216), or 63 percent, are so modified.

Table A-19 supplies the ad hoc categories created to describe the physical, social, and cultural worlds of the two plays and the frequency with which each category occurs. This table is based only on the homophoric function of the definite article. Tables A-20 through A-22 contain supplementary word lists to show what words were assigned to each category in Table A-19 and give the frequency of any word that occurs more than once.

Table A-23 shows that adjectival *-ing* words, like adjectives in general, decreased sharply in *Antony* although nominalized forms are relatively stable. The increase of determiners before nominal forms that characterizes *Antony* can be best appreciated by noting that the combined use of definite and possessive determiners before gerunds in this play (34) is triple that for *Richard II*, even though the over-all frequency of nominals is similar. Both sets of proportions in Table A-23 (viz., adjectival to nominal *-ing* forms; definite/possessive to other determiners) are significantly different. These passages illustrate the adjectival use of *-ing* forms:

Yield stinging nettles to mine enemies;
And when they from thy bosom pluck a flower,

Table A-18
Determiners Modifying References to the Physical Universe

	Nonspecific		Definite		Demonstrative		Possessive		Zero		Other		Total	
	$R2$	Ant.	$R2$	Ant.	$R2$	Ant.	$R2$	Ant.	$R2$	Ant.	$R2$	Ant.	$R2$	Ant.
World	3 .1304	0 –	13 .5652	44 .8627	6 .2609	4 .0784	1 .0435	2 .0392	0 –	0 –	0 –	1 .0196	23 .1271	51 .2372
Earth	3 .0341	0 –	34 .3864	31 .5536	20 .2273	3 .0536	18 .2045	1 .0179	13 .1477	20 .3571	2 .0227	1 .0179	90 .4972	56 .2605
Air	1 .0313	3 .0732	20 .6250	20 .4878	2 .0625	0 –	5 .1563	5 .1220	4 .1250	5 .1220	0 –	8 .1951	32 .1768	41 .1907
Fire	2 .2000	0 –	3 .3000	5 .6250	0 –	0 –	0 –	1 .1250	5 .5000	1 .1250	0 –	1 .1250	10 .0552	8 .0372
Water	2 .0769	1 .0167	9 .3462	35 .5833	1 .0385	0 –	3 .1154	2 .0333	10 .3846	22 .3667	1 .0385	0 –	26 .1436	60 .2791
Total	11 .0608	4 .0186	79 .4365	135 .6279	29 .1602	7 .0326	27 .1492	11 .0512	32 .1768	48 .2233	3 .0166	11 .0512	181	216

Table A-19
Semantic Categories Used to Describe Self-Evident Fictional World of the Plays

	Physical Universe						Total
	World	Earth	Air	Fire	Water	Space/Time	
R2	11	33	18	1	8	18	89
	.1236	.3708	.2022	.0112	.0899	.2022	
Ant.	44	29	17	4	28	24	146
	.3014	.1986	.1164	.0274	.1918	.1644	

	Society							
	Name	Person	Morality	Economy	Polity	Nation	Rank	General
R2	3	15	5	2	15	3	111	2	156
	.0192	.0962	.0321	.0128	.0962	.0192	.7115	.0128	
Ant.	13	17	18	8	18	6	24	11	115
	.1130	.1478	.1565	.0696	.1565	.0522	.2087	.0957	

	Culture					
	Objects	Places	Events	Language	Values	Ideas
R2	20	24	5	21	10	13	93
	.2151	.2581	.0538	.2258	.1075	.1398	
Ant.	42	20	20	19	39	25	165
	.2545	.1212	.1212	.1152	.2364	.1515	

> Guard it, I pray thee, with a lurking adder
> (*R2* 3.2.18-20)

> On each side her
> Stood pretty dimpled boys, like smiling Cupids,
> With divers-colour'd fans, whose wind did seem
> To glow the delicate cheeks which they did cool,
> And what they undid did.
> (*Ant.* 2.2.206-210)

The presence of *dimpled* and *divers-colour'd* in the passage from *Antony* serves as a reminder that, in contrast to present participial adjectives like *smiling*, adjectives formed from the past participle increased significantly in *Antony*.

The following is a list of words identified as agent nouns in *-er/-or*. In *Richard II*: *accuser, rider* (2), *jailer, feeder, flatterer* (4), *keeper-back, carver, torturer, executors, executioner, lie-giver, conveyers, hearers, actor, challenger, beggar* (3). In *Antony*: *world-sharers, reapers, dancer, haters, wishers, rhymers, boggler, jailer, teller, wearer, feeders, homager, breather,*

Table A-20
Nouns Designating the Self-Evident Physical World of the Plays

	World	Earth	Air	Fire	Water	Space/Time
R2	world (10)	earth (12)	heavens (2)	fire	sea (5)	Alps
	clime	fruit	sky (2)		bay	hours (2)
		bay trees	clouds (2)		rivers	Caucasus
		ground (8)	air (4)		water	close
		pines	wind (3)			west
		land (3)	sun (3)			Antipodes
		dust	moon			night
		corn	firmament			East (2)
		eagle				day (2)
		twigs				Occident
		birds				North
		pelican				spring
		lion				side
						time
						Holy Land
Ant.	world (42)	hedge	wind (3)	thunderbolt	sea (6)	time (5)
	elements	stag	pestilence (2)	lightning	ports (2)	present (2)
	orb	pasture	stars (2)	fire (2)	stream	East (3)
		ground	heavens (2)		tide	Alps
		dust	air (3)		borders	Mt. Misenum
		earth (8)	sun		puddle	hour
		land	moon (3)		water	April
		myrtleleaf	spheres		ocean (3)	year
		rose			slime	Mount
		herd			shore (3)	Nile
		dove			showers	minute
		estridge			swell	day (2)
		hill			harbour	morn (2)
		vales			sea-side	night
		waterflies			source	dark
		aspic (2)			river	
		dung			isle	
		breese			haven	
		courser's hair				
		cuckoo				
		olive				

Table A-21

Nouns Designating the Self-Evident Social World of the Plays

Name	Person	Morality	Economy	Polity	Nation	Rank	General
Bolingbroke (2)	death (2)	wise	servants	accuser	French	King (56)	people
Norfolk	soul (2)	wantons	gardeners	champion (2)	Welshmen (2)	Duke (23)	man
	end	happy		marshal		Earl (7)	
	heart (2)	creature		appellant		nobles (2)	
	sore	villain		enemy (2)		commons (5)	
	rheum			foe		Lords (9)	
	mind			torturer		Duchess	
	blood (2)			challenger		poor	
	palsy			traitor		Queen (2)	
	heels			friend		Prince (2)	
	bosom			rebels		Bishop	
				murderer		peers	
				conspirator		Abbott	
Caesar (5)	tongue	liar (2)	actor	messengers (4)	Roman (2)	Queen (14)	woman (2)
Pompey	heart (3)	fool	seedsman	ambassadors	Parthians	priests	man (6)
Antony (4)	dead	deserver	landlord	soldier	Egyptians	triumvirate	people
Brutus (2)	body	penitent	hangman	routed	Phoenicians	Emperor (4)	side*
Cassius	sickness	slave	comedians	horse (2)	Ptolemies	Vestal	brothers
	face (2)	fellow (3)	nurse (2)	legions		augurers	
	feet	boy (3)	task	army		plebeians	
	eye	negligent		van		Prince	
	mind	witch (2)		host			
	ear	sleeper		foe			
	soul	varlotry		guard (4)			
	death	discontents					
	end						
	view						

	Objects	Places	Events	Language	Values	Ideas
R2	gage	lists (2)	fight	note	sacrament (3)	chivalry
	trumpets	realm (3)	trial (3)	leave	Destinies	hollown
	harmony	presence	triumph-	sentence	Book of Life	office
	crown (6)	highway (2)	day	word (5)	hand of God	good
	balm	grave (3)		matter (6)	cross	executie
	throne (2)	commonwealth		name	font	right (2
	glass	way (2)		suit	devil (2)	ransom
	windows	court (3)		moans		law
	key	castle (2)		French		degree
	door (3)	Tower (2)		*The Beggar and*		hate
	clock	taverns		*the King*		fertility
	rod	stews		news (2)		truth
		stocks				
Ant.	poop	streets (4)	war (5)	dare	gods (29)	measure
	sails	field (6)	buffet	matter (3)	powers	state (5
	oars	city (3)	feast	advice	Nereides	pleasure
	helm	Capitol	battle	news (2)	Jove (2)	treason:
	tackle	way (2)	journey	points (2)	goddess	motive
	barge	garden	match	fame (2)	fate	need
	wharfs	marketplace (2)	disguise	report	ghosts	fancy
	dice	showplace	fight (4)	odds (2)	haunt	office
	cable		show	precedence	Mercury	good
	reels		occupa-	lot	huswife	cause (2
	vessels		tion	hint	Fortune	lowness
	Bacchanals		chares	question		mean
	wine (2)		fashion	story		virtue
	music		battery			nonpare
	holding					brim
	boat					rule
	ships					height
	cup (2)					right
	Egyptian admiral					truth (2
	Antoniad					
	rudder					
	monument (4)					
	bands					
	diadem					
	bell					
	noise					
	waste					
	darts					
	bed					
	torch					
	pyramid					
	club					
	eyes					
	drums					
	ruin					

Table A-23
Types and Modifiers of Words Ending in *-ing*

	Adjectival *-ing* Forms	Nominal *-ing* Forms
R2	98	52
Ant.	35	59

Determiners before Nominal *-ing* Forms			
	Definite	Possessive	Other	Total
R2	5	6	41	52
Ant.	7	17	35	59

deserver, partaker, plighter, revenger (2), *sworder, reconciler, runner, bringer, armourer, sleeper, master-leaver, surfeiter.*

Functional shift was not examined in *Richard II*, but in *Antony and Cleopatra*, these words were tentatively identified as instances of this phenomenon: *companion,* 1.2.30P; *fortune,* 1.2.78P; *purpose,* 1.2.184; *safe,* 1.3.55; *lank'd,* 1.4.71; *paragon,* 1.5.71; *unpeople,* 1.5.78; *ghosted,* 2.6.13; *jaded,* 3.2.34; *unqualitied,* 3.11.44; *unstate,* 3.13.30; *fever,* 3.13.138; *discandying,* 3.13.165; *saf'd,* 4.6.26; *carbuncl'd,* 4.8.28; *disponge,* 4.9.12; *spaniel'd,* 4.12.21; *discandy,* 4.12.22; *bark'd,* **4.12.23;** *over-topp'd,* 4.12.24; *dislimns,* 4.14.10; *window'd,* 4.14.73; *brooch'd,* 4.14.25; *palate,* 5.2.7; *words,* 5.2.191; *ballad,* 5.2.213; *boy,* 5.2.219; *propertied,* 5.2.83. No attempt was made to check them against the *OED* or similar sources; several may be coinages as well as instances of functional shift. Citations are to the Kittredge edition of the *Complete Works,* 1936.

The figures in Table A-24 were obtained by measuring the total occurrences of *and* in the two plays against the instances of nominal and verbal groups linked by this conjunction. Compound verbal groups are few, there being eleven in *Richard II* and six in *Antony and Cleopatra.* As the total count of *and* decreases in *Antony* so do the instances of group parataxis. The chi-square test shows a significant difference between the two sets of

Table A-24
Proportion of Groups Linked by *and* to
Total Instances of *and*

	Linked Groups	Total *and*
R2	224	692
Ant.	132	597

proportions χ^2 = 9.2728), thus validating in part F. E. Halliday's intuitive hypothesis that group parataxis is a characteristic of Shakespeare's middle style.

Tables A-25 through A-29 contain information about Cleopatra, Antony, Caesar, King Richard, and Bolingbroke that corresponds to the discussion of them on pages 160-179. The headings in Tables A-25 through A-29 are as follows: "Nonspecific," *a, an, another*; "Definite," *the*; "Demonstrative," *this, that, these, those*; "Possessives," *my/mine, thy/ thine, her, his, our* (sg.), *your* (sg.); "Name," *Antony, Antonius, Mark Antony, Antony's*, etc.; and "Zero." The last category includes references that are neither nominal groups introduced by a determiner nor the name of the character (e.g., *royal wench, sir, noble Emperor*, etc.). Throughout this discussion "reference" is used in a broad sense to include direct address, apostrophe, and all possible mention of a given character in the play. Tables A-25 through A-29 show the raw frequency and ratio of times when a character is mentioned by one of these modes of reference. Thus, in Table A-25, references to Cleopatra, one finds the frequency and ratio of times when Antony, Cleopatra herself, Caesar, and all other characters refer to her by the various determiners, by her name, or by some other term like *madam*.

To make the information in Tables A-25 through A-29 explicit, Tables B-8 through B-12 provide the location in the text for all headings except "Possessives" and "Name." The counts for Bolingbroke's name include only *Bolingbroke* and *Hereford*, for Caesar's name only references to Octavius, and for all names variants like *Antony's*. There is occasional overlap between proper names and determiners when a name is modified, as in *an Antony, my Richard*, or *the approaching Caesar*. These were counted twice, once for the appropriate determiner and once for the name. Similarly, there are occasional phrases like *those his goodly eyes*, a reference to Antony, introduced by both a demonstrative and a possessive and counted under each of these headings. References to more than one person are not counted at all (*our brows, our lips; chief factors for the gods* [*Ant*. 1.3.35-36; 2.6.10], etc.). On the other hand, some expressions are reciprocal and are taken to refer to two distinct characters. Thus *my cousin king* defines a mutual relationship between Bolingbroke and King Richard and is counted once under the references to Bolingbroke by himself and once under the references to Richard by Bolingbroke. This practice explains how a character can refer to himself in the second person, as when Antony says *Thy master dies thy scholar* (4.14.102). When a determiner has been deleted in a compound or a series the reference is counted as an instance of that determiner. Thus, *My manors, rents, revenues I forgo* (*R2* 4.1.212) is counted as three instances of the first singular determiner in the references by Richard to himself.

Table A-25
Determiners Introducing References to Cleopatra

Speaker	Nonspecific	Definite	Demonstrative	Possessives 1	Possessives 2	Possessives 3	Name	Zero	Total
Antony	6 .0618	8 .0824	9 .0927	19	22 .4742	5	7 .0721	21 .2164	97 .2449
Cleopatra	8 .0695	4 .0347	5 .0435	89	1 .7826	0	3 .0261	5 .0435	115 .2904
Caesar	1 .0294	3 .0882	0 —	0	6 .5000	11	9 .2647	4 .1176	34 .0858
Others	8 .0533	11 .0733	0 —	3	29 .3200	16	9 .0600	74 .4933	150 .3787
Total	23 .0581	26 .0656	14 .0353	111	58 .5075	32	28 .0707	104 .2626	396

Table A-26
Determiners Introducing References to Antony

Speaker	Nonspecific	Definite	Demonstrative	Possessives 1	2	3	Name	Zero	Total
Antony	14 .0782	10 .0558	4 .0223	125	11 .7933	6	8 .0447	1 .0056	179 .2901
Cleopatra	8 .0689	10 .0862	9 .0775	14	8 .3793	22	36 .3103	9 .0775	116 .1880
Caesar	4 .0437	5 .0746	0 —	3	10 .5522	24	20 .2985	1 .0149	67 .1086
Others	9 .0352	20 .0745	8 .0313	25	34 .4745	62	72 .2824	25 .0980	255 .4133
Total	35 .0567	45 .0729	21 .0340	167	63 .5575	114	136 .2204	36 .0583	617

Table A-27
Determiners Introducing References to Octavius Caesar

Speaker	Nonspecific	Definite	Demonstrative	Possessives 1	Possessives 2	Possessives 3	Name	Zero	Total
Antony	1 .0149	4 .0597	1 .0149	1	8 .3881	17	29 .4328	6 .0896	67 .2343
Cleopatra	2 .0426	2 .0426	0 —	6	6 .3617	5	22 .4681	4 .0851	47 .1643
Caesar	0 —	0 —	0 —	35	0 .8409	2	7 .1591	0 —	44 .1538
Others	3 .0234	6 .0469	0 —	9	8 .2188	11	85 .6641	6 .0469	128 .4476
Total	6 .0210	12 .0420	1 .0035	51	22 .3776	35	143 .5000	16 .0559	286

Table A-28
Determiners Introducing References to King Richard

Speaker	Nonspecific	Definite	Demonstrative	Possessives 1	Possessives 2	Possessives 3	Name	Zero	Total
Richard	16 .0678	13 .0551	9 .0381	174	6 .7669	1	8 .0339	9 .0381	236 .4322
Boling-broke	3 .0652	5 .1087	3 .0652	15	4 .5870	8	7 .1522	1 .0217	46 .0842
Others	10 .0379	38 .1439	1 .0038	43	83 .6439	44	24 .0909	21 .0795	264 .4835
Total	29 .0531	56 .1026	13 .0238	232	93 .6923	53	39 .0714	31 .0568	546

Table A-29
Determiners Introducing References to Bolingbroke

Speaker	Nonspecific	Definite	Demonstrative	Possessives			Name	Zero	Total
				1	2	3			
Richard	3	6	5	13	15	22	23	15	102
	.0294	.0588	.0490		.4902		.2255	.1471	.2237
Boling-broke	8	3	2	108	0	1	4	2	128
	.0625	.0234	.0156		.8516		.0313	.0156	.2807
Others	13	19	3	31	61	29	53	17	226
	.0575	.0841	.0133		.5354		.2345	.0752	.4956
Total	24	28	10	152	76	52	80	34	456
	.0526	.0614	.0219		.6140		.1754	.0746	

The heading "Zero" excludes proper names even though these normally lack a determiner. Typical references under this heading are titles like *sir* or *madam*, vocatives like *thou most beauteous inn* or *thou mine of bounty*, and references like *rare Egyptian*. There is a certain skewness derived from the fact that King Richard is often called *my liege* or *my lord* but Cleopatra is called *madam* and thus has a very high ratio of references under "Zero." Table A-30 provides specific examples of the kind of information provided by Tables A-25 through A-29.

Table 39 of the text provides figures for determiners before a proper name and for determiners followed by an adjective or a noun and a proper name. Reference and direct address are not distinguished, but all groups introduced by *the* are instances of reference, as are all but a few of the remainder. The names of mythic figures like *Fortune* were included but not place names (*our England*), groups (*the fugitive Parthians*), or titles (*the wasteful King*), but, had such items been included, *Antony* would still have outnumbered *Richard II*.

The complete list for *Richard II* is as follows: *my sweet Richard, the banish'd Bolingbroke, this traitor Bolingbroke, the banish'd Norfolk, the mounting Bolingbroke.* For *Antony*, the list includes *my Antony, my Octavia, her Aeneas, our Caesar, an Antony, this Seleucus, this Charmian, another Antony, her Antony, a very Antony, the curled Antony, my brave Mark Antony, that brave Caesar, the brave Antony, the valiant Caesar, the ne'er-lust-wearied Antony, the noble Antony, our courteous Antony, the good Brutus, a noble Lepidus, th' adulterous Antony, the lean and wrinkled Cassius, the mad Brutus, the boy Caesar, the full Caesar, the full-fortun'd Caesar, the strong-wing'd Mercury, the false huswife Fortune, the condemn'd Pompey, the scarce-bearded Caesar, the god Hercules, my good Alexas, some squeaking Cleopatra.*

Table A-31 indicates the frequency with which references to the ear and the knee occur both in *Richard II* and in other English history plays. Only *Richard III* and *1 Henry IV* approach the same proportions, and in both of these the raw frequencies are lower. Only in *Richard III* does the association of kneeling with flattery/hypocrisy and with a single character present itself as clearly as in *Richard II*, although there may be some hypocrisy in Suffolk's kneeling (*1H6* 5.3.194; *2H6* 1.1.10, 63). The other plays were not examined for such associations. It is of some interest that, apart from the speeches of Bolingbroke himself, knees and kneeling are associated with the speeches of Aumerle and the Duchess of York, who beg his mercy in the final act. This action may indicate that he will now be the target for such flattery as he himself had used to gain the crown. Table A-32 shows how often *ear* and *knee* are mentioned with reference to King Richard, Bolingbroke, and all other characters.

Table A-30

Examples of References to Antony Introduced by Various Determiners

Nonspecific	Definite	Demonstrative	Possessives	Name	Zero
a soldier's kiss	the firm Roman	this pine is bark'd	mine honour thy master his corrigible neck	I am Antony yet	heart, once be stronger
such another man	the solider's pole	that great med'cine	my man of men thy cheek his love	the weight of Antony	courteous lord
a man who is the abstract	the arm of mine own body	—	our great competitor your being in Egypt his foils	our will is Antony be took alive	good brother
a sworder	the libertine	this amorous surfeiter	my brave Emperor thy grand captain his judgment	he adores Mark Antony	great chief

Table A-31
References to *Ear* and *Knee* in Eight History Plays

	1H6	2H6	3H6	R3	R2	1H4	2H4	H5	Total
Ear	1	2	7	8	14	8	6	10	56
Knee	7	18	13	6	15	5	3	5	72

Table A-32
References to *Ear* and *Knee* by Major Characters in *Richard II*

	Richard	Bolingbroke	Others	Total
Ear	10	1	3	14
Knee	0	7	8	15

Tables A-33 and A-34 provide the data for the suggestion that reference to language is more characteristic of Bolingbroke than of Richard, while Richard is as preoccupied with feelings of grief as he is with reference to language. All possessive determiners used by Richard and Bolingbroke and by others in ascribing possessions to them were examined to create a list of nouns designating aspects of language and sorrow. The total frequency of these nouns in the speech of Richard and of Bolingbroke was then obtained and the results are given in Table A-33.

Table A-33
Terms of Language and Sorrow Used by King Richard and Bolingbroke

Language	Richard	Bolingbroke	Sorrow	Richard	Bolingbroke
Breath	4	5	*Care*	9	2
Commends	1	1	*Cross*	1	0
Conjuration	1	0	*Grief*	10	3
Demands	2	0	*Patience*	1	0
Discourse	0	0	*Sorrow*	7	2
Greeting	0	2	*Wretchedness*	1	0
Name	9	6			
Quarrel	0	0			
Sentence	2	0			
Speech	1	1			
Title	1	1			
Tongue	7	4			
Word	5	4			

Table A-34
Frequency of Terms of Language and Sorrow:
King Richard and Bolingbroke

	Language	Sorrow
Richard	33	29
Bolingbroke	25	7

The data are unsatisfactory for several reasons. Obviously, the decision about what words designate language and sorrow is arbitrary, but this situation obtains whenever attempts are made to classify meaning. Second, reference to language and sorrow will be found in phrases other than those introduced by possessive determiners. Some attempt has been made to solve this problem by including all instances of these words in the speeches of Richard and Bolingbroke, regardless of determiner. This procedure creates a third difficulty, however. One character may be speaking of the other's use of language, which happens when Richard speaks of *all the number of his fair demands*, meaning Bolingbroke's demands. Strictly speaking, this should be counted among Bolingbroke's uses of language. Similarly, it may be the case that a third person ascribes some use of language to Richard or to Bolingbroke. Thus, Northumberland speaks to Bolingbroke of *your fair discourse* and the Marshal asks him *what's thy quarrel*, and these could be added to Bolingbroke's use of language. Both these words have zero frequency in Table A-33 because the list was derived from a study of possessive determiners ascribed to Richard and Bolingbroke and then enlarged by counting the occurrences of such words in their speech.

The tally of entries in Table A-33 supplies the data for Table A-34. The proportions of A-34 are significantly different ($\chi^2 = 4.5362$), but this difference shows only that Bolingbroke's speeches contain a low frequency of references to sorrow. The significance of language in the speech of the two characters can best be assessed from ratios obtained by dividing the total lines spoken into the figures given under "Language." For King Richard 33/755 yields .0437 and for Bolingbroke 25/413 yields .0605.

Nominal-Group Structure

"Name" means proper nouns and adjectives designating persons, places, objects, and events. With the exception of *Fortune* and *Love* they include all mythological allusions and historical references. "Titles" are words like *Duke, Emperor, Sir,* and *Liege,* which normally indicate social status or rank. They do not include kinship terms like *husband, brother, uncle,* and so on. Names and titles in the prose lines of *Antony* were omitted in the

Table A-35
Format of Method Used to Obtain Statistical Data on Names

	Entry	Frequency	Syllables	Vocative	Reference	Person	Other
R2	Gloucester	3	2	0	3	1	0
	Gloucester's	7	2	0	7	1	0
	Gloucestershire	2	3	0	2	0	1
Ant.	Egypt	37	2	6	31	1	1
	Egyptian	8	3	0	8	1	1
	Egyptians	2	3	0	2	1	1
	Egypt's	3	2	0	3	0	1

tabulation. Counts were obtained by listing all occurrences of each name and each title in the Spevack concordance and recording information about them, as exemplified in Table A-35. The three entries from *Richard II* have a total frequency of twelve; those from *Antony* have a total frequency of fifty. Because each name is listed separately in the concordances, the counts are slightly inflated. Thus, *Sextus Pompeius*, which occurs as such three times in *Antony*, appears three times under *Pompeius* and three times under *Sextus*, making a total of two entries and six names. Similarly, *Henry, Duke of Cobham* consists of three entries, analyzed as two names and one title. Morphological variants, whether inflectional or derivational, are counted as separate entries.

Inappropriate meanings were eliminated by consulting the context of the name (*Mars/mars, Green/green, Grace/grace, Sovereign/sovereign*, etc.). A study of context also made it possible to determine whether a name was used in direct address or in reference and to decide whether or not it referred to a person. In some instances it clearly meant both place and person, as in *Egyptian cookery* and *O rare Egyptian*. Apostrophes like the last phrase cited or *Now, darting Parthia, art thou stroke* are included among the vocatives, as are instances of third person address (*Why is my lord enraged against his love?*). The latter do not change the rhythm as direct address does, but, since there are only nine instances of third person address in *Richard II* and thirteen in *Antony*, its inclusion among the vocatives does not change the argument that the high frequency of vocatives in *Antony* makes a significant contribution to the sound system of that play.

The count of syllables per word is not based simply on the entries but on the frequency of each entry. Thus, using the data from Table A-35, one can say that in *Richard II* words of two syllables occur a total of ten times and words of three syllables occur twice; in *Antony* words of two syllables occur forty times and words of three syllables occur ten times. Syllables per name were assigned intuitively, and those deemed ambiguous can be mentioned briefly here. In *Richard II* these words were assigned two syl- lables: *Berkeley, Ciceter, Gloucester, Hereford, Worcester.* These were assigned three syllables: *Abraham, Parliament, Phaëton,* and *Salisbury.* In *Antony,* the most problematic words were those ending in *-ia* or *-ius.* These were classified as three-syllabled words: *Cassius, Domitius, Fulvia, Phoenicia, Sossius, Thyreus.* These were assigned four syllables: *Brundu- sium, Cappodocia, Lycaonia, Nereides, Octavia, Sardinia. Thracian* counted as a word of two syllables.

Table A-36 shows the nine highest-ranking names in each play together with their frequency and syllables per name and their average frequency and average syllables per name. For the name *Caesar* there is no distinction between Julius and Octavius. Variations in syllables per name are due to the fact that all variants are included in the count (*Antony, Antonius; Rome, Roman,* etc.). Table A-37 gives the frequency and ratio of syllables per name; syllables per title are not included.

Table A-36
Statistical Data on the Most Frequent Names

	Richard II			*Antony and Cleopatra*	
Name	Frequency	Syllables	Name	Frequency	Syllables
God	67	1	Caesar	150	2
Bolingbroke	49	3	Antony	135	3-4
Richard	39	2	Egypt	50	2-3
Hereford	31	2-3	Rome	39	1-2
Gaunt	24	1	Cleopatra	28	4
Aumerle	20	2	Eros	26	2
Mowbray	20	2	Charmian	25	3
Norfolk	20	2	Pompey	26	2-3
York	20	1	Octavia	20	4
Total	290	–	Total	499	–
Average	32	1.7	Average	55	2.4-3.0

Table A-37
Frequency of Monosyllabic and Polysyllabic Names

	1		2		3		4		Total	
	Frequency	Ratio	Frequency	Ratio	Frequency	Ratio	Frequency	Ratio	Frequency	Ratio
R2	155	.2528	335	.5464	107	.1745	16	.0261	613	.9998
Ant.	41	.0501	337	.4124	315	.3855	124	.1517	817	.9997

Table A-38
Synecdoche in First Singular Possessive Groups

	Synecdochic	Other	Total
R2	47	449	496
Ant.	20	316	336

Table A-38 provides the basis for the statement that synecdoche decreased significantly in *Antony and Cleopatra* ($\chi^2 = 17.9044$). The data are derived only from a study of first person singular possessives (*my/mine*), which were classified as "Synecdochic" or as "Other." Line references to those first person possessives classified as synecdochic are provided in Table B-13.

The information in Table 36 is derived from the study of adjective-noun relations in Chapter Two. Using the definitions provided by George Landon, certain collocations were counted as metaphoric; using the criteria discussed in this section, others were classified as synecdochic. Table A-39

Table A-39
Proportion of First Singular Pronouns to Possessive Determiners

	First Person Pronouns	First Person Possessives	Total
R2	673	496	1,169
Ant.	840	336	1,176

provides some related evidence for the conviction that the relationship between part and whole shifts from *Richard II*, where the part (represented by the first person possessives *my/mine*) has greater preponderance in relation to the whole (represented by first person pronouns like *I, me,* and *mine*), to the greater emphasis on the whole that is found in *Antony*. The proportions in Table A-39 are significantly different: $\chi^2 = 492.9150$. The proportions in Table 36, synecdochic to metaphoric adjective-noun collocations, are also significantly different: $\chi^2 = 9.8203$.

Table A-40 gives the total number of nominal groups in each play that were introduced by the indefinite article (*a/an*) and the number of these that were followed by a qualifying phrase or clause.

Table 40 shows the frequency of each type of nominal-group structure among groups preceded by the demonstrative determiner. The first column, *h*, shows how many times the nominal group consisted only of the determiner and a noun (*this land, these hands*); the second shows how many times additional modifiers occurred in the structure (*that ancient*

Table A-40
Proportion of Qualified to Total Nonspecific Groups

	a/an + Head + (Qualifier)*	*a/an* + Head + Qualifier
R2	257	47
Ant.	284	84

*The heading of the first column gives the total of nominal groups introduced by the indefinite article. These groups may or may not have a qualifier, a fact expressed by using parentheses to designate the optional item.

castle, these strong Egyptian fetters); *hq* signifies that the nominal group consisted of the determiner, a nominal head, and a qualifier (*this tongue of mine, this cup I call'd for*); and the last indicates that the nominal group consisted of the demonstrative, one or more other modifiers, the head, and a qualifier (*that self mould that fashioned thee*). The first and last types increase in *Antony*; the decline in the second type can be attributed to the over-all decline of adjectives.

Demonstrative words (*this, that, these, those*), incidentally, function also as pronouns (*That I beheld* [*Ant.* 3.10.16]) and as binders (*Most probable / That so she died* [*Ant.* 5.2.356-357]). Pronoun and binder functions both increase in *Antony*, as shown in Table A-41. Prose lines are excluded. The binder function increases by ten, and groups of the type *so lated that I have lost my way* increase by eleven in *Antony*.

Table A-41
Frequency and Function of Demonstrative Words

	Pronoun	Binder	Determiner	Total
R2	185	82	234	501
Ant.	228	92	139	459

Table A-42 shows that in *Antony* monosyllabic adjectives increased in nominal groups introduced by the demonstrative, both in comparison to *Richard II* and in comparison to the over-all ratio of monosyllabic adjectives in *Antony* itself. Nine of the twenty monosyllabic adjectives are the single word *great*. In *Richard II* the proportion of monosyllabic to total adjectives in nominal groups introduced by a demonstrative determiner reflects quite exactly the proportion of monosyllabic to other adjectives in the entire play. In this play the word *great* occurs once in the twenty-six groups containing a monosyllabic adjective and introduced by the demonstrative determiner.

Table A-42
Frequency of Monosyllabic Adjectives in Adjective-Noun Collocations

	Demonstrative + Adjective + Noun			Total Adjective-Noun Collocations		
	Monosyllabic	Other	Total	Monosyllabic	Other	Total
R2	26	56	82	313	684	997
	.3170	.6829		.3139	.6860	
Ant.	20	28	48	248	399	647
	.4166	.5833		.3833	.6166	

Table A-43
Frequency and Types of Pronouns in the Plays

	Demonstrative	*Wh-* Relatives	Personal*	Total
R2	185	231	2,037	2,453
Ant.	228	316	3,217	3,761

*Personal pronoun counts exclude all determiners, such as *my*, *his*, etc., but the counts for these pronouns include all prose lines of *Antony*. On a rough estimate, however, there is one pronoun per line in each play and on this basis one can subtract a personal pronoun for each of the 268 prose lines of *Ant.* and still find that this play has approximately 1,000 more pronouns than *R2*. The counts for demonstrative and relative pronouns exclude prose. Relatives are always pronominal; these counts are based only on the *wh-*relatives and are taken from Table A-9.'

Table A-43 provides a measure of the extent to which substitution, here measured in terms of certain pronouns, is characteristic of each play. That pronouns increased markedly in *Antony and Cleopatra* may in part have some relationship to the history of English, but it certainly has a stylistic explanation as well. Substitution, or the use of pronouns, may be thought of as a feature of colloquial language. The language of the later play is more colloquial than the earlier in several respects (ellipses; verbless sentences), and, as noted on several occasions, colloquial features distinguish the speech of the protagonists from that of Caesar.

Ant. 2.2.196-231: North and Shakespeare

To obtain information about Shakespeare's use of relative clauses in his description of Cleopatra's barge, Shakespeare's text was compared in detail with that of his source. The passage from North is long, but the third of it cited below is sufficient to illustrate some important differences in syntax:

... she disdained to set forward otherwise but to take her barge in the river of Cydnus, the poop whereof was of gold, the sails of purple, and the oars of silver, which kept stroke in rowing after the sound of the music of flutes, howboys, citherns, viols, and such other instruments as they played upon in the barge. And now for the person of herself: she was laid under a pavilion of cloth of gold of tissue, apparelled and attired like the goddess Venus commonly drawn in picture; and hard by her, on either hand of her, pretty fair boys apparelled as painters do set forth god Cupid, with little fans in their hands, with the which they fanned wind upon her. (T. J. B. Spencer, ed., *Shakespeare's Plutarch*, p. 201)

Shakespeare omits several details (that Cleopatra would travel in no other way, the emphasis on the behavior of the crowds—which explains the difference in word count, the rumor that Venus was come to play with Bacchus), and he rearranges others, putting the reference to Cydnus before the speech begins and applying to the person of Cleopatra the idea that the feast was beyond description. Among additions are the idea that the barge resembled a throne on which Cleopatra was seated and that its color was reflected in the water, the graceful bends of Cleopatra's attendants, the famous crux *tended her i' th' eyes*, the important rivalry between fancy and nature, and all but one adjective. Among subjects of greatest novelty and embellishment are the idea that air and water are enamored of Cleopatra and the final description of Antony, whistling to the air, unable to say *no* to any woman, barbered ten times over, and paying his heart for *what his eyes eat only*. Incredible as it may seem to those accustomed to noting the similarity of these passages, 28 of the 53 clauses in Shakespeare's text contain either material not in North or material that has been radically transposed.

With respect to diction, the two passages have only 39 content words in common; these constitute 12 percent of the total words in North's description and 14 percent of Shakespeare's. In all, North has 335 words, 8 sentences, and 50 clauses; the average length of his sentences is 42 words and 5 clauses. Shakespeare has 272 words, 13 sentences, and 53 clauses; his average sentence is 21 words and 4 clauses long. The clauses average 5 words in length. The 16 relatives of North and the 14 in Shakespeare are as follows: (North) *otherwise but to take her barge; the poop whereof; the sails of purple; the oars of silver; which kept stroke; instruments as they played; Venus, commonly drawn in picture; boys apparelled; as painters do set forth; fans ... with the which; which are the mermaids; barge, out of the which; that perfumed; pestered with innumerable multitudes; when Cleopatra landed; where he found.* (Shakespeare) *the barge she sat in; which ... kept stroke; and made the water; which they beat; where we see; whose wind; which they did cool; what they undid; that yarely frame;*

which but for vacancy; and made a gap; which she entreated; whom ne'er the word; what his eyes eat only. Among relative clauses are included those introduced by *as, that, but* (equivalent to *than*), zero and *wh-* words. Among the latter are those where the word has been deleted by branching.

APPENDIX B

Citations to *Richard II* and *Antony and Cleopatra*

Choosing the Random Sample

Table B-1 gives a list of line references to the sample of sentences drawn randomly from *Richard II* and *Antony and Cleopatra*. To obtain the sample, the first and middle lines from each column of the Kittredge text were marked, and the sentence containing that line was selected. As an independent check on the percentage of the text being sampled, the total words in the resulting sample were counted. For *Richard II* the sample yields 14 percent of the total words, for *Antony* about 12 percent. The format of the text poses problems for sampling, but efforts were made to ensure that each act and scene received representation proportionate to its length.

"Sentence" is defined graphemically, that is, by the punctuation of Kittredge's text, with the modification that sentences beginning with a coordinating conjunction are expanded to include the preceding clause or clause complex. Thus, where the text reads *If he fill'd | His vacancy . . . Call on him for't! But to confound . . . (Ant.* 1.4.25-33), the sentence beginning *But to confound* was treated as coordinate with the preceding sentence. Since Kittredge seldom begins a sentence with a coordinating conjunction, this procedure renders his (presumed) editorial practice more consistent and in fact tampers with not more than half a dozen sentences in the entire sample of both plays.

Recognition Criteria for Relative Clauses

Table B-2 lists those *what* clauses classified as relatives. The criteria for distinguishing *what* relatives from indirect questions are spelled out in Huddleston: "In the relative construction, *what* can be replaced without any change of meaning by *that which*, but no such substitution is possible in the interrogative" (p. 203). An italicized reference means that the clause

Table B-1
Citations to the Random Sample of Sentences

Richard II		
Act	Scene	Lines
1	1	1-6; 18-19; 35-38; 58-66; 85-86; *98-108;** 128-131; 152-155; 175; 196-199
	2	10; 30-32; 47-53; 73
	3	11-13; 26-30; 54; 78; *102*; 119-120; 144; 160-165; 192; 213; 237-238; 255-257; 277-278
	4	*6-9*; 23-30; 54-56
2	1	7-8; 29; *40-54*; 67-68; 84; *104-108*; *126-127*; 148; 165-170; 194; 216-217; 238-240; 256; *277-288*; 291-298
	2	*14-20*; 34-35; 56-57; 76; 96; 117-118; 140
	3	4-7; 26-28; 45-49; *65-67*; 85; 106-107; 129-130; 153-159
	4	1-3; 21-24
3	1	1; 16-27; 38-39
	2	8-11; *29-32*; *47-53*; *71-74*; 91-92; 112-113; 132; *151-154*; 176-177; 200-203
	3	*1-3*; 16-17; *31-41*; 58-60; 77-81; *103-118*; 127-128; *147-159*; 190-191; 209
	4	*12-18*; *55-57*; 75-76; *98-99*; 102-103
4	1	9-10; 30; 42; 64; 84-85; *107-110*; *132-133*; 156-157; 177-178; 200; 222-227; 247-252; 270; 292-293; 315; 333-334
5	1	1; 38-39; *76-80*
	2	4-6; 46-47; 81
	3	1; 36-37; 74; 113-114
	4	3
	5	34-38; *76-80*; 108-109
	6	19-23

Antony and Cleopatra		
Act	Scene	Lines
1	1	1-2; 10; 17; 20-23; 29-32; 48
	2	20; 65-72; 91; 103-107; 119-120; 138-139; 183-184
	3	3-5; 19; 35-37; *49-54*; 78-79
	4	3-8; *25-33*; 44-47; 61-63
	5	4; 19-20; 33-34; 47-50; 55-58; 72-73

*Italicized entries indicate that the sentence contains a hypotactic group complex.

Table B-1
Citations to the Random Sample of Sentences (Cont'd)

Act	Scene	Lines
		Antony and Cleopatra
2	1	1-2; 24-27; 43-49
	2	12; *29-30*; 41-42; *57-61*; 81-83; 99-102; *127-133*; 144-146; 167-169; 186-188; 211-213; 227-229
	3	1-2; 10; 22-23; 38-40
	4	1-2
	5	4-5; 10-12; *26-30*; 50; 65-66; 82-84; 99; 117-118
	6	1-2; *14-19*; *32-33*; 49; 69; 89; 135-138
	7	37; 61-62; 72; 106-108; 133-134
3	1	1-3; 13-15; *30-34*
	2	12; 28-33; 44-46
	3	*4-6*; 22
	4	*1-10*
	5	7-12
	6	13-16; *48-53*; 90
	7	11-13; *42-49*; 65-67
	9	1-4
	10	6-7; 26-27
	11	7-8; 23-24; 49-50
	12	7-10
	13	7-10; *22-25*; 42-46; 79-81; 94-95; 110-115; 156-157; 172; 195-197
4	2	8; 21-23; 38-41
	3	12; 20
	4	14-15; 24
	5	2-3; 13-14
	6	16-18; *31-34*
	7	9-10
	8	1; *16-18*; *32-35*
	9	10; 28
	11	1-3
	12	6-9; *25-29*; 48-49
	14	*2-7*; *15-20*; 29-30; 51-52; 68; 88; 103; 119; 136-138
	15	9; 25-26; 46; 63; 69; *86-88*
5	1	9-12; 25-26; *40-48*; 66-68
	2	9-11; 25-28; 47-49; 62-64; 81; 95-97; 116-117 *134-136*; 153-154; 172-174; 189; 204-205; 223-224; 239-240; 263-264; 286; 306-308; 326; 343; 354-356

Table B-2
Citations to Relative Clauses Introduced by *What*

Richard II		
Act	Scene	Lines
1	1	*36;*† 46; 77; *87*
	3	122; 124; *204; 249; 286*
	4	27*
2	1	180; 209; *212; 242**
	2	24; *39*
	3	18*, 76*
	4	13
3	3	138; 139; *206;* 207
	4	*17; 18;* 82
4	1	9; 27
5	1	19
	4	1*
	5	55*; *97**
	6	47

Antony and Cleopatra		
Act	Scene	Lines
1	2	124*; *127;* 184
	4	14; 15; 78; 81
	5	16; 18; 49
2	1	*3*
	2	*19;* 42; 77; 139; 143; *210;* 231
	5	71*; 100; 103
	6	33 (2)
	7	129
3	1	30; 35*
	2	36; *58*
	4	37*;
	6	*34;* 48
	7	13
	10	27; 33
	11	53
	12	28
	13	61; 80; 118*; 142; 143; 148

†Italicized entries mean that the clause occurs in theme or topic position. Asterisks indicate that the clause is not classified as homophoric.

Table B-2
Citations to Relative Clauses Introduced by *What* (Cont'd)

Act	Scene	Lines
		Antony and Cleopatra
4	3	17
	7	3
	12	9
	14	28; 48; 96; 106; 121
	15	*86* (2)
5	1	51; 62*; 77
	2	52; *65*; 73; 107; 118*; 136*; 148; *180* (2)

was in marked position (theme or topic); asterisks indicate clauses that do not have homophoric reference. In *Antony*, in every case, this asterisk means that *what* has a modifying function; in *Richard II*, the asterisk signifies four modifying functions, one cataphoric reference, and two relatives that were not treated as homophoric, because of their archaic construction, exemplified by this passage:

> The King is not himself, but basely led
> By flatterers; and what they will inform,
> Merely in hate, 'gainst any of us all,
> That will the King severely prosecute
> 'Gainst us, our lives, our children, and our heirs.
> (2.1.241-245)

Even if they are added to the count of homophoric relatives in *Richard II*, those in *Antony* would still be doubled, so that the evidence for a marked increase in the later play would not be greatly affected.

In brief, Table B-2 shows that in *Richard II* there are thirty-three relative clauses introduced by *what*: thirteen of these are in marked position; seven are not classified as homophoric because they are modifiers (4), cataphoric (1), or problematic (2). In *Antony*, sixty-four are relatives; eleven of these are in marked position, and eight are not homophoric, because they have modifying functions.

Table B-3 provides line references for the temporal relative *when* clauses in the two plays. Interrogative- and indirect-question uses of *when* were few and easily identified in the two plays. If the subordinating conjunction *since*, or in some cases *if*, could replace *when* in a clause, it was classified as conditioning. All others were treated as adverbial relatives of time. Because all these clauses, whether with or without antecedent, contain the semantic category *time* and this semantic information is used to interpret

Table B-3

Citations to Relative Clauses Introduced by *When*

Richard II

Clauses without Antecedents

Act	Scene	Lines
1	1	*82F**
	2	*7F*; 61
	3	*303*
	4	10P; *49F*
2	1	*178P*
	2	*2P*
	3	29P; *100P*
3	2	*19F; 37; 41; 47F*
	3	56; 65
4	1	89F; 274F; *306P*
5	2	*2P*
	3	70F
	5	35P; 43; 73P

Clauses with Antecedents

Act	Scene	Lines
3	3	9
4	1	10P
5	5	76P; 78P

Antony and Cleopatra

Clauses without Antecedents

Act	Scene	Lines
1	1	32
	2	100
	3	*33P*; 62; 96
	4	*56P*; 65
	5	*30P*
2	2	*20*; 34; 72P; 88; 245
	3	24; 28; 37
	5	*8*; 88

*Italics indicate that the clause is in nonfinal position in the matrix clause. The letter *P* designates a clause classified as an instance of past time reference; *F* as an instance of future time reference; all others are considered neutral with respect to time.

Table B-3
Citations to Relative Clauses Introduced
by *When* (Cont'd)

Act	Scene	Lines
Clauses without Antecedents		
	6	*45P*; 76P; 78P
	7	*78F*; 89
3	1	15
	2	*54P; 56P*
	4	*6P; 9P; 33F*
	11	74
	13	*111; 179P; 199*
4	1	*7*
	2	*22P*
	9	*8F*
	12	*16F*
	14	*63F; 81P*; 82; *121P*
5	2	74; *85P; 177; 231F*
Clauses with Antecedents		
1	1	57
	2	114
	5	64; 74P
2	2	90P
	5	15P; 16P
	7	104
3	3	4
	4	16F
	10	12P
	13	9P; 83P; 90P; 145P
4	14	64F

the plays, all temporal relatives are included on this list whether they are homophoric or have an antecedent, but the two types are listed separately in the table.

In sum, there are twenty-eight instances of temporal clauses in *Richard II*; eight are future, twelve are past, and eight are neutral. From the viewpoint of reference, all but four are homophoric, and of these twenty-four homophoric relatives fourteen occur in marked position. In *Antony*, of the sixty-one temporal clauses eight are future, twenty-five are past, and the rest neutral. Sixteen have antecedents, and of the forty-five homophoric relatives twenty-five occur in marked position.

Instances of Deviant Constituent Sequence

Tables B-4 through B-7 cite the lines from *Richard II* and *Antony and Cleopatra* where various types of deviant sequence are to be found. Since these references were compiled manually, it was easier to use the edition of Kittredge as revised by Irving Ribner because the format in this edition is more readable and offers more space for marking the analysis of sequence than does the Kittredge edition of the *Complete Works*. The line numbering differs slightly from that of the 1936 Kittredge edition.

Determiner References to Major Characters

Tables B-8 through B-12 give the line references for the study of determiners and point of view undertaken in Chapter Four. Table B-13 gives the line references for instances of synecdoche that involve a nominal group introduced by a first possessive determiner. In all these tables, citations are to the Kittredge-Ribner edition of the plays.

Table B-4
Citations to Instances of Complement Theme

Richard II		
Act	Scene	Lines
1	1	18; 36; 41; 42; 46; 53; 82; 115; 122; 123; 126; 128; 142; 154; 164; 165; 166; 167 (2); 177; 180; 184
	2	73; 74
	3	35; 56; 61; 95; 144; 152; 159; 160; 181; 204; 218; 240; 241; 242; 248; 250; 251; 265
2	1	30; 82; 113; 126; 140; 150; 176 (2); 212; 234; 246; 247; 255; 268
	2	24; 39; 74; 115; 136
	3	19; 153; 170
3	1	31; 40
	2	1; 89; 98; 100; 104; 128; 144; 152; 191; 211
	3	116; 119; 206
	4	17; 18; 63; 68; 81
4	1	109; 160; 161; 188; 191; 194; 198; 211; 212; 213; 220; 288; 317; 321

Table B-4
Citations to Instances of Complement Theme (Cont'd)

Act	Scene	Lines
5	1	102
	2	9; 39; 54
	3	6; 8; 34; 105; 120; 124; 128; 136; 142
	5	4; 6; 28; 34; 41; 44; 113; 114; 117
	6	18; 29; 31; 41

Antony and Cleopatra

Act	Scene	Lines
1	1	28
	2	95; 109; 113; 122
	3	23; 89 (2)
	4	50; 66; 81
	5	26; **45**
2	1	17; 47
	2	51; 53; 76; 108; 150; 164; 205
	5	**34**
	6	1; 19; 61
	7	**34**; 70; 107
3	1	14
	2	19; 58
	3	4
	4	8
	5	20
	6	13; 14
	7	**16**; **32**; **34**; **50**; 58; 77
	11	38; 39; 59; 69
	12	11; 23
	13	52; 58
4	1	2; 11
	4	8; 30
	5	**10**
	6	33; 36
	8	5
	9	13
	12	18; 24; 36
	14	28; 102; 126
	15	4; 10; 20; 48; 49; 51; 64
5	1	6; 10; 28
	2	32; 51; 65; 87; 116; 118; 168; 180; 202; 287; 288; 303

Table B-5
Citations to Instances of Predicator-Adjunct-Complement Structures

		Richard II
Act	Scene	Lines
1	1	3; 45; 57; 70; 71; 74; 97; 102; 111; 132; 146; 161; 162; 175; 186
	2	9; 10; 30; 70; 72
	3	27; 37; 83; 89; 94; 116; 119; 131; 179; 180; 199; 258; 276; 301
2	1	34; 134; 149; 160; 202; 219; 275; 276; 291; 292; 293; 294; 300
	2	2; 4; 63; 101
	3	5; 49; 61; 144; 145; 171
3	1	1; 25; 38
	2	60; 172; 181
	3	14 (2); 126; 128
	4	2; 29; 34; 37; 51; 97
4	1	6; 50; 63; 84; 207; 208; 242; 243; 249; 259; 269; 307 (2); 319
5	1	29; 36; 39; 62
	2	16; 44; 98; 115
	3	51
	5	31
	6	2; 13; 16; 21; 48

		Antony and Cleopatra
Act	Scene	Lines
1	1	11 (2); 17; 23; 29; 40
	2	185
	3	19; 65; 69; 72; 83
	5	5; 71; 77
2	1	6; 23; 25; 35; 48
	2	56; 73; 99; 120; 159
	4	30
	5	51; 54; 86
	6	6; 38; 40; 44
	7	100

Table B-5
Citations to Instances of Predicator-Adjunct-Complement Structures (Cont'd)

Act	Scene	Lines
3	3	42
	5	13
	6	82
	7	23; 41; 47; 70; 80
	10	7; 20; 24
	12	8; 30
	13	44; 76; 80; 182; 183; 197
4	2	9
	4	22
	5	13
	6	29
	8	23
	12	4; 15; 26
	14	64; 73; 84; 85; 91; 98
5	1	38; 41; 57; 71
	2	25; 78; 104; 129; 143; 144; 186; 279; 354; 357

Table B-6
Citations to Instances of Nominal-Group Deviance

	Richard II	
Act	Scene	Lines
1	1	11; 51; 65; 78; 95; 123; 172; 173
	2	2; 27; 35; 50; 57
	3	38; 164; 240; 263; 267
	4	42
2	1	7; 11; 36; 89; 96; 130; 138; 139; 201; 202; 230; 234; 255
	2	12; 27 (2); 47; 82; 142
	3	19; 37; 130; 138; 147; 151
3	1	31
	2	64; 91; 104; 152; 206; 211; 215
	3	87; 105; 114; 200
	4	55; 81; 84
4	1	11; 44; 64; 66; 118; 146; 177; 205; 217; 274

Table B-6
Citations to Instances of Nominal-Group Deviance (Cont'd)

Act	Scene	Lines
5	1	31
	2	30; 31; 37; 39; 46; 56
	3	8; 34; 78
	5	16; 64; 108
	6	25; 37

Antony and Cleopatra

Act	Scene	Lines
1	1	18; 45
	2	105; 113; 122; 173 (2)
	3	28; 73
	4	22; 49; 51; 60; 77; 81
	5	4; 35; 42
2	1	28; 51
	2	53; 85; 89; 97; 121; 127; 145; 150; 155; 194
	4	2
	5	5; 23; 72; 78
3	1	2; 14
	3	4; 34
	4	23
	6	10; 19; 56
	7	24
	10	4
	11	19; 39; 58; 61
	12	1; 4; 7; 9; 26; 28; 32
	13	10; 32; 39; 49; 68; 71; 87; 154
4	1	13
	4	15
	6	30
	7	10
	8	35
	9	8
	12	8; 9; 23
	14	75; 77; 83; 84; 117; 136
	15	20; 48; 67
5	1	6; 54
	2	15; 18; 40; 41; 87; 236; 241; 244; 287; 303; 306; 308; 315; 317; 350; 353; 360 (2)

Table B-7
Citations to Instances of Verbal-Group Deviance

	Richard II	
Act	Scene	Lines
Predicator Theme		
1	3	58; 227; 308
2	1	252
3	3	207
	4	68
4	1	87
Other Types of Inversion		
5	3	84

	Antony and Cleopatra	
Act	Scene	Lines
Predicator Theme		
2	1	4
Other Types of Inversion		
1	3	65
2	1	3; 49
	2	35; 68; 171
3	4	9;
	12	12
4	15	14; 23
5	2	140

Table B-8
Citations to Determiners of Cleopatra

Act	Scene	Lines
		Nonspecific
1	1	6; 10; 13
	5	31
2	5	5; 29
	6	70
3	6	67; 95
	7	18
	10	14
	13	110; 116; 117
4	4	13
	12	28
	14	60
	15	73
5	2	16; 47; 227; 315; 325
		Definite
1	2	170
	4	6
2	1	37
	2	204
3	7	17
	11	42 (2); 46; 50
	12	20
	13	15; 39; 40; 98
4	4	7
	8	2
	12	47
	14	15; 46
5	1	9; 52; 66; 197; 319
	2	112; 309
		Demonstrative
1	2	109; 121
2	5	82
3	13	84; 125 (2); 174
4	8	12
	12	10; 25 (2)
5	2	51; 281; 303

Table B-8
Citations to Determiners of Cleopatra (Cont'd)

Act	Scene	Lines
		Zero
1	1	29; 48
	2	73; 77
	3	6; 24; 31; 39; 41; 86
	5	2; 4; 7; 13; 15; 34; 39; 43; 62
2	1	37
	2	218; 226
	5	7; 25 (2); 31; 36; 45; 49; 57; 60; 62; 66; 72; 74; 75; 91; 93; 108
3	3	7; 9; 11; 14; 16; 21; 29; 36; 44; 45; 51
	6	11
	7	23
	11	26; 32; 33 (2); 43; 51; 56; 72
	13	172
4	4	15; 29
	8	13; 19
	12	13; 30
	15	2; 18; 41; 45; 47; 68; 69 (2); 70 (4); 71
5	2	32; 37; 38; 39 (2); 48; 71; 75; 81; 94; 100; 110; 112; 114; 141; 145; 158; 185; 193; 198; 206; 307; 315; 317

Table B-9
Citations to Determiners of Antony

Act	Scene	Lines
		Nonspecific
1	1	13
	3	90
	4	9; 70
2	2	120
	5	14; 117
3	10	20
	12	15
	13	31; 44; 95
4	2	18; 30
	4	18; 30; 33
	5	16
	6	29
	8	21
	14	13; 42; 100; 101
	15	57 (2)
5	1	14; 31; 34
	2	76; 78; 87; 93; 99; 345
		Definite
1	1	9 (2); 12
	2	120
	3	38
	5	23 (2); 24; 43; 54; 69
2	1	23; 38
	2	14; 44; 85; 96; 129; 242
3	2	10
	6	93
	7	20; 42; 79
	10	19
	11	13; 14
	13	10
4	1	4
	2	6
	8	16
	14	106; 129
	15	54; 55; 63; 64; 65

Table B-9
Citations to Determiners of Antony (Cont'd)

Act	Scene	Lines
		Definite
5	1	18; 23 (2); 24; 45 (2)
	2	300
		Demonstrative
1	1	1; 2; 30; 58
	3	19; 30; 84
	5	36
2	1	33
	3	17
3	1	31
	13	17; 19
4	12	23; 46
	14	14; 85
	15	89 (2)
5	1	21
	2	301
		Zero
1	3	86; 95
	5	53; 59
2	7	115
3	2	12
	4	18
	7	41; 61
	11	30; 34 (2); 46; 50
	13	63 (2); 158
4	2	33
	4	10; 21; 24; 25
	5	9; 10
	6	32
	7	11
	8	16; 17
	14	1; 40; 80; 93; 117; 133
	15	21; 59

Table B-10
Citations to Determiners of Octavius Caesar

Act	Scene	Lines
Nonspecific		
1	–	–
2	–	–
3	2	53
	13	60
4	14	20
5	2	4; 22; 27
Definite		
1	1	21
2	–	–
3	2	9; 11
	7	52
	11	62
	13	17; 35; 72; 87
4	12	48
	15	24
5	2	113
Demonstrative		
1	–	–
2	–	–
3	–	–
4	12	14
5	–	–
Zero		
1	4	82
2	2	28; 74
	3	4; 8
	7	16
3	2	45; 61
	4	18
	6	96
	12	11
4	–	–
5	2	3; 115; 120; 306; 332

Table B-11
Citations to Determiners of King Richard

Act	Scene	Lines
		Nonspecific
1	–	–
2	1	198; 257
	2	8
3	1	8 (2); 9
	2	55; 88; 177; 210
	3	9; 25; 68; 71
4	1	234; 248; 250; 266; 306; 307; 318
5	1	4; 34; 35; 36; 50; 92
	2	35; 48
		Definite
1	1	70
	3	11; 118; 194; 205; 279; 280; 283
2	1	1; 69; 118; 134; 241; 257; 289
	2	2; 5; 13; 43; 102; 114; 127; 128; 133
	3	28; 96; 97; 157
	4	3; 6; 7
3	1	17
	2	57; 85
	3	3; 101; 121; 143; 144; 145; 155
	4	55; 67
4	1	4; 125; 172; 283; 285; 288
5	1	1; 11; 34; 83
	4	10; 110
	6	32
		Demonstrative
1	1	34
2	–	–
3	3	133
4	1	278; 281; 287; 296
5	4	2; 9
	5	7; 9; 19; 86; 117

Table B-11
Citations to Determiners of King Richard (Cont'd)

Act	Scene	Lines
		Zero
1	1	165
	2	37; 38; 41
	3	226
2	1	87; 97; 109; 113; 262
3	2	67; 83; 84; 210
	3	140; 182
	4	97
4	1	126 (3); 135; 193; 304; 305
5	1	12; 13; 20
	5	32; 66; 72; 73

Table B-12
Citations to Determiners of Bolingbroke

Act	Scene	Lines
		Nonspecific
1	1	61 (2); 114; 143; 144
	3	274; 309
2	1	193; 194; 239
	2	47
	3	47; 60; 89; 110; 120; 133
3	1	16; 27
	2	86
	3	119
4	1	162; 308
5	3	136
		Definite
1	1	17
	3	3; 52; 221; 256; 257
2	1	232; 261
	3	32; 36; 40; 137; 148

Table B-12
Citations to Determiners of Bolingbroke (Cont'd)

Act	Scene	Lines
		Definite
3	2	124
	3	130
4	1	174
5	1	56
	2	7; 45; 84; 99; 111
	3	23; 80
	4	1; 11
	5	110; 117
		Demonstrative
1	1	108 (2); 113; 147
	3	26
2	3	90
3	2	47 (2)
	3	135
4	–	–
5	5	89
		Zero
1	1	162; 186
	3	247; 249
2	1	192
	3	2; 70; 97; 124
3	3	16; 190; 194; 204; 208
4	1	107; 109; 112; 134; 181; 182; 220; 263 (2); 290; 299
5	1	63
	3	43; 76; 87; 91; 116; 119
	5	102
	6	30

Table B-13
Citations to Certain Instances of Synecdoche

	Richard II	
Act	Scene	Lines
1	1	37; 38; 46; 71; 121; 138; 160; 187; 190; 192
	2	74
	3	37; 91; 94; 173; 245; 263
2	1	120; 234
	2	11; 28
	3	50 (2); 98; 121
3	2	65; 92; 93 (2); 197
	3	48; 89; 90; 192; 193; 199
	4	7; 8
4	1	6; 249
5	2	92
	3	53 (2)
	5	97 (2); 109
	6	45

	Antony and Cleopatra	
Act	Scene	Lines
1	2	100; 123
	5	42
2	1	10
	2	92; 93 (2)
	3	3
	5	54
	7	73; 74
3	2	26
	6	59
	11	58
	13	179
4	5	16
	12	14; 47
	14	19; 57

BIBLIOGRAPHY

Abbott, Edwin A. *A Shakespearian Grammar*. London: Macmillan, 1879.
Alexander, Peter. *Alexander's Introductions to Shakespeare*. New York: W. W. Norton & Co., 1964.
Allport, Gordon W. *Personality: A Psychological Interpretation*. New York: Henry Holt & Co., 1937.
Badawi, M. M. "Euphemism and Circumlocution in *Macbeth*." In *Cairo Studies in English*, edited by Magdi Wahba, pp. 25-46. Cairo, 1960.
Bailey, Richard W. "Current Trends in the Analysis of Style." *Style* 1 (1967): 1-14.
Barish, Jonas A. *Ben Jonson and the Language of Prose Comedy*. Cambridge, Mass.: Harvard University Press, 1960.
Barthes, Roland. *Elements of Semiology*. Translated by Annette Lavers and Colin Smith. New York: Hill & Wang, 1968.
Beardsley, Monroe C. *Aesthetics from Classical Greek to the Present: A Short History*. New York and London: Macmillan, 1966.
Bennett, Paul E. "The Statistical Measurement of a Stylistic Trait in *Julius Caesar* and *As You Like It*." *Shakespeare Quarterly* 8 (1957): 33-50.
Berry, Francis. *The Poet's Grammar*. London: Routledge & Kegan Paul, 1958.
Blau, Herbert. "Language and Structure in Poetic Drama." *Modern Language Quarterly* 18 (1957): 27-34.
Borinski, Ludwig. "Konstante Stilformen in Shakespeares Prosa." *Deutsche Shakespeare-Gesellschaft West. Jahrbuch* 1969: 81-102.
Bradbrook, Muriel C. "Fifty Years of the Criticism of Shakespeare's Style: A Retrospect." *Shakespeare Survey* 7 (1954): 1-11.
Brower, Reuben A. *Hero and Saint: Shakespeare and the Graeco-Roman Heroic Tradition*. New York and Oxford: Oxford University Press, 1971.
Brown, Roger, and Albert Gilman. "The Pronouns of Power and Solidarity." In *Style in Language*, edited by Thomas A. Sebeok,

pp. 253-276. Cambridge, Mass., New York, and London: Technology Press of M.I.T. and John Wiley & Sons, 1957.

Buch, Kai Rander. "A Note on Sentence-Length as Random Variable." In *Statistics and Style*, edited by Lubomir Doleźel and Richard W. Bailey, pp. 76-79. New York: American Elsevier, 1969.

Burton, Dolores M. "The Grammar of Shakespeare's Roman Plays: A Linguistic Approach to the Problem of Style." *Shakespeare Newsletter* 15 (1965): v.

———. "Some Uses of a Grammatical Concordance." *Computers and the Humanities* 2 (1968): 145-154.

Chambers, E. K. *William Shakespeare: A Study of Facts and Problems*. 2 vols. Oxford: Clarendon Press, 1930.

Charney, Maurice. *Shakespeare's Roman Plays: The Function of Imagery in the Drama*. Cambridge, Mass.: Harvard University Press, 1961.

Chatman, Seymour, and Samuel R. Levin, eds. *Essays on the Language of Literature*. Boston: Houghton Mifflin Co., 1967.

Chomsky, A. Noam. *Aspects of the Theory of Syntax*. Cambridge, Mass.: M.I.T. Press, 1965.

———. *Syntactic Structures*. The Hague: Mouton & Co., 1957.

Clemen, Wolfgang. *The Development of Shakespeare's Imagery*. Cambridge, Mass., and London: Harvard University Press, 1951.

———. *Shakespeares Monologe*. Göttingen: Vandenhoeck and Ruprecht, 1964.

———. *Shakespeare's Soliloquies*. Cambridge: Modern Humanities Research Association, 1964.

Coppedge, Walter R. "Shakespeare's Oaths and Imprecations." *Dissertation Abstracts* 28 (1968): 2643A-2644A.

Crane, Milton. *Shakespeare's Prose*. Chicago and London: University of Chicago Press, 1951.

Croll, Morris W. *See* Patrick, J. Max, et al.

Cunningham, James V., ed. *The Problem of Style*. Greenwich, Conn.: Fawcett Publications, 1967.

Davie, Donald. *Articulate Energy: An Enquiry into the Syntax of English Poetry*. New York: Harcourt, Brace & Co., 1958.

Dent, R. W. "Imagination in *A Midsummer Night's Dream*." In *Shakespeare 400: Essays by American Scholars on the Anniversary of the Poet's Birth*, edited by James G. McManaway, pp. 115-129). New York: Holt, Rinehart, and Winston, 1964.

Doleźel, Lubomír. "A Framework for the Statistical Analysis of Style." In *Statistics and Style*, edited by Lubomír Doleźel and Richard W. Bailey, pp. 10-25. New York: American Elsevier, 1969.

————, and Richard W. Bailey, eds. *Statistics and Style*. New York: American Elsevier, 1969.

Dorfman, Eugene. *The Nareme in the Medieval Romance Epic: An Introduction to Narrative Structures*. Toronto: University of Toronto Press, 1969.

————. "The Structure of Narrative: A Linguistic Approach." *The History of Ideas Newsletter* 2 (1956): 63-67.

Dowden, Edward. *Shakspere: A Critical Study of His Mind and Art*. London: Routledge & Kegan Paul, 1875. Reprinted 1962.

Draper, John W. "Shakespeare's Use of the Grand Entry." *Neophilologus* 44 (1960): 128-135.

————. *The Tempo-Patterns of Shakespeare's Plays*. Heidelberg: Carl Winter, 1957.

Dunbar, Georgia S. "The Verse Rhythms of *Antony and Cleopatra*." *Style* 5 (1971): 231-245.

Dunn, Thomas A. *Philip Massinger: The Man and the Playwright*. London: Nelson, 1957.

Eagleson, Robert D. "A Linguistic, Stylistic Analysis of the Non-Finite Verb Clause in Shakespeare's Plays." Dissertation, University of London, 1970.

Ellegård, Alvar. *A Statistical Method for Determining Authorship: The Junius Letters, 1769-1772*. Göteborg: Gothenburg Studies in English, 1962.

Ellis-Fermor, Una. "Some Functions of Verbal Music in Drama." *Shakespeare-Jahrbuch* 90 (1954): 37-48.

Fairley, Irene. "Syntax as Style." In *Studies Presented to Roman Jakobson by his Students*, pp. 105-111. Cambridge, Mass.: Slavica Publishers, 1968.

Firth, J. R. "Modes of Meaning." *Essays and Studies by Members of the English Association* 4 (1951): 118-149.

————. "Techniques of Semantics." In his *Papers in Linguistics: 1934-1951*, pp. 7-33. London: Oxford University Press, 1957.

Foakes, R. A. "An Approach to *Julius Caesar*." *Shakespeare Quarterly* 5 (1954): 259-270.

————. "Contrasts and Connections: Some Notes on Style in Shakespeare's Comedies and Tragedies." *Shakespeare-Jahrbuch* 90 (1954): 69-81.

Garvin, Paul, ed. and trans. *A Prague School Reader on Esthetics, Literary Structure, and Style*. Washington, D.C.: Georgetown University Press, 1964.

Gleason, Harold A., Jr. "Probings into No Man's Land—The Marches of Linguistics and Stylistics." Lecture delivered at the Bowdoin College

Conference on Linguistics and English Stylistics, Brunswick, Maine, May 4-6, 1967.

Greyerz, Georg von. *The Reported Scenes in Shakespeare's Plays*. Bern: Fritz Pochon-Jent, 1965.

Groom, Bernard. *The Diction of Poetry from Spenser to Bridges*. Toronto: University of Toronto Press, 1955.

Guyol, Hazel S. "A Temperance of Language." *English Journal* 55 (1966): 316-319.

Halberg, Charles J. A., Jr., and John F. Devlin. *Elementary Functions*. Atlanta: Scott Foresman, 1967.

Halliday, F. E. *The Poetry of Shakespeare's Plays*. New York and London: Gerald Duckworth & Co., 1954.

Halliday, M. A. K. "Categories of the Theory of Grammar." *Word* 17 (1961): 241-292.

———. "Class in Relation to the Axes of Chain and Choice in Language." *Linguistics*, no. 2 (1963), pp. 5-15.

———. *A Course in Spoken English, Part Two: Intonation Exercises*. London: Oxford University Press, 1965.

———. "Descriptive Linguistics in Literary Studies." In *English Studies Today*, Third Series, edited by G. I. Duthie, pp. 25-39. Edinburgh: Edinburgh University Press, 1964.

———. "Linguistic Function and Literary Style: An Inquiry into the Language of William Golding's *The Inheritors*." In *Literary Style: A Symposium*, edited by Seymour Chatman, pp. 330-365. London and New York: Oxford University Press, 1971.

———. "The Linguistic Study of Literary Texts." In *Proceedings of the Ninth International Congress of Linguists*, edited by Horace G. Lunt, pp. 302-307. The Hague: Mouton & Co., 1964.

———. "Notes on Transitivity and Theme in English." *Journal of Linguistics* 3 (1967): 37-81, 199-244; 4 (1968): 179-215.

———. "Some Notes on Deep Grammar." *Journal of Linguistics* 2 (1966): 57-67.

———. "The Tones of English." *Archivum Linguisticum* 15 (1963): 1-28.

Hardison, O. B., ed. *English Literary Criticism: The Renaissance*. New York: Appleton-Century Crofts, 1963.

Hart, Alfred. "The Growth of Shakespeare's Vocabulary." *Review of English Studies* 19 (1943): 242-254.

———. "Vocabularies of Shakespeare's Plays." *Review of English Studies* 19 (1943): 128-140.

Havranek, Bohuslav. "The Functional Differentiation of the Standard Language." In *A Prague School Reader on Esthetics, Literary Structure, and Style*, edited and translated by Paul L. Garvin, pp. 3-16. Washington, D.C.: Georgetown University Press, 1964.

Hendricks, William O. Review of *Linguistic Structures in Poetry* by Samuel R. Levin. *Language* 42 (1966): 639-649.

Hildreth, Carson. "The Bacon-Shakespeare Controversy." *University of Nebraska Studies* 2 (1897): 147-162.

Hill, Archibald A. *Introduction to Linguistic Structures: From Sound to Sentence in English.* New York: Harcourt, Brace & World, 1957.

Hockett, Charles F. *A Course in Modern Linguistics.* New York: Macmillan Co., 1958.

———. *The State of the Art.* The Hague: Mouton & Co., 1968.

Householder, Fred W. Review of *Language and Style* by Stephen Ullmann. *Language* 42 (1966): 632-639.

Howard-Hill, Trevor H. *Concordances to the Text of the First Folio of Shakespeare's Plays.* Oxford: Clarendon Press, 1969.

Howe, Clara. "The Streaks of the Tulip—Shakespeare's Commentary on Death." *University of South Florida Quarterly* 3 (1964): 33-36.

Howell, Wilbur Samuel. *Logic and Rhetoric in England, 1500-1700.* New York: Russell and Russell, 1961.

Huddleston, Rodney D. *Handbook of Analysis: Clause and Clause Complex Survey.* Manual prepared for the Communication Research Centre Scientific English Analysis Programme. London: University College, 1966.

———. "Rank and Depth." *Language* 41 (1965): 574-586.

———, R. A. Hudson, E. O. Winter, and A. Henrici. *Sentence and Clause in Scientific English.* Report of the Research Project on "The Linguistic Properties of Scientific English." Communication Research Centre, Department of General Linguistics. London: University College, 1968.

Jakobson, Roman. "Closing Statement: Linguistics and Poetics." In *Style in Language*, edited by Thomas A. Sebeok, pp. 350-377. Cambridge, Mass., New York, and London: Technology Press of M.I.T. and John Wiley & Sons, 1960.

———. "Grammatical and Lexical Meaning." Lecture delivered on July 6, 1966, at the U.C.L.A. Linguistic Institute, Los Angeles, California.

———, and Lawrence G. Jones. *Shakespeare's Verbal Art in Th'Expence of Spirit.* The Hague: Mouton & Co., 1970.

———, and Claude Lévi-Strauss. *"Les Chats* de Baudelaire." *L'Homme* 3 (1962): 5-21.

Jespersen, Otto. *A Modern English Grammar on Historical Principles.* 7 vols. Heidelberg, 1909-1949. Reprinted London and Copenhagen: George Allen & Unwin, and Ejnar Munksgaard, 1961 and 1965.

Jorgensen, Paul A. "A Deed without a Name." In *Pacific Coast Studies in Shakespeare*, edited by Waldo F. McNeir and Thelma N. Greenfield, pp. 190-198. Eugene: Oregon University Press, 1966.

Katz, Jerrold J. *The Philosophy of Language*. New York and London: Harper & Row, 1966.

Klammer, Thomas P. "Multihierarchical Structure in a Middle English Breton Lay—A Tagmemic Analysis." *Language and Style* 4 (1971): 3-23.

Knight, G. W. *The Crown of Life*. London: Methuen, 1948.

——. *The Sovereign Flower*. London: Methuen, 1958.

——. *The Wheel of Fire*. London: Oxford University Press, 1930.

Kroeber, A. L. *Anthropology: Culture Patterns and Processes*. New York: Harcourt, Brace & Co., 1963.

——. "Parts of Speech in Periods of Poetry." *Publications of the Modern Language Association* 73 (1958): 309-314.

Lacan, Jacques. "The Insistence of the Letter in the Unconscious." *Yale French Studies* 36-37 (1966): 112-147.

Landon, George M. "The Grammatical Description of Poetic Word-Order in English Verse." *Language and Style* 1 (1969): 194-200.

——. "The Quantification of Metaphoric Language in the Verse of Wilfred Owen." In *Statistics and Style*, edited by Lubomír Doležel and Richard W. Bailey, pp. 170-177. New York: American Elsevier, 1969.

Langer, Susanne. *Feeling and Form*. New York: Scribner, 1953.

Lee, Donald W. *Functional Change in Early English*. Menasha, Wis.: Banta, 1948.

Levin, Harry. "Form and Formality in *Romeo and Juliet*." *Shakespeare Quarterly* 11 (1960): 3-11.

Levin, Samuel R. *Linguistic Structures in Poetry*. The Hague: Mouton & Co., 1962.

——. "Poetry and Grammaticalness." In *Proceedings of the Ninth International Congress of Linguists*, edited by Horace G. Lunt, pp. 308-314. The Hague: Mouton & Co., 1964.

Lothian, John M. *Shakespeare's Charactery: A Book of 'Characters' from Shakespeare*. Oxford: Blackwell, 1966.

McIntosh, Angus. "Language and Style." *Durham University Journal* 24 (1963): 116-123.

——, and Colin Williamson. "*King Lear*, Act I, Scene i: A Stylistic Note." *Review of English Studies* 14 (1963): 54-58.

Mack, Maynard. *King Lear in Our Time*. Berkeley and Los Angeles: University of California Press, 1965.

McNemar, Quinn. *Psychological Statistics*. 2d. ed. New York: Wiley, 1955.

Malkiel, Yakov. Review of *Style in Language*, edited by Thomas A.

Sebeok. *International Journal of American Linguistics* 28 (1962): 268-286.

Markels, Julian. *The Pillar of the World: Antony and Cleopatra in Shakespeare's Stylistic Development.* Columbus: Ohio State University Press, 1968.

Maxwell, J. C. "Peele and Shakespeare: A Stylometric Test." *Journal of English and Germanic Philology* 49 (1950): 557-561.

———. "The Technique of Invocation in 'King Lear.' " *Modern Language Review* 45 (1950): 142-147.

Mendenhall, T. C. "A Mechanical Solution of a Literary Problem." *Popular Science Monthly* 60 (1901): 97-105.

Miles, Josephine. *Eras and Modes in English Poetry.* Berkeley and Los Angeles: University of California Press, 1964.

———. "Eras in English Poetry." *Publications of the Modern Language Association* 70 (1955): 853-875.

Milic, Louis T. "Against the Typology of Styles." In *Essays on the Language of Literature,* edited by Seymour Chatman and Samuel R. Levin, pp. 442-450. Boston: Houghton Mifflin, 1967.

———. *A Quantitative Approach to the Style of Jonathan Swift.* The Hague: Mouton & Co., 1966.

Milner, Ian. "Shakespeare's Climactic Style." In *Charles University on Shakespeare,* edited by Zdněk Stříbrný and Jarmila Emmerová, pp. 151-158. Prague: Universita Karlova, 1966.

Mosteller, Frederick, and David L. Wallace. *Inference and Disputed Authorship: The Federalist.* Reading, Mass.: Addison-Wesley Publishing Co., 1964.

Muir, Kenneth. "Shakespeare and Rhetoric." *Shakespeare-Jahrbuch* 90 (1954): 49-68.

Mukařovský, Jan. "Standard Language and Poetic Language." In *A Prague School Reader on Esthetics, Literary Structure, and Style,* edited and translated by Paul L. Garvin, pp. 17-30. Washington, D.C.: Georgetown University Press, 1964.

Neilson, William A., and Ashley H. Thorndike. *The Facts about Shakespeare.* New York: Macmillan, 1913.

Nowottny, Winifred M. T. "Some Aspects of the Style of *King Lear.*" *Shakespeare Survey* 13 (1960): 49-57.

———. *The Language Poets Use.* New York: Oxford University Press, 1962.

———. "Lear's Questions." *Shakespeare Survey* 10 (1957): 90-97.

O'Donnell, Bernard. "Stephen Crane's *The O'Ruddy*: A Problem in Authorship Discrimination." In *The Computer and Literary Style,* edited by Jacob Leed, pp. 107-115. Kent, Ohio: Kent State University Press, 1966.

Ohmann, Richard. "Generative Grammars and the Concept of Literary Style." *Word* 20 (1964): 423-439.

———. "Mentalism in the Study of Literary Language." In *Proceedings of the Conference on Language and Language Behavior*, edited by Eric M. Zale, pp. 188-212. New York: Appleton-Century-Crofts, 1968.

———. "Prolegomena to the Analysis of Prose Style." In *Style in Prose Fiction: English Institute Essays, 1958*, edited by Harold C. Martin, pp. 1-24. New York: Columbia University Press, 1959.

Olson, Elder. *Tragedy and the Theory of Drama*. Detroit: Wayne State University Press, 1961.

Palmer, F. R. Review of *The State of the Art* by Charles F. Hockett. *Language* 45 (1969): 616-621.

Parker, David. "Verbal Moods in Shakespeare's Sonnets." *Modern Language Quarterly* 30 (1969): 331-339.

Partridge, A. C. *The Problem of Henry VIII Re-opened: Some Linguistic Criteria for the Two Styles Apparent in the Play*. Cambridge: Bowes and Bowes, 1949.

Patrick, J. Max, et al., eds. *Style, Rhetoric, and Rhythm: Essays by Morris W. Croll*. Princeton, N.J.: Princeton University Press, 1966.

Price, Hereward T. "Shakespeare's Parts of Speech." *San Francisco Quarterly* 18 (1952): 19-28.

Propp, Vladímir I. *Morphology of the Folktale*. Translated by Laurence Scott with an Introduction by Svatava Pirkova-Jakobson. 2nd ed. Austin: University of Texas Press, 1968.

Puttenham, George. *See* Willcock, Gladys Doidge, and Alice Walker, eds.

Quirk, Randolph. "Colloquial English and Communication." In *Studies in Communication*, pp. 169-182. London: Secker and Warburg, 1955.

———. "Descriptive Statement and Serial Relationship." *Language* 41 (1965): 205-217.

Rabkin, Norman. *Shakespeare and the Common Understanding*. New York and London: Free Press and Collier-Macmillan, 1968.

Rauh, Miriam Joseph, C.S.C. *Shakespeare's Use of the Arts of Language*. New York: Columbia University Press, 1947.

Redin, Mats. *Word Order in English Verse from Pope to Sassoon*. Uppsala: Almquist & Wiksells, 1925.

Riffaterre, Michael. "Criteria for Style Analysis." *Word* 15 (1959): 154-174.

———. "Stylistic Context." *Word* 16 (1960): 207-218.

Salmon, Vivian. Remarks in "The Critical Forum." *Essays in Criticism* 8 (1958): 327-334.

———. "Sentence Structure in Colloquial Shakespearian English." *Transactions of the Philological Society, 1965*, pp. 105-140.

Sedelow, Sally Y., and Walter A. Sedelow. "Categories and Procedures for Content Analysis in the Humanities." In *The Analysis of Communication Content*, edited by George Gerbner et al., pp. 487-499. New York: John Wiley & Sons, 1969.

Shakespeare, William. *Antony and Cleopatra*. Edited by John Dover Wilson. Cambridge: Cambridge University Press, 1968.

———. *The Complete Works of Shakespeare*. Edited by George Lyman Kittredge. Boston: Ginn & Co., 1936.

———. *King Richard II*. Edited by John Dover Wilson. Cambridge: Cambridge University Press, 1968.

———. *Shakespeare's Hamlet. The First Quarto, 1603*. Reproduced in facsimile from the copy in the Huntington Library. Cambridge, Mass.: Harvard University Press, 1931.

———. *Shakespeare's Hamlet. The Second Quarto, 1604*. Reproduced in facsimile from the copy in the Huntington Library. San Marino, Calif., 1938.

———. *The Tragedie of Anthonie, and Cleopatra*. Edited by Horace Howard Furness. A New Variorum Edition. Philadelphia: Lippincott, 1907.

———. *The Tragedy of Antony and Cleopatra*. Edited by G. L. Kittredge. Revised by Irving Ribner. Waltham, Mass.: Blaisdell Publishing Co., 1966.

———. *The Tragedy of King Richard the Second*. Edited by G. L. Kittredge. Revised by Irving Ribner. Waltham, Mass.: Blaisdell Publishing Co., 1966.

Skinner, B. F. "The Alliteration in Shakespeare's Sonnets: A Study in Literary Behavior." *The Psychological Record* 3 (1939): 186-192.

Smith, John Barstow. "A Computer-Assisted Analysis of Imagery in Joyce's *A Portrait of the Artist*." Dissertation, University of North Carolina at Chapel Hill, 1970.

Smith, Jonathan. "The Language of Leontes." *Shakespeare Quarterly* 19 (1968): 317-327.

Spencer, T. J. B., ed. *Shakespeare's Plutarch*. London: Penguin Books, 1964.

Spencer, Theodore. *Shakespeare and the Nature of Man*. New York: Macmillan Co., 1942.

Spevack, Marvin. *A Complete and Systematic Concordance to the Works of Shakespeare*. 6 vols. Hildesheim: Georg Olms, 1968-1970.

Spurgeon, Caroline F. E. *Shakespeare's Imagery and What It Tells Us*. Cambridge: Cambridge University Press, 1935.

Stein, Arnold. "*Macbeth* and Word-Magic." *Sewanee Review* 59 (1951): 271-284.

Stirling, Brents. "Bolingbroke's 'Decision.' " *Shakespeare Quarterly* 2 (1951): 27-34.

Tauber, Anne-Marie. *Die Sterbeszenen in Shakespeares Dramen.* Bern: Francke, 1964.

Tenney, Edward H. "Style." In *Dictionary of World Literature*, edited by Joseph T. Shipley, pp. 398-399. New York: Philosophical Library, 1953.

Thomas, Norman. "Comparative Stylometry in Shakespeare." *Shakespeare Newsletter* 15 (1965): 56.

Thomas, Owen. *Transformational Grammar and the Teacher of English.* New York: Holt, Rinehart, and Winston, 1965.

Thorne, James Peter. "Stylistics and Generative Grammars." *Journal of Linguistics* 1 (1965): 49-59.

Tilley, Morris Palmer. *A Dictionary of the Proverbs in England in the Sixteenth and Seventeenth Centuries.* Ann Arbor: University of Michigan Press, 1950.

Traversi, Derek. *Shakespeare: The Roman Plays.* Stanford, Calif.: Hollis and Carter, 1963.

Uitti, Karl D. *Linguistics and Literary Theory.* Englewood Cliffs, N.J.: Prentice-Hall, 1969.

Van Doren, Mark. *Shakespeare.* New York: Doubleday & Co., 1939.

Van Draat, P. Fijn. "Rhythm in English Prose." *Anglia* 36 (1912): 1-58.

Veltruský, Jiří. "Man and Object in the Theater." In *A Prague School Reader on Esthetics, Literary Structure, and Style*, edited and translated by Paul L. Garvin, pp. 83-91. Washington, D.C.: Georgetown University Press, 1964.

Vickers, Brian. *The Artistry of Shakespeare's Prose.* London and New York: Methuen, 1968.

Weidhorn, Manfred. "The Relation of Title and Name to Identity in Shakespearean Tragedy." *Studies in English Literature* 9 (1969): 303-319.

Wellek, René, and Austin Warren. *Theory of Literature.* New York: Harcourt, Brace & World, 1956.

Western, August. *On Sentence-Rhythm and Word-Order in Modern English.* Christina: Dybwad, 1908.

Willcock, Gladys Doidge, and Alice Walker, eds. *"The Arte of English Poesie" by George Puttenham.* Cambridge: Cambridge University Press, 1936.

Willey, Gordon R. "Archeological Theories and Interpretation: New World." In *Anthropology Today*, edited by A. L. Kroeber, pp. 361-385. Chicago: University of Chicago Press, 1952.

Williams, C. B. "A Note on Sentence-Length." In *Statistics and Style*, edited by Lubomír Doležel and Richard W. Bailey, pp. 69-75. New York: American Elsevier, 1969.

Yardi, M. R. "Statistical Approach to the Problem of Chronology." *Sānkhyā: The Indian Journal of Statistics* 7 (1946): 263-268.

Yule, G. Udny. *The Statistical Study of Literary Vocabulary*. Cambridge: Cambridge University Press, 1944.

INDEX

Abbott, Edwin A.: 293

abstract nouns: syntax of, 40, 58-59, 61n., 70-71, 99, 187-190, 214, 219, 281-282; selection of, 187n.; frequency of, 188-189, 219; mentioned, 147, 195, 203-204, 208, 221

adjective-noun collocations: 61, 63 and n., 70-71, 185-187, 219, 230, 278, 313. *See also* selection restrictions

adjectives: syntax of, 21, 62, 64, 159, 201, 278; comparative vs. superlative, 39, 65-67, 147, 153, 202, 215, 218, 279-280; position of, 62, 104, 116, 128, 131, 195, 204, 214, 278, 280; compound vs. multiple, 62, 212, 214, 217, 219, 278-279, 280; frequency of, 64, 69 and n., 158, 211-212, 215, 314; selection of, 278-279; mentioned, 59, 157, 163, 230. *See also* participial adjectives; prefixes; quantifying words; suffixes; word, syllables per

adjunct: examples of, 45, 66n., 117-118, 127, 131, 132-133, 142; position of, 84, 116-127 *passim*, 132, 133, 137, 141; types of, 122, 126-127, 141, 200, 216, 275; mentioned, 43, 104n., 142, 200, 213, 288, 289

adjunct theme: examples of, 81-82, 96n., 120-121, 134; defined, 119-120; rhythm of, 140, 142, 143n.; mentioned, 137, 210, 218, 291. *See also* complement theme

adverbial clause: *See wh-*relative clauses: *when, where*

Aeneid, The: 49, 272

aesthetics: 9-10, 12n.-13n., 15, 113, 115 and n., 144, 212n.

agent nouns: 155-157 *passim*, 199-200, 214, 218, 296, 300

Alexander, Peter: 233-234

Allport, Gordon W.: 15n.

alpha, governing element: defined, 44, 116; in group hypotaxis, 45-47, 50, 56, 215, 230, 284, 289; position of, 116, 118, 137, 215, 290. *See also* hypotaxis

ambiguity: 27n., 45-51, 56, 78, 84, 89, 213, 217, 230

anaphoric specification: 153n., 193-195

and: 158, 214, 300

animation: 70 and n., 281-282

antecedent: of pronoun, 45; of beta clauses, 46-47, 230, 284, 286; of relative clauses, 54 and n., 88, 210, 282-283, 286, 322-324; kinds of, 97 and n.-98

Antony and Cleopatra

—dramatic structure of: Roman vs. Egyptian worlds in, 55, 87 and n., 161, 253-260 *passim*, 264; structural aspects of, 57, 83-84, 152-154, 160, 233-238, 295-299; imagination in, 84, 233, 238-254, 261, 265-272; identity in, 86, 183-184, 220, 242-246, 262-263; attitude toward history in, 92-96, 154-